GUIDE TO LITERARY AGENTS
2018

Includes a one-year online subscription to **Guide to Literary Agents** on

WritersMarket.com

Where & How to Sell What You Write

THE ULTIMATE MARKET RESEARCH TOOL FOR WRITERS

To register your *Guide to Literary Agents 2018* and **start your one-year online subscription to listings related to literary agents**, scratch off the block below to reveal your activation code, then go to WritersMarket.com. Find the box that says "Purchased a Deluxe Edition?" then click on "Activate Your Account" and enter the activation code. It's that easy!

UPDATED MARKET LISTINGS FOR YOUR INTEREST AREA
EASY-TO-USE, SEARCHABLE DATABASE • RECORD-KEEPING TOOLS
PROFESSIONAL TIPS & ADVICE • INDUSTRY NEWS

Your purchase of *Guide to Literary Agents* gives you access to updated listings related to literary agents (valid through 12/31/18). For just $9.99, you can upgrade your subscription and get access to listings from all of our best-selling Market Books. Visit **WritersMarket.com** for more information.

WritersMarket.com

Where & How to Sell What You Write

Activate your WritersMarket.com subscription to get instant access to:

- **UPDATED LISTINGS FOR AGENTS AND AGENCIES:** Find additional listings that didn't make it into the book, updated contact information, and more. WritersMarket.com provides the most comprehensive database of verified agents available anywhere.

- **EASY-TO-USE, SEARCHABLE DATABASE:** Looking for a specific agent or agency? Just type in its name. Or widen your prospects with the Advanced Search. You can also search for listings that have been recently updated!

- **PERSONALIZED TOOLS:** Store your best-bet agent leads, and use our popular recording-keeping tools to track your queries. Plus, get new and updated agent listings, query reminders, and more every time you log in!

- **PROFESSIONAL TIPS & ADVICE:** From pay-rate charts to sample query letters, how-to articles to Q&As with literary agents, we all have the resources writers need.

YOU'LL GET ALL OF THIS WITH THE INCLUDED SUBSCRIPTION TO

WritersMarket.com

Where & How to Sell What You Write

◄ 27TH ANNUAL EDITION ►

GUIDE TO LITERARY AGENTS

2018

Cris Freese, Editor

WD
WRITER'S DIGEST
BOOKS
WritersDigest.com
Cincinnati, Ohio

Guide to Literary Agents 2018. Copyright © 2017 F + W Media, Inc. Published by Writer's Digest Books, an imprint of F+W Media, Inc., 10151 Carver Road, Suite 200, Blue Ash, Ohio 45242. Printed and bound in the United States of America. All rights reserved. No part of this book may be reproduced in any form or by any electronic or mechanical means including information storage and retrieval systems without permission in writing from the publisher, except by a reviewer, who may quote brief passages in a review.

Writer's Market website: www.writersmarket.com
Writer's Digest website: www.writersdigest.com

Distributed in Canada by Fraser Direct
100 Armstrong Avenue
Georgetown, Ontario, Canada L7G 5S4
Tel: (905) 877-4411

Distributed in the U.K. and Europe by F&W Media International
Brunel House, Newton Abbot, Devon, TQ12 4PU, England
Tel: (+44) 1626-323200, Fax: (+44) 1626-323319
E-mail: postmaster@davidandcharles.co.uk

ISSN: 1078-6945
ISBN-13: 978-1-4403-5266-9
ISBN-10: 1-4403-5266-6

Attention Booksellers: This is an annual directory of F + W Media, Inc. Return deadline for this edition is December 31, 2018.

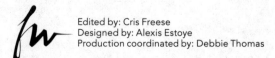

Edited by: Cris Freese
Designed by: Alexis Estoye
Production coordinated by: Debbie Thomas

CONTENTS

FROM THE EDITOR

When I first took over the role of editor of *Guide to Literary Agents* (both in print and online), I was overwhelmed by the enormous amount of information available to writers. I sought to determine the following: What does a writer absolutely need to know to get an agent, and get published? I settled on these things: A writer must know how to write a query letter and a synopsis, and if he is writing nonfiction, he must know how to write a book proposal.

But that's simple. Everyone knows that. And this information has been in this book for years. So I pushed further. First, a writer must write something worthwhile. So I included literary agent Paula Munier's wonderful piece on crafting the perfect first page. And I thought about editing, and the importance of conferences and critique groups. All of these items felt like necessary skills—or tools—for writers.

So I added a brand-new section to this book, **The Writer's Toolbox.** This section includes articles on the above information, along with a fantastic piece on the online opportunities for writers through hashtags and Twitter.

And to round out this new section, I added a genre specific roundtable from four fantastic agents on today's science fiction and fantasy market. But, if you're not interested in these genres, I've culled together a bevy of genre information for you online at writersdigest.com/GLA-18. Please check out this new feature, as I've highlighted other online articles throughout this book that can be of use for you.

When you're finished pouring over these articles, get ready for the listings and the New Agent Spotlights, packed with new agents who are actively building their client lists. Now's the time to begin your researchw—these agents are ready.

I hope you'll find this resource as fun and useful as I have in compiling it. Please stay in touch at my blog—www.guidetoliteraryagents.com/blog—and on Twitter (@Cris-Freese). And be sure to check out the fantastic new webinar on gettting an agent at www.writersmarket.com/2018-gla-webinar.

Cris Freese
Managing Editor, Writer's Digest Books & Writer's Market Series

HOW TO USE
GUIDE TO
LITERARY AGENTS

Searching for a literary agent can be overwhelming, whether you've just finished your first book or you have several publishing credits on your résumé. More than likely, you're eager to start pursuing agents and anxious to see your name on the spine of a book. But before you go directly to the listings in this book, take time to familiarize yourself with the way agents work and how you should approach them. By doing so, you will be more prepared for your search and ultimately save yourself effort and unnecessary angst.

READ THE ARTICLES

This book begins with feature articles organized into three sections: **Getting Started**, **Contacting Agents**, and **The Writer's Toolbox**. These articles explain how to prepare for representation, offer strategies for contacting agents, and arm you with vital tools in your journey. You may want to start by reading through each one and then refer back to relevant articles during each stage of your search.

Because there are many ways to make that initial contact with an agent, we've also provided an article called "Debut Authors Tell All." These personal accounts from just-published authors offer information and inspiration for any writer hoping to find representation.

DECIDE WHAT YOU'RE LOOKING FOR

A literary agent will present your work directly to editors or producers. It's the agent's job to get her client's work published or sold, and to negotiate a fair contract. In the **Literary Agents** listings section, we list each agent's contact information and explain both what type of work the agency represents and how to submit your work for consideration.

For face-to-face contact, many writers prefer to meet agents at conferences. By doing so, writers can assess an agent's personality, attend workshops, and have the chance to get more feedback on their work than they get by mailing or e-mailing submissions and waiting for a response. The **Conferences** section lists conferences agents and/or editors attend. In many cases, private consultations are available, and agents attend with the hope of finding new clients to represent.

UTILIZE THE EXTRAS

Aside from the articles and listings, this book offers a section of **Resources**. If you come across a term with which you aren't familiar, check out the Resources section for a quick explanation. Also, note the gray tabs along the edge of each page. The tabs identify each section so they are easier to flip to as you conduct your search.

Finally—and perhaps most importantly—there are the **Indexes** in the back of the book. These can serve as an incredibly helpful way to start your search because they categorize the listings according to different criteria. For example, you can look for literary agents according to their specialties (fiction/nonfiction genres).

LISTING POLICY AND COMPLAINT PROCEDURE

Listings in *Guide to Literary Agents* were originally compiled from detailed questionnaires and information provided by agents. However, the publishing industry is constantly in flux, and agencies change frequently. We rely on our readers for information about their dealings with agents, as well as changes in policies or fees that differ from what has been reported to the editor of this book. Write to the editor (*Guide to Literary Agents*, F+W, 10151 Carver Road, Suite 200, Cincinnati, OH 45242) or e-mail (cris.freese@fwmedia.com) if you have new information, questions, or problems dealing with the agencies listed.

Listings are published free of charge and are not advertisements. Although the information is as accurate as possible, the listings are not endorsements or guarantees by the editor or publisher of *Guide to Literary Agents*. If you feel you have not been treated fairly by an agent or representative listed in *Guide to Literary Agents*, we advise you to take the following steps:

- First try to contact the agency. Sometimes one letter or e-mail can clear up the matter. Politely relate your concern.
- Document all your correspondence with the agency. When you write to us with a complaint, provide the name of your manuscript, the date of your first contact with the agency, and the nature of your subsequent correspondence.

- We will keep your letter on file and attempt to contact the agency. The number, frequency, and severity of complaints will be considered when we decide whether or not to delete an agency's listing from the next edition.

NOTE: *Guide to Literary Agents* reserves the right to exclude any agency for any reason.

FREQUENTLY ASKED QUESTIONS

1. **Why do you include agents who are not seeking new clients?** Some agents ask that their listings indicate they are currently closed to new clients. We include them so writers know the agents exist and know not to contact them at this time.

2. **Why are some agents not listed?** Some agents may not have responded to our requests for information. We have taken others out of the book after we received complaints about them.

3. **Do I need more than one agent if I write in different genres?** It depends. If you have written in one genre and want to switch to a new style of writing, ask your agent if she is willing to represent you in your new endeavor. Occasionally an agent may feel she has no knowledge of a certain genre and will recommend an appropriate agent to her client. Regardless, you should always talk to your agent about any potential career move.

4. **Why don't you list more foreign agents?** Most American agents have relationships with foreign co-agents in other countries. It is more common for an American agent to work with a co-agent to sell a client's book abroad than for a writer to work directly with a foreign agent. If you decide to query foreign agents, make sure they represent American writers (if you're American). Some may request to receive submissions only from Canadians, for example, or from United Kingdom residents.

5. **Do agents ever contact a self-published writer?** If a self-published author attracts the attention of the media, or if his book sells extremely well, an agent might approach the author in the hope of representing him.

6. **Why won't the agent I queried return my material?** An agent may not answer your query or return your manuscript for several reasons. Perhaps you did not include a self-addressed, stamped envelope (SASE). Many agents will discard a submission without a SASE. Or the agent may have moved. To avoid using expired addresses, use the most current edition of *Guide to Literary Agents* or access the information online at www.writersmarket.com. Another possibility is that the agent is swamped with submissions. An agent can be overwhelmed with queries, especially if the agent recently has spoken at a conference or has been featured in an article or book. Also, some agents specify in their listings that they never return materials of any kind.

WHAT AN AGENT DOES

//

A writer's job is to write. A literary agent's job is to find publishers for her clients' books. Because publishing houses receive more and more unsolicited manuscripts each year, or do not accept unsolicited manuscripts, securing an agent is becoming increasingly necessary. But finding an eager and reputable agent can be a difficult task. Even the most patient writer can become frustrated or disappointed. As a writer seeking representation, you should prepare yourself before starting your search. Learn when to approach agents, as well as what to expect from an author/agent relationship. Beyond selling manuscripts, an agent must keep track of the ever-changing industry, writers' royalty statements, fluctuating market trends—the list goes on.

So you face the question: Do I need an agent? The answer, more often than not, is a resounding yes.

WHAT CAN AN AGENT DO FOR YOU?

For starters, today's competitive marketplace can be difficult to break into, especially for unpublished writers. Many larger publishing houses will only look at manuscripts from agents—and rightfully so, as they would be inundated with unsatisfactory writing if they did not. In fact, approximately 80 percent of books published by the five major houses are acquired through agents.

But an agent's job isn't just getting your book through a publisher's door. The following describes the various jobs agents do for their clients, many of which would be difficult for a writer to do without outside help.

BEFORE YOU SUBMIT YOUR NOVEL

- Finish your novel manuscript or short story collection. An agent can do nothing for fiction without a finished product. Never query with an incomplete novel.

- Revise your manuscript. Seek critiques from other writers or an independent editor to ensure your work is as polished as possible.
- Proofread. Don't ruin a potential relationship with an agent by submitting work that contains typos or poor grammar.
- Publish short stories or novel excerpts in literary journals, which will prove to prospective agents that editors see quality in your writing.
- Research to find the agents of writers whose works you admire or are similar to yours.
- Use the Internet and resources like *Guide to Literary Agents* to construct a list of agents who are open to new writers and looking for your category of fiction. (Jump to the listings sections of this book to start now.)
- Rank your list according to the agents most suitable for you and your work.
- Write your novel synopsis.
- Write your query letter. As an agent's first impression of you, this brief letter should be polished and to the point.
- Educate yourself about the business of agents so you will be prepared to act on any offer. This guide is a great place to start.

Agents Know Editors' Tastes and Needs

An agent possesses information on a complex web of publishing houses and a multitude of editors to ensure her clients' manuscripts are placed in the right hands. This knowledge is gathered through relationships she cultivates with acquisitions editors—the people who decide which books to present to their publisher for possible publication. Through her industry connections, an agent becomes aware of the specializations of publishing houses and their imprints, knowing that one publisher wants only contemporary romances while another is interested solely in nonfiction books about the military. By networking with editors, an agent also learns more specialized information—which editor is looking for a crafty, Agatha Christie–style mystery for his fall catalog, for example.

Agents Track Changes in Publishing

Being attentive to constant market changes and shifting trends is another major requirement of an agent. An agent understands what it may mean for clients when publisher A merges with publisher B and when an editor from house C moves to house D. Or what it means when readers—and therefore editors—are no longer interested in Westerns while thrillers are flying off the shelves.

Agents Get Your Work Read Faster

Although it may seem like an extra step to send your work to an agent instead of directly to a publishing house, the truth is that an agent can prevent you from wasting months sending manuscripts that end up in the wrong in-box or buried in an editor's slush pile. Editors rely on agents to save them time as well. With little time to sift through the hundreds of unsolicited submissions arriving weekly in the mail, an editor naturally prefers work that has already been approved by a qualified reader (i.e., the agent) who knows the editor's preferences. For this reason, many of the larger publishers accept agented submissions only.

Agents Understand Contracts

When publishers write contracts, they are primarily interested in their own bottom line, not the best interests of the author. Writers unfamiliar with contractual language may find themselves bound to a publisher with whom they no longer want to work. Or they may find themselves tied to a publisher who prevents them from getting royalties on their first book until subsequent books are written. Agents use their experiences and knowledge to negotiate a contract that benefits the writer while still respecting the publisher's needs. After all, more money for the author will almost always mean more money for the agent—another reason they're on your side.

Agents Negotiate—and Exploit—Subsidiary Rights

Beyond publication, a savvy agent keeps other opportunities for your manuscript in mind. If your agent believes your book also will be successful as an audio book, a Book-of-the-Month-Club selection, or even a blockbuster movie, she will take these options into consideration when shopping your manuscript. These additional opportunities for writers are called subsidiary rights. Part of an agent's job is to keep track of the strengths and weaknesses of different publishers' subsidiary rights offices to determine the deposition of these rights regarding your work. After contracts are negotiated, agents will seek additional moneymaking opportunities for the rights they kept for their clients.

Agents Get Escalators

An escalator is a bonus an agent can negotiate as part of the book contract. It is commonly given when a book appears on a best-seller list or if a client appears on a popular television show. For example, a publisher might give a writer a $30,000 bonus if he is picked for a book club. Both the agent and the editor know such media attention will sell more books, and the agent negotiates an escalator to ensure the writer benefits from this increase in sales.

Agents Track Payments

Because an agent receives payment only when the publisher pays the writer, it's in the agent's best interest to make sure the writer is paid on schedule. Some publishing houses are notorious for late payments. Having an agent distances you from any conflict regarding payment and allows you to spend time writing instead of making phone calls.

Agents Are Advocates

Besides standing up for your right to be paid on time, agents can ensure your book gets a better cover design, more attention from the publisher's marketing department, or other benefits you may not know to ask for during the publishing process. An agent can provide advice each step of the way, as well as guide you in your long-term writing career.

ARE YOU READY FOR AN AGENT?

Now that you know what an agent is capable of, ask yourself if you and your work are at a stage where you need an agent. Look at the "Before You Submit" lists for fiction and nonfiction writers in this article and judge how prepared you are for contacting an agent. Have you spent enough time researching or polishing your manuscript? Does your nonfiction book proposal include everything it should? Is your novel completely finished? Sending an agent an incomplete project not only wastes your time but also may turn off the agent in the process. Is the work thoroughly revised? If you've finished your project, set it aside for a few weeks, then examine it again with fresh eyes. Give your novel or proposal to critique group partners (or beta readers) for feedback.

Moreover, your work may not be appropriate for an agent. Most agents do not represent poetry, magazine articles, short stories, or material suitable for academic or small presses; the agent's commission does not justify spending time submitting these types of works. Those agents who do take on such material generally represent authors on larger projects first and then adopt the smaller items as a favor to the client.

If you believe your work is ready to be placed with an agent, make sure you're personally ready to be represented. In other words, consider the direction in which your writing career is headed. Besides skillful writers, agencies want clients with the ability to produce more than one book. Most agents say they're looking to represent careers, not books.

WHEN DON'T YOU NEED AN AGENT?

Although there are many reasons to work with an agent, some authors can benefit from submitting their own work directly to book publishers. For example, if your project focuses on a very specific topic, you may want to work with a small or specialized press. These houses usually are open to receiving material directly from writers. Small presses often can give more attention to writers than large houses can, providing editorial help, marketing expertise, and other advice. Academic books or specialized nonfiction books (such as a book about the history of Rhode Island) are good bets for unagented writers.

Beware, though, as you will now be responsible for reviewing and negotiating all parts of your contract and payment. If you choose this path, it's wise to use a lawyer or entertainment attorney to review all contracts. Lawyers who specialize in intellectual property can help writers with contract negotiations. Instead of earning a commission on resulting book sales, lawyers are paid only for their time.

And, of course, some people prefer working independently instead of relying on others. If you're one of these people, it's probably better to submit your own work instead of potentially butting heads with an agent. Let's say you manage to sign with one of the few literary agents who represent short story collections. If the collection gets shopped around to publishers for several months and no one bites, your agent may suggest retooling the work into a novel. Agents suggest changes—some bigger than others—and not all writers think their work is malleable. It's all a matter of what you're writing and how you feel about it.

BEFORE YOU SUBMIT YOUR NONFICTION BOOK

- Formulate a concrete idea for your book. Sketch a brief outline, making sure you'll have enough material for a book-length manuscript.
- Research works on similar topics to understand the competition and determine how your book is unique.
- Write sample chapters. This will help you estimate how much time you'll need to complete the work and determine whether or not your writing will need editorial help. You will also need to include a few sample chapters in the proposal itself.
- Publish completed chapters in journals and/or magazines. This validates your work to agents and provides writing samples for later in the process.
- Polish your nonfiction book proposal so you can refer to it while drafting a query letter—and so you'll be prepared when agents contact you.
- Brainstorm three to four subject categories that best describe your material.
- Use the Internet and resources like *Guide to Literary Agents* to construct a list of agents who are open to new writers and looking for your category of nonfiction.
- Rank your list. Research agent websites and narrow your list further, according to your preferences.
- Write your query. Give an agent an excellent first impression by describing your premise and your experience professionally and succinctly.
- Educate yourself about the business of agents so you can act on any offer.

ASSESSING CREDIBILITY

Many people wouldn't buy a used car without at least checking the odometer, and savvy shoppers would consult the blue books, take a test drive, and even ask for a mechanic's opinion. Much like the shrewd car shopper, you want to obtain the best possible agent for your writing, so you should research the business of agents before sending out query letters. Understanding how agents operate will help you find an agent appropriate for your work, as well as alert you about the types of agents to avoid.

Many writers take for granted that any agent who expresses interest in their work is trustworthy. They'll sign a contract before asking any questions and simply hope everything will turn out all right. We often receive complaints from writers regarding agents *after* they have lost money or have work bound by contract to an ineffective agent. If writers put the same amount of effort into researching agents as they did writing their full manuscripts, they would save themselves unnecessary angst.

The best way to educate yourself is to read all you can about agents and other authors. Organizations such as the Association of Authors' Representatives (AAR, www.aaronline .org), the National Writers Union (NWU, www.nwu.org), American Society of Journalists and Authors (ASJA, www.asja.org), and Poets & Writers, Inc. (www.pw.org) all have informational material on finding and working with an agent.

The magazine *Publishers Weekly* (www.publishersweekly.com) covers publishing news affecting agents and others in the publishing industry. The Publishers Lunch newsletter (www.publishersmarketplace.com) comes free via e-mail every workday and offers news on agents and editors, job postings, recent book sales, and more.

The Internet also has a wide range of sites where you can learn basic information about preparing for your initial contact, as well as specific details on individual agents. You can find online forums and listservs that keep authors connected and allow them to share experiences they've had with different editors and agents. Keep in mind, however, that not everything printed on the Web is fact; you may come across a writer who is bitter because an agent rejected his manuscript. Your best bet is to use the Internet only to *supplement* your other research.

Once you've established what your resources are, it's time to see which agents meet your criteria. Below are some of the key items to pay attention to when researching agents.

LEVEL OF EXPERIENCE

Through your research, you will discover the need to be wary of some agents. Anybody can go to the neighborhood copy center and order business cards that say "literary agent," but that title doesn't mean she can sell your book. She may lack the proper connections with others in the publishing industry, and an agent's reputation with editors can be a major strength or weakness.

Agents who have been in the business awhile have a large number of contacts and carry the most clout with editors. They know the ins and outs of the industry and are often able to take more calculated risks. However, veteran agents can be too busy to take on new clients or might not have the time to help develop an author. Newer agents, on the other hand, may be hungrier, as well as more open to unpublished writers. They probably have a smaller client list and are able to invest the effort to make your book a success.

If it's a new agent without a track record, be aware that you're taking more of a risk signing with her than with a more established agent. However, even a new agent should not be new to publishing. Many agents were editors before they were agents, or they worked at an agency as an assistant. This experience is crucial for making contacts in the publishing industry, and learning about rights and contracts. The majority of listings in this book explain how long the agent has been in business, as well as what she did before becoming an agent. After an agent has offered representation, you could ask her to name a few editors off the top of her head who she thinks may be interested in your work and why they sprang to mind. Has she sold to them before? Do they publish books in your genre?

If an agent has no contacts in the business, she has no more clout than you do. Without publishing prowess, she's just an expensive mailing service. Anyone can make photocopies, slide them into an envelope, and address them to "Editor." Unfortunately, without a contact name and a familiar return address on the envelope, or a phone call from a trusted colleague letting an editor know a wonderful submission is on its way, your work will land in the slush pile with all the other submissions that don't have representation. You can do your own mailings with higher priority than such an agent could.

PAST SALES

Agents should be willing to discuss their recent sales with you: how many, what type of books, and to what publishers. Keep in mind, though, that some agents consider this information confidential. If an agent does give you a list of recent sales, you can call the publishers' contracts department to ensure the sale was actually made by that agent. While it's true that even top agents are not able to sell every book they represent, an inexperienced agent who proposes too many inappropriate submissions will quickly lose her standing with editors.

You can also unearth details of recent sales on your own. Nearly all of the listings in this book offer the titles and authors of books with which the agent has worked. Some of them also note to which publishing house the book was sold. Again, you can call the publisher and confirm the sale. If you don't have the publisher's information, simply check to see if it's available on Amazon. You can also check your local library or bookstore to see if they carry the book. You may want to be wary of the agent if her books are nowhere to be found or are only available through the publisher's website. Distribution is a crucial component to getting published, and you want to make sure the agent has worked with competent publishers.

TYPES OF FEES

Becoming knowledgeable about the different types of fees agents may charge is vital to conducting effective research. Most agents make their living from the commissions they receive after selling their clients' books, and these are the agents we've listed. Be sure to ask about any expenses you don't understand so you have a clear grasp of what you're paying for. Here are some types of fees you may encounter in your research:

Office Fees
Occasionally, an agent will charge for the cost of photocopies and postage made on your behalf. This is acceptable, so long as she keeps an itemized account of the expenses and you've agreed on a ceiling cost. The agent should ask for office expenses only after agreeing to represent the writer. These expenses should be discussed up front, and the writer should receive a statement accounting for them. This money is sometimes returned to the author upon sale of the manuscript. Be wary if there is an upfront fee amounting to hundreds of dollars, which is excessive.

Reading Fees
Agencies that charge reading fees often do so to cover the cost of additional readers or the time spent reading that could have been spent selling. Agents also claim that charging reading fees cuts down on the number of submissions they receive. This practice can save the agent time and may allow her to consider each manuscript more extensively. Whether such promises are kept depends upon the honesty of the agency. You may pay a fee and

never receive a response from the agent, or you may pay someone who never submits your manuscript to publishers.

Officially, the Association of Authors' Representatives' (AAR) Canon of Ethics prohibits members from directly or indirectly charging a reading fee, and the Writers Guild of America (WGA) does not allow WGA signatory agencies to charge a reading fee to WGA members, as stated in the WGA's Artists' Manager Basic Agreement. A signatory may charge you a fee if you are not a member, but most signatory agencies do not charge a reading fee as an across-the-board policy.

WARNING SIGNS! BEWARE OF:

- Excessive typos or poor grammar in an agent's correspondence.
- A form letter accepting you as a client and praising generic things about your manuscript that could apply to any work. A good agent doesn't take on a new client very often, so when she does, it's a special occasion that warrants a personal note or phone call.
- Unprofessional contracts that ask you for money up front, contain clauses you haven't discussed, or are covered with amateur clip-art or silly borders.
- Rudeness when you inquire about any points you're unsure of. Don't employ any business partner who doesn't treat you with respect.
- Pressure, by way of threats, bullying, or bribes. A good agent is not desperate to represent more clients. She invites worthy authors but leaves the final decision up to them.
- Promises of publication. No agent can guarantee you a sale. Not even the top agents sell everything they choose to represent. They can only send your work to the most appropriate places, have it read with priority, and negotiate you a better contract if a sale does happen.
- A print-on-demand book contract or any contract offering no advance. You can sell your own book to an e-publisher anytime you wish without an agent's help. An agent should pursue traditional publishing routes with respectable advances.
- Reading fees from $25–$500 or more. The fee is usually nonrefundable, but sometimes agents agree to refund the money if they take on a writer as a client or if they sell the writer's manuscript. Keep in mind, however, that a payment for a reading fee does not ensure representation.
- No literary agents who charge reading fees are listed in this book. It's too risky of an option for writers, plus those who don't charge such fees have a stronger incentive to sell your work. After all, they don't make a dime until they make a sale. If you find that a literary agent listed in this book charges a reading fee, please contact the editor at cris.freese@fwmedia.com.

Critique Fees

Sometimes a manuscript will interest an agent, but the agent will point out areas requiring further development and offer to critique it for an additional fee. Like reading fees, payment of a critique fee does not ensure representation. When deciding if you will benefit from having someone critique your manuscript, keep in mind that the quality and quantity of comments vary from agent to agent. The critique's usefulness will depend on the agent's knowledge of the market. Also be aware that agents who spend a significant portion of their time commenting on manuscripts will have less time to actively market work they already represent.

In other cases, the agent may suggest an editor who understands your subject matter or genre, and has some experience getting manuscripts into shape. Occasionally, if your story is exceptional, or your ideas and credentials are marketable but your writing needs help, you will work with a ghostwriter or co-author who will either share a percentage of your commission or work with you at an agreed-upon cost per hour.

An agent may refer you to editors she knows, or you may choose an editor in your area. Many editors do freelance work and would be happy to help you with your writing project. Of course, before entering into an agreement, make sure you know what you'll be getting for your money. Ask the editor for writing samples, references, or critiques he's done in the past. Make sure you feel comfortable working with him before you give him your business.

An honest agent will not make any money for referring you to an editor. We strongly advise writers not to use critiquing services offered through an agency. Instead, try hiring a freelance editor or joining a writer's group until your work is ready to be submitted to agents who don't charge fees.

CRAFTING A QUERY

How to write a stand-out letter that gets agents' attention.

Kara Gebhart Uhl

Think of the hours, days, months, years you've spent writing your book. The thought you've put into plot, character development, scene setting, and backstory. The words you've kept. The words you've cut. The joy and frustration you've felt as you channeled Oscar Wilde: "I spent all morning putting in a comma and all afternoon taking it out."

And then you finish. You write "The End." You have a celebratory drink. You sleep.

But as any aspiring author knows, you haven't truly reached "The End." In terms of publishing, you've only just begun. And the next chapter in your publishing journey is your query. It's imperative you treat this chapter with as much attention to detail as you did to all the chapters in your book. Because a good query is your golden ticket. Your charmed demo tape. Your "in."

A query is a short, professional way of introducing yourself to an agent. If you're frustrated by this step, consider: Agents receive hundreds of submissions every month. Often they read these submissions on their own time—evenings, weekends, on their lunch break. Given the number of writers submitting—and the number of agents reading—it would simply be impossible for agents to ask for and read entire book manuscripts from every aspiring author. Instead, a query is a quick way for you to, first and foremost, pitch your book. But it's also a way to pitch yourself. If an agent is intrigued by your query, she may ask for a partial (say, the first three chapters of your manuscript). Or she may ask for the entire thing.

Remember all the time you've invested in your book. Take your time crafting your query. Yes, it's another step in a notoriously slow process. But it's necessary. Have you ever seen pictures of slush piles—those piles of unread queries on many well-known agents' desks? Imagine the size of those slush piles if they held full manuscripts instead of one-page query letters. Thinking of it this way, query letters begin to make more sense. And a well-crafted query just might help land all your well-placed commas into the public's hands.

Here we share with you the basics of a query, including its three parts and a detailed list of dos and don'ts.

PART I: THE INTRODUCTION

Whether you're submitting a 100-word picture book or a 90,000-word novel, you must be able to sum up the most basic aspects of your book in one sentence. Agents are busy. And they constantly receive submissions for types of work they don't represent. So up front they need to know that, after reading your first paragraph, the rest of your query is going to be worth their time.

An opening sentence designed to "hook" an agent is fine—if it's good and if it works. But this is the time to tune your right brain down and your left brain up—agents desire professionalism and queries that are short and to the point. Err on the side of formality with only a touch of whimsy. Tell the agent, in as few words as possible, what you've written, including title, genre, and length.

In the intro, you must also connect with the agent. Simply sending one hundred identical query letters out to "Dear Agent" won't get you published. Instead, your letter should be addressed not only to a specific agency but to a specific agent within that agency. (And double, triple, quadruple check that the agent's name is spelled correctly.)

When asked for submission tips, agents always mention the importance of making your letter personal. A good author-agent relationship is like a good marriage. It's important that both sides invest the time to find a good fit that meets their needs. So how do you connect with an agent you don't know personally? Research.

1. Make a Connection Based on a Book the Agent Already Represents

Most agencies have websites that list who and what they represent. Research those sites. Find a book similar to yours and explain that, because such-and-such book has a similar theme or tone, you think your book would be a great fit. In addition, many agents will list specific genres/categories they're looking for, either on their websites or in interviews. If your book is a match, state that.

2. Make a Connection Based on an Interview You Read

Search agents' names online and read any and all interviews they've given. Perhaps they mentioned a love for X and your book is all about X. Mention the specific interview. Prove that you've invested as much time researching them as they're about to spend researching you.

3. Make a Connection Based on a Conference You Both Attended

Was the agent you're querying the keynote speaker at a writing conference you were recently at? If so, mention it, and comment on an aspect of his speech you liked. Even better, did you meet the agent in person? Mention it, and if there's something you can say to jog her memory about the meeting, say it. Better yet, did the agent specifically ask you to send your manuscript? Mention it.

Finally, if you're being referred to a particular agent by an author the agent represents—that's your opening sentence. That referral is guaranteed to get your query placed at the top of the stack.

PART II: THE PITCH

Here's where you really get to sell your manuscript—but in only three to ten sentences. Consider a book's jacket flap and its role in convincing readers to plunk down $24.95 to buy what's in between those flaps. Like a jacket flap, you need to hook an agent in the confines of a very limited space. What makes your story interesting and unique? Is your story about someone's disappearance? Fine, but there are hundreds of stories about missing persons. Is your story about a teenager who has disappeared, and her frantic family and friends who are looking for her? Again, fine, but this story, too, already exists—in many forms. Is your story about a teenager who has disappeared, but her frantic family and friends who are looking for her don't realize that she ran away after finding out she was kidnapped as a baby and her biological parents are waiting for her in a secret place? *Now* you have a hook.

Practice your pitch. Read it out loud, not only to family and friends, but to people willing to give you honest, intelligent criticism. If you belong to a writing group, workshop your pitch. Share it with members of an online writing forum. Know anyone in the publishing industry? Share it with them. We're not talking about querying magazines here; we're talking about querying an agent who could become a lifelong partner. Spend time on your pitch. Write your pitch, put it aside for a week, then look at it again. Perfect it. Turn it into jacket-flap material so detailed, exciting, and clear that it would be near impossible to read your pitch and not want to read more. Use active verbs. Don't send a query simply because you finished a book. Send a query because you finished your pitch and you are ready to begin the next chapter of your publishing journey.

PART III: THE BIO

If you write fiction for adults or children, unless you're a household name or you've recently been a guest on some very big TV or radio shows, an agent is much more interested in your pitch than in who you are. If you write nonfiction, who you are—more specifically, your platform and publicity—is much more important. Regardless, these are key elements that must be present in every bio:

1. Publishing Credits

If you're submitting fiction, focus on your fiction credits—previously published works and short stories. That said, if you're submitting fiction and all your previously published work is nonfiction—articles, essays, etc.—that's still fine and good to mention. Don't be overly long about it. Mention your publications in bigger magazines or well-known literary journals. If you've never had anything published, don't say you lack official credits. Simply skip this altogether.

2. Contests and Awards

If you've won many, focus on the most impressive ones and those that most directly relate to your work. Don't mention contests you entered and weren't named in. Also, feel free to leave titles and years out.

3. MFAS

If you've earned or are working toward a master of fine arts in writing, say so and state the program. Don't mention English or journalism degrees, or online writing courses.

4. Large, Recognized Writing Organizations

Agents don't want to hear about your book club or the small critique group you meet with once a week. And they really don't want to hear about the online writing forum you belong to. But if you're a member of something like the Romance Writers of America (RWA), the Mystery Writers of America (MWA), the Society of Children's Book Writers and Illustrators (SCBWI), the Society of Professional Journalists (SPJ), the American Medical Writers, etc., say so. This shows you're serious about what you do and you're involved in groups that can aid with publicity and networking.

5. Platform and Publicity

If you write nonfiction, who you are and how you're going to help sell the book once it's published become very important. Why are you the best person to write it? What do you have now—public speaking engagements, an active website or blog, substantial cred in your industry—that will help you sell this book?

Finally, be cordial. Thank the agent for taking the time to read your query and consider your manuscript. Ask if you may send more, in the format she desires (partial, full, etc.).

Think back to the time you spent writing your book. The first draft wasn't your final. Don't fret too much over rejection slips. A line agents seemingly love to use on rejections is this: "Unfortunately, this isn't a right fit for me at this time, but I'm sure another agent will feel differently." It has merit. Your book—and query—can be good and still garner a rejection, for a myriad of reasons. Be patient. Keep pitching. And in the meantime, start writing that next book.

DOS AND DON'TS FOR QUERIES

DO:

- Keep the tone professional.
- Query a specific agent at a specific agency.
- Proofread. Double-check the spelling of the agency and the agent's name.
- Keep the query concise, limiting the overall length to one page (single-spaced, twelve-point type in a commonly used font).
- Focus on the plot, not your bio, when pitching fiction.
- Pitch agents who represent the type of material you write.
- Check an agency's submission guidelines to see how to query—for example, via e-mail or snail mail—and whether or not to include a SASE.
- Keep pitching, despite rejections.

DON'T:

- Include personal info not directly related to the book. For example, stating that you're a parent doesn't make you more qualified than someone else to write a children's book.
- Say how long it took you to write your manuscript. Some best-selling books took ten years to write—others, six weeks. An agent doesn't care how long it took—an agent only cares if it's good. Same thing goes with drafts—an agent doesn't care how many drafts it took you to reach the final product.
- Mention that this is your first novel or, worse, the first thing you've ever written. If you have no other publishing credits, don't advertise that fact. Don't mention it at all.
- State that your book has been edited by peers or professionals. Agents expect manuscripts to be edited, no matter how the editing was done.
- Bring up scripts or film adaptations—you're querying an agent about publishing a book, not making a movie.
- Mention any previous rejections.
- State that the story is copyrighted with the U.S. Copyright Office or that you own all rights. You already own all rights. You wrote it.

- Rave about how much your family and friends loved it. What matters is that the agent loves it.
- Send flowers or anything else except a self-addressed stamped envelope (and only if the SASE is required), if sending through snail mail.
- Follow up with a phone call. After the appropriate time has passed (many agencies say how long it will take to receive a response), follow up in the manner you queried—via e-mail or snail mail. And know that "no responses" do happen. After one follow-up and no response, cross the agent off your list.

KARA GEBHART UHL (pleiadesbee.com) writes and edits from Fort Thomas, KY.

SAMPLE QUERY 1: LITERARY FICTION

Agent's Comments: Jeff Kleinman (Folio Literary Management)

From: Garth Stein
To: Jeff Kleinman
Subject: Query: "The Art of Racing in the Rain" **①**

Dear Mr. Kleinman:

② Saturday night I was participating in a fundraiser for the King County Library System out here in the Pacific Northwest, and I met your client Layne Maheu. He spoke very highly of you and suggested that I contact you.

③ I am a Seattle writer with two published novels. I have recently completed my third novel, *The Art of Racing in the Rain*, and I find myself in a difficult situation: My new book is narrated by a dog, and my current agent **④** told me that he cannot (or will not) sell it for that very reason. Thus, I am seeking new representation.

⑤ *The Art of Racing in the Rain* is the story of Denny Swift, a race car driver who faces profound obstacles in his life, and ultimately overcomes them by applying the same techniques that have made him successful on the track. His story is narrated by his "philosopher dog," Enzo, who, having a nearly human soul (and an obsession with opposable thumbs), believes he will return as a man in his next lifetime.

⑥ My last novel, *How Evan Broke His Head and Other Secrets*, won a 2006 Pacific Northwest Booksellers Association Book Award, and since the award ceremony a year ago, I have given many readings, workshops, and lectures promoting the book. When time has permitted, I've read the first chapter from *The Art of Racing in the Rain*. Audience members have been universally enthusiastic and vocal in their response, and the first question asked is always: "When can I buy the book about the dog?" Also very positive.

⑦ I'm inserting, below, a short synopsis of *The Art of Racing in the Rain*, and my biography. Please let me know if the novel interests you; I would be happy to send you the manuscript.

Sincerely,
Garth Stein

① Putting the word *Query* and the title of the book on the subject line of an e-mail often keeps your e-mail from falling into the spam folder. **②** One of the best ways of starting out correspondence is figuring out your connection to the agent. **③** The author has some kind of track record. Who's the publisher, though? Were these both self-published novels, or were there reputable publishers involved? (I'll read on, and hope I find out.) **④** This seems promising, but also know this kind of approach can backfire, because we agents tend to be like sheep—what one doesn't like, the rest of us are wary of, too (or, conversely, what one likes, we all like). But in this case getting in the "two published novels" early is definitely helpful. **⑤** The third paragraph is the key pitch paragraph and Garth gives a great description of the book— he sums it up, gives us a feel for what we're going to get. This is the most important part of your letter. **⑥** Obviously it's nice to see the author's winning awards. Also good: The author's not afraid of promoting the book. **⑦** The end is simple and easy—it doesn't speak of desperation, or doubt, or anything other than polite willingness to help.

② SAMPLE QUERY 2: YOUNG ADULT
Agent's Comments: Ted Malawer (Upstart Crow Literary)

Dear Mr. Malawer:

I would like you to represent my 65,000-word contemporary teen novel *My Big Nose & Other Natural Disasters*.

① Seventeen-year-old Jory Michaels wakes up on the first day of summer vacation with her same old big nose, no passion in her life (in the creative sense of the word), and all signs still pointing to her dying a virgin. Plus, her mother is busy roasting a chicken for Day #6 of the Dinner For Breakfast Diet.

② In spite of her driving record (it was an accident!), Jory gets a job delivering flowers and cakes to Reno's casinos and wedding chapels. She also comes up with a new summer goal: saving for a life-altering nose job. She and her new nose will attract a fabulous boyfriend. Nothing like the shameless flirt Tyler Briggs, or Tom who's always nice but never calls. Maybe she'll find someone kind of like Gideon at the Jewel Café, except better looking and not quite so different. Jory survives various summer disasters like doing yoga after sampling Mom's Cabbage Soup Diet, Enforced Mother Bonding With Crazy Nose-Obsessed Daughter Night, and discovering Tyler's big secret. But will she learn to accept herself and maybe even find her passion in the creative (AND romantic!) sense of the word?

③ I have written for *APPLESEEDS, Confetti, Hopscotch, Story Friends, Wee Ones Magazine*, the *Deseret News, Children's Playmate*, and Blooming Tree Press' *Summer Shorts* anthology. I won the Utah Arts Council prize for *Not-A-Dr. Logan's Divorce Book*. My novels *Jungle Crossing* and *Going Native!* each won first prize in the League of Utah Writers contest. I currently serve as an SCBWI Regional Advisor.

④ I submitted *My Big Nose & Other Natural Disasters* to Krista Marino at Delacorte because she requested it during our critique at the summer SCBWI conference (no response yet).

Thank you for your time and attention. I look forward to hearing from you.

Sincerely,
Sydney Salter Husseman

① With hundreds and hundreds of queries each month, it's tough to stand out. Sydney, however, did just that. First, she has a great title that totally made me laugh. Second, she sets up her main character's dilemma in a succinct and interesting way. In one simple paragraph, I have a great idea of who Jory is and what her life is about—the interesting tidbits about her mother help show the novel's sense of humor, too. **②** Sydney's largest paragraph sets up the plot and the conflict, and introduces some exciting potential love interests and misadventures that I was excited to read about. Again, Sydney really shows off her fantastic sense of humor, and she leaves me hanging with a question that I needed an answer to. **③** She has writing experience and has completed other manuscripts that were prize worthy. Her SCBWI involvement—while not a necessity—shows me that she has an understanding of and an interest in the children's publishing world. **④** The fact that an editor requested the manuscript is always a good sign. That I knew Krista personally and highly valued her opinion was, as Sydney's main character Jory would say, "The icing on the cake."

SAMPLE QUERY 3: NONFICTION (SELF-HELP)
Agent's Comments: Michelle Wolfson (Wolfson Literary Agency)

Dear Ms. Wolfson:

1 Have you ever wanted to know the best day of the week to buy groceries or go out to dinner? Have you ever wondered about the best time of day to send an e-mail or ask for a raise? What about the best time of day to schedule a surgery or a haircut? What's the best day of the week to avoid lines at the Louvre? What's the best day of the month to make an offer on a house? What's the best time of day to ask someone out on a date? **2**

My book, *Buy Ketchup in May and Fly at Noon: A Guide to the Best Time to Buy This, Do That, and Go There*, has the answers to these questions and hundreds more.

3 As a longtime print journalist, I've been privy to readership surveys that show people can't get enough of newspaper and magazine stories about the best time to buy or do things. This book puts several hundreds of questions and answers in one place—a succinct, large-print reference book that readers will feel like they need to own. Why? Because it will save them time and money, and it will give them valuable information about issues related to health, education, travel, the workplace, and more. In short, it will make them smarter, so they can make better decisions. **4**

Best of all, the information in this book is relevant to anyone, whether they live in Virginia or the Virgin Islands; Portland, Oregon, or Portland, Maine. In fact, much of the book will find an audience in Europe and Australia.

5 I've worked as a journalist since 1984. In 1999, the Virginia Press Association created an award for the best news writing portfolio in the state—the closest thing Virginia had to a reporter-of-the-year award. I won it that year and then again in 2000. During the summer of 2007, I left newspapering to pursue book projects and long-form journalism.

6 I saw your name on a list of top literary agents for self-help books, and I read on your website that you're interested in books that offer practical advice. *Buy Ketchup in May and Fly at Noon* offers plenty of that. Please let me know if you'd like to read my proposal.

Sincerely,
Mark Di Vincenzo

1 I tend to prefer it when authors jump right into the heart of their book, the exception being if we've met at a conference or have some other personal connection. Mark chose clever questions for the opening of the query. All of those questions are, in fact, relevant to my life—with groceries, dinner, e-mail, and a raise—and yet I don't have a definitive answer to them. **2** He gets a little more offbeat and unusual with questions regarding surgery, the Louvre, buying a house, and dating. This shows a quirkier side to the book and also the range of topics it is going to cover, so I know right away there is going to be a mix of useful and quirky information on a broad range of topics. **3** By starting with "As a long time print journalist," Mark immediately establishes his credibility for writing on this topic. **4** This helps show that there is a market for this book and establishes the need for such a book. **5** Mark's bio paragraph offers a lot of good information. **6** It's nice when I feel like an author has sought me out specifically and thinks we would be a good fit.

④ SAMPLE QUERY 4: WOMEN'S FICTION
Agent's Comments: Elisabeth Weed (Weed Literary)

Dear Ms. Weed:

① Natalie Miller had a plan. She had a goddamn plan. Top of her class at Dartmouth. Even better at Yale Law. Youngest aide ever to the powerful Senator Claire Dupris. Higher, faster, stronger. This? Was all part of the plan. True, she was so busy ascending the political ladder that she rarely had time to sniff around her mediocre relationship with Ned, who fit the three Bs to the max: basic, blond, and boring, and she definitely didn't have time to mourn her mangled relationship with Jake, her budding rock star ex-boyfriend.

The lump in her right breast that Ned discovers during brain-numbingly bland morning sex? That? Was most definitely not part of the plan. And Stage IIIA breast cancer? Never once had Natalie jotted this down on her to-do list for conquering the world. When her (tiny-penised) boyfriend has the audacity to dump her on the day after her diagnosis, Natalie's entire world dissolves into a tornado of upheaval, and she's left with nothing but her diary to her ex-boyfriends, her mornings lingering over *The Price Is Right*, her burnt-out stubs of pot that carry her past the chemo pain, and finally, the weight of her life choices—the ones in which she might drown in if she doesn't find a buoy.

② *The Department of Lost and Found* is a story of hope, of resolve, of digging deeper than you thought possible until you find the strength not to crumble, and ultimately, of making your own luck, even when you've been dealt an unsteady hand.

③ I'm a freelance writer and have contributed to, among others, *American Baby, American Way, Arthritis Today, Bride's, Cooking Light, Fitness, Glamour, InStyle Weddings, Men's Edge, Men's Fitness, Men's Health, Parenting, Parents, Prevention, Redbook, Self, Shape, Sly, Stuff, USA Weekend, Weight Watchers, Woman's Day, Women's Health*, and ivillage.com, msn.com, and women.com. I also ghostwrote *The Knot Book of Wedding Flowers*.

If you are interested, I'd love to send you the completed manuscript. Thanks so much! Looking forward to speaking with you soon.

Allison Winn Scotch

① The opening sentence reads like great jacket copy, and I immediately know who our protagonist is and what the conflict for her will be. (And it's funny, without being silly.) **②** The third paragraph tells me where this book will land: upmarket women's fiction. (A great place to be these days!) **③** This paragraph highlights impressive credentials. While being able to write nonfiction does not necessarily translate over to fiction, it shows me that she is someone worth paying more attention to. And her magazine contacts will help when it comes time to promote the book.

⑤ SAMPLE QUERY 5: MAINSTREAM/COMEDIC FICTION
Agent's Comments: Michelle Brower (Folio Literary Management)

Dear Michelle Brower:

❶ "I spent two days in a cage at the SPCA until my parents finally came to pick me up. The stigma of bringing your undead son home to live with you can wreak havoc on your social status, so I can't exactly blame my parents for not rushing out to claim me. But one more day and I would have been donated to a research facility."

Andy Warner is a zombie.

After reanimating from a car accident that killed his wife, Andy is resented by his parents, abandoned by his friends, and vilified by society. Seeking comfort and camaraderie in Undead Anonymous, a support group for zombies, Andy finds kindred souls in Rita, a recent suicide who has a taste for consuming formaldehyde in cosmetic products, and Jerry, a 21-year-old car crash victim with an artistic flair for Renaissance pornography.

❷ With the help of his new friends and a rogue zombie named Ray, Andy embarks on a journey of personal freedom and self-discovery that will take him from his own casket to the SPCA to a media-driven, class-action lawsuit for the civil rights of all zombies. And along the way, he'll even devour a few Breathers.

Breathers is a contemporary dark comedy about life, or undeath, through the eyes of an ordinary zombie. In addition to *Breathers*, I've written three other novels and more than four dozen short stories—a dozen of which have appeared in small press publications. Currently, I'm working on my fifth novel, also a dark comedy, about fate.

Enclosed is a two-page synopsis and the first chapter of *Breathers*, with additional sample chapters or the entire manuscript available upon request. I appreciate your time and interest in considering my query and I look forward to your response.

Sincerely,
Scott G. Browne

❶ What really draws me to this query is the fact that it has exactly what I'm looking for in my commercial fiction—story and style. Scott includes a brief quote from the book that manages to capture his sense of humor as an author and his uniquely relatable main character (hard to do with someone who's recently reanimated). I think this is a great example of how query letters can break the rules and still stand out in the slush pile. I normally don't like quotes as the first line, because I don't have a context for them, but this quote both sets up the main concept of the book *and* gives me a sense of the character's voice. This method won't necessarily work for most fiction, but it absolutely is successful here. ❷ The letter quickly conveys that this is an unusual book about zombies, and being a fan of zombie literature, I'm aware that it seems to be taking things in a new direction. I also appreciate how Scott conveys the main conflict of his plot and his supporting cast of characters—we know there is an issue for Andy beyond coming back to life as a zombie, and that provides momentum for the story.

YOUR GUIDE TO AN EFFECTIVE NOVEL SYNOPSIS

How to summarize your story in a compelling way.

Chuck Sambuchino & the Editors of Writer's Digest

If your novel is complete and polished, it's time to write your query and synopsis. After that, you're ready to test the agent and editor waters.

How you submit your novel package will depend on each agent or publisher's specified submission guidelines. You'll find that some want only a query letter; others request a query letter and the complete manuscript; some prefer a query letter plus three sample chapters and a synopsis; and still others request a query letter, a few sample chapters, an outline, and a synopsis. All want an SASE (self-addressed, stamped envelope) with adequate postage, unless they request an electronic submission.

Be prepared to send at least a query letter, a synopsis, and three consecutive sample chapters. These are the most important—and most requested—parts of your novel package. You may not need to send them all in the same submission package, but you probably will need to use each of them at one time or another, so prepare everything before you start submitting. Here, we'll focus on what writers often find the most difficult component of their novel submission package: the synopsis.

DEFINING THE SYNOPSIS

The synopsis supplies key information about your novel (plot, theme, characterization, setting), while also showing how these coalesce to form the big picture. It quickly tells what your novel is about without making the editor or agent read the novel in its entirety.

There are no hard-and-fast rules about the synopsis. In fact, there's conflicting advice about the typical length of a synopsis. Most editors and agents agree, though: The shorter, the better.

When writing your synopsis, focus on the essential parts of your story, and try not to include sections of dialogue unless you think they're absolutely necessary. (It's okay to inject a few strong quotes from your characters, but keep them brief.) Finally, even though the synopsis is only a condensed version of your novel, it must seem complete.

Keep events in the same order as they happen in the novel (but don't break them down into individual chapters). Remember that your synopsis should have a beginning, a middle, and an ending (yes, you must tell how the novel ends to round out your synopsis).

That's what's required of a synopsis: You need to be concise, compelling, and complete, all at the same time.

CRAFTING TWO SYNOPSES

Because there is no definitive length to a synopsis, it's recommended you have two versions: a long synopsis and a short synopsis.

There used to be a fairly universal system regarding synopses. For every thirty-five or so pages of your manuscript, you would have one page of synopsis explanation, up to a maximum of eight pages. So if your book was 245 pages, double-spaced, your synopsis would be approximately seven pages. This was fairly standard and allowed writers a decent amount of space to explain their story. You should write a synopsis following these guidelines first. This will be your long synopsis.

The problem is that during the past several years, agents have become busier and busier, and now they want to hear your story now-now-now. Many agents today request a synopsis of no more than two pages. Some even say one page, but two pages is generally acceptable. To be ready to submit to these agents, you'll also need to draft a new, more concise synopsis—the short synopsis.

So once you've written both, which do you submit? If you think your short synopsis is tight and effective, always use that. However, if you think the long synopsis is actually more effective, then you will sometimes submit it instead. If an agent requests two pages max, send only the short one. If she says simply, "Send a synopsis," and you feel your longer synopsis is superior, submit the long one. If you're writing plot-heavy fiction, such as thrillers and mysteries, you might benefit a lot from submitting a longer, more thorough synopsis.

Your best bet on knowing what to submit is to follow the guidelines of the agency or publisher in question.

FORMATTING YOUR ELECTRONIC SUBMISSION

Some editors or agents might ask you to submit your synopsis via e-mail. The editor or agent can provide you with specific formatting guidelines indicating how she wants it sent and the type of files she prefers.

If an agent or editor does request an electronic submission, keep the following four points in mind:

- Follow the same formatting specs you would for a paper synopsis submission.
- When sending your synopsis via e-mail, put the name of your novel in the subject line (but don't use all caps).
- Send the synopsis as an attachment to your e-mail unless the editor or agent requests otherwise.
- Include a cover letter in the body of your e-mail. Your cover page and table of contents should go in the file along with the synopsis.

YOUR ESSENTIAL SYNOPSIS CHECKLIST

FORMATTING SPECS

- Use a 1-inch margin on all sides; justify the left margin only.
- Put your name and contact information on the top-left corner of the first page.
- Type the novel's genre, word count, and the word *Synopsis* in the top-right corner of the first page.
- Don't number the first page.
- Put the novel's title, centered and in all caps, about one-third of the way down the page.
- Begin the synopsis text four lines below the title.
- The text throughout the synopsis should be double-spaced (unless you plan to keep it to one or two pages, in which case single-spaced is okay).
- Use all caps the first time you introduce a character.
- After the first page, use a header on every page that contains your last name, your novel's title in all caps, and the word *Synopsis*, like so: Name/TITLE/Synopsis.
- After the first page, number the pages in the top-right corner on the same line as the header.
- The first line of text on each page after the first page should be three lines below the header.

OTHER DOS AND DON'TS

- **DO** keep in mind that this is a sales pitch. Make it a short, fast, and exciting read.
- **DO** establish a hook at the beginning of the synopsis. Introduce your lead character and set up a key conflict.

- **DO** introduce your most important character first.
- **DO** provide details about each of your central characters (age, gender, marital status, profession, etc.), but don't do this for every character—only the primary ones.
- **DO** include the characters' motivations and emotions.
- **DO** highlight pivotal plot points.
- **DO** reveal your novel's ending.
- **DON'T** go into detail about what happens; just tell the reader what happens as concisely as you can.
- **DON'T** inject long sections of dialogue.
- **DO** write in the third person, present tense, even if your novel is written in a different point of view.

CHUCK SAMBUCHINO (chucksambuchino.com) is an editor, best-selling humor book author, and an authority on how to get published. He is the editor of *Guide to Literary Agents 2017* and *Children's Writer's & Illustrator's Market 2017*. He is the author of the humor books *How to Survive a Garden Gnome Attack*; *Red Dog, Blue Dog*; and *When Clowns Attack*. In addition, Chuck has also written three writing-related titles: *Formatting and Submitting Your Manuscript 3rd Edition*, *Create Your Writer Platform*, and *Get a Literary Agent*.

NONFICTION BOOK PROPOSALS

Learn to pitch your nonfiction with confidence.

....

Chuck Sambuchino

A b*ook proposal* is a business plan that explains the details of a nonfiction book. Because your project is not complete during the pitching stages, the proposal acts as a blueprint and diagram for what the finished product will look like, as well as exactly how you will promote it when the product is in the marketplace.

Better yet, think about it like this: If you wanted to open a new restaurant and needed a bank loan, you would have to make a case to the bank as to why your business will succeed and generate revenue. A book proposal acts in much the same way. You must prove to a publisher that your book idea is a proven means to generate revenue—showing that customers will buy your worthwhile and unique product, and you have the means to draw in prospective customers.

"There are several factors that can help a book proposal's prospects: great writing, great platform, or great information, and ideally all three," says Ted Weinstein, founder of Ted Weinstein Literary. "For narrative works, the writing should be gorgeous, not just functional. For practical works, the information should be insightful, comprehensive, and preferably new. And for any work of nonfiction, of course, the author's platform is enormously important."

If you're writing a work of fiction (novel, screenplay, picture book) or memoir, the first all-important step is to simply finish the work, because agents and editors will consider it for publication based primarily on how good the writing is. On the other hand, when you have a nonfiction project of any kind, you do *not* need to finish the book to sell it. In fact, even if you're feeling ambitious and knock out the entire text, finishing the book will not help you sell it because all an editor really needs to see are several sample chapters that adequately portray what the rest of the book will be like.

THE STRUCTURE OF A BOOK PROPOSAL

A book proposal is made up of several key sections that flesh out the book, its markets, and information about the author. All of these important sections seek to answer one of the three main questions that every proposal must answer:

- What is the book, and why is it timely and unique?
- What is its place in the market?
- Why are you the best person to write and market it?

Every book proposal has several sections that allow the author to explain more about their book. Though you can sometimes vary the order of the sections, here are the major elements (and suggested order) that should be addressed before you pitch a nonfiction book to a literary agent.

Title Page
Keep it simple. Put your title and subtitle in the middle, centered, and put your personal contact information at the bottom right.

Table of Contents (with Page Numbers)
A nonfiction book proposal has several sections, and can run many pages, so this is where you explain everything the agent can find in the proposal, in case they want to jump around immediately to peruse different sections at different times.

Overview
This section gets its name because it's designed to be an overview of the entire proposal to come. It's something of a "greatest hits" of the proposal, where you discuss the concept and content, the evidence of need for this new resource in the market, and your platform. Overviews typically run up to three double-spaced pages and immediately make the case as to why this book is worthwhile for consideration and timely for readers *now*. Another way to think about this section is by imagining it as an extended query letter, because it serves the same purpose. If an agent likes your overview, she will review the rest of the document to delve deeper into both you and your ideas. The overview is arguably the most important part of the proposal. "Your overview is the sizzle in your nonfiction book proposal," says Michael Larsen of Larsen-Pomada Literary Agents. "If it doesn't sell you

and your book, agents and editors won't check the bones (the outline of your book) or try the steak (your sample chapter)."

Format

This section explains how the book will be formatted. Remember that your finished product does not physically exist, and all nonfiction books look different from one another in terms of appearance. So spell out exactly what it will look like. What is the physical size of the book? What is your estimated word count when everything is said and done? How long after the contract is signed will you be able to submit the finished product? Will there be sidebars, boxed quotes, or interactive elements? Will there be photos, illustrations, or other art? (If so, who will be responsible for collecting this art?)

Spinoffs (Optional

Some nonfiction projects lend themselves to things like sequels, spin-offs, subsidiary rights possibilities, and more. For example, when I pitched my political humor book for dog lovers, *Red Dog / Blue Dog*, this is the section where I mentioned the possibility of a tear-off calendar if the book succeeded, as well as a possible sequel, *Red Cat / Blue Cat*. Unlike other sections of a proposal, this one is optional, as some ideas will *not* lend themselves to more variations.

AN AGENT EXPLAINS THREE COMMON BOOK PROPOSAL PROBLEMS

1. **LACK OF A STORY ARC.** Many failed nonfiction proposals are mere surveys of a subject. The books that sell have strong characters who are engaged in some project that eventually is resolved. Don't do a book about slime mold. Do a book about the Slime Mold Guy who solved the mystery of slime mold.

2. **SKIMPINESS.** I like big fat proposals. Writers worry too much about how much reading editors have to do, and they self-defeatingly try to keep proposals short. Busy editors are not the problem. A great proposal will hook a reader within a few pages and keep that reader spellbound until the last page no matter how long. Short, skimpy proposals often quit before they can get me, or an editor, truly immersed and engaged. You aren't just informing us about your book; you are recruiting us into joining you on what is going to be a long and expensive expedition. If crazy, fire-eyed Christopher Columbus wants me to join him on his trip to the "Here Be Monsters" part of the ocean, I'd like to inspect his ships very, very carefully before I set sail. Editors are scared to buy books because they are so often wrong. Thoroughness builds confidence.

3. **EXTRAPOLATION.** Many proposals say, in effect, "I don't know all that much about this subject, but give me a six-figure contract, and I will go and find out everything

---

there is to know." I understand the problem writers face: How are they supposed to master a subject until after they've done the travels, interviews, and research? Nevertheless, unless you are already an established writer, you can't simply promise to master your subject. Book contracts go to those who have already mastered a subject. If you haven't mastered your subject, but you really think you deserve a book contract, try to get a magazine assignment so that you can do at least some of the necessary research, funded by the magazine. But if you're just winging it, I probably can't help you unless you have a superb platform.

Sidebar courtesy of literary agent Russell Galen (Scovil Galen Ghosh Literary Agency).

Chapter List

While you will be turning over only a few completed, polished chapters, agents still want to know exactly what will be in the rest of the book. So list out all your chapter concepts with a paragraph or so on the content of each. This section is important, as it shows that, although the book is not complete, the author has a clear path forward in terms of the exact content that will fill all the pages.

Sample Chapters

Although you do not have to finish the book before pitching nonfiction, you do have to complete up to four book chapters as an appropriate sample. The goal is to write chapters that you believe do a fine job of representing what the book is about. Typical sample chapters include the book's first chapter and others from different sections of the book. Your goal is to make these chapters represent what the final product will be like in both appearance and content. So if the book is going to be funny, your sample chapters better be humorous. If the book will be infused with art and illustrations, gather what images you can for these pages. The sample chapters are the one place in a proposal where the author can step out of "business mode" and into "writer mode," focusing on things like voice, humor, style, and more.

Target Audiences

You've probably heard before that "a book for everyone is a book for no one," so target your work to core audience groups. This section is your chance to prove an *evidence of need*. Or, as agent Mollie Glick of Creative Artists Agency says, "You want an original idea—but not too original."

For example, when I was listing audiences for my book, *How to Survive a Garden Gnome Attack*, they were (1) garden gnome enthusiasts, (2) gardeners, (3) survival guide parody lovers, and (4) humor book lovers. Note how I resisted the urge to say "Everyone everywhere loves a laugh, so I basically see the entire human population snatching this bad boy up at bookstores."

When I was pitching a book on historical theaters around the country, my audiences were (1) theater lovers, (2) historical preservationists in the regions where featured theaters are located, (3) nostalgia lovers, and (4) architecture buffs and enthusiasts. Again, the audiences were concise and focused. I proved I had researched and honed in on the exact pockets of people who would pay money for what I was proposing.

And once you identify these audiences, you must *quantify* them. If you want to write a book about the history of the arcade game Donkey Kong, a logical target audience would be "Individuals who currently play Donkey Kong"—but you must quantify the audience, because an agent has no idea if that audience size is 1,000 or 500,000. So tell them what it really is—and explain how you came to find that true number. You can find these quantifying numbers by seeing where such audiences get their news. For example, if www.donkeykongnews.com has a newsletter reach of 12,000 individuals, that is a proven number you can use. If the official Donkey Kong Twitter account has 134,000 followers, that will help you, as well. If *Classic Games Magazine* has a circulation of 52,000, that number can help you, too. "Use round, accurate numbers in your proposal," Larsen says. "If a number isn't round, qualify it by writing nearly, almost, or more than (not over). Provide sources for statistics if asked."

Comparative Titles

This is where you list any and all books that are similar to yours in the marketplace. What you're aiming for is showing that many books that have similarities to your title exist and have healthy sales, but no one book accomplishes everything yours will do. If you can show that, you've made an argument that your book is unique (and therefore worthwhile) and also that people have shown a history of buying such a book (and therefore the book is even more worthwhile). You're essentially trying to say "Books exist on Subject A and books exist on Subject B, but no book exists on Subject AB, which is exactly what my book, [*Title*], will do."

You can find comparative titles by searching through the appropriate bookshelf in Barnes & Noble or any local bookstore, as well as by scouring Amazon. Once you have your list, it's your time to write them all down—laying out details such as the publisher, title, year, and any signs of solid sales (such as awards or a good Amazon sales ranking). After you explain a book's specifics, you should quickly say why your book is different from it. At the same time, don't trash competing books. Because your book shares some similarity to it, you don't want your own work to come under fire.

Marketing/Writer Platform

This massively important section details all the many avenues you have in place to market the work to the audiences you've already identified. This section will list your social media channels, contacts in the media, personal marketing abilities, public speaking engagements, and much more. This section is of the utmost importance, as an agent needs to be assured you can currently market your book to thousands of possible buyers, if not more. Otherwise, the agent may stop reading the proposal. "Develop a significant following before you go out with your nonfiction book. If you build it, publishers will come," says agent Jeffery McGraw of The August Agency. "How visible are you to the world? That's what determines your level of platform. Someone with real platform is the go-to person in their area of expertise. If you don't make yourself known to the world as the expert in your field, then how will [members of the media] know to reach out to you? Get out there. Make as many connections as you possibly can."

Author Bio/Credentials

Here is your chance to explain what makes you qualified to write this book. Include things such as your degrees, memberships, endorsements, and more. Anything that qualifies you to write this book but is not technically considered "platform" should go in this section.

THE AGENT QUERY TRACKER

Submit smarter and follow up faster with these simple spreadsheets to revolutionize your record-keeping.

Tyler Moss

Everyone knows the real magic of writing comes from time spent in the chair, those sessions in which your fingertips flitting across the keyboard can barely keep pace with the electric current sparking through your brain.

Those in-between periods, full of administrative tasks—the querying, the tracking of payments, the day-to-day doldrums that occupy the interstitial moments of a writer's life—become an afterthought. But when such responsibilities are given short shrift, the inevitable result is disorganization—which at best can impede creativity and at worst can have dire consequences. Missed payments, embarrassing gaffes (querying the same agent twice, or realizing you have no record of where your previous agent submitted your last novel), and incomplete records come tax time are entirely avoidable headaches.

Still, organized record-keeping takes work. Which is why we decided to do it for you.

This does not have to mean you're about to start spending more time on these tasks—in fact, quite the opposite. Once you invest in a standard process up front, each future action will require little more than filling out a few cells in a spreadsheet. (Learn to love them as I have for their clean, quadrilateral beauty.)

You can use the simple guides on the following pages to customize forms of your own, whether you're querying an agent, tracking the places your agent is submitting, or working on your freelancing career between projects.

AGENT QUERY TRACKER

AGENT	**Example:** Booker M. Sellington		
AGENCY	The Booker M. Sellington Agency		
E-MAIL	BMS@bmsagency.com		
DATE QUERIED	8/1/16		
MATERIALS SENT	Query, Synopsis, first 10 pages		
DATE FOLLOWED UP	9/1/16		
RESPONSE	Request for additional materials		
ADDITIONAL MATE-RIALS REQUESTED	Full manuscript		
DATE FOLLOWED UP	10/15/16		
RESPONSE	Offer of representation		
NOTES	Specializes in thrillers		

Few writers hit the jackpot and manage to land a literary agent on their first query. As this process can take weeks or months, and as agency guidelines vary widely, it can be helpful to keep a detailed record of whom you have contacted, what agency they work for, what materials you've sent in, and the specifics of their responses. Customize your own tracker starting from these column headings:

- **AGENT, AGENCY & E-MAIL:** Where you are sending your query
- **POLICY AGAINST QUERYING MULTIPLE AGENTS AT AGENCY:** [Optional Field] Some agencies have a no-from-one-agent-means-no-from-the-whole-agency policy; noting this saves you time and embarrassment, particularly at larger firms where multiple reps might seem like a potential fit
- **DATE QUERIED & MATERIALS SENT:** When and what you submitted, always following guidelines (query letter, first ten pages, synopsis, proposal, etc.)
- **"NO RESPONSE MEANS NO" POLICY:** [Optional Field] Agents who specify in their guidelines that no response equates to a rejection, meaning you shouldn't follow up
- **DATE FOLLOWED UP:** In the event of no response and excluding those with the policy noted above
- **RESPONSE:** A rejection, a request to see more, or any constructive feedback
- **ADDITIONAL MATERIALS REQUESTED & DATE SENT:** Typically a full or partial manuscript is requested if your query garners interest

- **DATE FOLLOWED UP:** For a full or partial, follow up after at least four weeks if there's no response (unless you have an offer for representation elsewhere, in which case you'll follow up immediately to request a decision or withdraw your manuscript from consideration)
- **RESPONSE:** The agent's final feedback or response
- **NOTES:** Any helpful info on your interaction with the agent or agency, or feedback that could be addressed before additional querying (e.g., "The protagonist often behaves erratically and inconsistently," or "The manuscript could use a proofread")

If you opt to forgo seeking representation and instead are submitting directly to publishers that accept unagented submissions, then I suggest you make a separate spreadsheet to track that information, swapping the headings **AGENT** and **AGENCY** for **ACQUIRING EDITOR** and **IMPRINT/PUBLISHER**, respectively.

ORGANIZE YOUR QUERIES

Both versions of the tracker are available for download at writersdigest.com/GLA-18.

AGENT SUBMISSIONS TO PUBLISHER TRACKER

IMPRINT/PUBLISHER	**Example:** Pendant Publishing		
ACQUIRING EDITOR	Elaine Benes		
DATE SENT	8/1/16		
DATE FOLLOWED UP	9/1/16		
RESPONSE	Pass		
EDITOR'S COMMENTS	Says a "book about nothing" is not right for their Spring 2018 lineup		
ADDITIONAL NOTES	Suggests changes to plot in which the judge sentences protagonist to be the antagonist's butler		

After signing with an agent, it's critical to stay in close communication as she sends your manuscript to publishers. Such records allow you to stay involved in the direction of your career, gather essential data about the imprints your agent believes you'd be best suited for, and pinpoint commonalities or contradictions in feedback. And if you must someday sever ties with your agent, you'll have what you need to help your new representation pick up right where your old representation left off. Keep record of the following details:

- **IMPRINT/PUBLISHER, ACQUIRING EDITOR & DATE SENT:** The details of exactly where and when your agent submitted your manuscript
- **DATE FOLLOWED UP:** Date on which your agent followed up with the acquiring editor if you did not receive an initial response
- **RESPONSE:** Accepted, rejected, revise-and-resubmit request
- **EDITOR'S COMMENTS:** A one-line description highlighting any relevant feedback received
- **ADDITIONAL NOTES:** Miscellaneous information about the publisher, editor or the overall interaction between agent and publishing house

---

PRO TIP: SAVE SPREADSHEETS TO GOOGLE DRIVE

Recently I read a news story in which a writer in New Orleans ran into his burning home to save the manuscripts of two completed novels stored on his computer—the only place he had them saved. Luckily, he weathered the blaze and escaped with laptop in hand. Though we can admire his dedication to his work, there are any number of digital-age options that could've prevented this horrible scenario—among them, Google Drive.

The system is ideal for uploading a fresh document of your manuscript every time you make changes, storing files online in addition to on your computer (Google Drive has an online storage function similar to services such as Dropbox and Microsoft OneDrive).

Google Drive allows you to create documents, spreadsheets, slide shows, and more, all of which can be accessed from anywhere—laptop, tablet, smartphone—by logging into a free Google account. Such items are easily shared with your co-author, agent, or publicist for more efficient record keeping or file sharing. It's also a great place to create and modify the trackers from this article.

Simply log in to your account at google.com/drive (or create one for free), hit the New button in the top left corner of the interface and click on Google Sheets. This will open a new window with a clean spreadsheet, where you can then begin entering the appropriate column headings. Title the spreadsheet by clicking "Untitled spreadsheet" at the top of the page. Once complete, you'll be able to open up your Freelance Payment Tracker or Agent Query Tracker on any device with an Internet connection—far from flames or flood.

FREELANCE PITCH TRACKER

SUBJECT	**Example:** Essay about meeting Stephen King in the waiting room at the dentist		
PUBLICATION	*Writer's Digest*		
EDITOR	Tyler Moss		
E-MAIL	wdsubmissions@ fwmedia.com		
PITCH SUBMITTED	8/1/16		
FOLLOW UP	8/15/16		
RESULT	Accepted		
DEADLINE	10/15/16		
NOTES	$0.50 cents/word for 600 words		

For freelance writers, ideas are currency—but they don't exist in a vacuum. Once you've brainstormed a solid premise and started to pitch potential markets, the resulting interactions can quickly clutter your in-box. Avoid losing track by recording your pitches in a spreadsheet with the following column headings:

- **SUBJECT:** One-line description of your story idea
- **PUBLICATION:** Name of magazine, website, or newspaper you pitched to
- **EDITOR & E-MAIL:** Where you sent your pitch
- **PITCH SUBMITTED:** When the query was sent
- **FOLLOW UP:** The date on which you plan to follow up if you haven't received a response (typically two weeks later, unless the submission guidelines specify otherwise)
- **RESULT:** Accepted, rejected, asked to rework
- **DEADLINE:** If accepted, date story is due
- **NOTES:** Additional info, based on your interactions with the editor (e.g., "Publication pays too little," or "Editor rejected pitch, but encouraged pitching again soon")

In addition to keeping track of irons currently in the fire, this spreadsheet is invaluable for later looking up contact info of editors you haven't e-mailed in a while.

If you want to track submissions to literary journals, simply switch out the column headings **SUBJECT** and **PUBLICATION** with **STORY TITLE** and **JOURNAL**, respectively, ax the **FOLLOW UP** column (journals tend to operate on slower, more sporadic schedules, sometimes without full-time staff), and replace the **DEADLINE** column with **READING FEE** (so you can evaluate and track any submission expenses where applicable).

ORGANIZE YOUR FREELANCE LIFE

Find both the freelance pitch and journal versions of this pitch tracker available for download at writersdigest.com/GLA-18.

FREELANCE PAYMENT TRACKER

ARTICLE HEADLINE	Example: Tongue Tied		
PUBLICATION/URL	*Ball & String Magazine*		
PAYMENT	$500		
DATE PUBLISHED	July 2016		
TOTAL WORDS	1,000		
$/WORD	$0.40 cents/word		
INVOICE #	#2014-1		
INVOICE SUBMITTED	8/12/16		
PAID	8/30/16		

When you've been commissioned to write a piece, it's vital to document the status of your payment. Not only will it keep you from missing a check, but it's incredibly useful for noting what a publication has paid you in the past and comparing the rates of different publications for which you freelance—which can help you prioritize your time by targeting the most lucrative outlets. It's also a lifesaver come April 15.

As depicted in the example spreadsheet above, you can use the following column headings to trace the path of your payments:

- **HEADLINE:** Title of the finished, published piece
- **PUBLICATION/URL:** Outlet that published the article and, if applicable, the URL where the article can be found online
- **PAYMENT:** Total payment received for work
- **DATE PUBLISHED:** Date article went live online, or issue month if for a print magazine or journal
- **TOTAL WORDS & $/WORD:** Length of the piece and amount you were paid per word, found by dividing the total payment by the total number of words (a common standardization for freelance payment rates)

- **INVOICE # & SUBMITTED:** Unique number of the invoice you submitted for this particular article (if applicable), and date on which it was submitted
- **PAID:** Date on which you received the payment, most commonly via check or direct deposit

Of course, you can also use this same basic format to develop a spreadsheet that covers advances, royalties, speaking honoraria, etc. Use the basic format outlined here to construct your own customized version.

TYLER MOSS is the managing editor of *Writer's Digest*. Follow him on Twitter @tjmoss11.

THE ANATOMY OF A FIRST PAGE

A literary agent deconstructs the first page of several successful novels—and shows you what you need to stand out.

Paula Munier

FIERCE FIRST WORDS

The best story openings are fierce enough to grab the attention of readers, editors, and agents. This means keeping a lot of balls in the air. Skillful storytellers are master jugglers: They juggle voice, character, premise, setting, dialogue, conflict, point of view, style, and theme in an endless and seamless circle of story. They toss those story balls around with a fierceness we haven't quite experienced before. And thus we are compelled to read on.

A tall order.

Once I was in a writer's group where one of the writers was struggling with her opening. Margaret was a good storyteller, and while her story was solid, her opening did not work. Her first words were unworthy of the rest of her novel, and she knew it. She'd rewritten the first page a dozen times but remained unhappy with the results. She was stumped.

She stayed behind after everyone else had left, and we sat on my sofa and talked about the problem with the opening of her thriller.

"When in doubt," I said, "look to the masters." And I jumped up and went to my bookshelf, pulled down the first several thrillers I found, and stacked them on the coffee table.

We took turns reading aloud the first page of each novel. When we were finished, we looked at each other and grinned.

"Thanks," said Margaret. She went home and wrote a new opening. She published that book and several others since. (Check out *Under Fire, Under Oath,* and *Whitey on Trial* at www.margaretmclean.com.)

It worked for Margaret, and it will work for you. No matter what your genre, the quickest way to understand what constitutes a fierce beginning is to read the first words of several best-selling works. So let's pull seven stories off the shelf and take a hard look at the opening words.

Of course, the selections will be from my bookshelf since I am writing this article. Lucky for you, I have very eclectic tastes, so the odds are good that whatever genre you write in will be represented.

> All this happened, more or less. The war parts, anyway, are pretty much true. One guy I knew really *was* shot in Dresden for taking a teapot that wasn't his. Another guy I knew really *did* threaten to have his personal enemies killed by hired gunmen after the war. And so on. I've changed all the names.
>
> —*Slaughterhouse-Five*, by Kurt Vonnegut

> The first annoying thing is when I ask Dad what he thinks happened to Mom, he always says, "What's most important is for you to understand it's not your fault." You'll notice that wasn't even the question. When I press him, he says the second annoying thing, "The truth is complicated. There's no way one person can ever know everything about another person."
>
> Mom disappears into thin air two days before Christmas without telling me? Of course it's complicated. Just because it's complicated, just because you think you can't ever know everything about another person, it doesn't mean you can't try.
>
> It doesn't mean I can't try.
>
> —*Where'd You Go, Bernadette*, by Maria Semple

> LOG ENTRY: SOL 6
> I'm pretty much fucked.
>
> That's my considered opinion.
>
> Fucked.
>
> Six days into what should be the greatest two months of my life, and it's turned into a nightmare.
>
> I don't even know who'll read this. I guess someone will find it eventually. Maybe a hundred years from now.
>
> For the record … I didn't die on Sol 6. Certainly the rest of the crew thought I did, and I can't blame them. Maybe there'll be a day of national mourning for me, and my Wikipedia page will say, "Mark Watney is the only human being to have died on Mars."
>
> —*The Martian*, by Andy Weir

> I like to save things. Not important things like whales or people or the environment. Silly things. Porcelain bells, the kind you get at souvenir shops. Cookie cutters you'll never use, because who

needs a cookie in the shape of a foot? Ribbons for my hair. Love letters. Of all the things I save, I guess you could say my love letters are my most prized possession.

I keep my letters in a teal hatbox my mom bought me from a vintage store downtown. They aren't love letters that someone else wrote for me; I don't have any of those. These are ones I've written. There's one for every boy I've ever loved—five in all.

—*To All the Boys I've Loved Before*, by Jenny Han

April 1962
Porto Vergogna, Italy
The dying actress arrived in his village the only way one could come directly—in a boat that motored into the cove, lurched past the rock jetty, and bumped against the end of the pier. She wavered a moment in the boat's stern, then extended a slender hand to grip the mahogany railing; with the other, she pressed a wide-brimmed hat against her head. All around her, shards of sunlight broke on the flickering waves.

Twenty meters away, Pasquale Tursi watched the arrival of the woman as if in a dream. Or rather, he would think later, a dream's opposite: a burst of clarity after a lifetime of sleep.

—*Beautiful Ruins*, by Jess Walter

All the dying that summer began with the death of a child, a boy with golden hair and thick glasses, killed on the railroad tracks outside New Bremen, Minnesota, sliced into pieces by a thousand tons of steel speeding across the prairie toward South Dakota. His name was Bobby Cole. He was a sweet-looking kid and by that I mean he had eyes that seemed full of dreaming and he wore a half smile as if he was just about to understand something you'd spent an hour trying to explain. I should have known him better, been a better friend. He lived not far from my house and we were the same age. But he was two years behind me in school and might have been held back even more except for the kindness of certain teachers. He was a small kid, a simple child, no match at all for the diesel-fed drive of a Union Pacific locomotive.

—*Ordinary Grace*, by William Kent Krueger

"We should start back," Gared urged as the woods began to grow dark around them. "The wildlings are dead."

"Do the dead frighten you?" Ser Waymar Royce asked with just the hint of a smile.

Gared did not rise to the bait. He was an old man, past fifty, and he had seen the lordlings come and go. "Dead is dead," he said. "We have no business with the dead."

"Are they dead?" Royce asked softly. "What proof have we?"

"Will saw them," Gared said. "If he says they are dead, that's proof enough for me."

Will had known they would drag him into the quarrel sooner or later. He wished it had been later rather than sooner. "My mother told me that dead men sing no songs," he put in.

—*A Game of Thrones: Book One of A Song of Ice and Fire*, by George R.R. Martin

Each of these openings draws us in and compels us to read on. Each of these writers sets up the story, juggling voice, character, premise, setting, dialogue, conflict, point of view, style, and theme into that aforementioned seamless circle of story. Kurt Vonnegut does it in only fifty-seven words, but even the longest of these openings—the first paragraph of Krueger's *Ordinary Grace*—comes in at only 158 words. That's craftsmanship. Juggling at its best.

These are all smart writers who play to their strengths:

- Kurt Vonnegut relies on the uniqueness of his voice and the authority of his own experience to pull us into *Slaughterhouse-Five*, his psychedelic World War II classic about the absurdity of war.
- Maria Semple uses the irresistible premise of *Where'd You Go, Bernadette*—an abandoned child determined to find her mother in a world run by dissembling grown-ups—as hook, line, and sinker for us readers. And it works.
- Andy Weir serves up *The Martian*'s high-concept storyline—*Cast Away* on Mars—with style, and we fall in love with the profane astronaut recording what might be the rest of his brief life.
- Jenny Han opens with a lonely hearted teenage girl who writes her crushes love letters and hides them in a hatbox—but we know that somehow, some day soon, those letters are going to find their way into the wrong hands. We are actively worried about her, and so we keep on turning the pages of *To All the Boys I've Loved Before*.
- Jess Walter gives us a picture-perfect setup for sweet suffering in *Beautiful Ruins*: a dying actress, a village by the sea, a handsome Italian (Walter doesn't actually say that he's handsome, but he must be; mustn't he?), and love at first sight—the kind of story no romantic can resist.
- William Kent Krueger goes for broke in his first paragraph of *Ordinary Grace*, telling us in elegiac prose that "All the dying that summer began with the death of a child"—and setting the stage for our young hero's wrenching coming of age in this elegant and evocative literary mystery.
- George R.R. Martin builds a world readers fall in love with in very few words in his opening to *A Game of Thrones*, which seduces us with wildlings and lordlings and boys in a darkening woods inhabited by the dead. We aren't sure yet what it all means, but we are compelled to find out.

Deconstructing the First Page

In the examples we've just seen, not only do the writers grab and keep our attention, they answer the questions every reader asks as a story begins—questions that need to be answered, if the reader is to relax and enjoy the ride.

Think of driving a new automobile for the first time. Sure, you've driven a car before; you consider yourself a good driver. Still, in order to relax and enjoy the ride, you need to know a few things about this specific vehicle before you hit the road on a long journey: What kind of car is it? Will it take you where you want to go? Does it have four-wheel drive, automatic transmission, and cruise control? Where are the headlights, the emergency brake, and the turn signals? How worn are the tires?

Before you drive on down the road, you adjust the seat and rearview mirror and check out the controls. You consult a map or turn on the GPS. You find the radio station you prefer or plug in your mp3 player. You put on your seatbelt, turn on the ignition, and look both ways before you pull out into the street. Only then do you hit the gas and go.

Readers approach a new story in the same way. Like drivers, they're going on a journey, too. But before they settle into the story, they need to know:

- What kind of story is this?
- What is the story really about?
- Who is telling the story?
- Which character should they care about most?
- Where and when does the story take place?
- How should they feel about what's happening?
- Why should they care what happens next?

Answer these questions, and your readers will relax and enjoy the ride of your story. They'll read your first fierce words and breathe a sigh of relief and pleasure—that same sigh of relief and pleasure you breathe every time you open to the first page of a new book by your favorite author. You believe you are in good hands because you've read this writer before and enjoyed the experience, and you're looking forward to repeating that reading experience. You read the first fierce words of this new book, and they confirm your belief that this is a writer who knows how to drive. This is a journey worth your time and money.

You, too, can write a fierce beginning worth your readers' time and money, a beginning that allows your readers to settle in for the long haul as they turn the pages, heading farther down the road and deeper into the journey.

Let's take a harder look at those questions because these are the questions that, left unanswered or answered insufficiently, can blow your chances of hooking agents and editors, as well as readers.

What kind of story is this?

If you're writing science fiction, the story should read like science fiction. Andy Weir makes it perfectly clear on the first page of *The Martian* that he is writing science fiction when the main character tells us that people probably think he "is the only human being to have died on Mars."

NOTE: If you're thinking the title *The Martian* says it all, you're wrong. Readers (and agents, editors, publishers, and booksellers) hate it when the title sounds like one thing and the book turns out to be something else altogether. That's the sort of marketplace confusion that can derail a career. Your first words must reinforce the genre identity set by the title, or you'll lose the reader—and the sale.

Similarly, William Kent Krueger makes it clear in his first words that he's writing a crime novel: "All the dying that summer began with the death of a child …" Jenny Han writes about teenage girls thinking about teenage boys—what else could it be but a young-adult novel? Jess Walter shows us a man falling in love with a woman far above his station, and we fall in love with another love story. George R.R. Martin drops us into a dark world full of strange creatures, and we know we're reading a fantasy. Maria Semple gives us a precocious kid who ignores her father's prevarications and decides to find her mother on her own in classic book-club-best-seller form. Even Kurt Vonnegut makes it clear we're about to read a story unlike any we've read before, a story that defies classification as we know it—memoir, science fiction, war story, literary fiction, or … whatever it is, it's good.

As an agent, when I read a story opening that doesn't read like the genre the writer claims it to be, I pass—and fast—because I can only assume that the writer doesn't know his genre well enough to write a story that will appeal to that genre's readers.

Which means that I can't sell it.

Unless you're Kurt Vonnegut. But there's only one Kurt Vonnegut—and he's dead. May God rest his beautiful writer's soul.

If you're the next Kurt Vonnegut, then you probably don't need my advice. Then again, maybe you do. Either way, I'd like to hear from you.

QUERIES, SYNOPSES, & FIRST PAGES

Read Margaret Fortune's story of searching for a literary agent for ten years, and discover tips for querying, writing a synopsis, and mastering your first few pages at writersdigest .com/GLA-18.

What is the story really about?

Think about the last great book you read, the one you recommended to your best friend, your book club, or your writers' group. And when you did, your BFF/book clubber/writer asked, "What's it about?" The odds are good that you could answer in fifty words or less.

For me, that great book was *The Rosie Project* by Graeme Simsion. I recommended it to my friend Susan, who asked me: "What's it about?" And I said: "It's a romantic comedy about a genetics professor with Asperger's in Melbourne, Australia, who decides to use the scientific method to find himself the perfect wife."

But it just as easily could have been *The Martian*. In that case I would have said, "It's a science-fiction novel about an astronaut who gets stranded alone on Mars and how he tries to survive."

Or *Where'd You Go, Bernadette*: "It's a very funny novel about a girl in Seattle whose mother disappears right before Christmas and how she'll go to the ends of the earth—literally—to find her."

Or *Beautiful Ruins*: "It's a love story about an Italian guy from a remote coastal village who falls for a beautiful actress with a secret."

Or *To All the Boys I've Loved Before*: "It's a young-adult novel about a teenage girl yearning for love who writes secret letters to her crushes and then …"

Or *Ordinary Grace*: "It's a mystery about a Minnesota boy named Frank whose friend is run over by a train and how his death and the ones that follow affect Frank, Frank's family, and the whole town."

Or *Slaughterhouse-Five*: "It's a wild story about an American POW in Dresden during World War II. A lot of other crazy stuff happens, too, but I don't want to ruin it or you."

Or *A Game of Thrones*: "It's like Tolkien's Lord of the Rings and the Wars of the Roses had a love child—a fantasy about wildlings and lordlings and power and death and dragons and everything, man, just everything." Okay, okay, so *A Game of Thrones* is the exception to this rule.

The point is, in most of these stories, the opening makes it very clear what the story is about. Readers want to know what they're reading; they want to know that it's their kind of story. They don't want to wander around in a story that doesn't know what it is. That's a story going nowhere.

I can't sell a story going nowhere. Since becoming an agent, I've learned that if I can't say what a story is about in fifty words or less, I can't sell it. And even when I can describe it, if it isn't clear what the story is about from the very opening of the story, I still can't sell it.

Who is telling the story?

Consider the source. When you're writing a story, your point-of-view character is the source. So readers need to know right away who this POV character is. The POV character is often the protagonist. In five of our seven examples, the protagonist is telling the story from a first-person point of view.

First-person point of view is often the POV of choice for writers with a strong voice. I admit to being a sucker for a strong voice and thus a sucker for first-person point of view, which demands a strong voice. (**NOTE:** I am not alone in this. Agents, editors, and readers alike will follow a strong voice anywhere.)

In stories with multiple points of view, the POV character shifts from one character in one scene to another character in the next. In a mystery, say, the point of view may shift from hero to villain to victim and back again. Both *Beautiful Ruins* and *A Game of Thrones* are written in multiple third-person POV. Even so, the authors make it clear who's telling the story in the opening scene and in every scene thereafter.

Which character should readers care about most?

Readers always play favorites. They always prefer one character over all the others—and with any luck, that character is your protagonist. To put it another way, if you do your job right, the character that readers will care about most is your protagonist. They will fall in love with your heroine and follow her through hell and high water to "The End" (and beyond, should you be fortunate and skillful enough to create a series character that readers will pay to spend time with book after book).

The sooner you can make it perfectly clear who your heroine is and why readers should care about her, the better.

As readers, we can't help but care about an American prisoner of war stuck in Dresden during World War II (*Slaughterhouse-Five*), a forsaken child determined to find her mother (*Where'd You Go, Bernadette*), an astronaut marooned on Mars (*The Martian*), a teenage girl whose secret crushes won't stay secret for long (*To All the Boys I've Loved Before*), an Italian hotel-keeper destined for a doomed love (*Beautiful Ruins*), a boy whose friend is mysteriously killed by a train (*Ordinary Grace*), and a kid who's seen the dead wildlings for himself and wants to get the heck out of the dark woods, pronto (*A Game of Thrones*). These are all characters who (1) engage our sympathy and (2) find themselves in situations that command our attention.

Ask yourself why readers should care about your protagonist. What about your story opening will endear your readers to your hero? What about your heroine and/or her situation will evoke empathy on the part of the reader? What will resonate with readers?

One of the most common complaints I hear from editors when they pass on projects is this: "I just didn't fall in love with the protagonist." You want everyone who reviews your work—agents, editors, and readers—to fall in love with your hero. The sooner, the better. What you're aiming for in your story opening is love at first sight.

Where and when does the story take place?

Eudora Welty once said, "Every story would be another story, and unrecognizable as art, if it took up its characters and plot and happened somewhere else." Welty believed that "fiction depends for its life on place." The life of your story depends on place, too. That's why it's critical you ground your story in setting from the very beginning. Think of it as the establishing shot in a film.

Here are the opening settings in our examples:

- Dresden, Germany during World War II (*Slaughterhouse-Five*) **NOTE:** If you're thinking that the setting is really Ilium, New York, 1968 … well, fair enough. But the narrator (who may be in Ilium and may or may not be Billy Pilgrim or even Vonnegut himself) is talking about the war, and his imprisonment in Slaughterhouse-Five. It's complicated (in theory, if not in the reading) but compelling.

- Seattle, present day, Christmastime (*Where'd You Go, Bernadette*)
- Mars, Sol 6, sometime in the future [2035, according to readers determined enough to figure it out] (*The Martian*)
- Suburban Charlottesville, Virginia, present day (*To All the Boys I've Loved Before*)
- Porto Vergogna, Italy, April 1962 (*Beautiful Ruins*)
- New Bremen, Minnesota, summer of 1961 (*Ordinary Grace*)
- The haunted forest, another time and space (*A Game of Thrones*)

Each writer's approach to setting is as different as the settings themselves. Most are settings that are new to readers, as most of us did not survive the firebombing of Dresden or visit the Ligurian coast in 1962 or spend the summer of 1961 in small-town Minnesota. None of us has braved the haunted forest beyond the Wall in the North or the alien landscape of Mars. That's why the authors who take us to these places spend more time on setting throughout their stories.

The only settings here that most of us might be familiar with are the city of Seattle and the insular suburban world of the American teenager. So there's little mention of setting in these short opening excerpts of *Where'd You Go, Bernadette* and *To All the Boys I've Loved Before*. But within just a few pages of the former, Maria Semple will begin her hilarious satirizing of Seattle's coffee and Microsoft culture and foreshadow the Antarctic setting that plays such a prominent role later in the story. In the latter, Jenny Han uses the bland homogenous suburban landscape of American adolescence—McMansions and malls, Costcos and drive-throughs, school libraries and gymnasium pools—as a backdrop to the colorful and chaotic emotions of puberty.

What is your setting? How do you ground your story in that setting? What about that setting is unique to that story, and how does that setting help shape your story? Taking readers somewhere they've never been before—be it Mars, Antarctica, or New Bremen—is always an attraction, to agents, editors, and readers alike. If you're sending readers on a journey to somewhere more familiar than Winterfell, then you'll need to show them your singular view of that familiar place—as Maria Semple does in her farcical take on Seattle—or use that familiarity to highlight contrast, as Jenny Han does while chronicling angst-ridden teenagers in the humdrum of suburbia.

Wherever you place your story and however you distinguish that place, you should aim for creating a setting so well drawn that it becomes a character as compelling as any other in your story.

How should readers feel about what's happening?

Why do we love stories? Why do we read fiction and memoir? Sure, we want to be entertained; we want to learn about new people and places, but most of all, we want to feel something.

Art is meant to be cathartic—and your story is no different. The best stories are roller coasters of emotion for the reader, who hopes to be soothed and scared, enlightened and misled, teased and thrilled, angered and delighted, agitated and becalmed, embraced and spurned, reassured and unnerved, saddened, maddened, gladdened, and ultimately, moved.

The sooner you can evoke emotion in your readers, the sooner you draw them into your story. Make 'em laugh, make 'em cry, make 'em scream in fear and joy and surprise.

When the woods darken around Will in *A Game of Thrones*, we're afraid for him and what's to come. In *Ordinary Grace*, we share Frank's sympathy for his dead friend, his melancholy and bewilderment at the mysterious death, and his survivor's guilt. Lara Jean tells us about her secret love letters in *To All the Boys I've Loved Before*, and we remember the angst of our own teenage crushes and worry about what will happen to her when the letters are discovered. When Bee decides to find her mother in *Where'd You Go, Bernadette*, we feel the pain and confusion of her abandonment, and applaud her determination as we pray that she is not doomed to disappointment, for we have also suffered disappointment at the hands of our parents and we know how much it hurts. We watch Pasquale Tursi fall for the elusive and beautiful actress in *Beautiful Ruins*, and our hearts ache along with his. In *The Martian*, we feel as frustrated and frightened as Mark Watney when the weight of his impossible situation sinks in.

And when we read the tragicomic opening of *Slaughterhouse-Five*, as told by the narrator/Billy Pilgrim/Vonnegut, we feel like laughing and crying and screaming all at the same time.

So it goes.

Identify the emotion you need to evoke in your readers in your fierce first words. Evoke that emotion successfully, and you've engaged your readers—and the pull of that emotion will compel them on to the next page, and the next and the next.

Why should readers care what happens next?

This is a bigger—and more complicated—question than you may think. This question has to do with: (1) the action happening as the story opens, (2) the premise of the story, and (3) the big idea of the story itself.

These three factors all play into how much your readers will care about what happens next. And if they don't care what happens next, they won't read on—and you've lost them, possibly forever.

Sometimes all three factors are the same thing; sometimes they are very different things. Let's take a look at each in turn.

1. **THE ACTION HAPPENING AS THE STORY OPENS:** One of the main reasons that people stop reading is because nothing happens in those opening pages. Or at least

nothing *interesting enough* happens. The engine of narrative thrust must begin as your story begins and keep running hard until your story ends. Narrative thrust is the tight construction of story, line by line, beat by beat, event by event, pushing the action forward—and the reader with it. A lack of narrative thrust is the most common reason I pass on manuscripts because, as an agent, I know that the basic formula of commercial fiction is this: *No narrative thrust equals no sale.* Without narrative thrust to drive your plot, you have a story going nowhere. And, at the risk of repeating myself, no one will buy a story going nowhere.

2. **THE PREMISE OF THE STORY:** Premise is the basis, or the starting point, of a plot. Without a strong premise, you can't get your story off to a good start. You're grounded before you've even begun—a shuttle with no rocket boosters—and the reader is grounded with you. Your premise needs to be compelling enough to blast your story shuttle right into outer space, deep into the unknown territory of your narrative, where readers long to go.

3. **THE BIG IDEA OF THE STORY:** This is the idea that sells the story to agents, editors, and readers. It's the hook, what sets it apart from the competition, what persuades those agents, editors, and readers to invest in this story instead of a story written by one of the best-selling authors they already know and love. The big idea is what everyone is looking for; give me (or any agent) a big idea, and I have a great pitch. And pitching is how I sell books.

In B*eautiful Ruins*, two of these three factors are the same. The story opens with innkeeper Pasquale Tursi watching, mesmerized, as a boat carrying a beautiful and mysterious American actress pulls into the cove at Porto Vergogna. Tursi is smitten, and as a result, the trajectory of his life is forever changed. That's the opening action and the premise, but the story itself is far more complicated, weaving storylines, spanning decades, and hopping continents in what the *New York Times* called a "high-wire feat of bravura storytelling." As Jess Walter says, *Beautiful Ruins* is "a story about fame and how we all endeavor now to live our lives like movie stars, like celebrities, each of us an eager inner publicist managing our careers and our romances and our fragile self-images (our Facebook pages and LinkedIn profiles)." Or as I would have pitched it: *Love Story* meets *La Dolce Vita*—complete with Elizabeth Taylor and Richard Burton. Big idea, indeed.

Yet in *A Game of Thrones*, all three of these factors are different. The story opens with Will and dead wildlings and ends with a lethal encounter with one of a deadly race of creatures known only as the Others. The premise of the novel, however, is revealed nearly fifty pages later, when Ned Stark is named the Hand of the King, setting off a struggle for power—*a game of thrones*—that will last five volumes and counting. And the big idea of *A*

Game of Thrones is very big, colossal even: an epic fantasy that, as we've said, could best be described—and pitched—as "Lord of the Rings meets the Wars of the Roses."

Finally, in *The Martian*, all three of these factors are the same. The story opens with an astronaut alone on Mars, trying to figure out how he can survive. That's the action of the story opening, the premise, and the big idea.

What happens in your story opening? How does that relate to the premise of your story and the big idea that differentiates your story from all others?

PAULA MUNIER, senior literary agent and content strategist at Talcott Notch Literary, has created and marketed exceptional content in all formats across all markets for such media giants as WGBH, Fidelity, and Disney. A writer and editor before becoming an agent in 2012, she's always looking for good crime fiction, women's fiction, mainstream fiction, crossover YA, and high-concept SF/Fantasy, and nonfiction. She's written several books, including *Plot Perfect*, *Writing with Quiet Hands*, *The Writer's Guide to Beginnings*, and *Fixing Freddie*. Her first mystery, *Spare These Stones*, will debut from St. Martin's Press in 2018.

#HASHTAG HAPPY

Tweet your way to success with this handy guide to the best hashtags for writers.

....

compiled by the Editors of Writer's Digest

//

#MSWL

In the words of Jessica Sinsheimer, Manuscript Wish List co-founder and associate agent with Sarah Jane Freymann Literary Agency

HOW IT STARTED: Years ago, when I was a newer agent, I found that people would tell me about their wonderful manuscripts—exactly the sort of projects I wanted!—and then say, "Oh, but you aren't interested in projects like that." Because I hadn't sold [or mentioned those topics or genres] yet, no one knew I wanted them. I found myself having this discussion over and over—and figured that if I was having this problem, other agents would be, too.

I sent an e-mail to about twenty other agents, suggesting we spend a day tweeting about what we wanted. When that day came, amazingly, #MSWL began trending on Twitter. Quite suddenly, we had the attention of the writing world.

We've since expanded to several events a year, a full website at manuscriptwishlist .com, and now an online conference: The Manuscript Academy. Our mission is to give writers access to the knowledge and people who can make all the difference, to demystify the submission process, and to show that agents are, in fact, real people who want to help you. Often the difference between a request and a rejection is completely avoidable—a lost opportunity for everyone involved. I think we can all agree that education is power— and we want to bring that to as many people as possible.

WHY YOU SHOULD PAY ATTENTION: If you're looking for an agent, this is an excellent place to start. Agents are wonderfully complex people. We're always looking for something new to learn, to read about, to represent—that's how we keep things interesting and keep ourselves in business. I would wager that every agent has a passion that isn't represented in her current client list. You can look at a list of [desired] genres, sure—but if you're writing a steampunk romance with a strong female protagonist, wouldn't you love to know about agents looking for *exactly* that?

WHERE IT LIVES OFF TWITTER: You can find the fuller version of #MSWL—complete with searchable profiles, submission information, recent acquisitions, and upcoming events—on manuscriptwishlist.com. You can also find our free podcast (which features interviews with #MSWL agents, how-to tips, panels, and more) at manuscriptacademy.com/ourpodcast or in the iTunes store under the title "The Manuscript Academy."

WHEN TO FOLLOW: We host several events a year, all of them mentioned first on manuscriptwishlist.com and #MSWL. Join our mailing list to have those dates, and the newest agent and editor profiles, delivered to your in-box—and/or follow me on Twitter @jsinsheim for submissions tips, Q&As, free live publishing panels, and information about all of our events designed to connect writers, agents, and editors.

WHO IT CAN HELP THE MOST: Writers looking for agents are the most obvious fit—but it also helps those looking for inspiration for their next project. It has even helped agents find editors to purchase manuscripts. #MSWL can also help writers pinpoint editors open to direct submissions from unagented authors.

WHAT IT COULD DO FOR YOU: We have a long list of writers who are now agented, and published, thanks to #MSWL and manuscriptwishlist.com. It's often research that makes all the difference when pitching your work. #MSWL will enrich your agent search and give you the confidence of knowing you've given your work its best possible chance.

....

JESSICA SINSHEIMER is most excited about representing picture books, young adult, upmarket genre fiction (especially women's/romance/erotica, thrillers, and mysteries) and—on the nonfiction side—psychology, parenting, self-help, cookbooks, memoirs, and works that speak to life in the twenty-first century. She especially likes highbrow sentences with lowbrow content, smart/nerdy protagonists, vivid descriptions of food, picture books with nonhuman characters, and justified acts of bravery.

....

CONVERSATION STARTERS

#amwriting / #writing: Can you tweet and write at the same time? From the immense popularity of these hashtags, it seems so. Use them to connect with others who are at their keyboard in real time or simply to announce your solidarity before going off-line to focus.

#1linewed: Join the many writers sharing one line of their manuscripts on Wednesdays, in line with that week's theme as set by @RWAKissofDeath, or simply eavesdrop in search of inspiration.

#writerwednesday / #WW: These tweets highlight other writers worth following, in the spirit of paying it forward.

#fridayreads: Writing is all about the readers, after all—so why not join in this weekly status update by sharing what book is currently keeping you up at night?

#pubtip: Share or search using the hashtag for bite-size tips on publishing (but, of course, always check that the source is a knowledgeable one).

#writetip: Like #pubtip, but with writing.

#indieauthor: Connect with others who are interested in self-publishing or are actively doing so.

#askagent: Have a submissions question? It's worth a try to ask it with this hashtag and see whether you get an answer. Or, wait until you notice it trending on a day when agents are feeling generous, and hop in the conversation. (**NOTE:** Not recommended to directly pitch specific agents on Twitter, which is generally bad form outside of structured forums for doing so.)

#litchat: This more vague earmark tracks literary chat. —*WD Staff*

#PITCHWARS & #PITMAD

In the words of Brenda Drake, founder and best-selling author

HOW #PITCHWARS STARTED: The first Pitch Wars contest was in 2012. After running several contests for writers, I discovered that the requested pages or full manuscripts agents received [from the winners] often fell apart after the first few chapters. Then one fated day, I was watching "Cupcake Wars." A baker had an assistant help create beautiful cupcakes for the judges, and I thought: *That's what our writing community needed.* We needed experienced mentors (published and/or agented mentors, industry interns, and editors) to help writers who were getting rejections from literary agents work out what was failing in their manuscripts.

WHY YOU SHOULD PAY ATTENTION: Pitch Wars has had close to two hundred successes with writers finding agents and book deals [to date]. More than fifty authors were offered representation and/or publishing deals from our 2015 event, and our 2016 contest ended with twenty-four mentees signing with agents—and one snagging a publishing deal within the first month of the agent showcase ending!

WHERE IT LIVES OFF TWITTER: Pitch Wars has lived on my blog at brenda-drake.com/pitch-wars, but is moving to a website of its own at pitchwars.org. The site is currently under construction, and we hope to have it live by the time you read this. It will have numerous resources for writers, as well as a forum for Pitch Wars community [members] to hang out and help each other throughout the year.

HOW (& WHY) TO HOST YOUR OWN TWEET CHAT, by Crystal King

Imagine a party with lively and interesting conversation. Now imagine that party on Twitter, with dozens of participants asking questions and sharing information. Tweet chats are fantastic ways to network with other authors and readers.

Typical tweet chats start at a specific time, usually last an hour, and use a chat-specific hashtag to earmark each tweet (e.g., #bookchat). Joining a tweet chat is easy. Hosting one is a little trickier. Here are some tips and tricks:

- Participate in a few tweet chats before hosting your own. Find a chat through sites such as twubs.com/twitter-chats or tweetreports.com/twitter-chat-schedule.
- For fast-flowing chats, the native Twitter client can be clunky. Consider using a free service such as TweetChat, or free tools such as TweetDeck, Twitterfall, or Hootsuite to orchestrate things in real time.
- Choose a date and time wisely. Tweriod.com can tell you when your audience is most likely online.
- Unless you have a large Twitter following and can attract a crowd, inviting friends to help you keep the conversation going is advised.
- Decide on a format. Do you want to ask questions of all the participants, or do you want to invite influencer guests (for example, known authors, book bloggers, or experts in your topic) to answer the main questions, with the audience chiming in to ask their own?
- Promote your chat, using its predefined hashtag, the week before it takes place. Remind your audience again a few times in the hour leading up to the chat.

- Create visuals to help promote and advance the chat. (A tool such as canva
  .com can help.) Encourage participants to include images related to topics you
  are discussing, as tweets with images tend to draw more eyes.
- The best chats grow from predetermined questions that use a Q1, Q2 format
  alongside the hashtag. Answers should be prefaced with A1, A2, etc., and are
  best typed out in advance for simple cut and paste when the time comes. (If
  you're invited to participate as a special guest and are not serving as the primary host, request any predetermined questions in advance so you can prepare your answers.)
- Encourage participants to ask their own questions. Retweet the most interesting responses.
- Don't forget to check your @ mentions to see who is speaking to you directly. Follow interesting participants to encourage follow-backs and future
  conversation.

....

CRYSTAL KING (crystalking.com) is a social media professional, an instructor at GrubStreet writing center in Boston, and the author of the novel *Feast of Sorrow.*

....

WHEN TO FOLLOW: March is the best time to start following the contest. [Ultimately, during the submission window in August, you'll be applying directly to your top four choices of mentors, so you'll want plenty of time to meet all the prospective mentors, to learn more about how to present yourself and your work, and to make yourself known in the conversation thread ongoing under the hashtag.] Leading up to the submission window, we host critique workshops, mentor interviews, and a blog hop with the mentors' bios and what categories and genres they want to mentor.

WHO IT CAN HELP THE MOST: Writers with a finished, polished, and unpublished manuscript who are looking for agent representation.

WHAT IT COULD DO FOR YOU: Not only can it help your writing, but it can also get you noticed by many of the top literary agents in the industry.

MORE ON TWITTER CONTESTS

Read five tips on the benefits of Twitter contests, by agent Kaitlyn Johnson, at writersdigest.com/GLA-18.

HOW TO GET INVOLVED: Follow the website (and be sure to read the complete contest details there). Participate on the hashtag #PitchWars all year long to tap into a great community of writers helping writers and cheering each other on. Many writers have found close friends and critique partners on the feed. Mentors share advice, too. Submit your applications in August, and you never know—you might be our next success story!

SO WHAT ABOUT #PITMAD? #PitMad is solely a Twitter pitch party, hosted quarterly, and happens only on the hashtag. Dates are announced and pitching guidelines are posted in advance of each event at brenda-drake.com/pitmad. #PitMad has connected many writers with agents and publishers. (Success stories are featured at brenda-drake .com/pitmad-successes.)

WHEN TO FOLLOW: During the event: Each designated #PitMad day runs from 8 A.M. to 8 P.M. EST

WHO IT CAN HELP THE MOST: Writers with a finished, polished, and unpublished manuscript who are looking for agent representation or a publishing deal.

WHAT IT COULD DO FOR YOU: #PitMad is a fun way to pitch literary agents and get to know the community. Sometimes it's successful, sometimes not, but it's great practice. Jumping in a bigger pool and seeing if anyone bites helps writers see if they have their hook down [to an effective teaser]. Also, it helps writers learn how to focus on the main plot of their story and how to pitch it. [Agents "favorite" pitches to show interest, and sometimes a writer will garner interest from an agent/publisher who she wouldn't have thought to pitch.] It helps bring literary agents, editors, and writers together.

HOW TO GET INVOLVED: Prepare several 140-character pitches for your manuscript, making sure to include sub-hashtags for category and/or genre. Then, on the day of the Twitter pitch party, tweet your pitches. You get three tweets per manuscript, so be sure to spread them throughout the day. Easy!

BRENDA DRAKE (brenda-drake.com) is *The New York Times* best-selling author of *Thief of Lies*, *Guardian of Secrets*, *Touching Fate*, and *Cursing Fate*. She is passionate about hosting workshops and contests for writers. Find her on Twitter @brendadrake.

LOOK BEFORE YOU LEAP

Here's what every writer should know about revision and editing—from an agent's perspective.

Andrea Hurst & Sean Fletcher

As agents and editors, we spend a tremendous amount of time reading and evaluating submissions for possible representation. When we like a query letter and ask to see the full manuscript, we often don't make it beyond the first fifty pages for a multitude of reasons. Sadly, many of these books could have avoided rejection if they had gone through more thorough editing before submission.

It is our job and our passion to help authors create well-crafted, polished works and get them into print. But competition in the publishing landscape has changed so drastically in recent years that whether a writer is seeking traditional publication or self-publishing, the standards of quality are higher than ever. We're always surprised to hear authors say things like, "You're the first person to read this," or, "I had it copyedited. Isn't that enough?" This highlights just how important an outside perspective on the story can be. It's difficult for authors to accurately evaluate their own work without a fresh and skilled set of objective eyes reviewing it as well. Most authors are simply too close to the story to have a clear, impartial picture of its flaws.

POSITIONING YOURSELF FOR SUCCESS

You get only one chance to make an impression when you submit to an agent or editor. Your query letter must stand above the rest and show off your writing skills, and your manuscript must be as close to publication-ready as possible. This means there should be nothing unpolished about your work when it arrives in a submission in-box.

When an agent reads your query or sample pages and requests the full manuscript for consideration, it means she is intrigued by your premise. Now the importance of a well-developed story comes into play. At our agency, when we read requested work, we often make our decision regarding representation before finishing the entire book. It becomes apparent early on if the first act doesn't grab us, the characters aren't well developed, there's too much backstory, the plot drags or grammatical errors abound.

EDITING TIPS FROM AN AGENT

Literary agent Paula Munier shares some tips for a stronger beginning at writersdigest .com/GLA-18.

These are the sorts of issues that easily could have been addressed with developmental or (in the latter case) copyediting. Many authors seem to skip these steps before submission, in part because they don't understand their importance. Or they may recognize that they need help, but are unclear on the difference between a developmental edit and a copyedit. Whereas agents may be willing to help put a final shine on a solid story before shopping it to publishers, it is unlikely they will take on a book that requires in-depth reworking and was probably not ready to pitch in the first place. Instead, the manuscript will make a sharp right turn into the rejection pile.

It is frustrating to spend a great deal of time writing your book only to receive continual rejections. But while rejections come with the territory, sometimes they also help identify areas that need work. If you recognize those rejections for what they are, you can stop to address those areas before submitting further, thus improving your odds.

WHAT THE AGENT SAYS: *The idea is good, but it didn't pull me in.*
WHAT IT MIGHT MEAN: The book may take too long to get started, which is most often either a pacing problem or a sign that the story starts in the wrong place. Be wary, too, that you aren't spending those first pages telling rather than showing. Reassess your opening chapters and make sure they are the most dynamic entry point, giving readers a compelling reason to keep turning the pages.

WHAT THE AGENT SAYS: *I was not able to connect with the characters.*
WHAT IT MIGHT MEAN: Character motivations are weak or unclear, and/or characters are hard to relate to. On a mechanical level, dialogue is a common offender: When it's stilted or reads as overly scripted, it can make the people talking seem distant. In the broader

picture, remember that readers must care about your protagonist, her passions, and the issues she has to overcome in order to feel a connection.

WHAT THE AGENT SAYS: *The writing is strong, but it failed to hold my attention the whole way through.*

WHAT IT MIGHT MEAN: Usually this indicates incomplete plot threads or structural issues, a sagging middle, or lack of sufficient conflict. Raise the stakes. Make sure all of your subplots have a complete arc and take a closer look at the overall three-act structure of your story.

WHAT THE AGENT SAYS: *It had an unsatisfying ending.*

WHAT IT MIGHT MEAN: In a high-action thriller we worked with, we pointed out to the author that the main hero was unconscious during the final confrontation, which created a flat finish. This was easily remedied with a short rewrite of those chapters. Don't forget that the climax is as important as the entry.

WHAT THE AGENT SAYS: *Sorry, but this isn't for us.*

WHAT IT MIGHT MEAN: It very well may be a subjective judgment—or just not a good fit for what the agent is currently looking for. This could also reflect market concerns: He may think this area of your genre is saturated. Occasional vague rejections can be inevitable, but you can minimize them by being sure you tailor your submissions to agents' most up-to-date guidelines.

THE POWER OF EDITING

We recently received a submission from an author pitching us his first book in a self-published fantasy series that was selling fairly well. It didn't take more than a few pages of reading before we realized the work had not received a comprehensive edit. We were surprised to see confusing point-of-view switches, overuse of adverbs, and an excess of main characters. Our agency also offers an assisted (fee-based) publishing program for non-traditional authors, and when we worked with him to revisit the first book, then edit the second, he realized that he had skipped the crucial developmental editing phase and was excited by the improvement it offered. The rereleased books sold tens of thousands more copies and received much higher ratings.

From trying to get an agent, to finding a publisher, to attracting readers and ultimately receiving good reviews and sales, the goal of editing is to make your book the best it can be. Traditionally published books go through several stages of editing after the manuscript is acquired, including a developmental edit, a copyedit, and a thorough proofread. It is imperative that self-published books uphold that same standard. (For a detailed explanation of what each step of the process entails, see the sidebar "Understanding the Types of Editing.")

UNDERSTANDING THE TYPES OF EDITING

The following steps provide a basic overview of the editing process every book-length manuscript should undergo, whether you are working with a hired professional or a writing partner to get your work more submission-ready, preparing to self-publish, or signing on with a traditional publishing house (in which case the acquisitions editor will take the lead on shepherding your book through these steps yet again, involving you at every stage).

STEP 1: THE DEVELOPMENTAL EDIT

This is also known as content editing, story editing, structural editing, and substantive editing. At this stage the editor examines the big picture of the novel and determines how to improve it. Developmental editing focuses on:

- character arcs/development
- pacing
- story structure
- plot holes or inconsistencies
- strong beginning, middle, and end
- plausibility/believability
- clear transitions
- point of view
- showing vs. telling
- dialogue

A good editor has an understanding of what makes a story work overall, as well as the expectations of the genre you are writing in. For instance, romance has specific requirements that differ from horror or mystery. Young adult fiction often has a different voice and examines different themes than literary fiction. Memoirs frequently need assistance with the overall narrative arc in order to have broad appeal. (While a collection of disparate stories may have intense meaning to the writer, such retellings are often not written with the reader in mind.) Trust a professional editor proficient in your genre to help structure the story for the marketplace in the best way possible.

If you're pursuing this part of the process outside of a deal with a traditional publisher, finding a good developmental editor can be a journey unto itself. There is a big difference between an editor and your editor. An editor who worked well with another author may not have the right style for you. Take the time to find one who has the experience and knowledge your story needs, will be respectful of your voice, and demonstrates the ability to enhance your work.

STEP 2: THE COPYEDIT

After the developmental edit is complete, your story will go to a copyeditor.

Copyeditors are literature's cleanup crew. These are the folks who will go line by line and correct the following issues:

- grammar
- punctuation
- spelling
- redundant words
- inconsistencies/continuity errors
- awkward sentence structure

It's quite discouraging to finally launch your work only to have readers e-mail you with all the mistakes they found. Yes, this happens. You don't want to be the author who used the word *great* more than 150 times, or the one with a misspelled word in the very first line. If you're getting ready to submit and know that copyediting isn't your strong suit, or if you're self-publishing, we highly suggest that you find and work with a professional, experienced copyeditor. Don't assume that any English major will do: Many people consider themselves proficient in this detailed work, but they may not follow the standards of an accepted style guide, such as *The Chicago Manual of Style*, or know current usage in the market.

STEP 3: THE PROOFREAD

After a copyedit is complete, page proofs are generated for a final author review. (Self-published authors will sometimes save the final proofread until after they have created advanced reader copies [ARCs] for select readers.) A proofreader checks your manuscript for lingering errors, missed commas, typos, and the like. It may be tempting to skip this step, or to do it yourself—but we suggest you don't. By this stage, you've read the book so many times that you'll be blind to many lingering errors that an unfamiliar eye would be far more likely to catch.

FINDING YOUR TRIBE

One of the ways to get the most value out of working with an editor, whether that editor is a professional, a trusted friend, or a writing partner, is to make sure she is a good fit. Having the opportunity to work one-on-one or in small groups with other dedicated authors in your genre can be very effective.

- **JOINING A CRITIQUE GROUP:** In a critique group, writers who are serious about their craft, striving toward publication, or already published usually make the best partners. All groups have pros and cons, and sometimes advice from one member will conflict with another's opinion about your work. Ultimately you need to trust yourself and figure out whether this process moves your book forward sufficiently.

- **WORKING WITH A PROFESSIONAL EDITOR:** If you are unsure your manuscript is pitch-ready, or you are receiving consistent rejections but still unclear what the root of the problem is, it may be a good investment to hire a professional editor. You can find them through referrals, through advertisements in publications such as *Writer's Digest*, by checking the acknowledgments sections in books you enjoy, by contacting professional writing associations, or through networking at writing conferences.

  The best choice is an editor with high qualifications, experience in your genre, an understanding of what makes a book marketable, and favorable referrals you can contact. We practice and believe that effective editors are, above all, respectful in their suggestions. They keep the author's voice in the story rather than imposing their own. An author should leave the editing process feeling excited and inspired to revise—not discouraged or hopeless.

- **MAINTAINING EXPECTATIONS:** True professionals know and respect the amount of blood, sweat, tears, heart, and soul that goes into writing a book. A good editor—whether the voracious reader who happens to be your neighbor, an agent who's requested that you revise and resubmit, or someone you've hired—teaches, encourages, leads, and gives you a clear picture of what is not working and why.

  A note on perfection: There will inevitably be some mistakes in your book. There comes a point at which you have to accept that you did your best, but all books—even works from traditional publishers—contain (at minimum) minor errors.

SPECIAL CONSIDERATIONS FOR SELF-PUBLISHING AUTHORS

If you're releasing your work without the resources of a publishing house behind you, it's important to understand that editing plays a big part in refining your book and also will affect the way your book is received. This is important not only for your sales and reader reviews, but for your future publishing prospects—because agents and editors do scout self-published books in search of new authors they'd like to work with. If a self-published book has the magical mixture of great writing, good reviews, and marketability, you may have a golden ticket to representation or even an outright offer of a book deal.

> When scouting self-published books, we first look at the reviews. The more your work is exposed to readers, the more the chinks in the armor of the story begin to show. If there are consistent complaints—such as a slow plot, underdeveloped characters, or a predictable ending—we move on. If we like what we see, then we use the Amazon Preview feature to take a look at the opening pages. Just like potential buyers for your book, if we get hooked on those first chapters, we will contact you. And if the quality is not there, we will pass.

Whether you're publishing traditionally or on your own, good reviews can lead to awards and recognition. Bad reviews can cut an author's career short. In the end, a well-edited book stands the best chance for success, and a good editor can help turn that goal into a reality.

ANDREA HURST (andreahurst.com) has more than twenty-five years experience in the publishing business as a literary agent, editor, and best-selling Amazon author.

SEAN FLETCHER works with Andrea Hurst & Associates as an agent scout and editor.

TWEAKING & CRITIQUING

Try these five keys to making your writing group more effective.

Steven James

Critique groups can provide encouraging communities for writers and serve as a great way to get input on your works-in-progress.

They can also, however, steer authors in the wrong direction, propagate bad writing advice, and become caustic—even discouraging people to the point of tears.

The purpose of participating in a critique group isn't to get your work "ripped to shreds," but rather to improve your writing. While it might be helpful to "develop a tough skin," you also need a community that will provide appropriate feedback in a beneficial way.

Here are five keys to doing that with your group.

KEY 1: DETERMINE YOUR GOALS

There's nothing wrong with writers getting together to have lunch, to encourage each other, to develop friendships, or to keep each other accountable. But if your group exists to *help the members develop as professional writers*, it's vital for you to create an environment that facilitates that kind of growth.

The most helpful input will come from the most experienced people. So, if you find someone who's a gifted writing instructor, excellent! Consider hiring her to lead your group.

On the other hand, if you team up with mostly aspiring writers, their input can still be valuable—but don't expect expert advice from people who aren't experts yet. That would clearly be ill-advised and counterproductive.

They're certainly qualified as readers, so construct your meetings in a way that taps into their experience with the text rather than their expertise about writing. Which brings us to the next key ...

KEY 2: FOCUS ON SHARING FEEDBACK RATHER THAN GIVING ADVICE

When I was in high school, I had a basketball coach who would grab the ball from us if we were shooting poorly. "No, no, no," he'd say. "Do it like this." Then he would demonstrate how to shoot.

Later, when I played in college, the coach would watch us closely and then give us input. "Your shot looks flat. Keep an eye on the ball's arch. Also, watch that elbow. Try following through more—see how that works."

I learned a lot more from that second coach than the first one.

Sometimes, in their exuberance to help others, critique group members grab the ball and, in essence, say, "No, no, no. Do it like this." But that's never as effective as giving feedback to the writer so he can fix his own shot.

This might require a paradigm shift.

Instead of regarding the meeting as a place where writers come to get advice, think of it as a place where they come to get feedback. Group members aren't there to share their opinion of the writer's work, but their reaction to it.

This is a crucial difference.

For example, rather than telling the writer, "You should make the villain scarier" (advice), the person might say, "The villain didn't really scare me that much" (feedback).

In fact, it might be helpful to stop considering this a critique group altogether and think of it instead as a feedback forum. Group members aren't there to evaluate the writing, but to encounter it and respond. Because of that dynamic, they won't tell the writer what to write or how they would write it if it were their work. Saying things such as, "I think you should …" or, "If I were you, I would …" isn't allowed. No *shoulds*. No *woulds*.

Also, the partners' goal isn't to find instances where the writer has broken a "rule." Rather, they'll help pinpoint the places where their engagement with the story was disrupted. It's up to the author to take that input and use it as he wishes, keeping in mind the broader context of his work.

Then he'll have the information he needs to fix his own shot.

KEY 3: AGREE NOT TO DEFEND OR EXPLAIN

First of all, because no one is attacking your work, there's no need to defend it. No one is allowed to say, "But I was just trying to …" or "But that part of the story is true. It actually happened!"

Second, no clarifications.

A few years ago I visited an art museum at the Smithsonian Institution. One of the exhibits consisted of a canvas that was painted entirely blue except for a small triangle of red in the upper right-hand corner. The painting beside it looked like someone had simply dribbled paint onto the canvas and then framed it.

In wondering how either of these qualified as art, I asked myself, *What are they even supposed to mean?* Then I noticed small plaques hanging near the base of each painting. The plaques explained what the colors represented and what the artist was trying to communicate.

Well, that might be how the art world works, but it's not the way the literary world works.

There's no place at the end of a novel to clarify your use of imagery, your symbolism, or what you meant by your word choice. The book either stands or falls on its own—without any opportunity for explanation.

So, while you're getting feedback from your partners, you'll be testing the waters to see if your work-in-progress communicates what you intended. And that means you don't get to clarify or explain things. Ban such phrases as, "I wanted to show that …" or "What I meant was …" or "I was hoping to …"

Be receptive, rather than defensive. No arguing. No explaining.

No *buts*. No *whats*.

ROLE REMINDERS

FOR THE GROUP:

- Provide responsive feedback rather than criticism or advice.
- Help the writer understand how readers are experiencing the text.
- Target comments toward the writing rather than the writer.

FOR THE WRITER:

- Provide context. (Are members reading an essay you hope to submit to a specific market? A first chapter of a new novel?)
- Avoid taking feedback personally.
- Don't defend or clarify your narrative choices.

KEY 4: CREATE A SAFE ENVIRONMENT

When you open your critique group session, tell the members, "This is a safe place. People will likely be writing in different genres and have different views on cursing, religion, etc. Our role here is to listen, to learn, and not to judge. There won't be any negative consequences for your writing fumbles. You won't be rejected. No one will attack your work. We will be direct and honest, but never confrontational."

That takes the pressure off.

Focus should be on sharing works-in-progress; reading published (even self-published) work doesn't share the group's goals of forward movement, so those who don't have something new to share that week should resist the urge to bring something old just for the sake of reading something.

In order to save time, some writing groups e-mail the work prior to the meeting so members can read it beforehand. This can be effective, but inevitably someone forgets or runs out of time to look over the samples. Also, it can be harder for the author to provide necessary context (more on that in the next key).

Other groups have writers read their work aloud at meetings. If you want to use the reading-aloud approach, choose a person other than the writer to read each scene to the group. The author will naturally know when to pause and what inflection to give the text, whereas having someone else read it will allow the writer to hear how the story sounds and identify sections that might be confusing, or places where readers might stumble over the wording. This simple change alone can make a tremendous difference.

KEY 5: GIVE EVERYONE A CROWN

Using the acronym CROWN, you and your group can easily remember a system of moving through the feedback process in a positive, beneficial way: *C*ontext, *R*equests, *O*bservations, "*W*hat do you mean?" and *N*ew Ideas.

Context

Any critique that is given outside of the writing's broader context is bound to send you heading in the wrong direction, so the best approach is to begin by telling the group a little about your writing sample.

You might say, "This is the opening to a thriller that I expect will be three hundred pages long." Or, "This love scene takes place in the middle of my romance novel. Readers will be familiar with the two characters." Or, "In the climax of my young adult fantasy, the protagonist is getting chased by the Vapor Monster. I'm trying to make it as exciting as possible."

Keep things brief. Don't summarize the entire plot, just provide the context for the scene you're sharing.

Requests

Be honest and specific when you tell your group what kind of feedback you want.

- "I'm having trouble keeping the voice consistent. I feel like there might be some places where it sounds too stilted."
- "The dialogue doesn't seem to work. When we read it, can you note any places where you get lost or can't tell who's speaking?"
- "After we're done, I'd like to see if you can predict how the scene will end. I'm hoping to add a twist that readers won't anticipate in the next chapter."
- "I'm feeling discouraged. I need to keep my motivation up. Can you find any moments that really work or that seem emotionally resonant to you?"

Don't tell people, "Just look for anything that needs to be fixed." Usually that won't be as helpful. It will eat up a lot of time, and group members might start disagreeing with each other and end up giving you conflicting ideas on what is and is not "broken."

NOTE: Typos can become a distraction. Your friends aren't here to proofread your work for you. That's your job, so provide clean copy.

Observations

This is the heart of the feedback session. Now that everyone understands the context and what the writer is hoping to focus on, they can encounter the text and respond to it.

How you frame things matters. Most people thrive on affirmation but get discouraged when they're criticized. Hold fast to our earlier pledge to direct comments toward the writing, not the writer. Instead of "I hated how you had the main character insult that homeless man," you might say, "I stopped caring about the main character when he insulted that homeless man," or "It was hard for me to relate to the protagonist when he said those things." While the first response could easily cause the writer to feel defensive, the second two examples allow him to understand how a reader is experiencing his work.

Let me emphasize this one more time: Group members are here to give their reaction, not their opinion. Avoid value judgments ("I thought this scene was weak") and focus on what confused you, what promises you felt were being made, what distracted you from the story, or where your expectations went in the wrong direction.

- **CONFUSION:** "I'm confused. I thought the woman had decided to break up with her boyfriend. Did she change her mind?"
- **SETTING:** "I'm having a hard time picturing this scene. I might have missed something—I thought there were four people in the room, not three. What happened to Charlie?"
- **CONTINUITY:** "Two pages earlier, Francesca picked up the gun. Is she still carrying it? Did she set it down and I just didn't notice?"
- **ESCALATION:** "That dream sequence made me really worried, but then when the guy woke up, everything was solved and the tension was gone."

- **PROMISES/PAYOFF:** "With so many details about the woman's knife collection, I thought it would be vital to the story, but then it never came up again."
- **DIALOGUE:** "Both characters used the same idioms. They sounded the same to me when they spoke."
- **POLISH:** "This section at the end seems less fleshed out and detailed than the rest of the scene."

Of course, group members can and should also offer positive comments:

- "I thought it was cool how that engagement ring became such an important clue in the end."
- "That description of the mist-enshrouded forest seemed really vivid to me."
- "When she was walking alone through the parking garage, I could really feel the suspense. I didn't want her to get hurt."

Positive or negative, don't equate the number of comments or the amount of feedback with how good your work is. The information others provide doesn't necessarily correspond to the *quality* of your writing, but rather the *clarity* of your writing.

> **THICK SKIN**
>
> Discover six tips for learning how to handle and utilize critiques at writersdigest.com/GLA-18.

"What Do You Mean?"

After people have shared their feedback, the writer can ask for clarification about any comments she didn't understand. (Remember, no clarifying your own intent. The point isn't to make others understand your narrative choices, it's to help you understand what those choices are communicating to readers.)

Ask follow-up questions that will help you better understand the readers' experience with the text. Here are ten key areas you might address:

1. **CHARACTER INTENTION:** "Based on what you know, what would you say this character wants in this scene?"
2. **LOGIC:** "Did the ending seem contrived to you, or did it make sense?"
3. **BELIEVABILITY:** "Did you feel like this character would really do these things, or were there times he acted in a way that seemed unbelievable?"
4. **CAUSALITY:** "What step do you think he would naturally take next?"
5. **ANTICIPATION:** "What are you hoping will happen?"
6. **CONCERN:** "What are you worried about as you take in this scene?"

7. **EXPECTATION:** "What do you expect?"
8. **ENGAGEMENT:** "What might disappoint you if it happened in the following pages?"
9. **CONFUSION:** "What questions are you left with?"
10. **AUTHORIAL INTRUSION:** "Where was your engagement with the story disrupted?"

New Ideas

To conclude the session, if the writer desires, he can ask for help brainstorming solutions to plot problems. For instance, "I'm looking for a way to show how angry this guy is. Does anybody have any suggestions?"

At this point, group members can say, "You could …" However, the phrases "I would …" or "You should …" are still off-limits.

Time is a gift, so be appreciative that the people in your group are willing to invest some of their precious time trying to help you become more successful. End by thanking them for their feedback.

Throughout this process, remember that *all* writers in your group have likely invested many hours in their work. They're courageously offering pages for analysis. Respect that. Rather than viewing the work of others through a judgmental lens, let's create the kind of writing communities where growth can happen in a positive, encouraging way.

STEVEN JAMES is the critically acclaimed author of more than a dozen novels. When he's not writing or teaching fiction, you'll find him enjoying the mountains near his home in eastern Tennessee. His most recent book on the craft of writing is *Troubleshooting Your Novel*, from Writer's Digest Books.

KNOW *BEFORE* YOU GO

A workshop director and novelist shares 7 things *not* to do at a writing conference.

....

Sharon Short

You've finally made the big leap: registering to attend your first writing workshop or conference! Or perhaps you're a conference veteran—you've been to several and have another one (or two) on your calendar for the coming year. In either case, you probably have a list of all the things you want to do and achieve while you're there.

But just as important is keeping in mind what you *don't* want to do.

Sound negative? Ironically (and what writer doesn't love irony), having a list of *don'ts* will help you have a much more positive experience with your *dos*.

I know this firsthand, from both sides of the registration table. In addition to being an award-winning novelist, for the past seven years I've been executive director of the Antioch Writers' Workshop in Yellow Springs, Ohio. In addition to small events we host throughout the year, our most intensive is a weeklong summer workshop that draws more than one hundred writers as well as top-notch presenters.

As the person responsible for making the event run smoothly—from pre-conference planning through follow-up surveys with attendees—I've had an opportunity to observe year after year how participants can get the most out of the conference.

You can learn from my experience. Here are my top *what-not-to-do* tips to help you get the most out of any writing event, no matter its genre, focus, or length.

1. Don't View This One Conference as the Be All/End All of Your Writing Life

You're taking time to attend, perhaps precious vacation days from work or a weekend away from your family. You're spending money on the conference itself, not to mention any travel that comes with it. And let's not forget that it takes *courage* to attend a writing conference.

No wonder writers have high expectations, of both the conferences and themselves.

But no single event can give you all you need. With hope, most of your experience at a conference will be positive, inspiring, and helpful. Inevitably, though, something about the experience will be imperfect. Perhaps you won't learn as much as you'd hoped to from one of the top-billed speakers. Or the agent you really wanted to pitch cancelled at the last moment due to a family emergency.

Don't let disappointment overshadow this time. Remember: Each conference you attend is just one experience on a lifelong continuum of learning about writing and publishing that includes other workshops, books, magazines, classes, and writing groups.

Focus on the positives of the event, and you'll not only find the immediate experience more helpful, you'll also be pleasantly surprised by the more unexpected connections you make and lessons you learn that will likely extend well past the conference itself.

2. Don't Come With a Rigid List of Desired Outcomes

Perhaps you're attending because one of the instructors is known for her excellent dialogue, which happens to be a weak spot of yours. Or you want to meet like-minded writers in your area to create a monthly writing group. Maybe you're counting on an agent pitch to result in representation.

What's wrong with any of that? After all, you're investing in this event in order to advance yourself as a writer.

The problem with focusing on desired *outcomes* is that too many factors are out of your control. What if the speaker's talk barely addresses dialogue? What if the writers from your area all work during the time that you have free? What if the agent isn't interested?

Instead, create a flexible list of action items that focus on what you can do.

For example, the less-specific goal "Learn techniques to enhance my dialogue writing" frees you to focus on getting that information however you can—if not from the speakers, maybe from fellow attendees you engage with over lunch. "Network with writers from my area" means you'll be more likely to find one or two new writing buddies to connect with, even if not in a structured format. "Pitch to an agent and increase my confidence in my pitch" means that, whatever the outcome, you're positioning yourself to come away having learned something or improved a skill for the next opportunity.

<table>
<tr><td>

YOUR ESSENTIAL PACKING LIST

We've got a list of items you won't want to forget for your next conference at writersdigest.com/GLA-18.

</td></tr>
</table>

3. Don't Skip "Extras" or In-Between Moments

Often we writers are introverted. (I know I am!) As such, it's too easy to bypass the social hour, the faculty readings, or even random conversations at the breakfast table or between sessions in the hallway. However, I encourage you to push yourself out of your comfort zone and take in as many of these "extras" as possible. This is part of being open to the goodies that the writing universe may have to offer you, bonuses that you may not be seeking but that may have a huge positive impact on your future career.

Nineteen years before I joined the Antioch Writers' Workshop staff, I was a first-time attendee. As the end of the great but exhausting week neared, I was ready to withdraw into some much-needed alone time—but I pushed myself to go to the wrap-up party. There, I started chatting with another participant who I hadn't yet met, and enjoyed comparing notes about our experiences. It turned out he was a reporter for our local newspaper, and we stayed in touch, off and on, about our writing projects. Eventually, he entered the editorial side of the newspaper—and offered me an opportunity to try my hand at freelance column writing. The result? Ten years as a weekly humor columnist there, followed by five (and counting!) writing an arts column that focuses on writers and literary events in our area.

Good thing I decided to attend that party, huh?

4. Don't Be Exclusionary

It's understandably tempting to attend conferences with writer friends we already know—or to connect with one person early on and stick with him. But as my experience above illustrates, it's invaluable to chat with and get to know as many people as possible.

One of my joys as a director is staying in touch with many of our workshop participants long afterward. From that initial seed at our workshop, I've seen participants cheer one another on in their writing, share professional connections, create writing groups, and more.

It's also important to not be exclusionary about your genre (unless, of course, the event is genre specific). At workshops drawing multiple types of writers, get to know at least a few outside of your genre. This is about broadening your horizons, not narrowing them.

Though you're there to grow your own career, remember the experience is not all about you. Listen to other writers' thoughts. If instructors' books are for sale, buy one or two. As the adage goes, be a friend to make a friend.

5. Don't Try to Be an Exception

Before applying or registering for any conference, read the website in detail. Once you're enrolled, read conference e-mails closely. Perhaps this seems obvious, but I'm commonly asked for information that's readily available. Though I provide it cheerfully, I always feel a little worried for the writer. It's not just conference staff who expect writers to do the basic work of studying provided info before querying with a question. Agents and editors expect that, too.

If a seminar requires a maximum of twenty double-spaced manuscript pages, don't ask to submit fifty. It's not fair to other writers, not considerate to the instructors, and not in line with the seminar's goals. Likewise, most publishing professionals are fairly rigid about what they will—and won't—consider. If an agent wants one-page queries, sending a two-pager will make an impression—but it won't be a good one.

Follow the conference guidelines not only because it will make for a smoother experience but because it's good practice for the publishing world. If the guidelines rub you the wrong way, seek out a workshop that is a better fit for your needs.

That said, there are times when an exception is not unreasonable. For example, if you have a late flight, you can likely arrange a time to check in and pick up your registration materials beyond the stated window. Simply ask. Just remember that asking for any exception makes you stand out. Make that work in your favor by being courteous and saying thank you, whether or not the exception is granted.

6. Don't Forget to Take Care of Yourself

Think ahead about what you'll need for your own self-care at the event, such as special dietary needs. If those options aren't available, bring your own. If exercise is part of your wellness routine, build that into your conference schedule, particularly if the event runs more than a day or two.

And though we've discussed remaining present at the event, you can still nurture your introverted side by planning strategic five-, ten- or twenty-minute intervals to be alone, free-write, or meditate.

7. Don't Neglect to Follow Up

No matter how well you've prepared to be away for a conference (even if it's a local one), to-dos from your nonwriting life have a way of piling up while you're occupied. It's easy to plunge back into your routine, too quickly letting go of the inspiring and informative experience you've just had.

Make sure you allot time in your post-event schedule—a few hours at least—to process all you've gained. Review your notes. Make a list of follow-up to-dos, whether revising a scene based on new insights, sending requested pages to an editor, or learning more about a topic that caught your interest. Send "It was great to meet you!" notes to fellow writers, and don't be shy about pursuing opportunities to take those relationships further. Thank-yous to conference organizers are rarer than you might think and always appreciated.

As the weeks and months unfold, stay in touch with those with whom you found a particularly strong connection. Perhaps the best part of the conference experience is that it doesn't have to end when the event does.

SHARON SHORT is the author of several novels, including the award-winning *My One Square Inch of Alaska*. The executive director of the Antioch Writers' Workshop (antiochwritersworkshop .com), she also writes the Literary Life column for the *Dayton Daily News*.

SCIENCE FICTION & FANTASY TODAY

Four agents in the speculative genres share valuable information for breaking in.

....

Tyler Moss & Jessica Strawser

We asked four top agents in the speculative genres for their views on successful pitching, world-building, "series potential," and more. Here's what you need to know to break in—and stand out.

There are so many subgenres in this realm. How specific should writers be in attempting to label their work in their queries?

SCHNEIDER: Calling something an epic fantasy (or steampunk, or magical realism) is more helpful than calling something a fantasy novel and leaving it at that. But that doesn't mean digging up some obscure and precise subgenre; it's not particularly helpful to know that something is, say, carniepunk.

DIVER: I don't think it's necessary to pin your work down to a subgenre. You're querying agents who specialize in the field: It might be best to let the pro make the determination as to where your work will best fit.

GOTTLIEB: It is important to consider that certain subgenres of science fiction and fantasy have more of a struggle in the marketplace than others. For instance, if you're writing in urban fantasy, it might be better to refer to it as a *modern fantasy* or *contemporary fantasy*, since *urban fantasy* tends to struggle in the marketplace and therefore agents and publishers are reticent to take [it] on. An author might broadly refer to their work as *fantasy* in that instance and let the agent or publisher make an inference for themselves. When I pitch publishers, I'm careful to avoid what I refer to as "dirty words" in publishing.

GALEN: Writers seeking to break in are often so concerned with sounding salable that they put it before craft. It's off-putting. The more the writer seems focused on selling, the less genuine the craft tends to be. Talk to me about your ideas, your characters, your worlds: *That's* how to excite me.

MEET THE AGENT ROUNDTABLE

LUCIENNE DIVER joined The Knight Agency in 2008, after spending fifteen years with Spectrum Literary Agency. She has sold more than seven hundred titles, worked with every major publisher, and has a client list of more than forty authors spanning the commercial fiction genres, primarily fantasy, science fiction, romance, suspense, and young adult. Clients include such bestsellers and award-winners as Rachel Caine, Chloe Neill, Faith Hunter, N.K. Jemisin, Christina Henry, Ramez Naam, and many others. Visit knightagency. net and her blog, luciennediver.wordpress.com.

RUSSELL GALEN, an agent with Scovil Galen Ghosh Literary Agency, has made thousands of book, movie, TV, and subrights sales in his thirty-plus years as a literary agent. He divides his time between nonfiction (specializing in science and history) and fiction (specializing in science fiction, fantasy, and mainstream novels that incorporate genre elements). His list ranges from first-time sales for emerging writers to seven- and eight-figure deals for bestsellers.

MARK GOTTLIEB, an agent with Trident Media Group, is actively building his client list. He is excited to work directly with authors, helping to manage and grow their careers with all of the unique resources that are available to Trident. He has ranked No. 1 on Publishers Marketplace (publishersmarketplace.com) for agents' Overall Deals, as well as in categories such as Science Fiction/Fantasy, Children's, and Graphic Novels.

EDDIE SCHNEIDER is the vice president of JABberwocky Literary Agency, which he joined in 2008. His best-selling and award-winning clients include Brandon Sanderson (*Steelheart*) and Nancy Farmer (*The Ear, the Eye, and the Arm*). In addition to science fiction and fantasy, he is interested in YA and middle-grade (both realistic and fantastic), literary fiction and nonfiction, including science, nature, history, and social science. He is an Iowa graduate with a master's in publishing from New York University. Follow him on Twitter @eddieschneider.

How have the sci-fi and fantasy genres evolved in recent years, in terms of both writers/books and readers/audience?

GALEN: When I was growing up, being a sci-fi/fantasy reader was like being a member of a secret club. I remember visiting the home of a college English professor and stumbling on his stash of science fiction and being shocked that we had this in common. It was understood that regular people found science fiction/fantasy hard to read, pointless, uninteresting.

That hasn't completely changed, but it's changed a lot. I want my clients' books to be read by a wide audience. That means one thing: richly individualized characters caught in a web of conflict and drama. If the setting is a spaceship or a magical land, then we'll call it genre fiction, but anyone should be able to get caught up in the lives of such characters. Today, thanks to certain pioneering authors, some great books, and some great movies and TV series, the wall between genre and mainstream fiction has become not a wall, but a river. It can be forded or bridged.

DIVER: Primarily science fiction and fantasy has evolved into more modern sensibilities. For example, I don't think you'll find many books anymore where the men do all the fighting and the women are left behind—unless it's a period piece or there's a point being made about such a society. Fiction is ever evolving to comment on the times—political, social, economic. … Writers and readers of science fiction and fantasy have always been very sophisticated, and I don't think that any of that has changed, although it might be that modern novels are quicker to get to the point and faster paced.

GOTTLIEB: I am seeing more hard science fiction books and sci-fi thrillers published since the release of Andy Weir's *The Martian*. In fantasy, George R.R. Martin's Game of Thrones [series] has inspired a new readership, [as well as a] group of writers to create low fantasy, rather than something of the Tolkien milieu.

SCHNEIDER: Most significantly, they're more diverse. Conservatives in the genre community are suffering from a [sort of] identity crisis. … It's a classic "adapt or perish" situation, where the people who used to have the most power are on the cusp of losing it, and is a reflection of the changing demographics here in the U.S. They've tried to hijack awards and act like the little brother of GamerGate in a last gasp, but they're just swimming against the tide.

This wave of change, by the way, is one you want to surf as a reader. There's a broadening and deepening of the genres, a wider variety of writing styles and perspectives, exactly the sort of thing so many sci-fi and fantasy readers come to this section of the bookstore to read.

It feels like there are more epic fantasy novels than in years past, but also like heroic fantasy has taken a backseat to grittier fantasy. You can see it in the covers, with bright colors and fanciful art replaced with greater realism and more muted palettes. I feel like there's a lot of good historical fantasy lately, but that could be bias (I mean, I represent Marie Brennan …). We're seeing more stuff set outside of Northern European mythology, and a few retro novels, where the seventies and eighties are being mined (e.g., *Ready Player One* or my client Silvia Moreno-Garcia's *Signal to Noise*).

With science fiction, space opera is doing better than it had been. Military science fiction continues to be an entity unto itself—publishers are putting it out in mass market even as they scale back mass-market output in other subgenres. Most science fiction has been treading water, while fantasy has grown to become the more dominant commercial genre.

And then there are flash-in-the-pan trends, which I ignore as best I can (e.g., the proliferation of zombie novels about five years ago).

LOST IN SPACE?

Science fiction and fantasy not your genre? Don't worry, we've got you covered. Find a collection of important topics for other genres at writersdigest.com/GLA-18.

Can you describe the importance of world-building in speculative fiction? How pronounced or unique should an author's new world be?

GOTTLIEB: It's a fine line. The readership tends to expect a lot of world-building, hence why we see so many maps, glossaries/indexes/lists of key terms, dramatic personae, etc. On the other hand, the narrative can suffer from overbuilding. Such books are sometimes inaccessible to new readers of science fiction and fantasy, or just plain take away from the entertainment of the reading experience.

DIVER: To stand out in this market, you have to bring something unique to the table, whether it's the point of view, like in Ann Leckie's Ancillary series; the world and voice, like in N.K. Jemisin's *The Fifth Season*; or the most alien of alien species, like in *Blindsight* by Peter Watts. As an agent and as a reader, I want to feel that I'm stepping into a world, whether it's fantasy, science fiction, or a slantwise version of our own (as in urban fantasy), that is original, intriguing, and fully realized.

GALEN: It's the defining characteristic of science fiction/fantasy. No great world-building, no deal. I'm not seeking to turn my sci-fi/fantasy clients into mainstream writers. Take me to new worlds or don't take me at all.

But writers don't need to develop outrageous elements to get attention. Often it's the subtle elements that are most important. A built world should feel lived-in, complex, and inconsistent in the way that the real world is inconsistent. I'm more impressed with a futuristic lightbulb that burns out sooner than it's supposed to than I am with humans who have six heads.

That said, great world-building is bold. This might seem contradictory, but great world-building blends the quotidian details of life with dramatic feats of imagination.

SCHNEIDER: Whatever it is, the world an author creates for a fantasy or sci-fi novel should be clear. Neither genre requires that authors create a world from whole cloth, and most don't, but if you do, it shouldn't involve too many mental gymnastics for readers to get their bearings.

Traditional word count rules don't necessarily apply here. What's a benchmark for authors eyeing the tomes on their shelves and seeing their own pages near those lengths?

DIVER: There are certainly minimum and maximum lengths to be aware of, though they're more guidelines than rules. For example, it would be difficult to tell a truly epic story with high stakes and fantastic world-building in under 80,000 words. … The most important thing is to tell the story the way it needs to be told without short-changing the reader or keeping gratuitous bits that could be streamlined to keep the pace moving.

GOTTLIEB: Among established authors of science fiction and fantasy, you are correct that the normal book-length conventions (80,000–120,000 words) do not apply. On the other hand, an author making their debut in one of these genres will seldom get a good result by bucking the system.

A book in excess of 120,000 words costs more to produce, and it also needs to be priced higher to meet those costs. Conversely, a novella may cost less to produce, but the price margins are generally too small for major trade publishers. This is why we seldom see novellas and story collections unless they are from established authors.

SCHNEIDER: I do think it's a good idea to shoot for 90,000–120,000 words for fantasy, and 70,000–100,000 words for science fiction, but write the story you want to write and see where that leaves you. If [it] weighs in at more than 200,000 words or under 60,000 words, it's almost certainly going to need [to be] revised. And if you're an outlier within your subgenre, there has to be a good reason for it. So 200,000-word science fiction is going to have a harder time than 200,000-word epic fantasy.

GALEN: We're seeing less of the extremely long epic fantasy. Certain authors can still get away with 300,000-word blockbusters, but publishers prefer a maximum of 125,000–150,000. If a story cries out to be longer, we're most likely talking about multiple volumes. …

That said, some books just fly by, and it's not necessarily the supposedly fast-paced commercial ones. Some books you just can't stop reading. Would you tell Patrick Rothfuss to write shorter or to chop his work into more volumes? Of course not. Worry more about a gripping story and an accessible style than about length.

A lot of authors in these genres start out with a series in mind. How can a writer tell if her idea has the legs to carry multiple books? And should a query for Book One mention series potential?

SCHNEIDER: A quick way to determine this is to try to force yourself to write a paragraph describing the plot of the first, say, three books in the series. You don't have to be beholden to it, or an author who writes from outlines, to do this exercise. When you have paragraph synopses, does each story have its own individual arc? Is it connected to a larger arc that spans volumes? If not, the idea needs further exploration. But if it's there or mostly there, it probably has legs.

As for queries, yes, mention series potential. That's different from writing a multivolume series before seeking representation and then saying you have seven novels in your kaiju historical monster epic fantasy *Gojira With the Wind* (which, if you put all that in a query letter, is an example of being too specific about genre).

DIVER: I don't think an author should try specifically to write a series (or a stand-alone) due to any idea of the market. A concept either cries out to be written over the course of several books with a story arc big enough to support it—some threads that tie up satisfyingly in each book with others that demand more time and effort to resolve—or it doesn't. Writing two books where one is called for or three where a duology would do only means there's a sagging middle somewhere. An agent and/or editor can help in figuring that out if it's not clear-cut. But, yes, I think series potential should be mentioned if the author has more to say about that world and characters.

GALEN: I'm a huge fan of series both as a reader and as an agent. I look for books that have this potential. The problem is that everyone already knows that series are in demand, so when *writers say* their books have series potential, it seems like you're crying "series potential" because you know that's what everyone wants.

It's okay to mention series potential because it is the dominant form of our time, but I would just as soon not see the actual phrase "series potential." Don't talk to me in market speak. Tell me about your characters and the crisis they are trapped in, and make it seem serious, big. I will get the point that this is not going to end in one volume.

As for how to determine whether a story demands a series to begin with, the funny thing is that in science fiction and fantasy, they nearly always do. The world is full of stand-alones that wound up having many volumes (even written posthumously by collaborators) because readers wanted to return to worlds the writers built.

I assume there's series potential if the book is any good. I've never had a sci-fi or fantasy author say to me, "Future volumes? No, I've got no idea how I would go about doing that."

GOTTLIEB: Every good book should be left open-ended in order to create series potential within genre fiction. It is always good to replicate success wherever possible. Publishers like to build brands in authors, and fans are just as ravenous at digesting these series. Usually something with a sense of the epic has the makings of an ongoing saga. [Crafting] many characters with conflicts and interwoven lives is another way to go about that.

In my pitches … sometimes we let publishers know that the next books are planned and furnish them with titles/very short synopses. If Book Two is written or partially written, I may also let them know that is available at request, with the caveat that the second book is likely unedited. This sometimes allows for a multibook deal.

Writers are told not to write to trends, but the sci-fi/fantasy landscape seems to inspire trendsetters—from wizards to vampires. What are you seeing a demand for? What do you have a demand for—or want writers to be wary of?

DIVER: I'm not seeing any particular trend at the moment, unless it's for strong, original ideas with unique voices. What sets the trends is always something new, not something being done. I'd love to see ideas and worlds I'd never considered.

GALEN: I'm interested in *individuality*, not originality for its own sake. If you have a vampire who drinks only the blood of octopuses, so what? I see a lot of stunt originality. What is the individual inner nature of this vampire that means that I will enjoy him, even if I've read a thousand vampire novels already?

Does your work have fingerprints? Is it something only you could have written? Does it have a style—is it about individual passions and situations—that makes me feel I am getting to know you, a unique individual? If so I will want to represent it, even if it's about taking a ring to be destroyed or some cliché like that. Tropes go in and out of fashion. Just write the stories you want to write. If you are writing about authentic characters, we (agents, then editors, then readers) will care.

The biggest entertainment in New York City is not Broadway, the Philharmonic, or the Yankees: It's to go out to dinner with an interesting writer. These are the most interesting people on the planet. When they are able to decant that personality into a work of fiction, the rest of the world gets to experience for $24.95 what I get to experience for the going rate for a good meal for two in Manhattan. If they can't, I'm not going to be interested no matter how "original" it is.

GOTTLIEB: I enjoy working with authors that play with the status quo of genre conventions, while avoiding potential pitfalls of overcrowded genres. The difficult genres I'm finding in fantasy are high fantasy, urban fantasy, paranormal romance, cozy mysteries/ghost stories, and horror. I'm seeing that soft science fiction is struggling. Vampires and dystopian YA went out of style awhile ago. That is, of course, until someone comes along and turns one of those genres, or another genre deemed dead, on its head.

SCHNEIDER: I'm seeing sustained interest in epic fantasy, growing interest in fantasy and science fiction with thriller elements, and science fiction and fantasy written from non-Western cultural perspectives. That said, what I like the best are books that don't fit neatly into preconceived notions of a genre. We saw that with David Mitchell's *Cloud Atlas*, which jumped from genre to genre and time period to time period, then brought everything together with surprising grace. I tend to like novels that toe the line between literary and genre fiction, and that's a particularly well-known example.

What are the most common weaknesses in your sci-fi and fantasy submissions pile?

GALEN: Lack of individuality.

SCHNEIDER: Probably a tendency to be really derivative without realizing it, lack of awareness of the genre or proper query format, and overselling, by which I mean an author might declare their book the next Harry Potter or insist that a book is life-changing, contains the hidden secrets of the universe—and I'm not entirely kidding about that last thing.

GOTTLIEB: Myself and others also feel that the role-playing game community has informed sci-fi/fantasy writing in a negative way by detracting from some of the literary elements. On the flip side, I see a lot of science fiction/fantasy that reads like what a hippie would consider a great acid trip, but is essentially too smart for its own good to truly get noticed and understood by readers.

DIVER: I see a lot that's competently written, but the characters just don't come alive or invest me enough in their plight. Or novels where the stakes aren't high enough or the plotlines are too straightforward. I want to be surprised, challenged, and entertained, which sounds like a tall order, but I work with forty-seven authors already, so many have managed it!

What about a submission inspires confidence that you'll be able to find the work a home with a publisher?

GOTTLIEB: A well-written query letter is the start of trying to convince an agent that an author is destined for a publisher, since that indicates to me right away that an author knows how to speak about their work succinctly and in an interesting way. Plus it is usually a good indication that the manuscript will also be a good read. An author with advance praise from a notable author in their genre is also an excellent start. This type of "street cred" is important for a new author, along with award nominations, previous publications in journals or literary magazines, and a background in writing such as a Master of Fine Arts or teaching is great. I also love to see that authors have taken part in workshops or conferences.

SCHNEIDER: Generally speaking, it's in the narrative and the way authors present themselves. There isn't a magic formula or a gimmick or even subgenre that really works for me; I'm not someone that's actively looking for the same thing over and over. That said, if you have a project that wouldn't be out of place in the sci-fi or fantasy section but skews literary, the odds are in your favor.

DIVER: I'm inspired when I literally *can't* put a book down. I'll leave dishes in the sink. I'll bore friends and family talking about people they don't know and situations they've never read. In short, I'm pitching to everyone around me. If a book connects with me to that extent, it will connect with others. The biggest seller of books is still word of mouth, and the most successful books are those people can't stop talking about, agents included.

GALEN: The elusive quality of readability is the heart of everything we seek in publishing. It's amazing how often I find myself with a manuscript, or even a highly regarded published book, that is just hard to read. I read a few pages, then find myself checking Facebook or e-mail. Then there are other books you pick up thinking you've got half an hour before bed, and the next thing you know it's 3 A.M. and you're still reading.

I could maybe write a book about why some books have this readability and some don't, but when you encounter it, it's as obvious and recognizable as a mountain. This has nothing to do with gimmicks such as cliff-hangers, artificially juiced pacing, or crises that are transparently designed to evoke tension or sympathy. It's a way of writing. It's sentence structure, the balance between show and tell, the balance between prose and dialogue, the balance between narration and interior monologue, the balance between ideas and action, and many other things.

More than anything, it's about telling your story through the viewpoint of characters who you'd spend four hours with over dinner, then spend four more hours with the next night. If you can bring characters to life and invent a voice for them, so that they seem to be speaking in our heads as we read, you will have a highly readable manuscript. When I encounter that quality of readability in a book, I know I *cannot fail* as an agent. It's not confidence, it's certainty. I worry about failing as little as a hawk worries about falling when it jumps off a branch into the sky.

Without that, sure, I'll still take on and submit a well-crafted book that has many things going for it, but I'm never entirely confident.

Readability, man.

JESSICA STRAWSER (jessicastrawser.com) is the editorial director of *Writer's Digest*. Her debut novel, *Almost Missed You*, was published by St. Martin's Press in March 2017. Her second novel, *Not That I Could Tell*, will be published in March 2018.

DEBUT AUTHORS TELL ALL

Learn how nineteen first-time authors got published.

compiled by Cris Freese

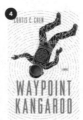

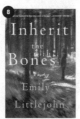

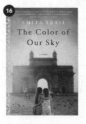
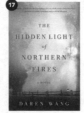

CHILDREN'S PICTURE BOOKS

❶ Ariel Bernstein

ARIELBERNSTEINBOOKS.COM

I Have a Balloon (September 2017, Paula Wiseman Books)

QUICK TAKE: When Monkey sees Owl's shiny red balloon, he offers to trade everything he has, including his sock. But when Owl points out that Monkey's sock has a star and a perfectly shaped hole, Monkey has a pretty tough decision to make. **WRITES FROM:** I grew up outside of Philadelphia, and I currently live in Northern New Jersey. **PRE-BOOK:** I was a stay-at-home mom when I started writing children's books. **TIME FRAME:** I first thought of the idea for my book during the 2015 SCBWI Winter Conference in New York. A couple days later, I sat down and wrote the story. Revisions usually take me a few months, but this story was ready after a couple weeks. **ENTER THE AGENT:** I submitted my story to Mary Cummings at Betsy Amtster Literary Agency by e-mail, so I was found in the slush pile. We talked on the phone, and I really liked the editorial feedback she gave me. I've been signed with Mary for about two years now, and it's been great working with her. **BIGGEST SURPRISE:** The biggest surprise is how different each book deal is. I've learned from my own book deals (one for the picture book, one for my chapter book series) with two different publishers, and from hearing what book deals have been like for other authors of children's books. Sometimes the process can be relatively smooth, but there can be plenty of unexpected delays and hiccups along the way. Publishing requires a never ending supply of patience! **WHAT I DID RIGHT:** I don't think every author or illustrator needs to attend a conference, but I know that attending the 2015 Winter SCBWI Conference is what pushed me in the right direction. Hearing from agents, editors, and published authors gave me a ton of insight into the current publishing world. I came out of the conference feeling much more informed, energized, and confident about where to go with my writing. What I'm doing right today is that I work with a wonderful critique group that helps me improve each manuscript over many, many revisions. **WHAT I WISH I WOULD HAVE DONE DIFFERENTLY:** I would have found critique partners right away. I spent too much time in the beginning trying to revise on my own. **PLATFORM:** I can be found at www.ArielBernsteinBooks.com and on Twitter at @ArielBBooks. I'm also a member of Picture The Books, a group of 2017 debut authors and illustrations (@PictureTheBooks, www.PictureTheBooks.com). **ADVICE FOR WRITERS:** Criticism can be hard to hear, but seriously taking in constructive feedback is one of the best ways to improve your manuscript. **NEXT UP:** I'm currently working on picture book manuscripts and a new chapter book.

WOMEN'S FICTION

② Kate Brandes
KATEBRANDES.COM

The Promise of Pierson Orchard (April 2017, Wyatt-Mackenzie Publishing)

QUICK TAKE: This story is *Erin Brockovich* meets *Promised Land*, about a Pennsylvania family threatened by betrayal, financial desperation, old flames, fracking, and ultimately finding forgiveness. **WRITES FROM:** Riegelsville, PA. **PRE-BOOK:** I worked as an environmental scientist. (I still do.) **TIME FRAME:** It took seven years from when I started writing the story until I got a publisher. I worked on it steadily during that time. **ENTER THE AGENT:** I had an offer from my publisher (Wyatt-MacKenzie Publishing) before I had an agent. Once I had the offer, I immediately sent e-mails to about thirty agents saying I had an interested publisher and was seeking representation. I had quick response from several agents. I ended up signing with my dream agent, Katie Shea Boutillier at The Donald Maass Agency. She then negotiated the deal with Wyatt-MacKenzie. **BIGGEST SURPRISE:** Writing has made me a more compassionate person. The best characters are complex, and they don't always do things that make sense. But every character has reasons for making the choices they make—just like people. **WHAT I DID RIGHT:** I asked for help even though it doesn't come naturally for me. This helped me build a writing community over several years and that has been the single most important thing in my writing career. **WHAT I WISH I WOULD HAVE DONE DIFFERENTLY:** I wish it wouldn't have taken me so long to call myself a writer. **PLATFORM:** I'm on Twitter, Facebook, and Instagram. I favor Instagram because I love to take pictures and I'm a visual person. **ADVICE FOR WRITERS:** Love your characters, especially the troubled ones. **NEXT UP:** I'm working on another women's fiction novel with an eco-bent, inspired in part by Edward Abbey's *The Monkey Wrench Gang*.

NONFICTION

③ Blaire Briody
BLAIREBRIODY.COM

The New Wild West (September 2017, St. Martin's Press)

QUICK TAKE: *The New Wild West* tells the story of how a small town in North Dakota suddenly became the new frontier of U.S. energy independence, told through the experiences of the families that have lived there for generations and the migrant laborers desperate to make a living. **WRITES FROM:** Santa Rosa, CA. **PRE-BOOK:** I was a writer and editor at *The Fiscal Times*, a business news site in New York. **TIME FRAME:** I'd been thinking about writing a book for a while, but I couldn't decide what it would be about. I stumbled across the idea for *The New Wild West* in late 2012 after reading about men who were so desperate for a job, they were traveling to North Dakota and living in a Walmart parking lot to work in the oil fields. It reminded me of *The Grapes of Wrath*, and I couldn't stop thinking about them. I told my photographer friend about it, and he said he wanted to go out there with me. That began the process of searching for funding to pay for a research trip, and in the back of my mind I thought, maybe this is my book. It took a few months to finally vocalize that I wanted to write a book about it, but as soon as I did, I was determined. I also knew that one short weeklong trip wouldn't be enough. We began a crowdfunding campaign through a start-up called FairStreet to raise funds, and I told my job I'd be quitting that summer to live in North Dakota. After the summer, I had enough material to finish the book proposal and I sold it in March 2014. Research and reporting took an additional year, and it was another year to finish the first draft of the manuscript. The total time from idea to final draft has been four-plus years. **ENTER THE AGENT:** I had recently raised $10,000 through crowdfunding to live in North Dakota for the summer. My boss at the time was incredibly supportive of the project, and she knew my goal was to turn it into a book. She introduced me to her agent, Laura Yorke with the Carol Mann Agency, before I left for North Dakota. Laura signed me on the spot. I didn't expect it to happen like that, but Laura was vital in helping me a craft a dynamite book proposal. **BIGGEST SURPRISE:** I've never written anything of this length before, and the process was completely different from magazine writing. I constantly underestimated how long things would take. And once I had a draft, there were so many delays and confusing aspects to the publishing process—plus, every publishing house seems to do things a little differently. There was certainly a learning curve, and I'm sure if I ever write a second book, the process will be smoother. **WHAT I DID RIGHT:** I love the characters that I ended up writing about. Having dynamic characters made the writing process so much easier. I chose them mostly because I enjoyed spending time with them. I debated picking a few people who had interesting scenarios but weren't all that engaging to be around, but I ultimately decided to go with people who I genuinely liked. I'm so glad I did because they turned out to be more interesting than I could've imagined. I only needed to hang around a little longer and dig deeper to peel back those layers. **WHAT I WISH I WOULD HAVE DONE DIFFERENTLY:** It was quite challenging to write a book while the story was still unfolding. When I started, I had no idea where the reporting was going to take me. I also didn't know when to stop reporting. I can see why some nonfiction writers take ten years to finish a book because the story never feels complete. Your characters are always changing and growing, and the scenarios they find themselves in are endlessly fascinating. For my own sanity, next time I may pick a topic that has a set beginning and ending. **PLATFORM:** Facebook and Twitter, though I rarely use Twitter for promotion and use it more as a reporting tool. My Facebook promotion and a few paid Facebook ads helped me raise the initial $10,000 for my crowdfunding campaign. **ADVICE FOR WRITERS:** Surround yourself with other passionate people who will boost your spirits when things get tough. There's a lot of negativity you have to wade through, especially at the beginning when you're receiving rejections. Even after someone said yes and bought my book proposal, it took me a while to let go of the rejections. Focus on the positive and believe in your work no matter what. **NEXT UP:** I'm taking a break! This book took a lot out of me—financially, emotionally, and physically—so I don't plan to start another book project for a while. I'm focusing on shorter, magazine-length pieces and teaching.

SCIENCE FICTION/THRILLER

4 Curtis C. Chen

CURTISCCHEN.COM

Waypoint Kangaroo (June 2016, Thomas Dunne Books)

QUICK TAKE: Meet Kangaroo. He's a superpowered secret agent who's about to face his toughest mission yet: Vacation. **WRITES FROM:** Vancouver, WA (near Portland, OR). **PRE-BOOK:** Though I dabbled in storytelling from a very young age, I started studying fiction writing much more seriously in 2008. Before that, I worked as a software engineer in Silicon Valley and watched a lot of *Star Trek*. **TIME FRAME:** I completed the first draft during National Novel Writing Month 2006. I worked on my first revisions between 2009 and 2011. I began querying agents in 2013 and signed with JABberwocky in 2014. The novel was sold to Thomas Dunne, in a two-book deal, in early 2015. It was published in the summer of 2016. The sequel is forthcoming in 2017. **ENTER THE AGENT:** My literary agent is Sam Morgan (who recently moved from JABberwocky to Foundry Literary + Media, and I went with him). He had the audacity to make me an offer of representation while he knew I was away from home and busy at the Clarion West six-week summer workshop. He wasn't even the agent I actually queried—that was Eddie Schneider! But the man knows comedy. Sam understood what I was doing with Kangaroo and really helped me whip the manuscript into shape. **BIGGEST SURPRISE:** I've been pleasantly surprised by how many of my wacky ideas people have listened to, considering I'm a newbie who knows very little about the publishing business. My editor actually asked me for cover ideas (and even let me hide a puzzle in there—see the next page for details), and his assistant and my publicist were invaluable in helping to schedule an international joint book tour with my pal Claire Humphrey, whose own first novel debuted the week before mine. **WHAT I DID RIGHT:** I research a lot, and doing my homework definitely helped when writing (and rewriting) my query letter. It still took a while to find the right agent, but I learned how to be patient and accept rejection from years of doing short story critiques. I've also learned how to ask for help when appropriate. No matter what stage of your writing career you're in, there are a lot of other writers out there in similar situations, and we are stronger together. **WHAT I WISH I WOULD HAVE DONE DIFFERENTLY:** I sometimes wish I hadn't waited so long to get started on certain projects or had otherwise focused my writing efforts differently. But all that time spent improving my craft—finishing NaNoWriMo eleven years in a row (2005–2015), writing a new flash fiction story every week for nearly five years (2008–2013)—got me to a level where I could actually do the work when facing external deadlines. **PLATFORM:** I'm on Twitter (@curtiscchen) and Facebook (/curtis.c.chen) the most; finding my other social media accounts is left as an exercise for the reader. I've also helped run Puzzled Pint since its inception in 2010 and utilized that experience to build a little puzzle hunt that launched with the book. The first clue is embedded in the cover image, and you'll find the "rabbit hole" at http://before.waypointkangaroo.com. **ADVICE FOR WRITERS:** Learn from everyone. Develop good habits. You are not the work. Persist. **NEXT UP:** The next book in the series, *Kangaroo Too*, launches on June 20, 2017. I'm also working on an untitled stand-alone novel that I hope we'll be able to announce soon!

LITERARY FICTION

⑤ Sophie Chen Keller

SOPHIECHENKELLER.COM

The Luster of Lost Things (August 2017, G.P. Putnam's Sons)

QUICK TAKE: A lonely twelve-year-old boy with a motor speech disorder has an uncanny ability to find lost things. When his mother's unusual dessert shop is jeopardized, he sets out on a quest through New York City to find the one thing that will save his home. **WRITES FROM:** New York. **PRE-BOOK:** My first short story was published in *Glimmer Train* when I was in high school. I wrote a few more short stories throughout college, stopped writing when I graduated in 2010 and started a corporate career in New York, and in 2014 left that career to dedicate myself to my passion for writing and work on this book. **TIME FRAME:** It took me four months to write the first draft of the book and find an agent. Then several rounds of revising with first my agent and then my editor. I'm lucky that they were enthusiastic, tireless, and all-around brilliant people. **ENTER THE AGENT:** I went about it the same way many of us writers do—I sent out cold query letters. The rest happened very quickly. One of the very first agents I e-mailed was Jeff Kleinman at Folio Literary Management, as he represented some of my favorite authors. The e-mail went out the day after Christmas, and before New Year's, I had signed with Jeff. It was a most auspicious way to ring in 2015. **BIGGEST SURPRISE:** That writing the book is just the first part in the process of publishing. I assumed that if I could just figure out how to write the book, the hard part would be done. Turns out that there are actually several parts—querying to find an agent, submitting to find an editor, revising and more revising, promoting and more promoting—and that each part is hard in its own way. **WHAT I DID RIGHT:** Believing that I could, most of the time. And developing and sticking to a writing schedule each day, because when I started doubting, well, I still had my schedule to stick to, so one way or another, those words were getting on the page. **WHAT I WISH I WOULD HAVE DONE DIFFERENTLY:** Plugging into a community of writers. It would have been great to have that source of wisdom and support throughout the process. **PLATFORM:** With my publisher's encouragement, I finally jumped—or, if we want to be precise here, was gently nudged overboard—into the Twitter and Instagram waters. I'm still learning how to swim, but at least I'm paddling along now. **ADVICE FOR WRITERS:** Be optimistic about what you're doing and be ambitious about what you can do. Then put in the work— set your end goal and your goals for each day, and go for it. **NEXT UP:** My second novel.

LITERARY THRILLER

6 Danya Kukafka

DANYAKUKAFKA.COM

Girl in Snow (August 2017, Simon & Schuster)

QUICK TAKE: A debut thriller about the mysterious death of a small-town golden girl and the secret lives of three people connected to her: the social misfit who loved her from afar, the rebellious girl who despised her, and the policeman investigating her death. **WRITES FROM:** Brooklyn, NY. **PRE-BOOK:** I was a student before I got into book publishing, where I now work as an assistant editor. **TIME FRAME:** The novel took about four and a half years to write. The first three years were spent writing alone, the fourth was with my agent, and I spent another eight months revising with my editor. **ENTER THE AGENT:** I'm represented by Dana Murphy at The Book Group, and she is an absolute dream. Our story is quite rare. I was an intern for The Book Group while I was doing my undergraduate degree at NYU; Dana, just a year or two out of school, was their assistant and my supervisor. I told her I was writing a novel, and when it was finally ready—just after I graduated from college— she offered to look at it. We worked together for a full year on the manuscript before we sent it out to editors. I was her first client! **BIGGEST SURPRISE:** I was surprised by how separate the publication aspect feels from the process of writing itself; I had expected it to fall in easily with writing, but they are two very different things. After all the excitement of getting a book deal, you still have to make the time to write, and it's still a very hard job to do—arguably, harder once there are external factors involved. **WHAT I DID RIGHT:** I made sure the book was as good as I could possibly make it before I sent it to my agent—and we both worked on it obsessively before we sent it to editors. I think people often make the mistake of sending too soon out of excitement, and it's worth taking the time to make sure that the book is as clean and lean and as readable as possible. You only get one chance to impress an editor (usually), and though I was anxious to get the book out, I'm so glad I waited and worked until the manuscript was absolutely ready. **WHAT I WISH I WOULD HAVE DONE DIFFERENTLY:** I wish I had appreciated the moments of actual writing. Now that the book is written, I often miss spending time with my characters. It's hard to let them go after spending so many years together. **PLATFORM:** I'm on Twitter and Instagram (@ danyakukafka). I don't use either explicitly for book promotion—but I do like being a part of a community of writers and funny Internet people. Goodreads is a wonderful resource, and in the moments of anxiety before my book came out, I especially loved watching early readers interact with my work. **ADVICE FOR WRITERS:** Don't be afraid to query young agents—they are keen, smart, and very hungry. Young agents at reputable agencies often have experienced mentors, and since they may not have a big client list yet, they can afford to be extra devoted and committed to the clients they do have. They are trying to launch their careers too, and if you have a good sale, it's a win for both of you. **NEXT UP:** I'm working on my next novel—it's been very freeing to start something new!

TROUBLE FINDING AN AGENT?

Are you struggling in your search for an agent? Check out writersdigest.com/GLA-18 for advice from author K.D. Proctor on submitting to small presses while querying.

MEMOIR

7 Ilana Kurshan
ILANAKURSHAN.COM
If All the Seas Were Ink (September 2017, St. Martin's Press)

QUICK TAKE: *If All the Seas Were Ink* is a memoir of one woman's journey through the Talmud, a vast compendium of ancient Jewish law and lore traditionally studied only by men. For nearly a decade Ilana Kurshan learned a page of Talmud every day, an experience she chronicles in this tale of heartache and humor, of love and loss, of marriage and motherhood, and of learning to put one foot in front of the other by turning page after page. **WRITES FROM:** Jerusalem, Israel. **PRE-BOOK:** I worked in publishing both in New York and in Jerusalem—as an editorial assistant, a foreign rights agent, an editor at *Lilith Magazine*, and a translator. **TIME FRAME:** My book began as a series of blog posts and magazine articles, which I published over the course of my seven and a half years of Talmud study. But I wrote the majority of the book while on maternity leave after the birth of my twins, when I had three kids under the age of two. Usually this meant trying to synchronize the kids' naps in the hope of getting some daytime working hours. But my kids are all good sleepers, and so most of this book was written at night, under cover of darkness, as I tried to shed light on the experience of seven years of Talmud study. **ENTER THE AGENT:** My agent is my boss at the literary agency where I work! In this regard I consider myself extremely lucky. **BIGGEST SURPRISE:** The first offer of publication that I received for my book came while I was in the hospital birthing my youngest daughter. My agent called me on my cell phone while I was in the delivery room! My husband commented that publishing a book is often compared to birthing a baby, but most people don't try to do both simultaneously. **WHAT I DID RIGHT:** My work on this book often felt like "stitching and unstitching" (as Yeats put it), writing one sentence only to delete it. And all too often it felt like it was all for naught, and at the end of the day all I had to show for it was a blank screen. But by the end of the process (if not always by the end of the day), I was glad I'd kept at it. **WHAT I WISH I WOULD HAVE DONE DIFFERENTLY:** I wish I had kept a record of my old drafts! There is a lot I wish I'd salvaged from the cutting room floor. **PLATFORM:** One of my closest friends created a website for me, where I post all my poetry, essays, and published articles. **ADVICE FOR WRITERS:** Read and reread the books and authors you love most! **NEXT UP:** I am trying to write a poem about every single page of the Talmud—a long-term project that has brought me much pleasure and has deepened my study of these texts. I am also preparing a course on my favorite Talmudic stories, which I'll be teaching in Jerusalem next year.

MYSTERY

❽ Emily Littlejohn

EMILYLITTLEJOHN.COM

Inherit the Bones (November 2016, Minotaur Books)

QUICK TAKE: Pregnant cop tracks killer in Colorado mountain town and discovers link to unsolved crime from thirty years prior. **WRITES FROM:** Denver, CO. **PRE-BOOK:** Librarian. **TIME FRAME:** I started writing *Inherit the Bones* five years ago. I knew I wanted to write a mystery set in a small Colorado town with a female lead. Very quickly on, I knew the main character would be a pregnant detective; there would be a present-day murder and an older, unsolved crime; and that the book would stand on its own while allowing room to be the first in a series. When I started writing, I was working full-time as a reference librarian, so I wrote on the weekends and in the evenings. At this rather slow pace, it took me about three years to finish the book. **ENTER THE AGENT:** I'm represented by the wonderful Pam Ahearn of The Ahearn Agency. After spending a number of weeks researching the query process, I crafted what I believed was a strong query and sent it off to a number of agents. I had early interest from several of them, including Pam. She believed in the story and once she agreed to represent me, she worked with me to get the book in the best shape possible before shopping the manuscript to editors. Her experience, connections, and critical eye were invaluable in getting a sale. **BIGGEST SURPRISE:** It takes a village to publish a book! If you're lucky enough to land with a great publisher, you'll find there is a whole team working to see your book succeed. That kind of support is crucial when you as a writer might be feeling insecure or nervous about the process. **WHAT I DID RIGHT:** One of the most important things that I did right was to listen to the ideas and edits suggested by my agent and editor. A debut author can't afford to have a large ego; the agents and editors you're working with have years of experience on you. If they suggest an ending might be too outlandish or question the motives of a character, listen to them. They know what they're talking about! Taking their advice only makes the story stronger. **WHAT I WISH I WOULD HAVE DONE DIFFERENTLY:** I wish I had started writing earlier in my life. I've had ideas floating in my head for years but I never made the commitment to sit down and actually write. I don't think successful writers are born talented; like anything, writing takes practice. So, I wish by this stage in my life I had accumulated more practice! **PLATFORM:** I have a website and maintain a presence on Facebook. For me, personally, I find Facebook to be the best way to engage online with readers and fans. The website is great for updating press, my biography, and upcoming appearances. **ADVICE FOR WRITERS:** Don't wait for the muse to strike. If you have a passion for storytelling and an idea that just won't leave your psyche, sit down and start to breathe some life into it. **NEXT UP:** I'm working on the first draft of the third book in the Gemma Monroe series, tentatively titled *Lost Lake*. I just finished reviewing copyedits to *A Season to Lie*, the second book in the series, which will be published in November 2017.

EPIC/HISTORICAL FANTASY

 Cass Morris

CASSMORRISWRITES.COM

From Unseen Fire (January 2018, DAW)

QUICK TAKE: I gave the ancient Romans magic to see what they'd do with it. Political, social, and romantic complications ensue. **WRITES FROM:** Western Virginia. **PRE-BOOK:** I started *From Unseen Fire* while working for the American Shakespeare Center as an educator, not long after finishing my Masters of Letters degree at Mary Baldwin University. **TIME FRAME:** *From Unseen Fire* began as a Nanowrimo project in 2011. I had been away from creative writing too long in favor of academic writing, and I needed to give myself a kick in the pants to get the fictional cogs turning again. I finished and edited it over the course of 2012, and in January 2013 began pitching to agents. By October 2013 I had signed with my agent. We went through some edits and were on submission by late 2014, and I got my deal with DAW in September 2015. **ENTER THE AGENT:** I'm represented by Connor Goldsmith of Fuse

Literary Agency. I found him through the Manuscript Wish List hashtag (#MSWL), where he indicated he was interested in complex heroines, unusual settings for fantasy novels, and interesting magical systems. He was the thirty-first agent I queried, and he almost immediately requested a full manuscript—which no one else had, which goes to show that it's really all about the right letter in front of the right eyes at the right time. I actually got "The Call" from him while I was at a theme park! It was easily one of the most surreal moments of my life—talking to someone offering me representation while standing next to a log flume and trying to tune out the oboes and tubas of the theme music in the background. **BIGGEST SURPRISE:** It. Is. Slow. I knew publishing was a slow industry going in, and I've still been surprised by how glacial the pace can feel sometimes. It's sort of neat in a way, though, that in this ultrarapid world, there are still tangible objects that take a long time and many hands to produce. **WHAT I DID RIGHT:** Learning how to roll with the punches and remain goodnatured is an important skill in this field, and I think I got pretty good at it. I made thematic playlists to pump me back up when I got rejected or felt like I was getting nowhere. **WHAT WISH I WOULD HAVE DONE DIFFERENTLY:** I wish I'd tapped into the writing community on Twitter much earlier. Especially in the science fiction and fantasy genres, there's an incredible group of women who are so supportive of each other, and you can learn so much about querying and publishing just from following the right people. The early stages of my journey might've gone a bit quicker if I'd figured out how to use that resource more swiftly. **PLATFORM:** I have a long background in fandom, so almost all of my social media platforms at least started out connected to my incurable geekery. You can find me on Twitter (@CassRMorris), Instagram (cassrmorris), Facebook (/CassMorrisWrites), Pinterest (reginalupae), and Patreon (CassRMorris). **ADVICE FOR WRITERS:** Perseverance is absolutely the key, every step of the way. It takes a lot of dedication to finish a book, more to edit it, more to polish a query letter, more and more and more to send that query letter out and take the rejections on the chin. Then yet more when you go out on submission. Then yet more when you have revisions from your editor. There will be times you will want to either throw a temper tantrum of epic proportions or crawl into a hole and never be seen again—but you can't. You have to be tough, and you have to keep going. Writing is an endurance sport, and the process of publication is the ultimate marathon. Remember to hydrate. **NEXT UP:** Book two! *From Unseen Fire* is the first in the Aven Cycle, so I owe DAW a couple more books.

CONTEMPORARY ROMANCE

(10) Priscilla Oliveras

PRISOLIVERAS.COM

His Perfect Partner (September 2017, Zebra Shout)

QUICK TAKE: Ad exec and single dad Tomás Garcia can't let himself think about Yazmine Fernandez, whose talent will take her away from Chicago and back to Broadway to fulfill the dreams her papi could not. But as their family lives become entwined, each unexpected intimacy and self-revelation brings them closer, igniting a fire neither can resist. **WRITES FROM:** Central Florida. **PRE-BOOK:** During the day, I work as a special projects manager/technical writer and teach an online romance writing course for ed2go. I write my novels in the early mornings or evenings and on weekends. **TIME FRAME:** *His Perfect Partner* was my MFA thesis manuscript at Seton Hill University, so I had quite a bit more time to polish and edit than I do with Books 2 and 3 in the Matched to Perfection series. I have about five months between deadlines for each book. **ENTER THE AGENT:** My agent is Rebecca Strauss with DeFiore & Company. I queried Rebecca right after I graduated from the Seton Hill University Writing Popular Fiction MFA program based on the recommendation of the program's current director. Rebecca read the full manuscript and we spoke over the phone—I had a list of important craft, industry, and career questions—before she offered representation and I ultimately accepted. **BIGGEST SURPRISE:** The stress is always there. Before signing a contract, the stress was about wondering when the right publisher would love my manuscript as much as I did. After signing, the stress has been meeting shorter deadlines, meeting others' expectations, and balancing looming deadlines with learning about book marketing. I often remind myself that this new stress is something I've worked for, so I need to enjoy it. **WHAT I DID RIGHT:** Thus far, it's staying on top of deadlines. Responding to publisher requests promptly and striving to be the type of author my publishers know they can rely on. On a personal level, it's been treating my writing like a job, sitting down to work every day, not only when I "feel like it." **WHAT I WISH I WOULD HAVE DONE DIFFERENTLY:** Ooh, hindsight … I wish I could have quieted the doubts when I started working on Book 2. These doubts slowed my progress. But I've been told by others that Book 2 in a debut series for a new author can often be a struggle. Knowing other authors have experienced similar issues helped me realize doubts are part of the business. I simply need to sit down and get words on the page like I have before. Then I can count on my editing, revising, and polishing skills to whip my manuscript into shape. **PLATFORM:** I'm on Twitter (@prisoliveras), Facebook (/prisoliveras), and Instagram (prisoliveras). My author platform/brand is contemporary romance with a Latina flavor. I write family stories. You'll find my social media accounts show readers why I write the stories and characters that I do, because my family and culture are important to me and that's what I enjoy sharing with my readers. **ADVICE FOR WRITERS:** Keep writing. Learn about our craft. Join professional organizations like Romance Writers of America. Network. Enter contests and/or work with a trusted critique group to get feedback. Don't be afraid to submit to agents and editors when you have a manuscript you've revised and polished. But above all, don't give up. Keep writing!

NEXT UP: I'm working on Book 2 (*Her Perfect Affair*, March 2018) and Book 3 (untitled, August 2018) in the Matched to Perfection series. After those two are submitted to my editor, I'll get started on the next series I have in mind.

WOMEN'S FICTION

11 Kristin Rockaway

KRISTINROCKAWAY.COM

The Wild Woman's Guide to Traveling the World (June 2017, Center Street)

QUICK TAKE: A twenty-something New Yorker with a severe case of wanderlust questions her prestigious career and perfectly ordered life after meeting a free-spirited American artist in Hong Kong. **WRITES FROM:** Encinitas, CA. **PRE-BOOK:** I worked in IT for fifteen years, first as a software developer, then as a manager. **TIME FRAME:** The novel began as a 500-word writing assignment for a fiction class I took in September of 2013. My instructor encouraged me to flesh it out into a longer piece, so I used it as a starting point for NaNoWriMo that year—but quickly grew discouraged at my inability to keep up with the word count, and set it aside. Several months later, I picked it back up with renewed commitment and began querying my final draft in March of 2015. **ENTER THE AGENT:** I'd been in the query trenches for about four months when I found my agent, Jennifer Johnson-Blalock, through an #MSWL tweet asking for "commercial women's fiction with standout plots." I sent her a query letter, and two months later, she offered me representation. **BIGGEST SURPRISE:** The pace. I had heard going into it that publishing was slow, but I didn't realize exactly how slow. It's very much a "hurry up and wait" process. I signed my publishing contract sixteen months before my book was released! **WHAT I DID RIGHT:** In this business, persistence is everything. Every time I received a rejection, I'd allow myself five minutes of self-pity before querying the next agent on my list. It's all about conquering self-doubt and not letting the rejections get you down. **WHAT I WISH I WOULD HAVE DONE DIFFERENTLY:** While I was writing my first draft, I spent a lot of time pointlessly obsessing over the market. Was my novel upmarket or commercial? Romance or women's fiction? None of those questions mattered until I had a finished novel in my hands. Once I stopped worrying about how I was going to sell my novel and just wrote the book of my heart, the words flowed—and I found an agent and editor who connected with it, too. **PLATFORM:** I have a presence on most of the big social media platforms—Facebook, Instagram, Pinterest, Goodreads—but I'm most active on Twitter. It's an excellent way to connect with readers, agents, editors, and other writers. I think Twitter is sort of like the water cooler for the publishing industry. **ADVICE FOR WRITERS:** Be patient, be gracious, and don't give up. **NEXT UP:** A story about women in tech, dating apps, and the search for true connection in a digitally detached world.

FANTASY

12 Isabelle Steiger

The Empire's Ghost (May 2017, Thomas Dunne Books)

QUICK TAKE: A once-great empire has been reduced to a patchwork of feuding kingdoms; in the midst of this political chaos, a sprawling cast of nobles and commoners fight to determine the fate of the entire continent. **WRITES FROM:** New York City. **PRE-BOOK:** I had just graduated from college and was working as an editorial assistant at a magazine. **TIME FRAME:** I started writing in early 2012. I'd always wanted to be a novelist, and the time seemed right to find out if I could actually finish a novel. I've always struggled with outlines, so I set myself a minimum daily word count and just jumped right in. It took approximately fourteen months to finish and edit the manuscript to the point where I was ready to shop it around. **ENTER THE AGENT:** I owe my agent to a chance encounter: Going to meet my father for lunch one afternoon, I ran into a friend of his on the street, a woman who had never met me. After he explained who I was and what I was trying to do, she insisted that I talk to the agent who'd gotten her own book published, David Vigliano, and introduced us via e-mail almost before I knew what had happened. I wasn't expecting anything to come of it: She'd recommended my manuscript without even asking for a summary, and her agency (then called Vigliano Associates) was one I had heard focused mostly on nonfiction. I've never been happier to be wrong. **BIGGEST SURPRISE:** I had no idea there was such a large amount of time between the editing of a manuscript and its publication. I'm sure veteran authors are used to dividing their imaginations between the book they're about to publish and the book they're currently writing (but won't publish for a year or more), but it was a new experience for me. **WHAT I DID RIGHT:** I did everything in my power to create a book that was representative of who I am as a thinker and storyteller—to write the kind of book I'd always wanted to read. I ignored any advice that wasn't actually about how to make the book better, but only about how to make it more generically appealing or how to make it compliant with a formula. Refusing to heed suggestions from people much more experienced than you are can certainly be nerveracking, even when you have others who are willing to support you. Though it took some time, my stubbornness paid off in the end. **WHAT I WISH I WOULD HAVE DONE DIFFERENTLY:** I wish I had done more research on how to write a query letter and which agents might be receptive to my manuscript before the manuscript was ready to send out, instead of waiting until afterward. While writing and editing, I felt like I was accomplishing something every day, only to hurry up and wait once I realized I didn't know enough to take the next step yet. **PLATFORM:** I'm not on any public social media accounts as of this writing. **ADVICE FOR WRITERS:** Perseverance is as vital to success as talent. While you're still struggling to get published, no one else is going to make you keep going, and you'll likely experience your share of self-doubt. When I was searching for an agent, my initial rejections made me worry my book was too unusual or unwieldy to sell. But the solution wasn't to change anything about the book—just to keep trying until I found the right place for it. **NEXT UP:** I'm under contract to write a trilogy, so I'm currently working on the sequel to *The Empire's Ghost*.

WOMEN'S FICTION/SUSPENSE

13 Jessica Strawser
JESSICASTRAWSER.COM
Almost Missed You (March 2017, St. Martin's Press)

QUICK TAKE: Violet and Finn were "meant to be," said everyone, always—until the day he packs up and vanishes in the middle of a family vacation, taking their son with him. Told through alternating viewpoints of Violet, Finn, and a mutual friend who gets pulled into their nightmare, *Almost Missed You* is a powerful story of love, secrets, missed connections, and the spaces between what's meant to be and what might have been. **WRITES FROM:** Cincinnati, OH. **PRE-BOOK:** Having held several editorial staff jobs in magazine and book publishing, I've been the chief editor of *Writer's Digest* since 2008, with occasional freelance bylines (including a Modern Love essay in *The New York Times*). But my path to becoming an author was not as straightforward as you might think. I had landed an agent for an earlier novel, but it never sold, and after about eighteen months of what my agent called "rave rejections," we parted ways. I'd written *Almost Missed You* while that first book was out on submission, and so found myself with a new manuscript but no representation. **TIME FRAME:** Having spent the previous five years or so rewriting the same (unsuccessful) novel over and over again, when I finally set it aside and started writing *Almost Missed You* in the summer of 2014, the story came together in a burst of creative energy—about ten intense months, including revision. **ENTER THE AGENT:** My pitch focused on *Almost Missed You* but noted that I had an earlier novel that had garnered some rejections as well before losing representation. Barbara Poelle asked me to send both, and about a month later I got the call: She did not think she could sell Book 1, but was head over heels for Book 2. I decided to trust her and table the first project for good—and she sold *Almost Missed You* in a preempt in just two weeks. **BIGGEST SURPRISE:** How important it is to have the right team behind you. The enthusiasm of a particular agent, editor, publicist, marketing team, etc., can make a world of difference in how a project is perceived, both at your publishing house and beyond. **WHAT I DID RIGHT:** Tried to focus on what I could control, shook off the setbacks, and kept trying.

WHAT I WISH I WOULD HAVE DONE DIFFERENTLY: Though I could have made my life easier by doing quite a few things differently, even my missteps were learning experiences that helped get me to where I am today—so I don't think I'd change much even if I could. **PLATFORM:** I'm a member of the Women's Fiction Writer's Association and, of course, the *Writer's Digest* community. I speak at writing conferences as much as my schedule allows (which isn't a ton, with two young kids) and actively pursue guest blog posts as well as freelance bylines, most recently with an essay for *Publishers Weekly* that went viral. I'm on Twitter (@jessicastrawser) and Facebook (/jessicastrawserauthor). **ADVICE FOR WRITERS:** Hold tight to whatever it is about writing that brings you joy, and don't give up. **NEXT UP:** Another hybrid of women's fiction and suspense, *Not That I Could Tell*, from St. Martin's Press in Spring 2018.

AN INSIDER'S LOOK

Revisit Jessica Strawser's journey to publication by reading her collection of blog posts at writersdigest.com/author/jessica-strawser. She shares everything from how she got her agent to surviving a copyedit and more.

MIDDLE GRADE

14 Ellie Terry
ELLIETERRY.COM
Forget Me Not (March 2017, Feiwel & Friends)

QUICK TAKE: *Forget Me Not* is a dual-POV verse novel about a girl named Calliope who tries to hide her Tourette syndrome from her new school, while trying to convince her mother not to move them yet again, especially after she meets Jinsong—the boy next door— who also happens to be the school's popular student body president. **WRITES FROM:** St. George, UT. **PRE-BOOK:** I've worked at two different chiropractor's offices (as a receptionist), a sourdough pizza joint, a family fun center, and a jewelry store. I was also a cheerleading coach and a baton twirling coach. Now I just write. **TIME FRAME:** I started drafting *Forget Me Not* in August 2013. It took about six months to get that first draft down and then another six months to revise it. In August 2014 I entered a contest called Pitch Wars and was chosen to be mentored by Joy McCullough-Carranza. I spent two intense months cutting out an entire POV and then I began querying agents with the manuscript. **ENTER THE AGENT:** In January 2015, I queried Steven Chudney. After he read the manuscript, we spoke on the phone and he gave me a lot of insights and suggestions on how to improve the plot and characters. I spent six weeks deleting and rewriting the last quarter of the novel, among other things, and I must have done a good job, because Steven e-mailed four days after I sent it with an offer of representation. **BIGGEST SURPRISE:** That there would be so much waiting. It was a long road to signing with an agent (eleven years of querying five middle-grade novels and forty picture books), but my debut sold very quickly (two-and-a-half weeks). So I assumed that once I had a book deal, things would just speed up! The truth is, you're always waiting on something. Hearing back from an agent, waiting on edit notes from your editor, waiting to see the draft of the cover, etc. It's best to sit back and enjoy the journey (and always be working on the next project, or two). **WHAT I DID RIGHT:** Connecting with other authors. Being able to talk to other debut authors as well as those further in their publishing journey proved to be invaluable for me. **WHAT I WISH I WOULD HAVE DONE DIFFERENTLY:** Worried less. There are so many things in publishing that are out of an author's control, and therefore provides plenty of opportunity for anxiety issues to grow. I wish I would have learned earlier that it's best to focus on the one thing I do have control over: writing the best stories I can. **PLATFORM:** I hang out on Facebook and Twitter, mostly. There aren't a whole lot of books for the middle-grade market that deal with characters who have Tourette syndrome. My platform is unique in that my debut novel deals with Tourette syndrome, and I myself am diagnosed with the condition. **ADVICE FOR WRITERS:** Read. Join a critique group. Read. Never give up. Read. Write lots of stories. Read. Take yourself seriously and those around will follow suit. Read. Don't be afraid to try new things. Also... read. **NEXT UP:** I am currently working on two MG projects—both verse novels—and both have boy main characters, so we'll see how that goes!

YOUNG ADULT

⑮ Angie Thomas
ANGIETHOMAS.COM
The Hate U Give (February 2017, Balzer + Bray)

QUICK TAKE: Sixteen-year-old Starr Carter navigates between the poverty-stricken neighborhood she has grown up in and the upper-crust suburban prep school she attends. Her life is upended when she is the sole witness to a police officer shooting her best friend, Khalil, who turns out to have been unarmed during the confrontation. **WRITES FROM:** Mississippi. **PRE-BOOK:** I was an assistant to a Bishop at a local mega church. **TIME FRAME:** I first wrote the book as a short story back in 2010/2011, and I put it aside for a few years. I started working on it as a full-length novel in December 2014/January 2015. It took me about five months of drafting and revising before I queried it. **ENTER THE AGENT:** I surprisingly got my agent through Twitter. The Bent Agency held a question-and-answer session. I was afraid to query my book because of the topic, so I asked if it was an appropriate book to query. Brooks Sherman responded by saying not only was it appropriate, but he asked to see it when I finished. I queried him a few weeks later. Not long after that, he made an offer of representation. Not too long after signing with him, we went on submission and ended up in a thirteen-publishing house auction. Not bad for a process that started with Twitter. **BIGGEST SURPRISE:** One of the biggest surprises about this process has been that waiting never ends. When you're sending queries and waiting for responses, you may think that once you get an agent, everything happens quickly. Not so much. Even once you get a publishing contract, there's more waiting. You soon learn that patience truly is key. **WHAT I DID RIGHT:** For years, I revised and queried a middle-grade project only to get rejection after rejection after rejection. During my third round of submissions, I decided to work on something new. That "something new" became *The Hate U Give*. Sometimes the next book is *the* book. **WHAT I WISH I WOULD HAVE DONE DIFFERENTLY:** I wish I would have moved on from my MG project sooner. Not that there's anything wrong with it, but sometimes when we're querying we can get so caught up in one project that we don't allow ourselves to even consider other options. Allow yourself to write other things. **PLATFORM:** I love Twitter (@acthomasbooks), and I am trying to use Instagram (@acwrites) a bit more. **ADVICE FOR WRITERS:** Don't fret over all of the nos (and there will be plenty of them)—all it takes is one yes. **NEXT UP:** I'm working on my second book. It's a YA contemporary, set in the same neighborhood as *The Hate U Give*, but it is not a sequel. That's all I can say for now.

LITERARY FICTION

16 Amita Trasi

AMITATRASI.COM

The Color of Our Sky (April 2017, William Morrow)

QUICK TAKE: A sweeping, emotional journey of two childhood friends in Mumbai, India—one trying to escape the brutal world of human trafficking and another on a mission to rescue her. **WRITES FROM:** Woodlands, TX. **PRE-BOOK:** I worked for about seven years in India in the field of human resources before I moved to the U.S. I traveled quite a bit for the first few years after arriving here. In 2009, I was attending one of the Arvon residential writing retreats (Moniack Mhor) in Inverness, Scotland, when this idea of two childhood friends came to me. These characters suddenly became so clear in my head that when I was leaving the place, I knew this was going to become a novel. **TIME FRAME:** I wrote in bits and pieces starting early 2010. I started writing from their birth in different class/caste systems (in a village vs. a city), and I wrote detailed scenes with them growing up and retaining their friendship for three decades. I wrote more than three hundred pages just to get to know my characters and the plot. Once I knew my characters well enough and the story I wanted to tell, I got rid of more than half the writing and worked through many drafts to start the novel at critical points in each character's life. It took me about four years to finish. **ENTER THE AGENT:** I sent my novel to many agents in the U.S. and received many rejection letters. A couple of agents came back to me with feedback and encouraged me to keep going. I self-published this book in 2015 and received an overwhelming positive feedback from bloggers and an interest from a Turkish publisher for translation rights. I went looking for an agent, once again, to represent me for the Turkish deal. Aroon Raman, a terrific author, recommended Priya Doraswamy of Lotus Lane agency and when I approached her to represent me for the translation rights, she read my book and suggested that we try to sell it to a traditional publisher. And she did a fabulous job! **BIGGEST SURPRISE:** I think the contrast between the efforts required to self-publish versus publish with one of the Big Five publishing houses shouldn't have been surprising, but it was amazing to experience the difference and have all the help I could get. The support I have from my publishing team at William Morrow is fantastic! **WHAT I DID RIGHT:** I went through many, many drafts through the four years I worked on this, which helped me get a polished book in front of an audience. I had good critique partners, editors, and proofreaders along the way. **WHAT I WISH I WOULD HAVE DONE DIFFERENTLY:** Nothing really. I'm quite pleased with the way it all turned out. I've tried my best, learned valuable lessons from my mistakes, and met wonderful people along the way. **PLATFORM:** Twitter (@AmitaTrasi) and Facebook (/amitatrasiauthor). **ADVICE FOR WRITERS:** With writing, the rule is there are no rules. This, and letting my intuition guide me through the entire process, has served me well. **NEXT UP:** I'm working on a second novel.

HISTORICAL FICTION

 Daren Wang

DARENWANG.COM

The Hidden Light of Northern Fires (August 2017, Thomas Dunne Books)

QUICK TAKE: A novel rooted in the remarkable, but little-known, true history of the only secessionist town north of the Mason Dixon Line. When escaped slave Joe Bell collapses in her father's barn, Mary Willis must ward off Confederate spies, copperheads, Joe's vengeful owner, and even her own brother to help the fugitive find his way to freedom. **WRITES FROM:** Decatur, GA. **PRE-BOOK:** I am the founding executive director of the Decatur Book Festival in Georgia. We started that in 2005 and held our first festival in 2006. We expect about eighty thousand attendees this year. Before that, I worked in public radio producing and hosting writer-related programs. **TIME FRAME:** I grew up in Town Line, the setting of the book, and heard stories about my house being on the Underground Railroad during that time. But sometime in 2007 or so, I Googled my old address and found an oral history of the family that built the house. It led me down a rabbit hole, and I spent a couple years

PHOTO © TOM MEYER

researching all I could about the history of Western New York. I became obsessed. A place I had always thought boring was suddenly imbued with magic. I'd find myself drinking with some writer and would become that jerk trying to get them to write the story I wanted to read. I embarrassed myself that way until I finally sat down and opened a blank document and started typing. That was probably around 2009. **ENTER THE AGENT:** I had gotten the last in a series of rejections from friends' agents when a publicist friend said it would be a good fit with Marly Rusoff and that I could use his name. Marly is such a legend that I was too intimidated to send it over the transom, even with the friends' name. A couple days later, the phone rang, and the voice on the other end said, "Hi Daren, this is Marly Rusoff." She was publishing Jonathan Odell's great book, *Miss Hazel and The Rosa Parks League*, on her own small imprint and needed some help promoting it here in Atlanta. I did what I could to help. She called me the Monday after his event to thank me, and I said, "I have a manuscript I was hoping to send you." She said she wasn't taking new clients, but I think I guilted her into reading it. I e-mailed it to her that afternoon, then settled in for the long wait. She called me on Wednesday to complain I had kept her up all night, and she'd come down with something as a result. The book literally made her sick, but she took it anyway. **BIGGEST SURPRISE:** I expected to be rejected, but I was surprised by the thought and care in the rejection letters. I could have pulled blurbs for the cover from some of them. I used to hear those stories about how some hugely successful novel had been rejected by dozens of editors and wonder what kind of fool had passed on the title. After going through the process, I understood that being good enough was only a starting point. Editors also ask themselves if they are the right fit to fix any problems, if they'll be able to champion a title within the house, if there is already a competing title scheduled for that season, and dozens of other questions. It is frustrating when you're in the midst of it, but there's reassurance, too. **WHAT I DID RIGHT:** I persevered. I gave the process time. Although I've worked with professional writers for a good chunk of my life, I have no formal training myself, not even a creative writing class. All those years were somewhat about crafting a novel, but also about teaching myself how to write. Long ago, I interviewed the great Larry Brown, and he talked about how he burned a pile of seven or so manuscripts in his backyard when he finally sold his first book. I kept that idea close to my heart, that turning myself into a writer would be a long slog. **WHAT I WISH I WOULD HAVE DONE DIFFERENTLY:** Although my style doesn't reflect it, I'm a disciple of Flannery O'Connor. In one of her letters, she said that when she was writing *Good Country People*, she had no idea that the bible salesman was going to steal Joy/Hulga's wooden leg until it happened. I fell in love with the idea that a writer should let the story come as he or she wrote. There's a reason that Flannery is best known for short stories. All in all, I think that conceit cost me close to three years of dead ends and wrong turns, and more than a dozen finished, polished chapters that ended up on the scrap heap. From now on, I'll outline. **PLATFORM:** Twitter sometimes, Facebook often. I can be a wordy son of a bitch. I need more than 140 characters. **ADVICE FOR WRITERS:** Unplug your Internet router before you sit down, then get behind the mule and plow. There's no substitute for just doing the work. **NEXT UP:** I'm so wrapped up in the history of upstate New York, I'm returning there for new one. I've started researching another nineteenth century story that is leading me down new rabbit holes.

LITERARY FICTION

18 Weike Wang

Chemistry (May 2017, Knopf)

QUICK TAKE: This is a coming-of-age novel of an Asian American graduate student in chemistry. **WRITES FROM:** New York City. **PRE-BOOK:** I went into graduate school for bio-statistics and cancer epidemiology. It was very different. If anything, it affirmed my passion for writing. **TIME FRAME:** The actual novel writing took a little under four months. The editing took a year or so. But before the four months of novel writing, I had written a two hundred-page draft that I just didn't like. So on July 29th, I remember distinctly, I tossed this draft out and started over. I think novel writing is different for everyone. I don't like having so many drafts on my computer, so I just save my edits over and over again such that I only have one draft and one other document of excess that came from the draft. I know I am supposed to outline before a novel, but usually I end up outlining when I am in the middle of it or when I am stuck. **ENTER THE AGENT:** I was lucky enough to have a teacher I greatly admire in both teaching and writing. She kindly introduced me to her agent and then the story unfolded. **BIGGEST SURPRISE:** Nothing really surprised me about the process. I knew the odds going in. But I think I was genuinely surprised by how nice and supportive everyone was once the ball started rolling. I was surprised that people actually found my writing funny. Sometimes when you write, it happens in this vacuum and you are not sure if it's good or not. Also the more times you read your own work, the less funny it becomes. **WHAT I DID RIGHT:** I found great mentors and teachers who really helped me become the writer I am. **WHAT I WISH I WOULD HAVE DONE DIF-FERENTLY:** I had done my MFA in fiction and doctorate in epidemiology simultaneously. There were a few months where I questioned my sanity. I don't know if I would want to do that again, but I also don't know how else I would have gained the confidence to write. My confidence came from realizing that I would write no matter what and I was happy doing it. **PLATFORM:** Nope. For some reason social media really stresses me out. **ADVICE FOR WRITERS:** Do not underestimate your own background. Every writer is different. I had often compared myself to this ideal artist type, you know, the free-spirited creative. I never saw myself like that so I never thought writing would work out for me. But then I realized that there was room for everyone. And the world of writing wouldn't be able to expand if there weren't new writers who could bring in new experiences and voices. **NEXT UP:** I am working on another novel and some short stories!

MEMOIR

19 Lauren Fern Watt

LAURENFERNWATT.COM

Gizelle's Bucket List (March 2017, Simon & Schuster)

QUICK TAKE: *Gizelle's Bucket List* is about my adventures with my English mastiff, Gizelle. Gizelle was my best friend through boyfriends, first jobs, my parent's divorce, and my mother's struggle with addiction, so when Gizelle got sick and I realized time with her was coming to an end, I designed a bucket list to make the most of the days we had left. **WRITES FROM:** Los Angeles and Nashville. **PRE-BOOK:** I worked in travel and fashion public relations, and did freelance travel journalism on the side. **TIME FRAME:** I began writing in January 2015 and finished editing around Christmas 2016. **ENTER THE AGENT:** I'm represented by Abrams Artists Agency. I signed with them after receiving media attention for a viral story I wrote about my dying dog's bucket list. **BIGGEST SURPRISE:** The biggest surprise I had with the writing process was how long it took, and how much bad writing it took to finally find the story that worked. I always heard people say "Writing a book is like running a marathon." But I didn't totally understand it until I wrote my own. Writing a book is a long journey with lots of ups and downs, some great moments, some painful moments, but I eventually learned if I promised myself I'd never quit, I'd cross the finish line. **WHAT I DID RIGHT:** I worked really hard. I didn't trade my writing time for anything and was disciplined with closing myself in rooms to work. I dated my laptop and gave up a lot of nights out with friends. I was determined to write the best book I possibly could. **WHAT I WISH I WOULD HAVE DONE DIFFERENTLY:** Perhaps what I did right is also what I wish I could do over. Sometimes I was too disciplined. It took me a while to realize that it was okay to write bad and that some writing days are harder than others and that's the way it is and always will be. I had a hard time peeling myself away from my computer. I put a lot of pressure on myself. But whenever I finally did step away from writing, I often thought of my best ideas! I love writing, but if I could do it over, I would have tried to take more deep breaths and reminded myself to enjoy the creative process and not get overly stressed about it. I would have tried to cheer myself on more, instead of being so hard on myself. **PLATFORM:** Instagram (@lfernwatt), Twitter (@ laurenfernwatt), and Facebook (/laurenfernwatt). I love travel and dogs, so my accounts are pretty pet/travel related. **ADVICE FOR WRITERS:** I think patience is key. There were a lot of days I had too many documents going for too many possible chapters and it felt chaotic and disorganized and like I would never, ever, ever finish. But I promised myself I would sit there until it came together … and it eventually did come together. I think determination is really important, but it's also important to be loving toward yourself throughout the process. Writing sometimes got lonely for me, and I loved to pick on myself and beat myself up if I couldn't make a deadline. One day when I was feeling particularly discouraged, I made signs that said, "Go Lauren!" and "You can do it!" and "No whining! Smile!" and hung them all over the room. This sounds so cheesy and dumb and embarrassing, but it did help. Writing sometimes felt overwhelming, but I try to remember how wonderful it is and that I do it because it is fun and I love it. And whenever I was positive about my process, the words came easier. **NEXT UP:** I'm in the process of planning a two-month North America road trip with my new rescue dog named Bette, and I hope to write about that.

NEW AGENT SPOTLIGHTS

Study new reps who are actively seeking to build their client list

//

One of the most popular columns on the Guide to Literary Agents Blog is "New Agent Alerts," a running series spotlighting new/newer literary reps who are open to queries and actively searching for clients.

Newer agents are golden opportunities for aspiring authors because of exactly that—they're still building their client lists. These agents are hungry to sign new clients, to start submitting to editors, and to sell books. While an established agent with forty clients may have little to no time to consider new writers' work (let alone help them shape it), a newer agent may be willing to sign a promising writer whose work is not a guaranteed huge payday.

THE PROS AND CONS OF NEWER AGENTS

It's common to ask the question, "Is it okay to sign with a new agent?" People value experience and wonder about a new agent's skill. The concern is an interesting one, so let's examine the positives and negatives of choosing a rep who's in her first few years of agenting.

Probable Pros
- They are actively building their client lists—and that means they are anxious to sign new writers and lock in those first several sales.
- They are willing to give your work a longer look. They may be willing to work with you on a project to get it ready for submission, whereas a more established agent has many clients and little time—they don't have a spare moment to help you shape your novel or proposal.

- With fewer clients under their wing, they will give you more attention than you would get from an established rep.
- If they've found their calling and don't seem like they're giving up anytime soon (and keep in mind, most do continue on as agents), you can have a decades-long relationship that pays off.
- They have little going against them. An established agent once told me that a new agent is in a unique position because they have no duds under their belt—their slates are clean.

Possible Cons

- They are less experienced in contract negotiations.
- They know fewer editors than a rep who's been in business for years, meaning there might be some bumps in the road to publication. This is a big, justified point—and writers' foremost concern.
- They are in a weaker position to demand a higher advance.
- New agents come and some go. This means if your agent is in business for a year or two and doesn't find the success for which they hoped, they might bail altogether. That leaves you without a home. If you sign with an agent who's been in business for fourteen years, however, chances are they won't quit tomorrow.

HOW CAN YOU DECIDE FOR YOURSELF?

1. FIND OUT IF THE AGENT IS PART OF A LARGER AGENCY. Agents share contacts and resources. If your agent is the new guy at an agency with five people, those other four agents will help him (and you) with submissions. In other words, he's new, but not alone.

2. LEARN WHERE THE AGENT CAME FROM. Has she been an apprentice at the agency for two years? Was she an editor for seven years and just switched to agenting? If she already has a few years in publishing under her belt, she's not as green as you may think. Agents don't become agents overnight.

3. ASK WHERE HE WILL SUBMIT THE WORK. This is a big one. If you fear the agent lacks proper contacts to move your work, be stragiht with him: "What editors do you see us submitting this book to, and have you sold to them before?" The question tests his plan for where to send the manuscript and get it in print.

4. ASK THE AGENT WHY SHE IS YOUR BEST OPTION. This is another straight-up question that gets right to the point. If she's new and has few (or no) sales at that point, she can't respond with "I sell tons of books and I make it rain cash money!! Dolla dolla bills, y'all!!!" She can't rely on her track record to entice you. So what's her sales pitch? Weigh her enthusiasm, her plan for the book, her promises of hard work, and anything else she tells you. In the publishing business, you want communication and enthusiasm from agents (and editors). Both are invaluable. What's the point of signing with a huge agent when she doesn't return your e-mails and considers your book last on her list of priorities for the day?

5. IF YOU'RE NOT SOLD, YOU CAN ALWAYS SAY NO. It's as simple as that. Always query new/newer agents because, at the end of the day, receiving an offer of representation doesn't mean you're obligated to accept.

NEW AGENT SPOTLIGHTS

Peppered throughout this book's large number of agency listings are sporadic "New Agent Alert" sidebars. (And due to spacing and timing of their becoming an agent or joining their agency, some of these sidebars include agents who you won't find in their agency listings (though they're still listed in the index)! Even more reason to read closely.) Look them over to see if these newer reps might be a good fit for your work. Always read personal information and submission guidelines carefully. Don't get rejected on a technicality because you submitted work incorrectly. Wherever possible, we have included a website address for their agency, as well as the Twitter handle for those reps that tweet.

Also, please note that all these agents were active and seeking clients at the time of this book's publication. It is not a guarantee that every agent is still in their respective position when you read this, nor that they have kept their query in-boxes open. We urge you to visit agency websites and double-check before you query. (This is always a good idea in any case.) Good luck!

GLOSSARY OF INDUSTRY TERMS

Your guide for every need-to-know term.

//

#10 ENVELOPE. A standard, business-size envelope.

ACKNOWLEDGMENTS PAGE. The page of a book on which the author credits sources of assistance—both individuals and organizations.

ACQUISITIONS EDITOR. The person responsible for originating and/or acquiring new publishing projects.

ADAPTATION. The process of rewriting a composition (novel, story, film, article, play) into a form suitable for some other medium, such as television or the stage.

ADVANCE. Money a publisher pays a writer prior to book publication, usually paid in installments, such as one-half upon signing the contract and one-half upon delivery of the complete, satisfactory manuscript. An advance is paid against the royalty money to be earned by the book. Agents take their percentage off the top of the advance as well as from the royalties earned.

ADVENTURE. A genre of fiction in which action is the key element, overshadowing characters, theme, and setting.

AUCTION. Publishers sometimes bid for the acquisition of a book manuscript with excellent sales prospects. The bids are for the amount of the author's advance, guaranteed dollar amounts, advertising and promotional expenses, royalty percentage, etc. Auctions are conducted by agents.

AUTHOR'S COPIES. An author usually receives about ten free copies of his hardcover book from the publisher; more from a paperback firm. He can obtain additional copies at a reduced price by using his author's discount (usually 50 percent of the retail price).

AUTOBIOGRAPHY. A book-length account of a person's entire life written by the subject himself.

BACKLIST. A publisher's list of books that were not published during the current season, but that are still in print.

BACKSTORY. The history of what has happened before the action in your story takes place, affecting a character's current behavior.

BIO. A sentence or brief paragraph about the writer; includes work, any publishing history, and educational experience.

BIOGRAPHY. An account of a person's life (or the lives of a family or close-knit group) written by someone other than the subject(s). The work is set within the historical framework (i.e., the unique economic, social, and political conditions) existing during the subject's life.

BLURB. The copy on paperback book covers or hardcover book dust jackets, either promoting the book and the author or featuring testimonials from book reviewers or well-known people in the book's field. Also called flap copy or jacket copy.

BOILERPLATE. A standardized publishing contract. Most authors and agents make many changes to the boilerplate before accepting the contract.

BOOK DOCTOR. A freelance editor hired by a writer, agent, or book editor who analyzes problems that exist in a book manuscript or proposal, and offers solutions to those problems.

BOOK PACKAGER. Someone who draws elements of a book together—from initial concept to writing and marketing strategies—and then sells the book package to a book publisher and/or movie producer. Also known as book producer or book developer.

BOUND GALLEYS. A prepublication, often paperbound, edition of a book, usually prepared from photocopies of the final galley proofs. Designed for promotional purposes, bound galleys serve as the first set of review copies to be mailed out. Also called bound proofs.

CATEGORY FICTION. A term used to include all types of fiction. See *genre*.

CLIMAX. The most intense point in the storyline of a fictional work.

CLIPS. Samples, usually from newspapers or magazines, of your published work. Also called tearsheets.

COMMERCIAL FICTION. Novels designed to appeal to a broad audience. These are often broken down into categories such as Western, mystery, and romance. See genre.

CONFESSION. A first-person story in which the narrator is involved in an emotional situation that encourages sympathetic reader identification, concluding with the affirmation of a morally acceptable theme.

CONFLICT. A prime ingredient of fiction that usually represents some obstacle to the main character's (i.e., the protagonist's) goals.

CONTRIBUTOR'S COPIES. Copies of the book sent to the author. The exact number of contributor's copies is often negotiated in the publishing contract.

CO-PUBLISHING. Arrangement where author and publisher share publication costs and profits of a book. Also called cooperative publishing.

COPYEDITING. Editing of a manuscript for writing style, grammar, punctuation, and factual accuracy.

COPYRIGHT. A means to protect an author's work. A copyright is a proprietary right designed to give the creator of a work the power to control that work's reproduction, distribution, and public display or performance, as well as its adaptation to other forms.

COVER LETTER. A brief letter that accompanies the manuscript being sent to an agent or publisher.

CREATIVE NONFICTION. Type of writing where true stories are told by employing the techniques usually reserved for novelists and poets, such as scenes, character arc, a three-act structure, and detailed descriptions. This category is also called "narrative nonfiction" or "literary journalism."

CRITIQUING SERVICE. An editing service offered by some agents in which writers pay a fee for comments on the salability or other qualities of their manuscript. Sometimes the critique includes suggestions on how to improve the work. Fees vary, as does the quality of the critique.

CURRICULUM VITAE (CV). Short account of one's career or qualifications.

DEADLINE. A specified date and/or time that a project or draft must be turned into the editor. A deadline factors into a preproduction schedule, which involves copyediting, typesetting, and production.

DEAL MEMO. The memorandum of agreement between a publisher and author that precedes the actual contract and includes important issues such as royalty, advance, rights, distribution, and option clauses.

DEUS EX MACHINA. A term meaning "God from the machine" that refers to any unlikely, contrived, or trick resolution of a plot in any type of fiction.

DIALOGUE. An essential element of fiction. Dialogue consists of conversations between two or more people, and can be used heavily or sparsely.

DIVISION. An unincorporated branch of a publishing house/company.

ELECTRONIC RIGHTS. Secondary or subsidiary rights dealing with electronic/multimedia formats (the Internet, CD-ROMs, electronic magazines).

EL-HI. Elementary to high school. A term used to indicate reading or interest level.

EROTICA. A form of literature or film dealing with the sexual aspects of love. Erotic content ranges from subtle sexual innuendo to explicit descriptions of sexual acts.

ETHNIC. Stories and novels whose central characters are African American, Native American, Italian American, Jewish, Appalachian, or members of some other specific cultural group. Ethnic fiction usually deals with a protagonist caught between two conflicting ways of life: mainstream American culture and his ethnic heritage.

EVALUATION FEES. Fees an agent may charge to simply evaluate or consider material without further guarantee of representation. Paying up-front evaluation fees to agents is never recommended and strictly forbidden by the Association of Authors' Representations. An agent makes money through a standard commission—taking 15 percent of what you earn through advances, sales of subsidiary rights, and, if applicable, royalties.

EXCLUSIVE. Offering a manuscript, usually for a set period of time, such as one month, to just one agent and guaranteeing that agent is the only one looking at the manuscript.

EXPERIMENTAL. Type of fiction that focuses on style, structure, narrative technique, setting, and strong characterization rather than plot. This form depends on the revelation of a character's inner being, which elicits an emotional response from the reader.

FAMILY SAGA. A story that chronicles the lives of a family or a number of related or interconnected families over a period of time.

FANTASY. Stories set in fanciful, invented worlds or in a legendary, mythic past that rely on outright invention or magic for conflict and setting.

FILM RIGHTS. May be sold or optioned by the agent/author to a person in the film industry, enabling the book to be made into a movie.

FLOOR BID. If a publisher is very interested in a manuscript, he may offer to enter a floor bid when the book goes to auction. The publisher sits out of the auction, but agrees to take the book by topping the highest bid by an agreed-upon percentage (usually 10 percent).

FOREIGN RIGHTS. Translation or reprint rights to be sold abroad.

FOREIGN RIGHTS AGENT. An agent who handles selling the rights to a country other than that of the first book agent.

GENRE. Refers to either a general classification of writing, such as a novel, poem, or short story, or to the categories within those classifications, such as problem novels or sonnets.

GENRE FICTION. A term that covers various types of commercial novels, such as mystery, romance, Western, science fiction, fantasy, thriller, and horror.

GHOSTWRITING. A writer puts into literary form the words, ideas, or knowledge of another person under that person's name. Some agents offer this service; others pair ghostwriters with celebrities or experts.

GOTHIC. Novels characterized by historical settings and featuring young, beautiful women who win the favor of handsome, brooding heroes while simultaneously dealing with some life-threatening menace—either natural or supernatural.

GRAPHIC NOVEL. Contains comic-like drawings and captions, but deals more with everyday events and issues than with superheroes.

HIGH CONCEPT. A story idea easily expressed in a quick, one-line description.

HI-LO. A type of fiction that offers a high level of interest for readers at a low reading level.

HISTORICAL. A story set in a recognizable period of history. In addition to telling the stories of ordinary people's lives, historical fiction may involve political or social events of the time.

HOOK. Aspect of the work that sets it apart from others and draws in the reader/viewer.

HORROR. A story that aims to evoke some combination of fear, fascination, and revulsion in its readers—either through supernatural or psychological circumstances.

HOW-TO. A book that offers the reader a description of how something is accomplished. It includes both information and advice.

IMPRINT. The name applied to a publisher's specific line of books.

IN MEDIAS RES. A Latin term meaning "into the midst of things" that refers to the literary device of beginning a narrative at a dramatic point in a story well along in the sequence of events to immediately convey action and capture reader interest.

IRC. International Reply Coupon. Buy at a post office to enclose with material sent outside the country to cover the cost of return postage. The recipient turns them in for stamps in their own country.

ISBN. This acronym stands for International Standard Book Number. ISBN is a tool used for both ordering and cataloging purposes.

JOINT CONTRACT. A legal agreement between a publisher and two or more authors that establishes provisions for the division of royalties their co-written book generates.

LIBEL. A form of defamation, or injury to a person's name or reputation. Written or published defamation is called "libel," whereas spoken defamation is known as "slander."

LITERARY. A book where style and technique are often as important as subject matter. In literary fiction, character is typically more important than plot, and the writer's voice and skill with words are both essential. Also called "serious fiction."

LOGLINE. A one-sentence description of a plot.

MAINSTREAM FICTION. Fiction on subjects or trends that transcend popular novel categories like mystery or romance. Using conventional methods, this kind of fiction tells stories about people and their conflicts.

MARKETING FEE. Fee charged by some agents to cover marketing expenses. It may be used to cover postage, telephone calls, faxes, photocopying or any other legitimate expense incurred in marketing a manuscript. Recouping expenses associated with submissions and marketing is the one and only time agents should ask for out-of-pocket money from writers.

MASS-MARKET PAPERBACKS. Softcover books, usually 4×7 inches, on a popular subject directed at a general audience and sold in groceries, drugstores, and bookstores.

MEMOIR. An author's commentary on the personalities and events that have significantly influenced one phase of his life.

MIDLIST. Those titles on a publisher's list expected to have limited sales. Midlist books are mainstream, not literary, scholarly or genre, and are usually written by new or relatively unknown writers.

MULTIPLE CONTRACT. Book contract that includes an agreement for a future book(s).

MYSTERY. A form of narration in which one or more elements remain unknown or unexplained until the end of the story. Subgenres include amateur sleuth, caper, cozy, heist, malice domestic, police procedural, etc.

NET RECEIPTS. One method of royalty payment based on the amount of money a book publisher receives on the sale of the book after the booksellers' discounts, special sales discounts, and returned copies.

NEW ADULT (NA). Novels with characters in their late teens or early twenties who are exploring what it means to be an adult.

NOVELIZATION. A novel created from the script of a popular movie and published in paperback. Also called a movie tie-in.

NOVELLA. A short novel or long short story, usually 20,000–50,000 words. Also called a "novelette."

OCCULT. Supernatural phenomena, including ghosts, ESP, astrology, demonic possession, paranormal elements, and witchcraft.

ONE-TIME RIGHTS. This right allows a short story or portions of a fiction or nonfiction book to be published again without violating the contract.

OPTION. The act of a producer buying film rights to a book for a limited period of time (usually six months or one year) rather than purchasing said rights in full. A book can be optioned multiple times by different production companies.

OPTION CLAUSE. A contract clause giving a publisher the right to publish an author's next book.

OUTLINE. A summary of a book's content (up to fifteen double-spaced pages); often in the form of chapter headings with a descriptive sentence or two under each one to show the scope of the book.

PICTURE BOOK. A type of book aimed at ages two to nine that tells the story partially or entirely with artwork, with up to one thousand words. Agents interested in selling to publishers of these books often handle both artists and writers.

PLATFORM. A writer's speaking experience, interview skills, website, and other abilities that help form a following of potential buyers for his book.

PROOFREADING. Close reading and correction of a manuscript's typographical errors.

PROPOSAL. An offer to an editor or publisher to write a specific work, usually consists of an outline, sample chapters, a marketing plan, and more.

PROSPECTUS. A preliminary written description of a book, usually one page in length.

PSYCHIC/SUPERNATURAL. Fiction exploiting—or requiring as plot devices or themes—some contradictions of the commonplace natural world and materialist assumptions about it (including the traditional ghost story).

QUERY. A letter written to an agent or a potential market to elicit interest in a writer's work.

READER. A person employed by an agent to go through the slush pile of manuscripts and scripts, and select those worth considering.

REGIONAL. A book faithful to a particular geographic region and its people, including behavior, customs, speech, and history.

RELEASE. A statement that your idea is original, has never been sold to anyone else, and that you are selling negotiated rights to the idea upon payment. Some agents may ask that you sign a release before they request pages and review your work.

REMAINDERS. Leftover copies of an out-of-print or slow-selling book purchased from the publisher at a reduced rate. Depending on the contract, a reduced royalty or no royalty is paid to the author on remaindered books.

REPRINT RIGHTS. The right to republish a book after its initial printing.

ROMANCE. A type of category fiction in which the love relationship between a man and a woman pervades the plot. The story is told from the viewpoint of the heroine, who meets a man (the hero), falls in love with him, encounters a conflict that hinders their relationship, and then resolves the conflict with a happy ending.

ROYALTIES. A percentage of the retail price paid to the author for each copy of the book that is sold. Agents take their percentage from the royalties earned and from the advance.

SASE. Self-addressed, stamped envelope. It should be included with all postal mail correspondence and submissions.

SCHOLARLY BOOKS. Books written for an academic or research audience. These are usually heavily researched, technical, and often contain terms used only within a specific field.

SCIENCE FICTION. Literature involving elements of science and technology as a basis for conflict or as the setting for a story.

SERIAL RIGHTS. The right for a newspaper or magazine to publish sections of a manuscript.

SIMULTANEOUS SUBMISSION. Sending the same query or manuscript to several agents or publishers at the same time.

SLICE OF LIFE. A type of short story, novel, play, or film that takes a strong thematic approach, depending less on plot than on vivid detail in describing the setting and/or environment and the environment's effect on characters involved in it.

SLUSH PILE. A stack of unsolicited submissions in the office of an editor, agent, or publisher.

STANDARD COMMISSION. The commission an agent earns on the sales of a manuscript. The commission percentage (usually 15 percent) is taken from the advance and royalties paid to the writer.

SUBAGENT. An agent handling certain subsidiary rights, usually working in conjunction with the agent who handled the book rights. The percentage paid the book agent is increased to pay the subagent.

SUBSIDIARY. An incorporated branch of a company or conglomerate (for example, Crown Publishing Group is a subsidiary of Random House, Inc.).

SUBSIDIARY RIGHTS. All rights other than book publishing rights included in a book publishing contract, such as paperback rights, book club rights, and movie rights. Part of an agent's job is to negotiate those rights and advise the writer on which to sell and which to keep.

SUSPENSE. The element of both fiction and some nonfiction that makes the reader uncertain about the outcome. Suspense can be created through almost any element of a story, including the title, characters, plot, time restrictions, and word choice.

SYNOPSIS. A brief summary of a story, novel, or play. As a part of a book proposal, it is a comprehensive summary condensed in a page or page-and-a-half, single-spaced. Unlike a query letter or logline, a synopsis is a front-to-back explanation of the work—and will give away the story's ending.

TERMS. Financial provisions agreed upon in a contract, whether between writer and agent, or writer and editor.

TEXTBOOK. Book used in school classrooms at the elementary, high school, or college level.

THEME. The point a writer wishes to make. It poses a question—a human problem.

THRILLER. A story intended to arouse feelings of excitement or suspense. Works in this genre are highly sensational, usually focusing on illegal activities, international espionage, sex, and violence.

TOC. Table of Contents. A listing at the beginning of a book indicating chapter titles and their corresponding page numbers. It can also include chapter descriptions.

TRADE BOOK. Either a hardcover or softcover book sold mainly in bookstores. The subject matter frequently concerns a special interest for a more general audience.

TRADE PAPERBACK. A softbound volume, usually 5×8 inches, published and designed for the general public; available mainly in bookstores.

TRANSLATION RIGHTS. Sold to a foreign agent or foreign publisher.

UNSOLICITED MANUSCRIPT. An unrequested manuscript sent to an editor, agent, or publisher.

VET. A term used by editors when referring to the procedure of submitting a book manuscript to an outside expert (such as a lawyer) for review before publication. Memoirs are frequently vetted to confirm factual accuracy before the book is published.

WESTERNS/FRONTIER. Stories set in the American West, almost always in the nineteenth century, generally between the antebellum period and the turn of the century.

YOUNG ADULT (YA). The general classification of books written for ages twelve to sixteen. They run forty thousand to eighty thousand words and include category novels—adventure, sports, paranormal, science fiction, fantasy, multicultural, mysteries, romance, etc.

LITERARY AGENTS

//

Literary agents listed in this section do not charge for reading or considering your manuscript or book proposal. It's the goal of an agent to find salable manuscripts: Her income depends on finding the best publisher for your manuscript.

Since an agent's time is better spent meeting with editors, she will have little or no time to critique your writing. Agents who don't charge fees must be selective and often prefer to work with established authors, celebrities, or those with professional credentials in a particular field.

SUBHEADS

Each agency listing is broken down into subheads to make locating specific information easier. In the first section, you'll find contact information for each agency. Additional information in this section includes the size of each agency, its willingness to work with new or unpublished writers, and its general areas of interest.

MEMBER AGENTS: Agencies comprised of more than one agent list member agents and their individual specialties. This information will help you determine the appropriate person to whom you should send your query letter.

REPRESENTS: This section allows agencies to specify what nonfiction and fiction subjects they represent. Make sure you query only those agents who represent the type of material you write.

Look for the key icon to quickly learn an agent's areas of specialization. In this portion of the listing, agents mention the specific subject areas they're currently seeking as well as those subject areas they do not consider.

HOW TO CONTACT: Most agents open to submissions prefer an initial query letter that briefly describes your work. You should send additional material only if the agent requests it. In this section, agents also mention if they accept queries by fax or e-mail, if they consider simultaneous submissions, and how they prefer to obtain new clients.

TERMS: Provided here are details of an agent's commission, whether a contract is offered and for how long, and what additional office expenses you might have to pay if the agent agrees to represent you. Standard commissions range from 10–15 percent for domestic sales and 15–25 percent for foreign or dramatic sales (with the difference going to the co-agent who places the work).

RECENT SALES: Some agencies have chosen to list recent book sales in their listing. To get to know an agency better, investigate these published titles and learn about writing styles that the agency has bonded with.

WRITERS CONFERENCES: A great way to meet an agent is at a writers conference. Here agents list the conferences they usually attend. For more information about a specific conference, check the Conferences section starting on page 270.

TIPS: In this section, agents offer advice and additional instructions for writers.

SPECIAL INDEXES

LITERARY AGENTS SPECIALTIES INDEX: This index (page 293) organizes agencies according to the subjects they are interested in receiving. This index should help you compose a list of agents specializing in your areas. Cross-referencing categories and concentrating on agents interested in two or more aspects of your manuscript might increase your chances of success.

AGENTS INDEX: This index (page 324) provides a list of agents' names in alphabetical order, along with the name of the agency for which they work. Find the name of the person you would like to contact, and then check the agency listing.

A+B WORKS

Website: http://aplusbworks.com. **Contact:** Amy Jameson, Brandon Jameson. Estab. 2004.

○ Ms. Jameson began her career in New York with esteemed literary agency Janklow & Nesbit Associates, where she launched Shannon Hale's career.

MEMBER AGENTS Amy Jameson (middle-grade, young adult).

REPRESENTS novels. **Considers these fiction areas:** middle-grade, young adult.

HOW TO CONTACT Query via online submission form. "Due to the high volume of queries we receive, we can't guarantee a response." Accepts simultaneous submissions.

⊘ DOMINICK ABEL LITERARY AGENCY, INC.

146 W. 82nd St., #1A, New York NY 10024. (212)877-0710. **E-mail:** agency@dalainc.com. **Website:** dalainc.com. **Contact:** Dominick Abel. Estab. 1975. Member of AAR. Represents 50 clients.

REPRESENTS fiction, novels. **Considers these nonfiction areas:** business, true crime. **Considers these fiction areas:** action, adventure, crime, detective, mystery, police.

HOW TO CONTACT Query via e-mail. No attachments. "If you wish to submit fiction, describe what you have written and what market you are targeting (you may find it useful to compare your work to that of an established author). Include a synopsis of the novel and the first two or three chapters. If you wish to submit nonfiction, you should, in addition, detail your qualifications for writing this particular book. Identify the audience for your book and explain how your book will be different from and better than already published works aimed at the same market." Accepts simultaneous submissions. Responds in 2-3 weeks.

ADAMS LITERARY

7845 Colony Rd., C4 #215, Charlotte NC 28226. (704)542-1440. **Fax:** (704)542-1450. **E-mail:** info@adamsliterary.com. **Website:** www.adamsliterary.com. **Contact:** Tracey Adams, Josh Adams. Adams Literary is a full-service literary agency exclusively representing children's and young adult authors and artists. Estab. 2004. Member of AAR, SCBWI, WNBA.

MEMBER AGENTS Tracey Adams, Josh Adams, Lorin Oberweger.

REPRESENTS **Considers these fiction areas:** middle-grade, picture books, young adult.

⌐ Represents "the finest children's book and young adult authors and artists."

HOW TO CONTACT **Submit through online form on website only.** Send e-mail if that is not operating correctly. All submissions and queries should first be made through the online form on website. Will not review—and will promptly recycle—any unsolicited submissions or queries received by mail. Before submitting work for consideration, review complete guidelines online, as the agency sometimes shuts off to new submissions. Accepts simultaneous submissions. Responds in 6 weeks if interested. "While we have an established client list, we do seek new talent—and we accept submissions from both published and aspiring authors and artists."

TERMS Agent receives 15% commission on domestic sales; 20% on foreign sales. Offers written contract.

RECENT SALES *The Cruelty*, by Scott Bergstrom (Feiwel & Friends); *The Little Fire Truck*, by Margery Cuyler (Christy Ottaviano); *Unearthed*, by Amie Kaufman and Meagan Spooner (Disney-Hyperion); *A Handful of Stars*, by Cynthia Lord (Scholastic); *Under Their Skin*, by Margaret Peterson Haddix (Simon & Schuster); *The Secret Horses of Briar Hill*, by Megan Shepherd (Delacorte); *The Secret Subway*, by Shana Corey (Schwartz & Wade); *Impyrium*, by Henry Neff (HarperCollins).

TIPS "Guidelines are posted (and frequently updated) on our website."

BRET ADAMS LTD. AGENCY

448 W. 44th St., New York NY 10036. (212)765-5630. **Fax:** (212)265-2212. **Website:** bretadamsltd.net. A full-service boutique theatrical agency representing writers, directors, and designers. Member of AAR.

MEMBER AGENTS Bruce Ostler, Mark Orsini, Alexis Williams.

REPRESENTS theatrical stage play, stage plays. **Considers these script areas:** stage plays, theatrical stage plays.

⌐ Handles theatre projects. No books. Cannot accept unsolicited material.

HOW TO CONTACT Use the online submission form. Because of this agency's submission policy and interests, it's best to approach with a professional recommendation from a client. Accepts simultaneous submissions.

THE AHEARN AGENCY, INC.

2021 Pine St., New Orleans LA 70118. (504)861-8395. **Fax:** (504)866-6434. **E-mail:** pahearn@aol.com. **Website:** www.ahearnagency.com. **Contact:** Pamela G. Ahearn. Memberships include MWA, RWA, ITW. Represents 30 clients.

○ Prior to opening her agency, Ms. Ahearn was an agent for 8 years and an editor with Bantam Books.

REPRESENTS novels. **Considers these fiction areas:** crime, detective, romance, suspense, thriller.

⚷ Handles general adult fiction, specializing in women's fiction and suspense. Does not deal with any nonfiction, poetry, juvenile material, or science fiction.

HOW TO CONTACT Query with SASE or via e-mail. Please send a one-page query letter stating the type of book you're writing, word length, where you feel your book fits into the current market, and any writing credentials you may possess. Please do not send ms pages or synopses if they haven't been previously requested. If you're querying via e-mail, send no attachments unless requested. Accepts simultaneous submissions. Responds in 2 months on submissions, 4 months on queries. Obtains most new clients through recommendations from others, solicitations, conferences.

TERMS Agent receives 15% commission on domestic sales; 20% commission on foreign sales. Offers written contract, binding for 1 year; renewable by mutual consent.

RECENT SALES *Black-Eyed Susans*, by Julia Heaberlin; *The Art of Sinning*, by Sabrina Jeffries; *The Comfort of Black*, by Carter Wilson; *Flirting with Felicity*, by Gerri Russell; *The Iris Fan*, by Laura Joh Rowland; *The Loner*, by Kate Moore; *Can't Find My Way Home*, by Carlene Thompson.

WRITERS CONFERENCES Romance Writers of America, Thrillerfest, Bouchercon.

TIPS "Be professional! Always send in exactly what an agent/editor asks for—no more, no less. Keep query letters brief and to the point, giving your writing credentials and a very brief summary of your book. If one agent rejects you, keep trying—there are a lot of us out there!"

● AITKEN ALEXANDER ASSOCIATES

291 Gray's Inn Rd., Kings Cross, London WC1X 8QJ United Kingdom. (020)7373-8672. **Fax:** (020)7373-6002. **E-mail:** reception@aitkenalexander.co.uk, submissions@aitkenalexander.co.uk. **Website:** www.aitkenalexander.co.uk. Estab. 1976.

MEMBER AGENTS Gillon Aitken; Clare Alexander (literary, commercial, memoir, narrative nonfiction, history); **Matthew Hamilton** (literary fiction, suspense, music, politics, **sports**); Gillie Russell (middle-grade, young **adult**); **Mary Pachnos; Anthony Sheil; Lucy Luck** (quality fiction and **nonfiction**); **Lesley Thorne; Matias Lopez Portillo; Shruti Debi; Leah Middleton**.

REPRESENTS nonfiction, novels. **Considers these nonfiction areas:** creative nonfiction, memoirs, music, politics, sports. **Considers these fiction areas:** commercial, literary, mainstream, middle-grade, suspense, thriller, young adult.

⚷ "We specialize in literary fiction and nonfiction." Does not represent illustrated children's books, poetry, or screenplays.

HOW TO CONTACT "If you would like to submit your work to us, please e-mail your covering letter with a short synopsis and the first 30 pages (as a Word document) to submissions@aitkenalexander.co.uk indicating if there is a specific agent who you would like to consider your work. Although every effort is made to respond to submissions, if we have not responded within three months, please assume that your work is not right for the agency's list. Please note that the Indian Office does not accept unsolicited submissions." Accepts simultaneous submissions. Obtains most new clients through recommendations from others, solicitations.

RECENT SALES *A Country Row, A Tree*, by Jo Baker (Knopf); *Noonday*, by Pat Barker (Doubleday); *Beatlebone*, by Kevin Barry (Doubleday); *Spill Simmer Falter Wither*, by Sara Baume (Houghton Mifflin).

AMBASSADOR LITERARY AGENCY

P.O. Box 50358, Nashville TN 37205. (615)370-4700. **Website:** www.ambassadorspeakers.com/acp/index.aspx. **Contact:** Wes Yoder. Represents 25-30 clients.

○ Prior to becoming an agent, Mr. Yoder founded a music artist agency in 1973; he established a speakers bureau division of the company in 1984.

REPRESENTS nonfiction, novels. **Considers these nonfiction areas:** inspirational, religious, spirituality. **Considers these fiction areas:** contemporary issues, religious.

> "Ambassador's Literary department represents a select list of best-selling authors and writers who are published by the leading religious and general market publishers in the United States and Europe."

HOW TO CONTACT Authors should e-mail a short description of their ms with a request to submit their work for review. Official submission guidelines will be sent if we agree to review a ms. Direct all inquiries and submissions to info@ambassadoragency.com. Accepts simultaneous submissions.

BETSY AMSTER LITERARY ENTERPRISES

6312 SW Capitol Hwy. #503, Portland OR 97239. **E-mail:** b.amster.assistant@gmail.com (for adult titles), b.amster.kidsbooks@gmail.com (for children's and young adult). **Website:** www.amsterlit.com. **Contact:** Betsy Amster (adult), Mary Cummings (children's and young adult). Estab. 1992. Member of AAR. Represents more than 65 clients.

> Prior to opening her agency, Ms. Amster was an editor at Pantheon and Vintage for 10 years and served as editorial director for the Globe Pequot Press for 2 years. Prior to joining the agency, Mary Cummings served as education director at the Loft Literary Center in Minneapolis for 14 years, overseeing classes, workshops, and conferences. She curated the annual Festival of Children's Literature and selected judges for the McKnight Award in Children's Literature.

REPRESENTS nonfiction, novels, juvenile books. **Considers these nonfiction areas:** autobiography, business, cooking, creative nonfiction, cultural interests, decorating, design, foods, gardening, health, history, horticulture, how-to, interior design, investigative, medicine, memoirs, money, multicultural, parenting, popular culture, psychology, self-help, sociology, women's issues. **Considers these fiction areas:** crime, detective, family saga, juvenile, literary, middle-grade, multicultural, mystery, picture books, police, suspense, thriller, women's, young adult.

> "Actively seeking strong narrative nonfiction, particularly by journalists; outstanding literary fiction (the next Jennifer Haigh or Jess Walter); witty, intelligent commerical women's fiction (the next Elinor Lipman); mystery and thriller that open new worlds to us; high-profile self-help and psychology, preferably research-based; and cookbooks and food narratives by West Coast-based chefs and food writers with an original viewpoint and national exposure." Also actively seeking picture books and middle-grade novels. Does not want to receive poetry, romances, western, science fiction, action/adventure, screenplays, fantasy, techno-thriller, spy capers, apocalyptic scenarios, or political or religious arguments.

HOW TO CONTACT "For fiction or memoirs, please embed the first three pages in the body of your e-mail. For nonfiction, please embed the overview of your proposal." For children's and young adult, see submission requirements online. "For picture books, please embed the entire text in the body of your e-mail. For novels, please embed the first three pages." Accepts simultaneous submissions. Responds in 1 month to queries. Responds in 2 months to mss. Obtains most new clients through recommendations from others, solicitations, conferences.

TERMS Agent receives 15% commission on domestic sales. Agent receives 20% commission on foreign sales. Offers written contract, binding for 1 year; 3-month notice must be given to terminate contract. Charges for photocopying, postage, messengers, galleys/books used in submissions to foreign and film agents and to magazines for first serial rights. (Please note that it is rare to incur much in the way of expenses now that most submissions are made by e-mail.)

RECENT SALES Betsy Amster: *Kachka: The Recipes, Stories, and Vodka that Started a Russian Food Revolution*, by Bonnie Morales (Flatiron); *It Takes One to Tango*, by Winifred Reilly (Touchstone); *Plus One*, by Christopher Noxon (Prospect Park Books); **Mary Cummings**: *Warren & Dragon's 100 Friends*, by Ariel Bernstein (Viking Children's); *Animals Spell Love: I Love You in Sixteen Languages*, by David Cundy (David R. Godine); *Monster Trucks*, by Joy Keller (Holt Children's).

THE ANDERSON LITERARY AGENCY

(917)363-6829. **E-mail:** giles@andersonliteraryagency.com. **Website:** www.andersonliteraryagency.com. **Contact:** Giles Anderson. Estab. 2000.

Owner and founder Giles Anderson started the agency in 2000 after working several years at The Waxman Literary Agency, Zephyr Press, and The Carnegie Council for Ethics in International Affairs.

MEMBER AGENTS Giles Anderson.

"Over time my interests have increasingly turned to books that help us understand people, ideas, and the possibility of change. From an examination of the religious beliefs of a founder to the science of motivation, I'm looking for books that surprise, inform, and inspire."

HOW TO CONTACT Send query via e-mail. Accepts simultaneous submissions.

RECENT SALES *Mindset: The New Psychology of Success*, by Carol S. Dweck, Ph.D.; *9 Things Successful People Do Differently*, by Heidi Grant Halverson; *Reality-Based Leadership*, by CY Wakeman.

APONTE LITERARY AGENCY

E-mail: agents@aponteliterary.com. **Website:** aponteliterary.com. **Contact:** Natalia Aponte. Member of AAR. Signatory of WGA.

MEMBER AGENTS Natalia Aponte (any genre of mainstream fiction and nonfiction, but she is especially seeking women's novels, historical novels, supernatural and paranormal fiction, fantasy novels, political and science thriller); **Victoria Lea** (any category, especially interested in women's fiction, science fiction, speculative fiction).

REPRESENTS novels. **Considers these fiction areas:** fantasy, historical, paranormal, science fiction, supernatural, thriller, women's.

Actively seeking women's novels, historical novels, supernatural and paranormal fiction, fantasy novels, political and science thriller, science fiction and speculative fiction. In nonfiction, will look at any genre with commercial potential.

HOW TO CONTACT E-query. Accepts simultaneous submissions. Responds in 6 weeks if interested.

RECENT SALES *The Nightingale Bones*, by Ariel Swan; *An Irish Doctor in Peace and at War*, by Patrick Taylor; *Siren's Treasure*, by Debbie Herbert.

ARCADIA

31 Lake Place N., Danbury CT 06810. **E-mail:** arcadialit@sbcglobal.net. **Contact:** Victoria Gould Pryor. Member of AAR.

REPRESENTS Considers these nonfiction areas: biography, current affairs, health, history, medicine, psychology, science.

"We're not seeking new clients at this time."

HOW TO CONTACT No unsolicited submissions.

THE AUGUST AGENCY, LLC

Website: www.augustagency.com. **Contact:** Cricket Freemain, Jeffery McGraw. Estab. 2004. Represents 25-40 clients.

Before opening The August Agency, Ms. Freeman was a freelance writer, magazine editor and independent literary agent. Mr. McGraw worked as an editor for HarperCollins and publicity manager for Abrams.

MEMBER AGENTS Cricket Freeman, Jeffery McGraw.

REPRESENTS novels. **Considers these nonfiction areas:** art, biography, business, current affairs, history, memoirs, popular culture, politics, sociology, true crime, creative nonfiction, narrative nonfiction, academic works. **Considers these fiction areas:** crime, mainstream.

"At this time, we are not accepting the following types of submissions: self-published works, screenplays, children's books, genre fiction, romance, horror, westerns, fantasy, science fiction, poetry, short story collections."

HOW TO CONTACT Currently closed to submissions.

THE AXELROD AGENCY

55 Main St., P.O. Box 357, Chatham NY 12037. (518)392-2100. **E-mail:** steve@axelrodagency.com. **Website:** www.axelrodagency.com. **Contact:** Steven Axelrod. Member of AAR. Represents 15-20 clients.

Prior to becoming an agent, Mr. Axelrod was a book club editor.

MEMBER AGENTS Steven Axelrod, representation; **Lori Antonson**, subsidiary rights.

REPRESENTS novels. **Considers these fiction areas:** crime, mystery, New Adult, romance, women's.

This agency specializes in women's fiction and romance.

HOW TO CONTACT Query via e-mail. Accepts simultaneous submissions. Obtains most new clients through recommendations from others.

TERMS Agent receives 15% commission on domestic sales; 20% commission on foreign sales. No written contract.

WRITERS CONFERENCES RWA National Conference.

AZANTIAN LITERARY AGENCY

Website: www.azantianlitagency.com. **Contact:** Jennifer Azantian. Estab. 2014.

○   Prior to her current position, Ms. Azantian was with Sandra Dijkstra Literary Agency.

REPRESENTS novels. **Considers these fiction areas:** fantasy, horror, middle-grade, science fiction, urban fantasy, young adult.

☞   Actively seeking fantasy, science fiction, and psychological horror for adult, young adult, and middle-grade readers.

HOW TO CONTACT To submit, send your query letter, 1-2 page synopsis, and first 10-15 pages all pasted in an e-mail (no attachments). Please note in the e-mail subject line if your work was requested at a conference, is an exclusive submission, or was referred by a current client. Accepts simultaneous submissions. Responds within 6 weeks. Check the website before submitting to make sure Ms. Azantian is currently open to queries.

BARONE LITERARY AGENCY

385 North St., Batavia OH 45103. (513)732-6740. **Fax:** (513)297-7208. **E-mail:** baroneliteraryagency@roadrunner.com. **Website:** www.baroneliteraryagency.com. **Contact:** Denise Barone. Represents Cathy Bennett, Rebekah Purdy, Michele Barrow-Belisle, Angharad Jones, Denise Gwen, Laurie Albano, Robert E. Hoxie, Rhonda Vincent, Anna Snow, and Jennifer Petersen Fraser. Estab. 2010. Member of AAR. Signatory of WGA. RWA represents 10 clients.

REPRESENTS nonfiction, novels. **Considers these nonfiction areas:** memoirs, theater, young adult. **Considers these fiction areas:** action, adventure, cartoon, comic books, commercial, confession, contemporary issues, crime, detective, erotica, ethnic, experimental, family saga, fantasy, feminist, frontier, gay, glitz, hi-lo, historical, horror, humor, inspirational, juvenile, lesbian, literary, mainstream, metaphysical, military, multicultural, multimedia, mystery, New Adult, New Age, occult, paranormal, plays, police, psychic, regional, religious, romance, satire, science fiction, short story collections, spiritual, sports, supernatural, suspense, thriller, translation, urban fantasy, war, westerns, women's, young adult.

☞   Actively seeking adult contemporary romance. Does not want textbooks.

HOW TO CONTACT "We are no longer accepting snail mail submissions; send a query letter via e-mail instead. If I like your query letter, I will ask for the first three chapters and a synopsis as attachments." Accepts simultaneous submissions. "I make every effort to respond within 4 weeks." Obtains new clients by queries/submissions via e-mail only.

TERMS 15% commission on domestic sales; 20% on foreign sales. Offers written contract.

RECENT SALES *All The Glittering Bones*, by Anna Snow (Entangled Publishing); *Devon's Choice*, by Cathy Bennett (Clean Reads); *Molly's Folly*, by Denise Gwen (Clean Reads); *In Deep*, by Laurie Albano (Solstice Publishing).

WRITERS CONFERENCES Lori Foster's Reader and Author Get Together, West Chester, Ohio; A Weekend with the Authors, Nashville, Tennessee. Willamette Writers Conference, Portland, Oregon.

TIPS "The best writing advice I ever got came from a fellow writer who wrote 'Learn how to edit yourself' when signing her book to me."

BAROR INTERNATIONAL, INC.

P.O. Box 868, Armonk NY 10504. **E-mail:** heather@barorint.com. **Website:** www.barorint.com. **Contact:** Danny Baror, Heather Baror-Shapiro. Represents 300 clients.

MEMBER AGENTS Danny Baror, Heather Baror-Shapiro.

REPRESENTS fiction. **Considers these fiction areas:** fantasy, literary, science fiction, young adult, adult fiction, commerical.

☞   This agency represents authors and publishers in the international market. Currently representing commercial fiction, literary titles, science fiction, young adult, and more.

HOW TO CONTACT Submit by e-mail or mail (with SASE); include a cover letter and a few sample chapters. Accepts simultaneous submissions.

🌑 LORELLA BELLI LITERARY AGENCY (LBLA)

54 Hartford House, 35 Tavistock Crescent, Notting Hill, London, England W11 1AY United Kingdom. (44)(207)727-8547. **Fax:** (44)(870)787-4194. **E-mail:** info@lorellabelliagency.com. **Website:** www.lorella-belliagency.com. **Contact:** Lorella Belli. Estab. 2002. Membership includes AAA (the British Association of Authors Agents), Crime Writers' Association, Romantic Novelists Association, The Book Society, Women in Publishing.

REPRESENTS nonfiction, fiction, novels, juvenile books. **Considers these nonfiction areas:** autobiography, biography, cooking, current affairs, diet/nutrition, history, memoirs, multicultural, popular culture, psychology, science, self-help, sports, translation, travel, true crime, women's issues, young adult. **Considers these fiction areas:** action, adventure, commercial, contemporary issues, crime, detective, family saga, feminist, historical, inspirational, literary, mainstream, multicultural, mystery, New Adult, police, romance, suspense, thriller, women's, young adult.

    ⌐ This agency handles adult fiction, adult nonfiction, and young adult. Does not want to receive children's picture books, fantasy, science fiction, screenplays, short stories, poetry, academic, or specialist books.

HOW TO CONTACT E-query. Do not send a proposal or ms before it's requested. Please send an initial brief query via e-mail. Accepts simultaneous submissions.

TERMS Agent receives 15% commission on domestic sales; 20% commission on foreign sales.

RECENT SALES Follow us on Twitter and Facebook to see all sales.

THE BENT AGENCY

E-mail: info@thebentagency.com. **Website:** www.thebentagency.com. **Contact:** Jenny Bent, Molly Ker Hawn, Gemma Cooper, Louise Fury, Beth Phelan, Victoria Lowes, Heather Flaherty. Estab. 2009. Member of AAR.

    ◯ Prior to forming her own agency, Ms. Bent was an agent and vice president at Trident Media Group.

MEMBER AGENTS Jenny Bent (adult fiction, including women's fiction, romance, crime/suspense; particularly likes novels with magical or fantasy elements that fall outside genre fiction; young adult and middle-grade fiction; memoir; humor); **Molly Ker Hawn** (young adult and middle-grade books, including contemporary, historical, fantasy, science fiction, thriller, mystery); **Gemma Cooper** (all ages of children's and young adult books, including picture books; likes historical, contemporary, thriller, mystery, humor, science fiction); **Louise Fury** (children's fiction: picture books, literary middle-grade, all young adult; adult fiction: speculative fiction, suspense/thriller, commercial fiction, all subgenres of romance including erotic; nonfiction: cookbooks, pop culture); **Beth Phelan** (young adult, thriller, suspense and mystery, romance and women's fiction, literary and general fiction, cookbooks, lifestyle, pets/animals); **Victoria Lowes** (romance and women's fiction, thriller and mystery, young adult); **Heather Flaherty** (young adult, middle-grade fiction: all genres; select adult fiction: upmarket fiction, women's fiction, female-centric thriller; select nonfiction: pop culture, humorous, social media-based projects, teen memoir).

REPRESENTS nonfiction, novels, short story collections, juvenile books. **Considers these nonfiction areas:** animals, cooking, creative nonfiction, foods, juvenile nonfiction, popular culture, women's issues, young adult. **Considers these fiction areas:** adventure, commercial, crime, erotica, fantasy, feminist, historical, horror, humor, juvenile, literary, mainstream, middle-grade, multicultural, mystery, New Adult, picture books, romance, short story collections, suspense, thriller, women's, young adult.

HOW TO CONTACT For Jenny Bent, e-mail queries@thebentagency.com; for Molly Ker Hawn, e-mail hawnqueries@thebentagency.com; for Gemma Cooper, e-mail cooperqueries@thebentagency.com; for Louise Fury, e-mail furyqueries@thebentagency.com; for Beth Phelan, e-mail phelanagencies@thebentagency.com; for Victoria Lowes, e-mail lowesqueries@thebentagency.com; for Heather Flaherty, e-mail flahertyqueries@thebentagency.com. "Tell us briefly who you are, what your book is, and why you're the one to write it. Then include the first 10 pages of your material in the body of your e-mail. We respond to all queries, please resend your query if you haven't had a response within 4 weeks." Accepts simultaneous submissions.

RECENT SALES *Caraval* by Stephanie Garber (Flatiron); *Rebel of the Sands* by Alwyn Hamilton

(Viking Children's/Penguin BFYR); *My Perfect Me* by J.M.M. Nuanez (Kathy Dawson Books/Penguin BFYR); *The Square Root of Summer* by Harriet Reuter Hapgood (Roaring Brook/Macmillan); *Dirty Money* by Lisa Renee Jones (Simon & Schuster); *True North* by Liora Blake (Pocket Star).

BIDNICK & COMPANY

E-mail: bidnick@comcast.net. **Website:** www.publishersmarketplace.com/members/bidnick. **Contact:** Carole Bidnick. Estab. 1997.

○ Prior to becoming an agent, Ms. Bidnick was a founding member of Collins Publishers and vice president of HarperCollins, San Francisco.

REPRESENTS nonfiction. **Considers these nonfiction areas:** cooking.

⌐ This agency specializes in cookbooks and commercial nonfiction.

HOW TO CONTACT Send queries via e-mail only. Accepts simultaneous submissions.

RECENT SALES *Burma Superstar Cookbook*, by Desmond Tan and Kate Leahy (Ten Speed); *The Healthiest Diet on the Planet*, by Dr. John McDougall and Mary McDougall (Harper One); *The Road to Sparta*, by Dean Karnazes (Rodale); *The Bold Dry Garden*, by Johanna Silver (Timber Press); *Foreign Cinema Cookbook*, by Gayle Pirie and John Clark (Abrams); *Hungry*, by Christine O'Brien (St. Martin's Press).

VICKY BIJUR LITERARY AGENCY

27 W. 20th St., Suite 1003, New York NY 10011. E-mail: queries@vickybijuragency.com. **Website:** www.vickybijuragency.com. Estab. 1988. Member of AAR.

○ Vicky Bijur worked at Oxford University Press and with the Charlotte Sheedy Literary Agency. Books she represents have appeared on the *New York Times Bestseller List* and in the *New York Times* Notable Books of the Year, *Los Angeles Times* Best Fiction of the Year, and *Washington Post* Book World Rave Reviews of the Year.

MEMBER AGENTS Vicky Bijur, Alexandra Franklin.

REPRESENTS nonfiction, novels. **Considers these nonfiction areas:** memoirs. **Considers these fiction areas:** commercial, literary, mystery, New Adult,

thriller, women's, young adult, campus novels, coming-of-age.

⌐ "We are not the right agency for screenplays, picture books, poetry, self-help, science fiction, fantasy, horror, or romance."

HOW TO CONTACT "Please send a query letter of no more than 3 paragraphs on what makes your book special and unique, a very brief synopsis, its length and genre, and your biographical information, along with the first 10 pages of your manuscript. Please let us know in your query letter if it is a multiple submission, and kindly keep us informed of other agents' interest and offers of representation. If sending electronically, paste the pages in an e-mail, as we don't open attachments from unfamiliar senders. If sending by hard copy, please include an SASE for our response. If you want your material returned, include an SASE large enough to contain pages and enough postage to send back to you." Accepts simultaneous submissions. "We generally respond to all queries within 8 weeks of receipt."

RECENT SALES *That Darkness*, by Lisa Black; *Long Upon the Land*, by Margaret Maron; *Daughter of Ashes*, by Marcia Talley.

DAVID BLACK LITERARY AGENCY

335 Adams St., Suite 2707, Brooklyn NY 11201. (718)852-5500. **Fax:** (718)852-5539. **Website:** www.davidblackagency.com. **Contact:** David Black, owner. Estab. 1989 Member of AAR. Represents 150 clients.

MEMBER AGENTS David Black; Jenny Herrera; Gary Morris; Joy E. Tutela (narrative nonfiction, memoir, history, politics, self-help, investment, business, science, women's issues, LGBTQ issues, parenting, health and fitness, humor, craft, cooking and wine, lifestyle and entertainment, commercial fiction, literary fiction, Middle-grade, young adult); **Susan Raihofer** (commercial fiction and nonfiction, memoir, pop culture, music, inspirational, thriller, literary fiction); **Sarah Smith** (memoir, biography, food, music, narrative history, social studies, literary fiction).

REPRESENTS nonfiction, novels. **Considers these nonfiction areas:** biography, business, cooking, crafts, gay/lesbian, health, history, humor, inspirational, memoirs, music, parenting, popular culture, politics, science, self-help, sociology, sports, women's issues. **Considers these fiction areas:** commercial, literary, middle-grade, thriller, young adult.

HOW TO CONTACT "To query an individual agent, please follow the specific query guidelines outlined in the agent's profile on our website. Not all agents are currently accepting unsolicited queries. To query the agency, please send a 1-2 page query letter describing your book, and include information about any previously published works, your audience, and your platform." Do not e-mail your query unless an agent specifically asks for an e-mail. Accepts simultaneous submissions. Responds in 2 months to queries.

RECENT SALES Some of the agency's bestselling authors include: Erik Larson, Stuart Scott, Jeff Hobbs, Mitch Albom, Gregg Olsen, Jim Abbott, John Bacon.

JUDY BOALS, INC.

262 W. 38th St., #1207, New York NY 10018. (212)500-1424. **Fax:** (212)500-1426. **Website:** www.judyboals.com. **Contact:** Judy Boals. "Serving and supporting the artistry of our clients with a positive and holistic business practice."

HOW TO CONTACT Query by referral or invitation only. Accepts simultaneous submissions.

BOND LITERARY AGENCY

4340 E. Kentucky Ave., Suite 471, Denver CO 80246. (303)781-9305. **E-mail:** queries@bondliteraryagency.com. **Website:** www.bondliteraryagency.com. **Contact:** Sandra Bond. The agency is small, with a select list of writers. Represents adult and young adult fiction, both literary and commercial, including mystery and women's fiction. Nonfiction interests include narrative, health, science, biography, and business.

○ Prior to her current position, Ms. Bond worked with agent Jody Rein.

MEMBER AGENTS Sandra Bond, agent (fiction: adult commercial and literary, mystery/thriller/suspense, women's, historical, young adult; nonfiction: narrative, history, science, business); **Becky LeJeune**, associate agent (fiction: horror, mystery/thriller/suspense, science fiction/fantasy, historical, general fiction, young adult).

REPRESENTS nonfiction, novels, juvenile books. **Considers these nonfiction areas:** biography, business, history, juvenile nonfiction, popular culture, science, young adult. **Considers these fiction areas:** commercial, crime, detective, family saga, fantasy, historical, horror, juvenile, literary, mainstream,

middle-grade, multicultural, mystery, police, science fiction, suspense, thriller, urban fantasy, women's, young adult.

⌐ Agency does not represent romance, poetry, young reader chapter books, children's picture books, or screenplays.

HOW TO CONTACT Please submit query by e-mail (absolutely no attachments unless requested). No unsolicited mss. "We will let you know if we are interested in seeing more material. No phone calls, please." Accepts simultaneous submissions.

RECENT SALES *Betrayal at Iga*, by Susan Spann; *Border Bandits, Border Raids*, by W.C. Jameson; *Among the Lesser Gods*, by Margo Catts; *Imagine*, by Federico Pena; *The Past Is Never Dead*, by Tiffany Quay Tyson.

BOOK CENTS LITERARY AGENCY, LLC

364 Patteson Dr., #228, Morgantown WV 26505. **E-mail:** cw@bookcentsliteraryagency.com. **Website:** www.bookcentsliteraryagency.com. **Contact:** Christine Witthohn. Estab. 2005. Member of AAR, RWA, MWA, SinC, KOD.

REPRESENTS novels, juvenile books. **Considers these nonfiction areas:** cooking, gardening, travel, women's issues. **Considers these fiction areas:** commercial, literary, mainstream, multicultural, mystery, New Adult, paranormal, romance, suspense, thriller, urban fantasy, women's, young adult.

⌐ Actively seeking upmarket fiction, commercial fiction (particularly if it has crossover appeal), women's fiction (emotional and layered), romance (single title or category), mainstream mystery/suspense, thriller (particularly psychological), and young adult. For a detailed list of what this agency is currently searching for, visit the website. Does not want to receive third-party submissions, previously published titles, short stories/novellas, erotica, inspirational, historical, science fiction/fantasy, horror/pulp/slasher thriller, middle-grade, children's picture books, poetry, or screenplays. Does not want stories with priests/nuns, religion, abuse of children/animals/elderly, rape, or serial killers.

HOW TO CONTACT Submit via form on website. Does not accept mail or e-mail submissions. Accepts simultaneous submissions.

NEW AGENT SPOTLIGHT

KRISTY HUNTER
THE KNIGHT AGENCY

www.knightagency.net
@KristySHunter

ABOUT KRISTY: With a degree in Women & Gender Studies and English Literature from Vanderbilt University, Kristy moved to New York City immediately after graduation to try her hand at publishing. She completed the Columbia Publishing Course and worked in the city for several years—first at Grove/Atlantic and then at Random House Children's Books—before deciding it was time to make the move back down south. She now takes advantage of her new surroundings by being outside as much as possible with her French bulldog, Gummi.

CURRENTLY SEEKING: Kristy is currently accepting submissions from a wide variety of genres, including women's fiction, mystery, historical romance, romance, young adult, and middle grade. Having spent significant time in the south and New York City, she particularly likes books set in these regions. She also enjoys books that feature horses, boarding schools, sisters, and sororities—to name just a few.

HOW TO SUBMIT: The Knight Agency is a green agency and, therefore, only accepts emailed queries. Paper queries submitted via US Mail or any other means (including Fax, Fed-Ex/UPS and even door-to-door delivery) will not be reviewed nor returned. All queries should be sent to Submissions@KnightAgency.net. Your submission should include a 1-page query letter and the first 5 pages of your manuscript. All text must be contained in the body of your e-mail.

TIPS Sponsors the International Women's Fiction Festival in Matera, Italy. See www.womensfictionfestival.com for more information. Ms. Witthohn is also the U.S. rights and licensing agent for leading French publisher Bragelonne, German publisher Egmont, and Spanish publisher Edebe. For a list of upcoming publications, leading clients, and sales, visit www.publishersmarketplace.com/members/BookCents.

THE BOOK GROUP

20 W. 20th St., Suite 601, New York NY 10011. (212)803-3360. **E-mail:** submissions@thebookgroup.com. **Website:** www.thebookgroup.com. Estab. 2015. Member of AAR. Signatory of WGA.
MEMBER AGENTS Julie Barer; Faye Bender; **Brettne Bloom** (fiction: literary and commercial fiction, select young adult; nonfiction, including cookbooks, lifestyle, investigative journalism, history, biography, memoir, psychology); **Elisabeth Weed**

(upmarket fiction, especially plot-driven novels with a sense of place); **Rebecca Stead** (innovative forms, diverse voices, open-hearted fiction for children, young adults, adults); **Dana Murphy** (story-driven fiction with a strong sense of place, narrative nonfiction/essays with a pop-culture lean, young adult with an honest voice).

REPRESENTS Considers these nonfiction areas: biography, cooking, history, investigative, memoirs, psychology. **Considers these fiction areas:** commercial, literary, mainstream, women's, young adult.

☞ Please do not send poetry or screenplays.

HOW TO CONTACT Send a query letter and 10 sample pages to submissions@thebookgroup.com, with the first and last name of the agent you are querying in the subject line. All material must be in the body of the e-mail, as the agents do not open attachments. "If we are interested in reading more, we will get in touch with you as soon as possible." Accepts simultaneous submissions.

RECENT SALES *This Is Not Over*, by Holly Brown; *Perfect Little World*, by Kevin Wilson; *City of Saints & Thieves*, by Natalie C. Anderson; *The Runaway Midwife*, by Patricia Harman; *Always*, by Sarah Jio; *The Young Widower's Handbook*, by Tom McAllister.

BOOKS & SUCH LITERARY MANAGEMENT

52 Mission Circle, Suite 122, PMB 170, Santa Rosa CA 95409. **E-mail:** representation@booksandsuch. com. **Website:** www.booksandsuch.com. **Contact:** Janet Kobobel Grant, Wendy Lawton, Rachel Kent, Mary Keeley, Rachelle Gardner. Estab. 1996. Member of CBA, American Christian Fiction Writers. Represents 250 clients.

○ Prior to founding the agency, Ms. Grant was an editor for Zondervan and managing editor for Focus on the Family. Ms. Keeley previously was an acquisitions editor for Tyndale publishers. Ms. Kent has worked as an agent for 10 years. Ms. Gardner worked as an editor at NavPress, at General Publishing Group in rights and marketing, and at Fox Broadcasting Company as special programming coordinator before becoming an agent.

REPRESENTS nonfiction, novels, novellas, juvenile books. **Considers these nonfiction areas:** autobiography, biography, business, cooking, creative nonfiction, cultural interests, current affairs, foods, inspirational, juvenile nonfiction, memoirs, parenting, popular culture, religious, self-help, spirituality, true crime, women's issues, young adult. **Considers these fiction areas:** action, adventure, commercial, crime, family saga, frontier, historical, inspirational, juvenile, literary, mainstream, middle-grade, mystery, New Adult, religious, romance, spiritual, suspense, women's, young adult.

☞ This agency specializes in general and inspirational fiction and nonfiction, and in the Christian booksellers market. Actively seeking well-crafted material that presents Judeo-Christian values, if only subtly.

HOW TO CONTACT Query via e-mail only; no attachments. Accepts simultaneous submissions. Responds in 1 month to queries. "If you don't hear from us asking to see more of your writing within 30 days after you have sent your e-mail, please know that we have read and considered your submission but determined that it would not be a good fit for us." Obtains most new clients through recommendations from others, conferences.

TERMS Agent receives 15% commission on domestic sales; 20% commission on foreign sales. Offers written contract; two-month notice must be given to terminate contract. No additional charges.

RECENT SALES A full list of this agency's clients (and the awards they have won) is on the agency website.

WRITERS CONFERENCES Mount Hermon Christian Writers Conference, American Christian Fiction Writers Conference, San Francisco Writers Conference.

TIPS "Our agency highlights personal attention to individual clients that includes coaching on how to thrive in a rapidly changing publishing climate, grow a career, and get the best publishing offers possible."

BOOKENDS LITERARY AGENCY

Website: www.bookendsliterary.com. **Contact:** Jessica Faust, Kim Lionetti, Jessica Alvarez, Moe Ferrara, Tracy Marchini, Beth Campbell. Estab. 1999. Member of AAR, RWA, MWA, SCBWI. Represents 50+ clients.

MEMBER AGENTS Jessica Faust (women's fiction, mystery, thriller, suspense, young adult); **Kim Lionetti** (romance, women's fiction, young adult); **Jessica Alvarez** (romance, women's fiction, erotica, romantic suspense); **Beth Campbell** (fantasy, science fiction, young adult, suspense, romantic suspense, mystery); **Moe Ferrara** (middle-grade, young adult, adult: romance, science fiction, fantasy, horror); **Tracy Marchini** (picture book, middle-grade, young adult: fiction, nonfiction).

REPRESENTS nonfiction, novels, juvenile books. **Considers these nonfiction areas:** art, business, creative nonfiction, ethnic, how-to, inspirational, juvenile nonfiction, money, self-help, women's issues, young adult, picture book, middle-grade. **Considers these fiction areas:** adventure, crime, detective, erotica, fantasy, gay, historical, horror, juvenile, lesbian, mainstream, middle-grade, multicultural, mystery, paranormal, picture books, police, romance, science fiction, supernatural, suspense, thriller, urban fantasy, women's, young adult.

> "BookEnds is currently accepting queries from published and unpublished writers in the areas of romance, mystery, suspense, science fiction and fantasy, horror, women's fiction, picture books, middle-grade, and young adult. In nonfiction we represent titles in the following areas: current affairs, reference, business and career, parenting, pop culture, coloring books, general nonfiction, and nonfiction for children and teens." BookEnds does not represent short fiction, poetry, screenplays, or techno-thriller.

HOW TO CONTACT Visit website for the most up-to-date guidelines and current preferences. BookEnds agents accept all submissions through their personal Query Manager forms. These forms are accessible on the agency website under Submissions. Accepts simultaneous submissions. "Our response time goals are 6 weeks for queries and 12 weeks on requested partials and fulls."

BOOKSTOP LITERARY AGENCY

67 Meadow View Rd., Orinda CA 94563. (925)254-2664. **E-mail:** info@bookstopliterary.com. **Website:** www.bookstopliterary.com. Represents authors and illustrators of books for children and young adults. Estab. 1984.

REPRESENTS nonfiction, fiction, novels, short story collections, juvenile books, poetry books. **Considers these nonfiction areas:** juvenile nonfiction, young adult. **Considers these fiction areas:** hi-lo, middle-grade, picture books, plays, poetry, young adult.

> "Special interest in Hispanic, Asian-American, African-American, and multicultural

writers. Also seeking quirky picture books, clever adventure/mystery novels, eye-opening nonfiction, heartfelt middle-grade, unusual teen romance."

HOW TO CONTACT Send:cover letter, entire ms for picture books, first 10 pages of novels; proposal and sample chapters OK for nonfiction. E-mail submissions: Paste cover letter and first 10 pages of ms into body of e-mail and send to info@bookstopliterary.com. Send sample illustrations only if you are an illustrator. Illustrators: send postcard or link to online portfolio. Do not send original artwork. Accepts simultaneous submissions.

TERMS Agent receives 15% commission on domestic sales. Offers written contract, binding for 1 year.

⊘ GEORGES BORCHARDT, INC.

136 E. 57th St., New York NY 10022. (212)753-5785. **Website:** www.gbagency.com. Estab. 1967. Member of AAR. Represents 200+ clients.

MEMBER AGENTS Anne Borchardt, Georges Borchardt, Valerie Borchardt, Samantha Shea.

REPRESENTS nonfiction, novels, short story collections, novellas. **Considers these nonfiction areas:** art, biography, creative nonfiction, current affairs, history, literature, philosophy, politics, religious, science.

> This agency specializes in literary fiction and outstanding nonfiction.

HOW TO CONTACT No unsolicited submissions. Obtains most new clients through recommendations from others.

TERMS Agent receives 15% commission on domestic sales; 20% commission on foreign sales. Offers written contract.

RECENT SALES *The Relive Box and Other Stories* by T.C. Boyle; *Nutshell* by Ian McEwan; *Sisters* by Lily Tuck.

BRADFORD LITERARY AGENCY

5694 Mission Center Rd., #347, San Diego CA 92108. (619)521-1201. **E-mail:** queries@bradfordlit.com. **Website:** www.bradfordlit.com. **Contact:** Laura Bradford, Natalie Lakosil, Sarah LaPolla, Monica Odom. Estab. 2001. Member of AAR, RWA, SCBWI, ALA. Represents 130 clients.

MEMBER AGENTS Laura Bradford (romance: historical, romantic suspense, paranormal, category, contemporary, erotic; mystery, women's fiction, thriller/suspense, middle-grade, young adult);

Natalie Lakosil (children's literature from picture book through teen and New Adult, contemporary and historical romance, cozy mystery/crime, upmarket women's/general fiction, select children's nonfiction); **Sarah LaPolla** (YA, middle-grade, literary fiction, science fiction, magical realism, dark/psychological mystery, literary horror, upmarket contemporary fiction); **Monica Odom** (nonfiction by authors with demonstrable platforms in the areas of pop culture, illustrated/graphic design, food and cooking, humor, history and social issues; narrative nonfiction, memoir, literary fiction, upmarket commercial fiction, compelling speculative fiction and magic realism, historical fiction, alternative histories, dark and edgy fiction, literary psychological thriller, illustrated/picture books).

REPRESENTS nonfiction, fiction, novels, juvenile books. **Considers these nonfiction areas:** biography, cooking, creative nonfiction, cultural interests, foods, history, humor, juvenile nonfiction, memoirs, parenting, popular culture, politics, self-help, women's issues, women's studies, young adult. **Considers these fiction areas:** commercial, crime, ethnic, gay, historical, juvenile, lesbian, literary, mainstream, middle-grade, multicultural, mystery, New Adult, paranormal, picture books, romance, science fiction, thriller, women's, young adult.

☛ Laura Bradford does not want to receive poetry, screenplays, short stories, westerns, horror, new age, religion, crafts, cookbooks, or gift books. Natalie Lakosil does not want to receive inspirational novels, memoir, romantic suspense, adult thriller, poetry, or screenplays. Sarah LaPolla does not want to receive nonfiction, picture books, inspirational/spiritual novels, romance, or erotica. Monica Odom does not want to receive genre romance, erotica, military, poetry, or inspirational/spiritual works.

HOW TO CONTACT Accepts e-mail queries only. For submissions to Laura Bradford or Natalie Lakosil, send to queries@bradfordlit.com. For submissions to Sarah LaPolla, send to sarah@bradfordlit.com. For submissions to Monica Odom, send to monica@bradfordlit.com. The entire submission must appear in the body of the e-mail and not as an attachment. The subject line should begin as follows: "QUERY: (the title of the ms or any short message that is important)." For fiction: e-mail a query letter along with the first chapter of ms and a synopsis. Include the genre and word count in your query letter. Nonfiction: e-mail full nonfiction proposal, including a query letter and a sample chapter. Accepts simultaneous submissions. Responds in 4 weeks to queries, 10 weeks to mss. Obtains most new clients through queries.

TERMS Agent receives 15% commission on domestic sales; 25% commission on foreign sales. Offers written contract. Charges for extra copies of books for foreign submissions.

RECENT SALES Sold 115 titles in the last year, including *Snowed in with Murder*, by Auralee Wallace (St. Martin's); *All the Secrets We Keep*, by Megan Hart (Montlake); *The Notorious Bargain*, by Joanna Shupe (Avon); *Allegedly*, by Tiffany Jackson (Katherine Tegen Books); *Wives of War*, by Soraya Lane (Amazon).

WRITERS CONFERENCES RWA National Conference, Romantic Times Booklovers Convention.

BRANDT & HOCHMAN LITERARY AGENTS, INC.

1501 Broadway, Suite 2310, New York NY 10036. (212)840-5760. **Fax:** (212)840-5776. **Website:** brandthochman.com. **Contact:** Gail Hochman. Member of AAR. Represents 200 clients.

MEMBER AGENTS Gail Hochman (literary fiction, idea-driven nonfiction, literary memoir, children's books); **Marianne Merola** (fiction, nonfiction and children's books with strong and unique narrative voices); **Bill Contardi** (voice-driven young adult and middle-grade fiction, commercial thriller, psychological suspense, quirky mystery, high fantasy, commercial fiction, memoir); **Emily Forland** (voice-driven literary fiction and nonfiction, memoir, narrative nonfiction, history, biography, food writing, cultural criticism, graphic novels, young adult fiction); **Emma Patterson** (fiction from dark literary novels to upmarket women's and historical fiction; narrative nonfiction, including memoir, investigative journalism, popular history; young adult fiction); **Jody Kahn** (literary and upmarket fiction; narrative nonfiction, particularly books related to sports, food, history, science, pop culture—including cookbooks; literary memoir, journalism); **Henry Thayer** (nonfiction on a wide variety of subjects; fiction that inclines toward the literary). The e-mail addresses and specific likes of each of these agents is listed on the agency website.

REPRESENTS nonfiction, novels. **Considers these nonfiction areas:** biography, cooking, current affairs, foods, health, history, memoirs, music, popular culture, science, sports, narrative nonfiction, journalism. **Considers these fiction areas:** fantasy, historical, literary, middle-grade, mystery, suspense, thriller, women's, young adult.

> No screenplays or textbooks.

HOW TO CONTACT "We accept queries by e-mail and regular mail; however, we cannot guarantee a response to e-mailed queries. For queries via regular mail, be sure to include a SASE for our reply. Query letters should be no more than 2 pages and should include a convincing overview of the book project and information about the author and his or her writing credits. Address queries to the specific Brandt & Hochman agent whom you would like to consider your work. Agent e-mail addresses and query preferences may be found at the end of each agent profile on the Agents page of our website." Accepts simultaneous submissions. Obtains most new clients through recommendations from others.

TERMS Agent receives 15% commission on domestic sales; 20% commission on foreign sales.

RECENT SALES This agency sells 40-60 new titles each year. A full list of their hundreds of clients is on the agency website.

TIPS "Write a letter that will give the agent a sense of you as a professional writer—your long-term interests as well as a short description of the work at hand."

THE BRATTLE AGENCY

P.O. Box 380537, Cambridge MA 02238. (617)721-5375. **E-mail:** christopher.vyce@thebrattleagency.com; submissions@thebrattleagency.com. **Website:** thebrattleagency.com. **Contact:** Christopher Vyce. Member of AAR. Signatory of WGA.

> Prior to being an agent, Mr. Vyce worked for the Beacon Press in Boston as an acquisitions editor.

REPRESENTS nonfiction, fiction. **Considers these nonfiction areas:** art, cultural interests, history, politics, sports, race studies, American studies. **Considers these fiction areas:** literary, graphic novels.

HOW TO CONTACT Query by e-mail. Include cover letter, brief synopsis, brief CV. Accepts simultaneous submissions. Responds to queries in 72 hours. Responds to approved submissions in 6-8 weeks.

BARBARA BRAUN ASSOCIATES, INC.

7 E. 14th St., #19F, New York NY 10003. **Fax:** (212)604-9023. **E-mail:** bbasubmissions@gmail.com. **Website:** www.barbarabraunagency.com. **Contact:** Barbara Braun. Member of AAR, Authors Guild, PEN Center USA.

REPRESENTS nonfiction, novels. **Considers these nonfiction areas:** architecture, art, biography, design, film, history, photography, politics, psychology, women's issues, social issues, cultural criticism, fashion, narrative nonfiction. **Considers these fiction areas:** commercial, historical, literary, multicultural, mystery, thriller, women's, young adult, art-related fiction.

> "Our fiction is strong on stories for women, art-related fiction, historical and multicultural stories, and to a lesser extent, mystery and thriller. We are interested in narrative nonfiction and current affairs books by journalists, as well as young adult literature." Does not represent poetry, science fiction, fantasy, horror, or screenplays.

HOW TO CONTACT "We no longer accept submissions by regular mail. Please send all queries via e-mail, marked 'Query' in the subject line. Your query should include a brief summary of your book, word count, genre, any relevant publishing experience, and the first 5 pages of your manuscript pasted into the body of the e-mail. (No attachments—we will not open these.)" Accepts simultaneous submissions.

TERMS Agent receives 15% commission on domestic sales; 20% commission on foreign sales. No reading fees.

TIPS "Our clients' books are represented throughout Europe, Asia, and Latin America by various sub-agents. We are also active in selling motion picture rights to the books we represent and work with various Hollywood agencies."

BRESNICK WEIL LITERARY AGENCY

115 W. 29th St., Third Floor, New York NY 10001. (212)239-3166. **Fax:** (212)239-3165. **E-mail:** query@bresnickagency.com. **Website:** bresnickagency.com. **Contact:** Paul Bresnick.

> Prior to becoming an agent, Mr. Bresnick spent 25 years as a trade book editor.

MEMBER AGENTS Paul Bresnick; Susan Duff (women's health, food and wine, fitness, humor,

NEW AGENT SPOTLIGHT

LAUREN SPIELLER
TRIADA US LITERARY AGENCY

www.triadaus.com
@laurenspieller

ABOUT LAUREN: Lauren Spieller is an author and literary agent living in Brooklyn. Before joining Triada US, she worked in literary scouting, and as an editorial consultant. She is the author of *The Wanderings of Dessa Rose* (Simon & Schuster Books for Young Readers, 2018).

SHE IS SEEKING: Middle grade and young adult fiction, as well as commercial adult fiction. Whatever the age group or genre, Lauren welcomes diverse voices. In MG, she's drawn to heartfelt contemporaries, exciting adventures, contemporary fantasy, and magical realism. Some of her favorite recent novels include *Rules for Stealing Stars*, *George*, *My Seventh-Grade Life In Tights*, *The Seventh Wish*, and *Rooftoppers*. In YA, she'd love to find authentic teen voices in any genre. Her recent favorites include *Dumplin'*, *Scorpio Races*, *Since You've Been Gone*, *Feed*, *The Lunar Chronicles*, *Six of Crows*, and *Simon vs. The Homo Sapiens Agenda*.

In adult fiction, Lauren is seeking commercial fiction, particularly twisted thrillers in the vein of Lauren Beukes and Gillian Flynn, and immersive fantasies, such as *The Night Circus*, *The Miniaturist*, *The Rook*, and *A Darker Shade of Magic*. She is also interested in Women's Fiction and pop-culture non-fiction.

HOW TO SUBMIT: Please send a concise summary of your work, along with the first ten pages in the body of an email to lauren@triadaus.com.

---

memoir); **Lisa Kopel** (narrative nonfiction, memoir, pop culture, commercial and literary fiction); **Matthew MiGangi** (music, American history, sports, politics, weird science, pop/alternative culture, video games, fiction).
REPRESENTS nonfiction, novels. **Considers these nonfiction areas:** foods, health, history, humor, memoirs, music, popular culture, politics, science, sports, women's issues, fitness, pop/alternative culture, video games. **Considers these fiction areas:** commercial, literary.

Matthew DiGangi does not represent young adult, middle-grade, or books for children.
HOW TO CONTACT Electronic submissions only. For fiction, submit query and 2 chapters. For nonfiction, submit query with proposal. Accepts simultaneous submissions.

✪ RICK BROADHEAD & ASSOCIATES LITERARY AGENCY
47 St. Clair Ave. W., Suite 501, Toronto ON M4V 3A5 Canada. (416)929-0516. **E-mail:** info@rbalit-

erary.com. **E-mail:** submissions@rbaliterary.com. **Website:** www.rbaliterary.com. **Contact:** Rick Broadhead, president. Estab. 2002. Membership includes Authors Guild. Represents 125 clients.

○ With an MBA from the Schulich School of Business, one of the world's leading business schools, Rick Broadhead is one of the few literary agents in the publishing industry with a business and entrepreneurial background, one that benefits his clients at every step of the book development and contract negotiation process.

REPRESENTS nonfiction. **Considers these nonfiction areas:** biography, business, current affairs, environment, health, history, humor, medicine, military, popular culture, politics, science, self-help, relationships, pop science, security/intelligence, natural history.

⌐ The agency is actively seeking compelling proposals from experts in their fields, journalists, and authors with relevant credentials and an established media platform (TV, web, radio, print experience/exposure). Does not want to receive fiction, screenplays, children's, poetry at this time.

HOW TO CONTACT Query with e-mail. Include a brief description of your project, your credentials, and contact information. Accepts simultaneous submissions.

TIPS "Books rarely sell themselves these days, so I look for authors who have a 'platform' (media exposure/experience, university affiliation, recognized expertise, etc.). Remember that a literary agent has to sell your project to an editor, and then the editor has to sell your project internally to his or her colleagues (including the marketing and sales staff), and then the publisher has to sell your book to the book buyers at the chains and bookstores. You're most likely to get my attention if you write a succinct and persuasive query letter that demonstrates your platform and credentials, the market potential of your book, and why your book is different."

BROWER LITERARY & MANAGEMENT

110 Wall Street, 2-047, New York NY 10005. (646)854-6073. **E-mail:** kimberly@browerliterary.com. **Website:** browerliterary.com. Estab. 2016. Member of AAR. Signatory of WGA.

MEMBER AGENTS Kimberly Brower, kimberly@browerliterary.com (currently closed to unsolic-

ited queries); **Jess Dallow,** jess@browerliterary.com (YA and adult commercial fiction, romance, family stories, thriller, mystery, women's fiction); **Aimee Ashcraft,** aimee@browerliterary.com (upmarket and literary fiction, specifically historical fiction, women's fiction, young adult—all genres).

REPRESENTS fiction, novels. **Considers these fiction areas:** commercial, historical, literary, mystery, romance, thriller, women's, young adult.

HOW TO CONTACT "When sending queries, e-mail with "QUERY: [Manuscript/Project Title]" in the subject line and include a query letter, a full synopsis (summarize the entire book), and first chapter pasted into the e-mail, double-spaced. No attachments, please." Accepts simultaneous submissions. Responds in 6 8 weeks.

RECENT SALES *Rose Colored Glasses*, by Brianna Wolfson (Mira); *Riot Street*, by Tyler King (Forever Yours); *Everyday Watercolor*, by Jenna Rainey (Ten Speed Press).

ANDREA BROWN LITERARY AGENCY, INC.

E-mail: andrea@andreabrownlit.com, caryn@andreabrownlit.com, lauraqueries@gmail.com, jennifer@andreabrownlit.com, kelly@andreabrownlit.com, jennl@andreabrownlit.com, jamie@andreabrownlit.com, jmatt@andreabrownlit.com, kathleen@andreabrownlit.com, lara@andreabrownlit.com, soloway@andreabrownlit.com. **Website:** www.andreabrownlit.com. Member of AAR.

○ Prior to opening her agency, Ms. Brown served as an editorial assistant at Random House and Dell Publishing and as an editor with Knopf.

MEMBER AGENTS Andrea Brown, president; **Laura Rennert,** executive agent; **Caryn Wiseman,** senior agent; **Jennifer Laughran,** senior agent; **Jennifer Rofé,** senior agent; **Kelly Sonnack,** agent; **Jamie Weiss Chilton,** agent; **Jennifer Mattson,** agent; **Kathleen Rushall,** agent; **Lara Perkins,** associate agent, digital manager; **Jennifer March Soloway,** assistant agent.

REPRESENTS nonfiction, fiction, juvenile books. **Considers these nonfiction areas:** juvenile nonfiction, young adult, narrative. **Considers these fiction areas:** juvenile, picture books, young adult, middle-grade, all juvenile genres.

⌐ Specializes in all kinds of children's books— illustrators and authors. 98% juvenile books.

Considers nonfiction, fiction, picture books, young adult.

HOW TO CONTACT For picture books, submit a query letter and complete ms in the body of the e-mail. For fiction, submit a query letter and the first 10 pages in the body of the e-mail. For nonfiction, submit proposal, first 10 pages in the body of the e-mail. Illustrators: submit a query letter and 2-3 illustration samples (in JPEG format), link to online portfolio, and text of picture book, if applicable. "We only accept queries via e-mail. No attachments, with the exception of JPEG illustrations from illustrators." Visit the agents' bios on our website and choose only *one* agent to whom you will submit your e-query. Send a short e-mail query letter to that agent with "QUERY" in the subject field. Accepts simultaneous submissions. "If we are interested in your work, we will certainly follow up by e-mail or by phone. However, if you haven't heard from us within 6 to 8 weeks, please assume that we are passing on your project." Obtains most new clients through referrals from editors, clients and agents. Check website for guidelines and information.

TERMS Agent receives 15% commission on domestic sales; 25% commission on foreign sales. Offers written contract.

RECENT SALES *The Scorpio Races*, by Maggie Stiefvater (Scholastic); *The Future of Us*, by Jay Asher; *Triangles*, by Ellen Hopkins (Atria); *Crank*, by Ellen Hopkins (McElderry/S&S); *Burned*, by Ellen Hopkins (McElderry/S&S); *Impulse*, by Ellen Hopkins (McElderry/S&S); *Glass*, by Ellen Hopkins (McElderry/S&S); *Tricks*, by Ellen Hopkins (McElderry/S&S); *Fallout*, by Ellen Hopkins (McElderry/S&S).

CURTIS BROWN, LTD.

10 Astor Place, New York NY 10003. (212)473-5400. **Fax:** (212)598-0917. **Website:** www.curtisbrown. com. **Contact:** Ginger Knowlton. Represents authors and illustrators of fiction, nonfiction, picture books, middle-grade, young adult. Member of AAR. Signatory of WGA.

MEMBER AGENTS Noah Ballard (literary debuts, upmarket thriller and narrative nonfiction, and always on the lookout for honest and provocative new writers); **Ginger Clark** (science fiction, fantasy, paranormal romance, literary horror, young adult and middle-grade fiction); **Kerry D'Agostino** (a

wide range of literary and commercial fiction; narrative nonfiction, memoir); **Katherine Fausset** (literary fiction, upmarket commercial fiction, journalism, memoir, popular science, narrative nonfiction); **Holly Frederick**; **Peter Ginsberg**, president; **Elizabeth Harding**, vice president (represents authors and illustrators of juvenile, middle-grade, young adult fiction); **Steve Kasdin** (commercial fiction, including mystery/thriller, romantic suspense—emphasis on the suspense—and historical fiction; narrative nonfiction, including biography, history, and current affairs; young adult fiction, particularly if it has adult crossover appeal; not interested in science fiction/fantasy, memoirs, vampires, writers trying to capitalize on trends); **Ginger Knowlton**, executive vice president (authors and illustrators of children's books in all genres); **Timothy Knowlton**, CEO; **Jonathan Lyons** (biography, history, science, pop culture, sports, general narrative nonfiction, mystery, thriller, science fiction and fantasy, young adult fiction); **Laura Blake Peterson**, vice president (memoir and biography, natural history, literary fiction, mystery, suspense, women's fiction, health and fitness, children's and young adult, faith issues, popular culture); **Maureen Walters**, senior vice president (primarily women's fiction and nonfiction, parenting and child care, popular psychology, inspirational/motivational volumes, a few medical/nutrition books); **Mitchell Waters** (literary and commercial fiction and nonfiction, including mystery, history, biography, memoir, young adult, cookbooks, self-help, popular culture); **Monika Woods**.

REPRESENTS NONFICTION, novels. **Considers these nonfiction areas:** biography, computers, cooking, current affairs, ethnic, health, history, humor, memoirs, popular culture, psychology, science, self-help, spirituality, sports. **Considers these fiction areas:** fantasy, horror, humor, juvenile, literary, mainstream, middle-grade, mystery, paranormal, picture books, religious, romance, spiritual, sports, suspense, thriller, women's, young adult.

HOW TO CONTACT Please refer to the Agents page on the website for each agent's submission guidelines. Accepts simultaneous submissions. Responds in 3 weeks to queries, 5 weeks to mss. Obtains most new clients through recommendations from others, solicitations, conferences.

TERMS Agent receives 15% commission on domestic sales; 20% on foreign sales. Offers written con-

tract; 75-day notice must be given to terminate contract. Charges for some postage (overseas, etc.).
RECENT SALES This agency prefers not to share information on specific sales.

🗩 CURTIS BROWN (AUST) PTY LTD

P.O. Box 19, Paddington NSW 2021 Australia. (+61)(2)9361-6161. **Fax:** (+61)(2)9360-3935. **E-mail:** reception@curtisbrown.com.au, submission@curtisbrown.com.au. **Website:** www.curtisbrown.com.au.

○   "Prior to joining Curtis Brown, most of our agents worked in publishing or the film/theatre industry in Australia and the United Kingdom."

MEMBER AGENTS Fiona Inglis, managing director/agent; Tara Wynne, agent; Pippa Masson, agent; Clare Forster, agent; Grace Heifetz, agent.

⌇   "We are Australia's oldest and largest literary agency representing a diverse range of Australian and New Zealand writers and estates."

HOW TO CONTACT "Please refer to our website for information regarding ms submissions, permissions, theatre rights requests, and the clients and estates we represent. We are not currently looking to represent poetry, short stories, stage/screenplays, picture books, or translations. We do not accept e-mailed or faxed submissions. No responsibility is taken for the receipt or loss of mss." Accepts simultaneous submissions.

MARIE BROWN ASSOCIATES, INC.

412 W. 154th St., New York NY 10032. (212)939-9725 for Marie Brown, (678)515-7907 for Janell Walden Agyeman. **Fax:** (212)939-9728. **E-mail:** info@janellwaldenagyeman.com. **Website:** www.janellwaldenagyeman.com. **Contact:** Marie Brown, Janell Walden Agyeman. Estab. 1984. Authors Guild, Independent Book Publishers Association, SCBWI.

MEMBER AGENTS Marie Brown, Janell Walden Agyeman (middle-grade, young adult, and New Adult fiction featuring multicultural protagonists in contemporary or historical settings; narrative nonfiction that illuminates the experiences of people of color or enlightened responses to the human journey).

REPRESENTS nonfiction, novels, juvenile books. **Considers these nonfiction areas:** creative nonfiction, cultural interests, education, ethnic, history, inspirational, juvenile nonfiction, memoirs, multicultural, popular culture, spirituality, sports, wom-

en's studies, young adult. **Considers these fiction areas:** contemporary issues, ethnic, hi-lo, historical, juvenile, literary, mainstream, middle-grade, multicultural, New Adult, paranormal, picture books, supernatural, urban fantasy, women's, young adult.

⌇   Ms. Brown's special interests include sports and performing arts. Ms. Agyeman's special interests include spirituality and cultural issues. Actively seeking debut fiction for adults (literary and popular) and for young readers. Ms. Brown does not want to receive genre fiction or poetry. Ms. Agyeman does not want to receive true crime, high fantasy, thriller, or poetry.

HOW TO CONTACT "We are closed to unsolicited submissions from time to time; check the website to confirm our review status before querying. Marie Brown will consider hard-copy materials submitted according to her guidelines (on website). Janell Agyeman welcomes e-mailed queries when she is open to unsolicited submissions. Check the website for her current submissions review policy before sending queries." Responds within 3 months. Primarily obtains new clients through recommendations and conferences.

TERMS Agent receives 15% commission on domestic sales; 20% commission on foreign sales. Offers written contract.

RECENT SALES *The Man in 3B*, by Carl Weber; *Pushout*, by Monique Morris; *Born Bright*, by C. Nicole Mason; *Degree Zombie Zone*, by Patrik Henry Bass; *Harlem Renaissance Party*, by Faith Ringgold; *Stella by Starlight*, by Sharon M. Draper.

TIPS "Have your project professionally edited and/or critiqued before submitting; show us your very best work."

BROWNE & MILLER LITERARY ASSOCIATES

52 Village Place, Hinsdale IL 60521. (312)922-3063. **E-mail:** mail@browneandmiller.com. **Website:** www.browneandmiller.com. **Contact:** Danielle Egan-Miller, president. Founded in 1971 by Jane Jordan Browne, Browne & Miller Literary Associates is the Chicago area's leading literary agency. Danielle Egan-Miller became president of the agency in 2003 and has since sold hundreds of books with a heavy emphasis on commercial adult fiction. Her roster includes several *New York Times* best-selling authors and numerous prize- and award-winning writers.

She loves a great story well told. Estab. 1971. Member of AAR, RWA, MWA, Authors Guild.

○ Prior to joining the agency as Jane Jordan Browne's partner, Danielle Egan-Miller worked as an editor.

REPRESENTS nonfiction, novels. **Considers these fiction areas:** commercial, crime, detective, erotica, family saga, historical, inspirational, literary, mainstream, mystery, police, religious, romance, suspense, thriller, women's, Christian/inspirational fiction.

⌗ Browne & Miller is most interested in literary and commercial fiction, women's fiction, women's historical fiction, literary-leaning crime fiction, dark suspense/domestic suspense, romance of most subgenres, including time travel, Christian/inspirational fiction by established authors, and a wide range of platform-driven nonfiction by nationally recognized author-experts. Does not want to receive young adult or middle-grade. "We do not represent picture books, horror, science fiction or fantasy, short stories, poetry, original screenplays, articles, or software."

HOW TO CONTACT Query via e-mail only; no attachments. Do not send unsolicited mss. Accepts simultaneous submissions.

TRACY BROWN LITERARY AGENCY

P.O. Box 772, Nyack NY 10960. **Fax:** (914)931-1746. **E-mail:** tracy@brownlit.com. **Contact:** Tracy Brown. Estab. 2003. Represents 35 clients.

○ Prior to becoming an agent, Mr. Brown was a book editor for 25 years.

REPRESENTS nonfiction. **Considers these nonfiction areas:** biography, current affairs, health, history, psychology, travel, women's issues.

⌗ Specializes in thorough involvement with clients' books at every stage of the process from writing to proposals to publication. Actively seeking serious nonfiction. Does not want to receive young adult, science fiction, or romance.

HOW TO CONTACT Submit outline/proposal, synopsis, and author bio. Accepts simultaneous submissions. Responds in 2 weeks to queries. Obtains most new clients through referrals.

TERMS Agent receives 15% commission on domestic sales; 20% commission on foreign sales. Offers written contract.

SHEREE BYKOFSKY ASSOCIATES, INC.

P.O. Box 706, Brigantine NJ 08203. **E-mail:** shereebee@aol.com. **Website:** www.shereebee.com. **Contact:** Sheree Bykofsky. Sheree Bykovsky is the author or coauthor of more than 30 books, including *The Complete Idiot's Guide to Getting Published, 5th Edition*. As an adjunct professor, she teaches publishing at Rosemont College, NYU, and offers her all-day preconference pitch workshop at writers conferences, libraries, and other venues around the country. Janet Rosen is the former president of the NYC chapter of the Women's National Book Association. Her writing has appeared in *Glamour, Publishers Weekly, Paper*, and other print and online publications. Estab. 1991. Member of AAR, Author's Guild, Atlantic City Chamber of Commerce, PRC Council. Represents 1,000+ clients.

○ Prior to opening her agency, Sheree Bykofsky served as executive editor of Stonesong Press and managing editor of Chiron Press. Janet Rosen worked as associate book editor at *Glamour* and as the senior books and fiction editor at *Woman* before turning to agenting at Sheree Bykofsky Associates, where she represents a range of nonfiction and a limited amount of fiction.

MEMBER AGENTS Sheree Bykofsky, Janet Rosen.
REPRESENTS nonfiction, novels, scholarly books. **Considers these nonfiction areas:** Americana, animals, anthropology, architecture, art, autobiography, biography, business, child guidance, cooking, crafts, creative nonfiction, cultural interests, current affairs, dance, decorating, diet/nutrition, design, economics, education, environment, ethnic, film, foods, gardening, gay/lesbian, government, health, history, hobbies, how-to, humor, inspirational, language, law, literature, medicine, memoirs, metaphysics, military, money, multicultural, music, New Age, parenting, philosophy, photography, popular culture, politics, psychology, recreation, regional, religious, science, self-help, sex, sociology, software, spirituality, sports, technology, theater, translation, travel, true crime, war, women's issues, creative nonfiction. **Considers these fiction areas:** commercial, contemporary issues, crime, detective, literary, mainstream, mystery, women's. **Considers these script areas:** Dramatic rights represented by Joel Gotler.

NEW AGENT SPOTLIGHT

ANNIE HWANG

FOLIO LITERARY MANAGEMENT

www.foliolit.com
@AnnieAHwang

ABOUT ANNIE: Originally from Los Angeles, Annie first worked in journalism before moving to New York to pursue her love of book publishing. Since joining Folio Literary Management she has had the pleasure of working with both debut and seasoned authors alike.

CURRENTLY SEEKING: She specializes in all categories of literary and upmarket fiction. She's especially drawn to historical novels and psychological thrillers. In addition, she loves working with debut authors who have a gift for storytelling and are able immerse her deep within a well-built world in the space of a few sentences. Braided narratives, layered plots, and characters with deep emotional resonance all occupy a strong place in her heart . Annie is also open to nonfiction in the categories of pop science, diet/health/fitness, food, lifestyle, humor, pop culture, and select narrative nonfiction.

HOW TO SUBMIT: Please submit queries to annie@foliolit.com. Please include the query letter and first ten pages of your manuscript or proposal in the body of the email. "Please be sure to write 'Query' in the subject line as this will ensure I do not miss your letter."

This agency is seeking nonfiction, both prescriptive and narrative, and some fiction. Prescriptive nonfiction: primarily health and business. Narrative nonfiction: pop culture, biography, history, popular and social science, language, music, cities, medicine, fashion, military, and espionage. Fiction: women's commercial fiction (with a literary quality) and mystery. Does not want to receive poetry, children's, screenplays, westerns, science fiction, or horror.

HOW TO CONTACT Query via e-mail to submitbee@aol.com. "We only accept e-queries. We respond only to those queries in which we are interested. No attachments, snail mail, or phone calls, please. We do not open attachments." Fiction: one-page query, one-page synopsis, and first three pages of ms in body of the e-mail. Nonfiction: one-page query in the body of the e-mail. Accepts simultaneous submissions. Responds in 1 month to requested mss. Obtains most new clients through referrals but still reads all submissions closely.

TERMS AGENT receives 15% commission on domestic sales; 10% commission on foreign sales, plus international co-agent receives another 10%. Offers written contract, binding for 1 year. Charges for international postage.

RECENT SALES *Virtual Billions: The Genius, the Drug Lord, and the Ivy League Twins Behind the Rise of Bitcoin*, by Eric Geissinger (Prometheus Books); *Thank You, Teacher: Grateful Students Tell the Stories of the Teachers Who Changed Their Lives*, by Holly and Bruce Holbert (New World Library); *The Type B Manager: Leading Successfully in a Type A World*, by Victor Lipman (Prentice Hall).

KIMBERLEY CAMERON & ASSOCIATES

1550 Tiburon Blvd., #704, Tiburon CA 94920. (415)789-9191. **Website:** www.kimberleycameron. com. **Contact:** Kimberley Cameron. Member of AAR. Signatory of WGA.

○ Kimberley Cameron & Associates (formerly The Reece Halsey Agency) has had an illustrious client list of established writers, including Aldous Huxley, Upton Sinclair, William Faulkner, and Henry Miller.

MEMBER AGENTS Kimberley Cameron; Elizabeth Kracht (temporarily closed to submissions); Amy Cloughley (literary and upmarket fiction, women's, historical, narrative nonfiction, travel or adventure memoirs); Mary C. Moore (fantasy, science fiction, upmarket "book club," genre romance, thriller with female protagonists, stories from marginalized voices); Lisa Abellera (currently closed to unsolicited submissions); Douglas Lee (only accepting submissions via conference and in-person meetings in the Bay Area).

REPRESENTS Considers these nonfiction areas: animals, environment, health, memoirs, science, spirituality, travel, true crime, narrative nonfiction. **Considers these fiction areas:** commercial, fantasy, historical, literary, mystery, romance, science fiction, thriller, women's, young adult, LGBTQ.

○— "We are looking for a unique and heartfelt voice that conveys a universal truth."

HOW TO CONTACT Prefers queries via site. Only query one agent at a time. For fiction, fill out the correct submissions form for the individual agent and attach the first 50 pages and a synopsis (if requested) as a Word doc or PDF. For nonfiction, fill out the correct submission form of the individual agent and attach a full book proposal and sample chapters (includes the first chapter and no more than 50 pages) as a Word doc or PDF. Accepts simultaneous submissions. Obtains new clients through recommendations from others, solicitations.

CYNTHIA CANNELL LITERARY AGENCY

54 W. 40th St., New York NY 10018. (212)396-9595. **Website:** www.cannellagency.com. **Contact:** Cynthia Cannell. "The Cynthia Cannell Literary Agency is a full-service literary agency in New York City active in both the national and the international publishing markets. We represent the authors of literary fiction as well as memoir, biography, historical fiction, popular science, self-improvement, spirituality, and nonfiction on contemporary issues." Estab. 1997. Member of AAR, Women's Media Group, Authors Guild/

○ Prior to forming the Cynthia Cannell Literary Agency, Ms. Cannell was the vice president of Janklow & Nesbit Associates for 12 years.

REPRESENTS nonfiction, fiction. **Considers these nonfiction areas:** biography, current affairs, memoirs, self-help, spirituality.

○— Does not represent screenplays, children's books, illustrated books, cookbooks, romance, category mystery, or science fiction.

HOW TO CONTACT "Please query us with an e-mail or letter. If querying by e-mail, send a brief description of your project with relevant biographical information, including publishing credits (if any), to info@cannellagency.com. Do not send attachments. If querying by conventional mail, enclose an SASE." Responds if interested. Accepts simultaneous submissions.

RECENT SALES Check the website for an updated list of authors and sales.

CAPITAL TALENT AGENCY

1330 Connecticut Ave. NW, Suite 271, Washington DC 20036. (202)429-4785. **Fax:** (202)429-4786. **E-mail:** literary.submissions@capitaltalentagency. com. **Website:** capitaltalentagency.com/html/literary.shtml. **Contact:** Cynthia Kane. Estab. 2014. Member of AAR. Signatory of WGA.

○ Prior to joining CTA, Ms. Kane was involved in the publishing industry for more than 10 years. She has worked as a development editor for different publishing houses and individual authors and has seen more than 100 titles to market.

MEMBER AGENTS Cynthia Kane, Roger Yoerges, Michelle Muntifering, J. Fred Shiffman.
REPRESENTS nonfiction, fiction, movie scripts, stage plays.

HOW TO CONTACT "We accept submissions only by e-mail. We do not accept queries via postal mail or fax. For fiction and nonfiction submissions, send a query letter in the body of your e-mail. Please note that while we consider each query seriously, we are unable to respond to all of them. We endeavor to respond within 6 weeks to projects that interest us." Accepts simultaneous submissions. Responds in 6 weeks

MARIA CARVAINIS AGENCY, INC.

Rockefeller Center, 1270 Avenue of the Americas, Suite 2915, New York NY 10020. (212)245-6365. **Fax:** (212)245-7196. **E-mail:** mca@mariacarvainisagency.com. **E-mail:** mca@mariacarvainisagency.com. **Website:** www.mariacarvainisagency.com. Estab. 1977. Member of AAR, Authors Guild, Women's Media Group, ABA, MWA, RWA. Represents 75 clients.

Prior to opening her agency, Ms. Carvainis spent more than 10 years in the publishing industry as a senior editor with Macmillan, Basic Books, Avon Books, and Crown Publishers. Ms. Carvainis has served as a member of the AAR Board of Directors and as the AAR treasurer, as well as serving as chair of the AAR Contracts Committee. She presently serves on the AAR Royalty Committee.

MEMBER AGENTS Maria Carvainis, president/literary agent; **Elizabeth Copps**, associate agent.

REPRESENTS nonfiction, novels. **Considers these nonfiction areas:** biography, business, history, memoirs, popular culture, psychology, science. **Considers these fiction areas:** action, adventure, commercial, contemporary issues, crime, family saga, historical, horror, humor, juvenile, literary, mainstream, middle-grade, multicultural, mystery, romance, suspense, thriller, women's, young adult.

The agency does not represent screenplays, children's picture books, science fiction, or poetry.

HOW TO CONTACT If you would like to query the agency, please send a query letter, a synopsis of the work, first 5-10 pages, and note of any writing credentials. Please e-mail queries to mca@mariacarvainisagency.com. All attachments must be either Word documents or PDF files. The agency also accepts queries by mail to Maria Carvainis Agency, Inc., Attention: Query Department. If you want the materials returned to you, please enclose a SASE; otherwise, please be sure to include your e-mail address. There is no reading fee. Accepts simultaneous submissions. Responds to queries within 1 month. Obtains most new clients through recommendations from others, conferences, query letters.

TERMS Agent receives 15% commission on domestic sales; 20% commission on foreign sales. Offers written contract. Charges clients for foreign postage.

RECENT SALES *Someone To Love*, by Mary Balogh (Signet); *Sting*, by Sandra Brown (Grand Central); *Enraptured*, by Candace Camp (Pocket Books); *If You Only Knew*, by Kristan Higgins (HQN Books); *Palindrome*, by E.Z. Rinsky (Witness Impulse); *Almost Paradise*, by Corabel Shofner (Farrar Straus & Giroux Books for Young Readers).

CHALBERG & SUSSMAN

115 W. 29th St., Third Floor, New York NY 10001. (917)261-7550. **Website:** www.chalbergsussman.com. Member of AAR. Signatory of WGA.

Prior to her current position, Ms. Chalberg held a variety of editorial positions and was an agent with The Susan Golomb Literary Agency. Ms. Sussman was an agent with Zachary Shuster Harmsworth. Ms. James was with The Aaron Priest Literary Agency.

MEMBER AGENTS Terra Chalberg; Rachel Sussman (narrative journalism, memoir, psychology, history, humor, pop culture, literary fiction); **Nicole James** (plot-driven fiction, psychological suspense, uplifting female-driven memoirs, upmarket self-help, lifestyle books); **Lana Popovic** (young adult, middle-grade, contemporary realism, speculative fiction, fantasy, horror, sophisticated erotica, romance, select nonfiction, international stories).

REPRESENTS nonfiction, fiction, novels. **Considers these nonfiction areas:** history, humor, memoirs, popular culture, psychology, self-help, narrative journalism. **Considers these fiction areas:** erotica, fantasy, horror, literary, middle-grade, romance, science fiction, suspense, young adult, contemporary realism, speculative fiction.

HOW TO CONTACT To query by e-mail, please contact one of the following: terra@chalbergsussman.com, rachel@chalbergsussman.com, nicole@chalbergsussman.com, lana@chalbergsussman.com. To query by regular mail, please address your letter to one agent and include SASE. Accepts simultaneous submissions.

RECENT SALES The agents' sales and clients are listed on the website.

CHASE LITERARY AGENCY

242 W. 38th St., 2nd Floor, New York NY 10018. (212)477-5100. **E-mail:** farley@chaseliterary.com. **Website:** www.chaseliterary.com. **Contact:** Farley Chase. "After starting out at *The New Yorker*, I moved to The New Press and later became an editor at Talk Miramax Books. I spent 8 years as a literary agent at the Waxman Literary Agency, and I founded Chase Literary Agency in 2012. I live in NYC with my wife and dog and am a graduate of Macalester College. Over my more than 13 years as a literary agent and 19 years in publishing, I've been fortunate to work with distinguished authors of fiction and nonfiction. They include winners of the Pulitzer Prize, MacArthur fellows, members of Congress, Olympic gold medalists, and members of the Baseball Hall of Fame."

MEMBER AGENTS Farley Chase.

REPRESENTS nonfiction, fiction, novels. **Considers these nonfiction areas:** agriculture, Americana, animals, anthropology, archeology, architecture, autobiography, biography, business, creative nonfiction, cultural interests, current affairs, design, education, environment, ethnic, film, foods, gay/lesbian, health, history, how-to, humor, inspirational, investigative, juvenile nonfiction, language, law, literature, medicine, memoirs, metaphysics, military, money, multicultural, music, philosophy, popular culture, politics, recreation, regional, satire, science, sex, sociology, sports, technology, translation, travel, true crime, war, women's issues, women's studies. **Considers these fiction areas:** commercial, historical, literary, mystery.

No romance, science fiction, or young adult.

HOW TO CONTACT E-query farley@chaseliterary.com. If submitting fiction, please include the first few pages of the ms with the query. "I do not respond to queries not addressed to me by name. I'm keenly interested in both fiction and nonfiction. In fiction, I'm looking for both literary or commercial projects in either contemporary or historical settings. I'm open to anything with a strong sense of place, voice, and especially plot. I don't handle science fiction, romance, supernatural, or young adult. In nonfiction, I'm especially interested in narratives in history, memoir, journalism, natural science, military history, sports, pop culture, and humor. Whether by first-time writers or longtime journalists, I'm excited by original ideas, strong points of view, detailed research, and access to subjects that give readers fresh perspectives on things they think they know. I'm also interested in visually driven and illustrated books. Whether they involve photography, comics, illustrations, or art, I'm taken by creative storytelling with visual elements, four color or black and white." Accepts simultaneous submissions.

RECENT SALES *Devil in the Grove: Thurgood Marshall, the Groveland Boys, and the Dawn of a New America*, by Gilbert King (Harper); *Heads in Beds: A Reckless Memoir of Hotels, Hustles, and So-Called Hospitality*, by Jacob Tomsky (Doubleday); *And Every Day Was Overcast*, by Paul Kwiatowski (Black Balloon); *The Badlands Saloon*, by Jonathan Twingley (Scribner).

CHENEY ASSOCIATES, LLC

78 Fifth Ave., 3rd Floor, New York NY 10011. (212)277-8007. **Fax:** (212)614-0728. **E-mail:** submissions@cheneyliterary.com. **Website:** www.cheneyliterary.com. **Contact:** Elyse Cheney, Adam Eaglin, Alex Jacobs, Alice Whitwham.

● Prior to her current position, Ms. Cheney was an agent with Sanford J. Greenburger Associates.

MEMBER AGENTS Elyse Cheney; Adam Eaglin (literary fiction and nonfiction, including history, politics, current events, narrative reportage, biography, memoir, popular science); Alexander Jacobs (narrative nonfiction [particularly in the areas of history, science, politics, and culture], literary fiction, crime, memoir); Alice Whitwham (literary and commercial fiction, voice-driven narrative nonfiction, cultural criticism, journalism).

REPRESENTS nonfiction, novels. **Considers these nonfiction areas:** biography, cultural interests, current affairs, history, memoirs, politics, science, narrative nonfiction, narrative reportage. **Considers these fiction areas:** commercial, crime, family saga, historical, literary, short story collections, suspense, women's.

HOW TO CONTACT Query by e-mail or snail mail. For a snail mail response, include a SASE. Include up to 3 chapters of sample material. Do not query more than one agent. Accepts simultaneous submissions.

RECENT SALES *The Love Affairs of Nathaniel P.*, by Adelle Waldman (Henry Holt & Co.); *This Town*, by Mark Leibovich (Blue Rider Press); *Thunder & Lightning*, by Lauren Redniss (Random House).

THE CHUDNEY AGENCY

72 N. State Rd., Suite 501, Briarcliff Manor NY 10510. (914)465-5560. **E-mail:** steven@thechudney-agency.com. **Website:** www.thechudneyagency.com. **Contact:** Steven Chudney. Estab. 2001.

○ Prior to becoming an agent, Mr. Chudney held various sales positions with major publishers.

REPRESENTS novels. **Considers these fiction areas:** historical, juvenile, literary, middle-grade, picture books, young adult.

⚬— "At this time, the agency is only looking for author/illustrators (one individual) who can both write and illustrate wonderful picture books. The author/illustrator must really know and understand the needs and wants of the child reader! Storylines should be engaging and fun, with a hint of a life lesson and cannot be longer than 800 words. With chapter books, middle-grade, and teen novels, I'm primarily looking for quality contemporary literary fiction: novels that are exceedingly well-written, with wonderful settings and developed, unforgettable characters. I'm looking for historical fiction that will excite me, young readers, editors, and reviewers, and that will introduce us to unique characters in settings and situations, countries, and eras we haven't encountered too often yet in children's and teen literature."

HOW TO CONTACT No snail mail submissions. Queries only. Submit proposal package, 4-6 sample chapters. For children's, submit full text and 3-5 illustrations. Accepts simultaneous submissions. Responds if interested in 2-3 weeks to queries.

WM CLARK ASSOCIATES

186 Fifth Ave., Second Floor, New York NY 10010. (212)675-2784. **E-mail:** general@wmclark.com. **Website:** www.wmclark.com. **Contact:** William Clark. Estab. 1997. Member of AAR.

○ Prior to opening WCA, Mr. Clark was an agent at the William Morris Agency.

REPRESENTS nonfiction, novels. **Considers these nonfiction areas:** architecture, art, autobiography, biography, cultural interests, current affairs, dance, design, ethnic, film, history, inspirational, memoirs, music, popular culture, politics, religious, science, sociology, technology, theater, translation, travel. **Considers these fiction areas:** contemporary issues, ethnic, historical, literary, mainstream, young adult.

⚬— "William Clark represents a wide range of titles across all formats to the publishing, motion picture, television, and multimedia fields. Offering individual focus and a global reach, we move quickly and strategically on behalf of domestic and international clients ranging from authors of award-winning, best-selling narrative nonfiction to authors in translation, chefs, musicians, and artists. The agency undertakes to discover, develop, and market today's most interesting content and the talent that creates it, and forge sophisticated and innovative plans for self-promotion, reliable revenue streams, and an enduring creative career. Agency does not represent screenplays or respond to screenplay pitches. It is advised that before querying you become familiar with the kinds of books we handle by browsing our Book List, which is available on our website."

HOW TO CONTACT Accepts queries via online query form only. "We will endeavor to respond as soon as possible as to whether or not we'd like to see a proposal or sample chapters from your manuscript." Responds in 1-2 months to queries.

TERMS Agent receives 15% commission on domestic sales; 20% commission on foreign sales. Offers written contract.

FRANCES COLLIN, LITERARY AGENT

P.O. Box 33, Wayne PA 19087-0033. **E-mail:** queries@francescollin.com. **Website:** www.francescollin.com. Estab. 1948. Member of AAR. Represents 50 clients.

○ Sarah Yake has been with the agency since 2005 and handles foreign and subrights as well as her own client list. She holds an M.A. in English Literature and has been a sales rep for a major publisher and a bookstore manager. She currently teaches in the Rosemont College Graduate Publishing Program.

MEMBER AGENTS Frances Collin, Sarah Yake.
REPRESENTS nonfiction, fiction, novels. **Considers these nonfiction areas:** art, autobiography, biog-

NEW AGENT SPOTLIGHT

ANNA WORRALL
THE GERNERT COMPANY

www.thegernertco.com
@annaworrall

ABOUT ANNA: Anna is the Director of Marketing and Social Media and a literary agent at The Gernert Company, which she joined in 2010. After graduating from NYU with a degree in history, she worked in the marketing department at an academic publisher in her native Philadelphia before moving to Hungary, where she taught conversational English and traveled extensively.

CURRENTLY SEEKING: She's looking to represent smart women's literary and commercial fiction, psychological thrillers, and narrative nonfiction.

HOW TO SUBMIT: Queries by e-mail should be directed to: info@thegernertco.com. Please indicate in your letter which agent you are querying. You can visit the OUR TEAM section of the website to get a sense of who might be a good fit for your work. If you have previously corresponded with one of their agents and choose to query another, please let them know of any communication history in your letter. Please do not send e-mails directly to individual agents, even if their email addresses are available elsewhere online. The agency asks that you do not phone the office regarding unsolicited manuscripts for any reason.

raphy, creative nonfiction, cultural interests, history, literature, memoirs, popular culture, science, sociology, travel, women's issues, women's studies. **Considers these fiction areas:** adventure, commercial, experimental, feminist, historical, juvenile, literary, middle-grade, multicultural, science fiction, women's, young adult.

• Actively seeking authors who are invested in their unique visions and who want to set trends, not chase them. "I'd like to think that my authors are unplagiarizable by virtue of their distinct voices and styles." Does not want previously self-published work. Query with new mss only, please.

HOW TO CONTACT "We ask that writers send a traditional query e-mail describing the project and copy and paste the first 5 pages of the manuscript into the body of the e-mail. We look forward to hearing from you at queries@francescollin.com. Please send queries to that e-mail address. Any queries sent to another e-mail address within the agency will be deleted unread." Accepts simultaneous submissions. Responds in 1-3 weeks for initial queries, longer for full mss.

⊘ **COMPASS TALENT**
(646)376-7747. **Website:** www.compasstalent.com. **Contact:** Heather Schroder. Founded by Heather Schroder after over 25 years as an agent at ICM

Partners, Compass is dedicated to working with authors to shape their work and guide their careers through each stage of the publication process. Member of AAR. Signatory of WGA.

REPRESENTS Considers these nonfiction areas: cooking, creative nonfiction, foods, memoirs. **Considers these fiction areas:** commercial, literary, mainstream.

HOW TO CONTACT This agency is currently closed to unsolicited submissions. Accepts simultaneous submissions.

RECENT SALES A full list of agency clients is available on the website.

DON CONGDON ASSOCIATES INC.

110 William St., Suite 2202, New York NY 10038. (212)645-1229. **Fax:** (212)727-2688. **E-mail:** dca@doncongdon.com. **Website:** doncongdon.com. Estab. 1983. Member of AAR.

MEMBER AGENTS Christina Concepcion (crime fiction, narrative nonfiction, political science, journalism, history, books on cities, classical music, biography, science for a popular audience, philosophy, food and wine, iconoclastic books on health and human relationships, essays, arts criticism); **Michael Congdon** (commercial and literary fiction, suspense, mystery, thriller, history, military history, biography, memoir, current affairs, narrative nonfiction [adventure, medicine, science, nature]); **Katie Grimm** (literary fiction, historical, women's fiction, short story collections, graphic novels, mystery, young adult, middle-grade, memoir, science, academic); **Katie Kotchman** (business [all areas], narrative nonfiction [particularly popular science and social/cultural issues], self-help, success, motivation, psychology, pop culture, women's fiction, realistic young adult, literary fiction, psychological thriller); **Maura Kye-Casella** (narrative nonfiction, cookbooks, women's fiction, young adult, self-help, parenting); **Susan Ramer** (literary fiction, upmarket commercial fiction [contemporary and historical], narrative nonfiction, social history, cultural history, smart pop culture [music, film, food, art], women's issues, psychology and mental health, memoir).

REPRESENTS nonfiction, novels, short story collections. **Considers these nonfiction areas:** art, biography, business, cooking, creative nonfiction, cultural interests, current affairs, film, foods, history, humor, literature, medicine, memoirs, military, multicultural, music, parenting, philosophy, popular culture, politics, psychology, science, self-help, sociology, sports, women's issues, young adult. **Considers these fiction areas:** crime, hi-lo, historical, literary, middle-grade, mystery, short story collections, suspense, thriller, women's, young adult.

➤ Susan Ramer: "Not looking for romance, science fiction, fantasy, espionage, mystery, politics, health/diet/fitness, self-help, or sports." Katie Kotchman: "Please do not send screenplays or poetry."

HOW TO CONTACT "For queries via e-mail, you must include the word 'query' and the agent's full name in your subject heading. Please also include your query and sample chapter in the body of the e-mail, as we do not open attachments for security reasons. Please query only one agent within the agency at a time. If you are sending your query via regular mail, please enclose a SASE for our reply. If you would like us to return your materials, please make sure your postage will cover their return." Accepts simultaneous submissions.

RECENT SALES This agency represents many best-selling clients, such as David Sedaris and Kathryn Stockett.

THE DOE COOVER AGENCY

P.O. Box 668, Winchester MA 01890. (781)721-6000. **E-mail:** info@doecooveragency.com. **Website:** www.doecooveragency.com. Represents 150+ clients.

MEMBER AGENTS Doe Coover (general nonfiction, including business, cooking/food writing, history, biography, health, science); **Colleen Mohyde** (literary and commercial fiction, general nonfiction); **Frances Kennedy**.

REPRESENTS nonfiction, novels. **Considers these nonfiction areas:** creative nonfiction. **Considers these fiction areas:** commercial, literary.

➤ The agency specializes in narrative nonfiction, particularly biography, business, cooking and food writing, health, history, popular science, social issues, gardening, and humor; literary and commercial fiction. The agency does not represent poetry, screenplays, romance, fantasy, science fiction, or unsolicited children's books.

HOW TO CONTACT Accepts queries by e-mail only. Check website for submission guidelines. No unsolicited mss. Accepts simultaneous submissions. Responds within 6 weeks. Responds only if additional material is required. Obtains most new clients through solicitation and recommendation.

TERMS Agent receives 15% commission on domestic sale; 10% of original advance commission on foreign sales. No reading fees.

RECENT SALES *Lessons from a Grandfather*, by Jacques Pepin (Houghton Mifflin Harcourt); *Lift Off*, by Donovan Livingston (Speigel & Grau); *World Food*, by James Oseland (Ten Speed Press); *Biography of Garry Trudeau*, by Steven Weinberg (St. Martin's Press); *A Welcome Murder*, by Robin Yocum (Prometheus Books).

⊙ JILL CORCORAN LITERARY AGENCY

2150 Park Place, Suite 100, El Segundo CA 90245. **Website:** jillcorcoranliteraryagency.com. **Contact:** Jill Corcoran. Estab. 2013.

MEMBER AGENTS Jill Corcoran, Adah Nuchi, Silvia Arienti, Eve Porinchak.

REPRESENTS nonfiction, novels, juvenile books. **Considers these nonfiction areas:** business, how-to, juvenile nonfiction, true crime, young adult. **Considers these fiction areas:** commercial, crime, juvenile, middle-grade, picture books, romance, young adult.

- Actively seeking picture books, middle-grade, young adult, crime novels, psychological suspense, and true crime. Does not want to receive screenplays, chapbooks, or poetry.

HOW TO CONTACT Please go online to the agency submissions page and submit to the agent you feel would best represent your work. Accepts simultaneous submissions.

CORVISIERO LITERARY AGENCY

275 Madison Ave., at 40th, 14th Floor, New York NY 10016. **E-mail:** query@corvisieroagency.com. **Website:** www.corvisieroagency.com. **Contact:** Marisa A. Corvisiero, senior agent and literary attorney. "We are a boutique literary agency founded by Marisa A. Corvisiero, Esq. This agency is a place where authors can find professional and experienced representation." *Does not accept unsolicited mss.* Member of AAR. Signatory of WGA.

MEMBER AGENTS Marisa A. Corvisiero, senior agent and literary attorney (contemporary romance, thriller, adventure, paranormal, urban fantasy, science fiction, Middle-grade, young adult, picture books, Christmas themes, time travel, space science fiction, nonfiction, self-help, science business); Saritza Hernandez, senior agent (all kinds of romance, GLBT, young adult, erotica); **Doreen Thistle** (do not query); **Cate Hart** (YA, fantasy, magical realism, Middle-grade, mystery, fantasy, adventure, historical romance, LGBTQ, erotic, history, biography); **Veronica Park** (dark or edgy young adult/NA, commercial adult, adult romance and romantic suspense, funny and/or current/controversial nonfiction); **Vanessa Robins** (New Adult, human, young adult, thriller, romance, science fiction, sports-centric plots, memoirs, cultural/ethnic/sexuality, humor, medical narratives); **Kelly Peterson** (Middle-grade, fantasy, paranormal, science fiction, young adult, steampunk, historical, dystopian, sword and sorcery, romance, historical romance, adult, fantasy, romance); **Justin Wells**; **Kaitlyn Johnson**.

REPRESENTS nonfiction, fiction, novels. **Considers these nonfiction areas:** biography, business, history, medicine, memoirs, science, self-help, spirituality. **Considers these fiction areas:** adventure, erotica, fantasy, gay, historical, lesbian, middle-grade, mystery, paranormal, picture books, romance, science fiction, suspense, thriller, urban fantasy, young adult, magical realism, steampunk, dystopian, sword and sorcery.

HOW TO CONTACT Accepts submissions via e-mail only. Include 5 pages of complete and polished ms pasted into the body of an e-mail and a 1-2 page synopsis. For nonfiction, include a proposal instead of the synopsis. Put "Query for [Agent]" in the e-mail subject line. Accepts simultaneous submissions.

⊘ RICHARD CURTIS ASSOCIATES, INC.

200 E. 72nd St., Suite 28J, New York NY 10021. (212)772-7363. **Fax:** (212)772-7393. **E-mail:** info@ curtisagency.com. **Website:** www.curtisagency.com. Member of AAR, RWA, MWA, ITW, SFWA. Represents 100 clients.

- Prior to becoming an agent, Mr. Curtis authored blogs, articles, and books on the publishing business and help for authors.

REPRESENTS nonfiction, novels, juvenile books. **Considers these nonfiction areas:** biography, business, current affairs, dance, gay/lesbian, health, history, how-to, investigative, literature, military, music, politics, psychology, science, sports, theater, true crime, war, women's issues, young adult. **Considers these fiction areas:** commercial, fantasy, romance, science fiction, thriller, young adult.

Actively seeking nonfiction (but no memoir), women's fiction (especially contemporary), thriller, science fiction, middle-grade, and young adult.

HOW TO CONTACT Submit a query letter by mail (with SASE) or e-mail. Do not include sample material unless requested. Accepts simultaneous submissions.

TERMS Agent receives 15% commission on domestic sales; 25% commission on foreign sales. Offers written contract. Charges for photocopying, express mail, international freight, book orders.

RECENT SALES Sold 100 titles in the last year, including *The Library* by D.J. MacHale, *War Dogs* by Greg Bear, and *The Drafter* by Kim Harrison.

D4EO LITERARY AGENCY

7 Indian Valley Rd., Weston CT 06883. (203)544-7180. **Fax:** (203)544-7160. **Website:** www.d4eoliteraryagency.com. **Contact:** Bob Diforio. Estab. 1990.

Prior to opening his agency, Mr. Diforio was a publisher.

MEMBER AGENTS Bob Diforio, Joyce Holland, Pam Howell, Quressa Robinson, Kelly Van Sant.

REPRESENTS nonfiction, novels. **Considers these nonfiction areas:** biography, business, health, history, humor, money, psychology, science, sports. **Considers these fiction areas:** adventure, detective, erotica, juvenile, literary, mainstream, middle-grade, mystery, New Adult, romance, sports, thriller, young adult.

HOW TO CONTACT Each of these agents has a different submission e-mail and different tastes regarding how they review material. See all on their individual agent pages on the agency website. Responds in 1 week to queries if interested. Obtains most new clients through recommendations from others.

TERMS Offers written contract, binding for 2 years; automatic renewal unless 60 days notice given prior to renewal date. Charges for photocopying and submission postage.

LAURA DAIL LITERARY AGENCY, INC.

350 Seventh Ave., Suite 2003, New York NY 10001. (212)239-7477. **E-mail:** ldail@ldlainc.com. **E-mail:** queries@ldlainc.com. **Website:** www.ldlainc.com. Member of AAR.

MEMBER AGENTS Laura Dail, Tamar Rydzinski, Elana Roth Parker.

REPRESENTS nonfiction, fiction, novels, juvenile books. **Considers these nonfiction areas:** biography, cooking, creative nonfiction, current affairs, government, history, investigative, juvenile nonfiction, memoirs, multicultural, popular culture, politics, psychology, sociology, true crime, war, women's studies, young adult. **Considers these fiction areas:** commercial, crime, detective, fantasy, feminist, historical, juvenile, mainstream, middle-grade, multicultural, mystery, thriller, women's, young adult.

Specializes in women's fiction, literary fiction, young adult fiction, and both practical and idea-driven nonfiction. "Tamar is not interested in prescriptive or practical nonfiction, humor, coffee table books, or children's books (meaning anything younger than middle-grade). She is interested in everything else that is well written and has great characters, including graphic novels." "Due to the volume of queries and mss received, we apologize for not answering every e-mail and letter. None of us handles children's picture books or chapter books. No New Age. We do not handle screenplays or poetry."

HOW TO CONTACT "If you would like, you may include a synopsis and no more than 10 pages. If you are mailing your query, please be sure to include a self-addressed, stamped envelope; without it, you may not hear back from us. To save money, time, and trees, we prefer queries by e-mail to queries@ldlainc.com. We get a lot of spam and are wary of computer viruses, so please use the word 'Query' in the subject line and include your detailed materials in the body of your message, not as an attachment." Accepts simultaneous submissions. Responds in 2-4 weeks.

DANIEL LITERARY GROUP

601 Old Hickory Blvd., #56, Brentwood TN 37027. **E-mail:** greg@danielliterarygroup.com. **E-mail:** submissions@danielliterarygroup.com. **Website:** www.danielliterarygroup.com. **Contact:** Greg Daniel. Represents 45 clients.

Prior to becoming an agent, Mr. Daniel spent 10 years in publishing—6 at the executive level at Thomas Nelson Publishers.

REPRESENTS nonfiction. **Considers these nonfiction areas:** autobiography, biography, business, child guidance, current affairs, economics, environment, film, health, history, how-to, humor, inspirational, medicine, memoirs, parenting, popular culture, religious, satire, self-help, sports, theater, women's issues, women's studies.

☞ "We take pride in our ability to come alongside our authors and help strategize about where they want their writing to take them in both the near and long term. Forging close relationships with our authors, we help them with such critical factors as editorial refinement, branding, audience, and marketing." The agency is open to submissions in almost every popular category of nonfiction, especially if authors are recognized experts in their fields. No fiction, screenplays, poetry, science fiction/fantasy, romance, children's, or short stories.

HOW TO CONTACT Query via e-mail only. Submit publishing history, author bio, key selling points; no attachments. Check the agency's online submission guidelines before querying or submitting, as they do change. Please do not query via telephone. Accepts simultaneous submissions. Responds in 2-3 weeks to queries.

DARHANSOFF & VERRILL LITERARY AGENTS

133 W. 72nd St., Room 304, New York NY 10023. (917)305-1300. **E-mail:** submissions@dvagency. com. **Website:** www.dvagency.com. "We are most interested in literary fiction, narrative nonfiction, memoir, sophisticated suspense, and both fiction and nonfiction for younger readers. Please note that we do not represent theatrical plays or film scripts." Member of AAR.

MEMBER AGENTS Liz Darhansoff, Chuck Verrill, Michele Mortimer, Eric Amling.

REPRESENTS nonfiction, novels. **Considers these nonfiction areas:** creative nonfiction, juvenile nonfiction, memoirs, young adult. **Considers these fiction areas:** literary, middle-grade, suspense, young adult.

HOW TO CONTACT Send queries via e-mail. Accepts simultaneous submissions.

RECENT SALES A full list of clients is available on the website.

LIZA DAWSON ASSOCIATES

350 Seventh Ave., Suite 2003, New York NY 10001. (212)465-9071. **E-mail:** querycaitie@lizadawsonassociates.com. **Website:** www.lizadawsonassociates.

com. **Contact:** Caitie Flum. Member of AAR, MWA, Women's Media Group. Represents 50+ clients.

○ Prior to becoming an agent, Ms. Dawson was an editor for 20 years, spending 11 years at William Morrow as vice president and 2 years at Putnam as executive editor. Ms. Blasdell was a senior editor at HarperCollins and Avon. Ms. Johnson-Blalock was an assistant at Trident Media Group. Ms. Flum was the coordinator for the Children's Book of the Month club.

MEMBER AGENTS Liza Dawson, queryliza@lizadawsonassociates.com (plot-driven literary and popular fiction, historical, thriller, suspense, history, psychology [both popular and clinical], politics, narrative nonfiction, memoirs); Caitlin Blasdell, querycaitlin@lizadawsonassociates.com (science fiction, fantasy [both adult and young adult], parenting, business, thriller, women's fiction; Hannah Bowman, queryhannah@lizadawsonassociates.com (commercial fiction [especially science fiction and fantasy, young adult] nonfiction [mathematics, science, and spirituality]); Jennifer Johnson-Blalock, queryjennifer@lizadawsonassociates.com (nonfiction, particularly current events, social sciences, women's issues, law, business, history, the arts and pop culture, lifestyle, sports, food; commercial and upmarket fiction, especially thriller/mystery, women's fiction, contemporary romance, young adult, middle-grade); Caitie Flum, querycaitie@lizadawsonassociates.com (commercial fiction, especially historical, women's fiction, mystery, crossover fantasy, young adult, middle-grade; nonfiction [theater, current affairs, pop culture].

REPRESENTS nonfiction, novels. **Considers these nonfiction areas:** agriculture, Americana, animals, anthropology, archeology, architecture, art, autobiography, biography, business, computers, cooking, creative nonfiction, cultural interests, current affairs, environment, ethnic, film, gardening, gay/lesbian, history, humor, investigative, juvenile nonfiction, memoirs, multicultural, parenting, popular culture, politics, psychology, religious, science, sex, sociology, spirituality, theater, travel, true crime, women's issues, women's studies, young adult. **Considers these fiction areas:** action, adventure, commercial, contemporary issues, crime, detective, ethnic, family saga, fantasy, feminist, gay, histori-

NEW AGENT SPOTLIGHT

JANNA BONIKOWSKI
THE KNIGHT AGENCY

www.knightagency.com
@jannabonikowski

ABOUT JANNA: Janna Bonikowski joined the Knight Agency with several years of experience as both an independent editor and a freelance editor for Lyrical Press/Kensington. Though her Bachelor's degree focused on business and economics, her passion for books made a career in publishing inevitable.

Raised on a steady supply of books including everything from *Little House on the Prairie* to *Trixie Belden* to *Anne of Green Gables,* Janna has since moved on, expanding her reading diet to multiple genres: romance, women's fiction, literary/commercial fiction, suspense, young adult, and historical fiction. With such a wide range of literary loves, she manically adds to her to-be-read pile every new-release Tuesday, supporting the economy one book purchase at a time.

SHE IS SEEKING: Women's fiction, romance, historical fiction, literary/commercial fiction, young adult, suspense.

HOW TO SUBMIT: Submissions should be sent to submissions@knightagency.net and addressed to Janna. A one-page query and the first five pages of the manuscript should be included in the body of the email.

cal, horror, humor, juvenile, lesbian, mainstream, middle-grade, multicultural, mystery, New Adult, police, romance, science fiction, supernatural, suspense, thriller, urban fantasy, women's, young adult.

This agency specializes in readable literary fiction, thriller, mainstream historicals, women's fiction, young adult, middle-grade, academics, historians, journalists, and psychology. **HOW TO CONTACT** Query by e-mail only. No phone calls. Each of these agents has specific submission requirements, which you can find online at the agency's website. Obtains most new clients through recommendations from others, conferences, queries.

TERMS Agent receives 15% commission on domestic sales; 20% commission on foreign sales. Offers written contract.

THE JENNIFER DE CHIARA LITERARY AGENCY

299 Park Ave., Sixth Floor, New York NY 10171. (212)739-0803. **E-mail:** jenndec@aol.com. **Website:** www.jdlit.com. **Contact:** Jennifer De Chiara. Estab. 2001.

MEMBER AGENTS Jennifer De Chiara, jenndec@aol.com (fiction: literary, commercial, women's fiction [no bodice-rippers, please], chick lit, mystery, suspense, thriller, funny/quirky picture books, middle-grade, young adult; nonfiction: celebrity memoirs and biography, LGBTQ, memoirs, arts and performing arts, behind-the-scenes-type books, popular culture); **Stephen Fraser**, fraserstephena@gmail.com (one-of-a-kind picture books, strong chapter book series, whimsical, dramatic, or humorous middle-grade, dramatic or high-concept young adult, powerful and unusual nonfiction on a broad range of topics); **Marie Lamba**, marie.jdlit@gmail.com (young adult and middle-grade fiction, general and women's fiction, some memoir; interested in established illustrators and picture book authors); **Roseanne Wells**, queryroseanne@gmail.com (literary fiction, young adult, middle-grade, narrative nonfiction, select memoir, science (popular or trade, not academic), history, religion (not inspirational), travel, humor, food/cooking, and similar subjects); **Victoria Selvaggio**, vselvaggio@windstream.net (board books, picture books, chapter books, middle-grade, young adult, New Adult, adult; nonfiction and fiction in all genres); **Damian McNicholl**, damianmcnichollvarney@gmail.com (accessible literary, historical [except naval, World War II, romance], legal thriller, offbeat/quirky, memoir, narrative nonfiction [especially biography, investigative journalism, cultural, legal, LGBTQ]); **Alexandra Weiss**, alexweiss.jdlit@gmail.com (voice-driven young adult stories, especially contemporary, science fiction, paranormal; quirky and fun middle-grade and children's books, magical realism, literary fiction).

REPRESENTS nonfiction, novels, juvenile books. **Considers these nonfiction areas:** art, autobiography, biography, child guidance, cooking, creative nonfiction, cultural interests, current affairs, dance, film, foods, gay/lesbian, health, history, humor, investigative, juvenile nonfiction, literature, memoirs, multicultural, parenting, philosophy, popular culture, politics, psychology, religious, science, self-help, sex, spirituality, technology, theater, travel, true crime, war, women's issues, women's studies, young adult. **Considers these fiction areas:** commercial, contemporary issues, crime, detective, ethnic, family saga, fantasy, feminist, gay, historical, horror, humor, inspirational, juvenile, lesbian, literary, mainstream, middle-grade, multicultural, mystery, New Adult, New Age, paranormal, picture books, science fiction, suspense, thriller, urban fantasy, women's, young adult.

HOW TO CONTACT Each agent has specific e-mail submission instructions; check the website for updates, as policies do change. Accepts simultaneous submissions. Obtains most new clients through recommendations from others, conferences, query letters.
TERMS Agent receives 15% commission on domestic sales. Offers written contract.

DEFIORE & COMPANY

47 E. 19th St., Third Floor, New York NY 10003. (212)925-7744. **Fax:** (212)925-9803. **E-mail:** info@defliterary.com, submissions@defliterary.com. **Website:** www.defliterary.com. Member of AAR. Signatory of WGA.

Prior to becoming an agent, Mr. DeFiore was publisher of Villard Books (1997-1998), editor-in-chief of Hyperion (1992-1997), editorial director of Delacorte Press (1988-1992), and an editor at St. Martin's Press (1984-1988).

MEMBER AGENTS Brian DeFiore (popular nonfiction, business, pop culture, parenting, commercial fiction); **Laurie Abkemeier** (memoir, parenting, business, how-to/self-help, popular science); **Matthew Elblonk** (young adult, popular culture, narrative nonfiction); **Caryn Karmatz-Rudy** (popular fiction, self-help, narrative nonfiction); **Adam Schear** (commercial fiction, humor, young adult, smart thriller, historical fiction, quirky debut literary novels, popular science, politics, popular culture, current events); **Meredith Kaffel Simonoff** (smart upmarket women's fiction, literary fiction [especially debut], literary thriller, narrative nonfiction, nonfiction about science and tech, sophisticated pop culture/humor books); **Rebecca Strauss** (literary and commercial fiction, women's fiction, urban fantasy, romance, mystery, young adult, memoir, pop culture, select nonfiction); **Lisa Gallagher** (fiction, nonfiction); **Nicole Tourtelot** (narrative and prescriptive nonfiction, food, lifestyle, wellness, pop culture, history, humor, memoir, select young adult adult fiction); **Ashely Collom** (women's fiction, children's and young adult, psychological thriller, memoir, politics, photography, cooking, narrative nonfiction, LGBTQ issues, feminism, occult); **Miriam Altshuler** (adult literary and commercial fiction, narrative nonfiction, middle-grade, young adult, memoir, narrative nonfiction, self-help, family sagas, historical novels); **Reiko Davis** (adult literary and upmarket fiction, narrative nonfiction, young adult, middle-grade, memoir).

REPRESENTS nonfiction, novels, short story collections, juvenile books, poetry books. **Considers these nonfiction areas:** autobiography, biography, business, child guidance, cooking, economics, foods, gay/lesbian, how-to, inspirational, money, multicultural, parenting, photography, popular culture, politics, psychology, religious, science, self-help, sex, sports, technology, travel, women's issues, young adult. **Considers these fiction areas:** comic books, commercial, ethnic, feminist, gay, lesbian, literary, mainstream, middle-grade, mystery, paranormal, picture books, poetry, romance, short story collections, suspense, thriller, urban fantasy, women's, young adult.

☞ "Please be advised that we are not considering dramatic projects at this time."

HOW TO CONTACT Query with SASE or e-mail to submissions@defliterary.com. "Please include the word 'query' in the subject line. All attachments will be deleted; please insert all text in the body of the e-mail. For more information about our agents, their individual interests, and their query guidelines, please visit our About Us page on our website." Accepts simultaneous submissions. Obtains most new clients through recommendations from others.

TERMS Agent receives 15% commission on domestic sales; 20% commission on foreign sales. Offers written contract; 10-day notice must be given to terminate contract. Charges clients for photocopying and overnight delivery (deducted only after a sale is made).

JOELLE DELBOURGO ASSOCIATES, INC.

101 Park St., Montclair NJ 07042. (973)773-0836. **Fax:** (973)783-6802. **E-mail:** joelle@delbourgo.com. **E-mail:** submissions@delbourgo.com. **Website:** www.delbourgo.com. "We are a boutique agency representing a wide range of nonfiction and fiction. Nonfiction: narrative, research-based and prescriptive nonfiction, including history, current affairs, education, psychology and personal development, parenting, science, business and economics, diet and nutrition, and cookbooks. Adult and young adult commercial and literary fiction, some middle-grade. We do not represent plays, screenplays, poet-

ry and picture books." Member of AAR. Represents more than 500 clients.

○ Prior to becoming an agent, Ms. Delbourgo was an editor and senior publishing executive at HarperCollins and Random House. She began her editorial career at Bantam Books, where she discovered the Choose Your Own Adventure series. Joelle Delbourgo brings more than three decades of experience as an editor and agent. Jacqueline Flynn was the executive editor at Amacom for more than 15 years.

MEMBER AGENTS Joelle Delbourgo, Jacqueline Flynn.

REPRESENTS nonfiction, fiction, novels. **Considers these nonfiction areas:** Americana, animals, anthropology, archeology, autobiography, biography, business, child guidance, cooking, creative nonfiction, current affairs, dance, decorating, diet/nutrition, design, economics, education, environment, film, gardening, gay/lesbian, government, health, history, how-to, humor, inspirational, interior design, investigative, juvenile nonfiction, literature, medicine, memoirs, military, money, multicultural, music, parenting, philosophy, popular culture, politics, psychology, science, self-help, sex, sociology, spirituality, sports, translation, travel, true crime, war, women's issues, women's studies. **Considers these fiction areas:** adventure, commercial, contemporary issues, crime, detective, fantasy, feminist, juvenile, literary, mainstream, middle-grade, military, mystery, New Adult, New Age, romance, science fiction, thriller, urban fantasy, women's, young adult.

☞ "We are former publishers and editors with deep knowledge and an insider perspective. We have a reputation for individualized attention to clients, strategic management of authors' careers, and creating strong partnerships with publishers for our clients." Do not send scripts, picture books, or poetry.

HOW TO CONTACT It's preferable if you submit via e-mail to a specific agent. Query 1 agent only. No attachments. Put the word "Query" in the subject line. "While we do our best to respond to each query, if you have not received a response in 60 days, you may consider that a pass. Please do not send us copies of self-published books unless requested. Let us know if you are sending your query to us exclusively or if this is a multiple submission. For nonfiction, let us know if a proposal and sample chapters are available; if not, you should probably wait to send your query when you have a completed proposal. For fiction and memoir, embed the *first* 10 pages of manuscript into the e-mail after your query letter. Please, no attachments. If we like your first pages, we may ask to see your synopsis and more manuscript. Please do not cold call us or make a follow-up call unless we call you." Accepts simultaneous submissions.

TERMS Agent receives 15% commission on domestic sales; 20% commission on foreign sales and television/film adaptations. Offers written contract. Charges clients for postage and photocopying.

RECENT SALES *Witness: Lessons from Elie Wiesel's Classroom*, by Ariel Burger; *After Anatevka: A Sequel to Fiddler on the Roof*, by Alexandra Silber; *UnSelfie: The Habits of Empathy*, by Dr. Michele Borba (Touchstone/Simon & Schuster); *The Prisoner*, by Ben H. Winters (Mulholland/Little Brown); The Guardian Herd novels, by Jennifer Lynn Alvarez.

WRITERS CONFERENCES Unicorn Conference.

TIPS "Do your homework. Do not cold call. Read and follow submission guidelines before contacting us. Do not call to find out if we received your material. No e-mail queries. Treat agents with respect, as you would any other professional, such as a doctor, lawyer, or financial advisor."

J DE S ASSOCIATES, INC.

9 Shagbark Rd., Norwalk CT 06854. (203)838-7571. **E-mail:** jdespoel@aol.com. **Website:** www.jdesassociates.com. **Contact:** Jacques de Spoelberch. Estab. 1975.

⊙ Prior to opening his agency, Mr. de Spoelberch was an editor with Houghton Mifflin, and launched International Literary Management for the International Management Group.

REPRESENTS novels. **Considers these nonfiction areas:** biography, business, cultural interests, current affairs, economics, ethnic, government, health, history, law, medicine, metaphysics, military, New Age, politics, self-help, sociology, sports, translation. **Considers these fiction areas:** crime, detective, frontier, historical, juvenile, literary, mainstream, mystery, New Age, police, suspense, westerns, young adult.

HOW TO CONTACT "Brief queries by regular mail and e-mail are welcomed for fiction and nonfiction, but kindly do not include sample proposals or other material unless specifically requested to do so." Accepts simultaneous submissions. Responds in 2 months to queries. Obtains most new clients through recommendations from authors and other clients.

TERMS Agent receives 15% commission on domestic sales; 20% commission on foreign sales. Charges clients for foreign postage and photocopying.

RECENT SALES Joshilyn Jackson's new novel, *A Grown-Up Kind of Pretty* (Grand Central); Margaret George's final Tudor historical, *Elizabeth I* (Penguin); the fifth in Leighton Gage's series of Brazilian thrillers, *A Vine in the Blood* (Soho); Genevieve Graham's romance, *Under the Same Sky* (Berkley Sensation); Hilary Holladay's biography of the early Beat Herbert Huncke, *American Hipster* (Magnus); Ron Rozelle's *My Boys and Girls Are in There: The 1937 New London School Explosion* (Texas A&M); the concluding novel in Dom Testa's young adult science fiction series, *The Galahad Legacy* (Tor); and Bruce Coston's new collection of animal stories, *The Gift of Pets* (St. Martin's Press).

SANDRA DIJKSTRA LITERARY AGENCY

1155 Camino del Mar, PMB 515, Del Mar CA 92014. **E-mail:** elise@dijkstraagency.com. **E-mail:** queries@dijkstraagency.com. **Website:** www.dijkstraagency.com. The Dijkstra Agency was established over 30 years ago and is known for guiding the careers of many best-selling fiction and nonfiction authors, including Amy Tan, Lisa See, Maxine Hong Kingston, Chitra Divakaruni, Eric Foner, and Marcus Rediker. "We handle nearly all genres, except for poetry." Please see www.dijkstraagency.com for each agent's interests. Member of AAR, Authors Guild, Organization of American Historians, RWA. Represents 100+ clients.

MEMBER AGENTS Sandra Dijkstra, president (adult), **Elise Capron** (adult), **Jill Marr** (adult), **Thao Le** (adult, young adult), **Roz Foster** (adult, young adult), **Jessica Watterson** (subgenres of adult and New Adult romance, women's fiction), **Suzy Evans** (adult, young adult), and **Jennifer Kim** (adult and young adult).

REPRESENTS nonfiction, fiction, novels, short story collections, juvenile books, scholarly books. **Considers these nonfiction areas:** Americana, animals, anthropology, art, biography, business, creative nonfiction, cultural interests, current affairs, design, economics, environment, ethnic, gardening, government, health, history, juvenile nonfiction, literature, memoirs, multicultural, parenting, popular culture, politics, psychology, science, self-help, sports, true crime, women's issues, women's studies, young adult, narrative. **Considers these fiction areas:** commercial, contemporary issues, detective, family saga, fantasy, feminist, historical, horror, juvenile, literary, mainstream, middle-grade, multicultural, mystery, New Adult, romance, science fiction, short story collections, sports, suspense, thriller, urban fantasy, women's, young adult.

HOW TO CONTACT "Please see guidelines on our website, www.dijkstraagency.com. Please note that we only accept e-mail submissions. Due to the large number of unsolicited submissions we receive, we are only able to respond those submissions in which we are interested." Accepts simultaneous submissions. Responds to queries of interest within 6 weeks.

TERMS Works in conjunction with foreign and film agents. Agent receives 15% commission on domestic sales; 20% commission on foreign sales. Offers written contract. No reading fee.

TIPS "Remember that publishing is a business. Do your research and present your project in as professional a way as possible. Only submit your work when you are confident that it is polished and ready for primetime. Make yourself a part of the active writing community by getting stories and articles published, networking with other writers, and getting a good sense of where your work fits in the market."

⊙ DONADIO & OLSON, INC.

40 W. 27th St., Fifth Floor, New York NY 10001. (212)691-8077. **Fax:** (212)633-2837. **E-mail:** neil@donadio.com. **E-mail:** mail@donadio.com. **Website:** http://donadio.com. **Contact:** Neil Olson. Member of AAR.

MEMBER AGENTS Neil Olson (no queries); Edward Hibbert (no queries); Carrie Howland, carrie@donadio.com (adult literary fiction, narrative nonfiction, young adult, middle-grade, picture books).

REPRESENTS nonfiction, novels. **Considers these nonfiction areas:** creative nonfiction. **Considers these fiction areas:** literary, middle-grade, picture books, young adult.

    ☛ This agency represents mostly fiction and is very selective.

HOW TO CONTACT "Please send a query letter and the first three chapters/first 25 pages of the manuscript to mail@donadio.com. Please allow a minimum of 1 month for a reply. Accepts simultaneous submissions.

DONAGHY LITERARY GROUP

(647)527-4353. **E-mail:** stacey@donaghyliterary.com. **E-mail:** query@donaghyliterary.com. **Website:** www.donaghyliterary.com. **Contact:** Stacey Donaghy. "Donaghy Literary Group provides full-service literary representation to our clients at every stage of their writing careers. Specializing in commercial fiction, we seek middle-grade, young adult, New Adult, and adult novels."

    ◗ Prior to opening her agency, Ms. Donaghy served as an agent at the Corvisiero Literary Agency. Before this, she worked in training and education, acquiring and editing academic materials for publication and training. Ms. Noble interned for Jessica Sinsheimer of Sarah Jane Freymann Literary Agency. Ms. Miller previously worked in children's publishing with Scholastic Canada and also interned with Bree Ogden during her time at the D4EO Agency. Ms. Ayers-Barnett is a former associate editor for Pocket Books, acquisitions editor for Re.ad Publishing, and a freelance book editor for New York Book Editors. Mr. Franks is a former bookseller and book club organizer for The Mysterious Bookshop in New York City, freelance editor for mysteriouspress.com, and proofreader for Europa Editions.

MEMBER AGENTS Stacey Donaghy (romantic suspense, LGBTQ, thriller, mystery, contemporary romance, erotic romance, young adult); Valerie Noble (historical, science fiction, fantasy [think Kristin Cashore and Suzanne Collins] for young adults and adults); Sue Miller (YA, urban fantasy, contemporary romance); Amanda Ayers Barnett (mystery/thriller, middle-grade, young adult, New Adult, women's fiction); Alex Franks (contemporary fiction, literary fiction, science fiction, espionage, thriller, mystery).

REPRESENTS fiction. **Considers these fiction areas:** commercial, crime, detective, erotica, ethnic, family saga, fantasy, feminist, gay, historical, horror, juvenile, lesbian, literary, mainstream, middle-grade, multicultural, mystery, New Adult, paranor-

NEW AGENT SPOTLIGHT

MELISSA NASSON
RUBIN PFEFFER CONTENT

www.rpcontent.com
@melissabnasson

ABOUT MELISSA: Melissa Nasson has spent her life living in and around Boston, attending college at Boston University (Go Terriers!). While studying at Boston University School of Law, she realized that becoming a literary agent would combine her passion for books with her legal background, and she began interning at Zachary Shuster Harmsworth, and later at East-West Literary Agency and Rubin Pfeffer Content. After taking the bar exam in 2012, Melissa worked as a foreign rights intern at Perseus Books Group before starting as contracts director at Beacon Press. Now, she continues her work at Beacon Press while actively building her list as an associate agent at Rubin Pfeffer Content. Melissa loves dogs, craft beer, making pickles, tending to her tiny vegetable garden, and her pet tortoise, Norton.

SHE IS SEEKING: Melissa is seeking middle-grade and young adult fiction and nonfiction. She is also accepting picture book queries. She is open to all genres, but has a special love for fantasy and science fiction. She enjoys unexpected settings and loves a good romantic angle. For nonfiction, she'd love to see manuscripts that bring to light untold stories from history, particularly featuring individuals from marginalized groups. Above all, she wants to see strong, polished writing, fully developed and multifaceted characters, and fresh concepts. Tip: Melissa is not a good fit for bathroom humor.

HOW TO SUBMIT: Please e-mail a query letter and the first 50 pages of your manuscript as a Word doc or PDF to melissa@rpcontent.com.

---

mal, police, psychic, romance, science fiction, sports, supernatural, suspense, thriller, urban fantasy, women's, young adult.
HOW TO CONTACT Query via e-mail, no attachments. Visit agency website for submission guidelines and for team to view agent bios. Do not e-mail agents directly. Accepts simultaneous submissions. Responds in 6-8 weeks to queries. Responds in 8-12 weeks to mss. Time may vary during holidays and closures.
TERMS Agent receives 15% commission on domestic sales; 20% commission on foreign sales. Offers written contract; 30-day notice must be given to terminate contract.
WRITERS CONFERENCES Romantic Times Booklovers Convention, Windsor International

Writers Conference, OWC Ontario Writers Conference, SoCal Writers Conference, WD Toronto Writer's Workshop.

TIPS "Only submit to one DLG agent at a time; we work collaboratively and often share projects that may be better suited to another agent at the agency."

JIM DONOVAN LITERARY

5635 SMU Blvd., Suite 201, Dallas TX 75206. **E-mail:** jdliterary@sbcglobal.net. **Contact:** Melissa Shultz, agent. Estab. 1993. Represents 34 clients.

MEMBER AGENTS Jim Donovan (American, military, and Western history; biography, sports, popular reference, popular culture, literary, thriller, mystery); **Melissa Shultz** (American, military, and Western history; biography, sports, popular reference, popular culture, literary, thriller, mystery, parenting, women's issues).

REPRESENTS nonfiction, fiction, novels. **Considers these nonfiction areas:** biography, current affairs, health, history, investigative, literature, military, parenting, popular culture, science, sports, war, women's issues. **Considers these fiction areas:** action, adventure, commercial, crime, detective, frontier, historical, mainstream, multicultural, mystery, police, suspense, thriller, war, westerns.

› This agency specializes in commercial fiction and nonfiction. Does not want to receive poetry, children's, science fiction, fantasy, short stories, memoir, inspirational, or anything else not listed above.

HOW TO CONTACT "For nonfiction, I need a well-thought-out query letter telling me about the book: what it does, how it does it, why it's needed now, why it's better or different than what's out there on the subject, and why the author is the perfect writer for it. For fiction, the novel has to be finished, of course; a short (2- to 5-page) synopsis—not a teaser, but a summary of all the action, from first page to last—and the first 30-50 pages is enough. This material should be polished to as close to perfection as possible." Accepts simultaneous submissions. Responds in 2 weeks to queries, 1 month to mss. Obtains most new clients through recommendations from others.

TERMS Agent receives 15% commission on domestic sales. Agent receives 20% commission on foreign sales. Offers written contract, binding for 1 year; 30-day notice must be given to terminate contract. This agency charges for things such as overnight delivery and manuscript copying. Charges are discussed beforehand.

RECENT SALES *The Road to Jonestown*, by Jeff Guinn (S&S); *The Earth Is All That Lasts*, by Mark Gardner (HarperCollins); *As Good as Dead*, by Stephen Moore (NAL); *James Monroe*, by Tim McGrath (NAL); *The Greatest Fury*, by William C. Davis (NAL); *The Hamilton Affair*, by Elizabeth Cobbs (Arcade); *Resurrection Pass*, by Kurt Anderson (Kensington).

TIPS "Get published in short form—magazine reviews, journals, etc.—first. This will increase your credibility considerably and make it much easier to sell a full-length book."

⊘ DOYEN LITERARY SERVICES, INC.

E-mail: topseller@barbaradoyen.com. **Website:** www.barbaradoyen.com. **Contact:** B.J. Doyen, president.

Prior to opening her agency, Ms. Doyen worked as a published author, teacher, and guest speaker, and wrote and appeared in her own weekly TV show airing in 7 states. She is also the coauthor of *The Everything Guide to Writing a Book Proposal* (Adams 2005) and *The Everything Guide to Getting Published* (Adams 2006).

REPRESENTS nonfiction. **Considers these nonfiction areas:** business, crafts, current affairs, diet/nutrition, economics, gardening, health, history, hobbies, horticulture, law, medicine, military, money, parenting, psychology, science, self-help, women's issues.

› This agency specializes in nonfiction. Seeking business, health, science, how-to, self-help—adult nonfiction suitable for the major trade publishers. Does not want to receive pornography, screenplays, children's books, fiction, or poetry.

HOW TO CONTACT Send an e-mailed **query letter** initially. "Please read the website before submitting a query. Send no unsolicited attachments." Accepts simultaneous submissions. Responds quickly to e-mailed queries.

TERMS Agent receives 15% commission on domestic sales. Offers written contract.

TIPS "Please read our website to better understand how we work and what we are looking for in a query. Please, no snail mail queries."

DUNHAM LITERARY, INC.

110 William St., Suite 2202, New York NY 10038. (212)929-0994. **E-mail:** query@dunhamlit.com.

Website: www.dunhamlit.com. **Contact:** Jennie Dunham. Estab. 2000. Member of AAR, SCBWI. Represents 50 clients.

○ Prior to opening her agency, Ms. Dunham worked as a literary agent for Russell & Volkening. The Rhoda Weyr Agency is now a division of Dunham Literary, Inc.

MEMBER AGENTS Jennie Dunham, Bridget Smith.

REPRESENTS nonfiction, fiction, novels, short story collections, juvenile books. **Considers these nonfiction areas:** anthropology, archeology, art, biography, creative nonfiction, cultural interests, environment, health, history, language, literature, medicine, memoirs, multicultural, parenting, popular culture, politics, psychology, science, sociology, technology, women's issues, women's studies, young adult. **Considers these fiction areas:** family saga, fantasy, gay, historical, humor, juvenile, literary, mainstream, middle-grade, multicultural, mystery, New Adult, picture books, science fiction, short story collections, sports, urban fantasy, women's, young adult, Westerns, horror, genre romance, poetry.

HOW TO CONTACT E-mail queries preferred, with all materials pasted in the body of the e-mail. Attachments will not be opened. Paper queries are also accepted. Please include a SASE for response and return of materials. If submitting to Bridget Smith, please include the first 5 pages with the query. Accepts simultaneous submissions. Responds in 4 weeks to queries, 2 months to mss. Obtains most new clients through recommendations from others, solicitations.

TERMS Agent receives 15% commission on domestic sales; 20% commission on foreign sales.

RECENT SALES Sales include *The Bad Kitty Series*, by Nick Bruel (Macmillan); *The Christmas Story*, by Robert Sabuda (Simon & Schuster); *The Gollywhopper Games* and sequels, by Jody Feldman (HarperCollins); *First & Then*, by Emma Mills (Macmillan); *Learning Not To Drown*, by Anna Shinoda (Simon & Schuster); *Gangsterland*, by Tod Goldberg (Counterpoint); *A Shadow All of Light*, by Fred Chappell (Tor); *Forward from Here*, by Reeve Lindbergh (Simon & Schuster).

DUNOW, CARLSON, & LERNER AGENCY

27 W. 20th St., Suite 1107, New York NY 10011. (212)645-7606. **E-mail:** mail@dclagency.com. **Website:** www.dclagency.com. Member of AAR.

MEMBER AGENTS Jennifer Carlson (narrative nonfiction writing and journalism: current events and ideas, cultural history; literary and upmarket commercial fiction); **Henry Dunow** (literary, historical, strongly written commercial fiction and voice-driven nonfiction across a range of area:–narrative history, biography, memoir, current affairs, cultural trends and criticism, science, sports); **Erin Hosier** (nonfiction: popular culture, music, sociology, memoir); **Betsy Lerner** (nonfiction: psychology, history, cultural studies, biography, current events, business; fiction: literary, dark, funny, voice driven); **Yishai Seidman** (fiction: literary, postmodern, thriller; nonfiction: sports, music, pop culture); **Amy Hughes** (nonfiction: history, cultural studies, memoir, current events, wellness, health, food, pop culture, biography; literary fiction); **Eleanor Jackson** (literary, commercial, memoir, art, food, science, history); **Julia Kenny** (adult, middle-grade, young adult, especially interested in dark, literary thriller and suspense); **Edward Necarsulmer IV** (strong new voices in teen & middle-grade, picture books); **Stacia Decker**; **Arielle Datz** (adult, young adult, middle-grade, literary and commercial; nonfiction: essays, unconventional memoir, pop culture, sociology).

REPRESENTS nonfiction, fiction, novels, short story collections. **Considers these nonfiction areas:** art, biography, creative nonfiction, cultural interests, current affairs, foods, health, history, memoirs, music, popular culture, psychology, science, sociology, sports. **Considers these fiction areas:** commercial, literary, mainstream, middle-grade, mystery, picture books, thriller, young adult.

HOW TO CONTACT Query via snail mail with SASE or by e-mail; e-mail preferred. Paste 10 sample pages below query letter. No attachments. Will respond only if interested. Accepts simultaneous submissions. Responds in 4-6 weeks if interested.

RECENT SALES A full list of agency clients is on the website.

DYSTEL, GODERICH & BOURRET LLC

1 Union Square W., Suite 904, New York NY 10003. (212)627-9100. **Fax:** (212)627-9313. **Website:** www.dystel.com. Estab. 1994. Member of AAR, SCBWI. Represents 600+ clients.

MEMBER AGENTS Jane Dystel; Miriam Goderich, miriam@dystel.com (literary and commercial fiction, genre fiction, narrative nonfiction, pop culture, psychology, history, science, art, business books, biography/memoir); **Stacey Glick**, sglick@dystel.com (adult narrative nonfiction: memoir, parenting, cooking and food, psychology, science, health and wellness, lifestyle, current events, pop culture; young adult, middle-grade, children's nonfiction, select adult contemporary fiction); **Michael Bourret**, mbourret@dystel.com (middle-grade and young adult fiction, commercial adult fiction, and all sorts of nonfiction, from practical to narrative; especially interested in food and cocktail related books, memoir, popular history, politics, religion [though not spirituality], popular science, current events); **Jim McCarthy**, jmccarthy@dystel.com (literary women's fiction, underrepresented voices, mystery, romance, paranormal fiction, narrative nonfiction, memoir, paranormal nonfiction); **Jessica Papin**, jpapin@dystel.com (plot-driven literary and smart commercial fiction, narrative nonfiction: history, medicine, science, economics, women's issues); **Lauren Abramo**, labramo@dystel.com (humorous middle-grade and contemporary young adult, upmarket commercial adult fiction and well-paced literary fiction; adult narrative nonfiction: pop culture, psychology, pop science, reportage, media, contemporary culture; in nonfiction, has a strong preference for interdisciplinary approaches, and in all categories especially interested in underrepresented voices); **John Rudolph**, jrudolph@dystel.com (picture book author/illustrators, middle-grade, young adult, select commercial fiction, and narrative nonfiction—especially in music, sports, history, popular science, "big think," performing arts, health, business, memoir, military history, humor); **Sharon Pelletier**, spelletier@dystel.com (smart commercial fiction: upmarket women's fiction, domestic suspense, literary thriller; strong contemporary romance novels, compelling nonfiction projects, especially feminism and religion); **Michael Hoogland**, mhoogland@dystel.com (thriller, science fiction and fantasy, young adult, upmarket women's fiction, narrative nonfiction); **Erin Young**, eyoung@dystel.com (YA/Middle-grade, literary and intellectual commercial thriller, memoirs, biography, sport and science narratives); **Amy Bishop**, abishop@dystel.com (commercial and literary women's fiction, fiction from diverse authors, historical fiction, young adult, personal narratives, biography); **Kemi Faderin**, kfaderin@dystel.com (smart, plot-driven young adult, historical fiction/nonfiction, contemporary women's fiction, and literary fiction).

REPRESENTS Considers these nonfiction areas: animals, art, autobiography, biography, business, cooking, cultural interests, current affairs, ethnic, foods, gay/lesbian, health, history, humor, inspirational, investigative, medicine, memoirs, metaphysics, military, New Age, parenting, popular culture, politics, psychology, religious, science, sports, women's issues, women's studies. **Considers these fiction areas:** commercial, ethnic, gay, lesbian, literary, mainstream, middle-grade, mystery, paranormal, romance, suspense, thriller, women's, young adult.

⚬— "We are actively seeking fiction for all ages, in all genres." No plays, screenplays, or poetry.

HOW TO CONTACT Query via e-mail and put "Query" in the subject line. "Synopses, outlines, or sample chapters (say, 1 chapter or the first 25 pages of your manuscript) should either be included below the cover letter or attached as a separate document. We won't open attachments if they come with a blank e-mail." Accepts simultaneous submissions. Responds in 6 to 8 weeks to queries, in 8 weeks to mss. Obtains most new clients through recommendations from others, solicitations, conferences.

TERMS Agent receives 15% commission on domestic sales; 19% commission on foreign sales. Offers written contract.

TIPS "DGLM prides itself on being a full-service agency. We're involved in every stage of the publishing process, from offering substantial editing on mss and proposals to coming up with book ideas for authors looking for their next project, negotiating contracts, and collecting monies for our clients. We follow a book from its inception through its sale to a publisher, its publication, and beyond. Our commitment to our writers does not, by any means, end when we have collected our commission. This is one of the many things that makes us unique in a very competitive business."

EDEN STREET LITERARY

P.O. Box 30, Billings NY 12510. **E-mail:** info@edenstreetlit.com. **E-mail:** submissions@edenstreetlit.com. **Website:** www.edenstreetlit.com. **Contact:** Liza Voges. Eden Street represents over 40 authors and author-illustrators of books for young readers from preschool through young adult. Its books have won numerous awards over the past 30 years. Eden Street prides itself on tailoring services to each client's goals, working in tandem with them to achieve literary, critical, and commercial success. Welcomes the opportunity to work with additional authors and illustrators. This agency gives priority to members of SCBWI. Member of AAR. Signatory of WGA. Represents over 40 clients.

REPRESENTS nonfiction, fiction, novels, juvenile books. **Considers these fiction areas:** juvenile, middle-grade, picture books, young adult.

HOW TO CONTACT E-mail a picture book ms or dummy, a synopsisand 3 chapters of a Middle-grade or young adult novel, or a proposal and 3 sample chapters for nonfiction. Accepts simultaneous submissions. Responds only to submissions of interest.

RECENT SALES *Dream Dog*, by Lou Berger; *Biscuit Loves the Library*, by Alyssa Capucilli; *The Scraps Book*, by Lois Ehlert; *Two Bunny Buddies*, by Kathryn O. Galbraith; *Between Two Worlds*, by Katherine Kirkpatrick.

JUDITH EHRLICH LITERARY MANAGEMENT, LLC

146 Central Park W., 20E, New York NY 10023. (646)505-1570. **Fax:** (646)505-1570. **E-mail:** jehrlich@judithehrlichliterary.com. **Website:** www.judithehrlichliterary.com. Judith Ehrlich Literary Management LLC, established in 2002 and based in New York City, is a full-service agency. "We represent nonfiction and fiction, both literary and commercial, for the mainstream trade market. Our approach is very hands-on, editorial, and constructive with the primary goal of helping authors build successful writing careers. Special areas of interest include compelling narrative nonfiction, outstanding biography and memoirs, lifestyle books, works that reflect our changing culture, women's issues, psychology, science, social issues, current events, parenting, health, history, business, and prescriptive books offering fresh information and advice. We also seek and represent stellar commercial and literary fiction, including romance and other women's fiction, historical fiction, literary mystery, and select thriller. Our agency deals closely with all major and independent publishers. When appropriate, we place our properties with foreign agents and co-agents at leading film agencies in New York and Los Angeles." Estab. 2002. Member of the Authors' Guild, American Society of Journalists and Authors.

○ Prior to her current position, Ms. Ehrlich was a senior associate at the Linda Chester Agency and is an award-winning journalist. She is the co-author of *The New Crowd: The Changing of the Jewish Guard on Wall Street* (Little, Brown).

MEMBER AGENTS Judith Ehrlich, jehrlich@judithehrlichliterary.com (upmarket, literary, and quality commercial fiction, nonfiction: narrative, women's, business, prescriptive, medical and health-related topics, history, current events).

REPRESENTS nonfiction, fiction, novels, short story collections, juvenile books. **Considers these nonfiction areas:** animals, art, autobiography, biography, business, creative nonfiction, cultural interests, current affairs, diet/nutrition, health, history, how-to, humor, inspirational, investigative, juvenile nonfiction, memoirs, parenting, photography, popular culture, politics, psychology, science, self-help, sociology, true crime, women's issues, young adult. **Considers these fiction areas:** adventure, commercial, contemporary issues, crime, detective, family saga, historical, humor, juvenile, literary, middle-grade, mystery, picture books, short story collections, suspense, thriller, women's, young adult.

➥ Does not want to receive novellas, poetry, textbooks, plays, or screenplays.

HOW TO CONTACT E-query, with a synopsis and some sample pages. The agency will respond only if interested. Accepts simultaneous submissions.

RECENT SALES *The Bicycle Spy*, by Yona Zeldis McDonough (Scholastic); *The House on Primrose Pond*, by Yona McDonough (NAL/Penguin); *You Were Meant for Me*, by Yona McDonough (NAL/Penguin); *Echoes of Us: The Hybrid Chronicles*, Book 3 by Kat Zhang (HarperCollins); *Once We Were: The Hybrid Chronicles* Book 2, by Kat Zhang (HarperCollins).

EINSTEIN LITERARY MANAGEMENT

27 W. 20th St., #1003, New York NY 10011. (212)221-8797. **E-mail:** info@einsteinliterary.com. **E-mail:** submissions@einsteinliterary.com. **Website:** http://einsteinliterary.com. **Contact:** Susanna Einstein. Estab. 2015. Member of AAR. Signatory of WGA.

○ Prior to her current position, Ms. Einstein was with LJK Literary Management and the Einstein Thompson Agency.

MEMBER AGENTS Susanna Einstein, Susan Graham, Shana Kelly.

REPRESENTS nonfiction, fiction, novels, short story collections, juvenile books. **Considers these nonfiction areas:** cooking, creative nonfiction,

NEW AGENT SPOTLIGHT

KIRA WATSON

EMMA SWEENEY AGENCY, LLC

www.emmasweeneyagency.com
@KiraWatsonESA

ABOUT KIRA: Kira Watson graduated from Hunter College where she earned a BA in English (with a focus on Creative Writing) and a BA in Russian Language & Culture.

SHE IS SEEKING: Kira is particularly interested in children's literature (young adult & middle grade) with a strong narrative voice, well-crafted storylines, and memorable characters. Within young adult & middle-grade, Kira is actively seeking realistic fiction, speculative fiction, magic realism, thriller/mystery, horror, fantasy, and historical fiction. Stories with folklore elements, complex villains, morally enigmatic (and very flawed) protagonists, medieval literature influences, and taboo subjects are bound to catch Kira's attention.

HOW TO CONTACT: "We accept only electronic queries, and ask that all queries be sent to queries@emmasweeneyagency.com. Please begin your query with a succinct (and hopefully catchy) description of your plot or proposal. Always include a brief cover letter telling us how you heard about ESA, your previous writing credits, and a few lines about yourself. We cannot open any attachments unless specifically requested, and ask that you paste the first 10 pages of your proposal or novel into the text of your e-mail."

memoirs, blog-to-book projects. **Considers these fiction areas:** comic books, commercial, crime, fantasy, historical, juvenile, literary, middle-grade, mystery, picture books, romance, science fiction, suspense, thriller, women's, young adult.

⚷— "As an agency we represent a broad range of literary and commercial fiction, including upmarket women's fiction, crime fiction, historical fiction, romance, and books for middle-grade children and young adults, including picture books and graphic novels. We also handle nonfiction, including cookbooks, memoir, and narrative, and blog-to-book

projects. Please see agent bios on the website for specific information about what each of ELM's agents represents." Does not want poetry, textbooks, or screenplays.

HOW TO CONTACT Please submit a query letter and the first 10 double-spaced pages of your manuscript in the body of the e-mail (no attachments). Does not respond to mail queries, telephone queries, or queries that are not specifically addressed to agency. Accepts simultaneous submissions. Responds in 6 weeks if interested.

THE LISA EKUS GROUP, LLC

57 North St., Hatfield MA 01038. (413)247-9325. **Fax:** (413)247-9873. **E-mail:** info@lisaekus.com. **Website:** www.lisaekus.com. **Contact:** Sally Ekus. This agency specializes in cookbooks, health and wellness, culinary narrative. Member of AAR.

MEMBER AGENTS Lisa Ekus, Sally Ekus.

REPRESENTS nonfiction. **Considers these nonfiction areas:** cooking, diet/nutrition, foods, health, how-to, humor, women's issues, occasionally health/well-being and women's issues, humor, lifestyle.

> "Please note that we do not handle fiction, poetry, or children's books. If we receive a query for titles in these categories, please understand that we do not have the time or resources to respond."

HOW TO CONTACT "For more information about our literary services, visit http://lisaekus.com/services/literary-agency. Submit a query via e-mail or through our contact form on the website. You can also submit complete hard copy proposal with title page, proposal contents, concept, bio, marketing, TOC, etc. Include SASE for the return of materials." Accepts simultaneous submissions. Responds in 4-6 weeks.

RECENT SALES "Please see the regularly updated client listing on our website."

TIPS "Please do not call. No phone queries."

ETHAN ELLENBERG LITERARY AGENCY

155 Suffolk St., #2R, New York NY 10002. (212)431-4554. **E-mail:** agent@ethanellenberg.com. **Website:** http://ethanellenberg.com. **Contact:** Ethan Ellenberg. This agency specializes in commercial fiction and nonfiction. Estab. 1984. Member of AAR, Science Fiction and Fantasy Writer's of America, SCBWI, RWA, MWA.

MEMBER AGENTS Ethan Ellenberg, president; Evan Gregory, senior agent; Bibi Lewis, associate agent (YA, women's fiction).

REPRESENTS nonfiction, fiction. **Considers these nonfiction areas:** biography, cooking, current affairs, health, history, memoirs, New Age, popular culture, psychology, science, spirituality, true crime, adventure. **Considers these fiction areas:** commercial, ethnic, fantasy, literary, middle-grade, mystery, picture books, romance, science fiction, thriller, women's, young adult, general.

> "We specialize in commercial fiction and children's books. In commercial fiction, we want to see science fiction, fantasy, romance, mystery, thriller, women's fiction; all genres welcome. In children's books, we want to see everything: picture books, early reader, middle-grade, and young adult. We do some nonfiction: history, biography, military, popular science, and cutting-edge books about any subject." Does not want to receive poetry, short stories, or screenplays.

HOW TO CONTACT Query by e-mail. Paste all of the material in the order listed. Fiction: query letter, synopsis, first 50 pages. Nonfiction: query letter, book proposal. Picture books: query letter, complete ms, 4-5 sample illustrations. Illustrators: query letter, 4-5 sample illustrations, link to online portfolio. Will not respond unless interested. Accepts simultaneous submissions. Responds in 2 weeks.

EMERALD CITY LITERARY AGENCY

2522 North Proctor St., Suite 359, Tacoma WA 98406. **E-mail:** Mandy@EmeraldCityLiterary.com, QueryLinda@EmeraldCityLiterary.com, querylindsay@emeraldcityliterary.com. **Website:** https://emeraldcityliterary.com. "Emerald City Literary Agency is a boutique literary agency located just outside of Seattle, Washington—otherwise known as the Emerald City; hence, the agency's name. But our location isn't the only reason we chose this moniker. The desire to be published might just be the biggest dream you can imagine. And if you found this website, then you must have something in common with Dorothy and her trio of new friends—you're on a journey to find someone who can grant your greatest wish." Estab. 2015.

MEMBER AGENTS Mandy Hubbard (closed to submissions); Linda Epstein (picture books, middle-grade and young adult fiction, children's nonfiction); Lindsay Mealing (science fiction, fantasy, young adult); Kirsten Wolf (contracts manager).

REPRESENTS nonfiction, fiction, novels, juvenile books. **Considers these nonfiction areas:** juvenile nonfiction. **Considers these fiction areas:** fantasy, middle-grade, picture books, science fiction, young adult.

> Linda Epstein: no adult literature. Lindsay Mealing: no middle-grade, nonfiction, short fiction, or adult fiction outside the science fiction and fantasy genres.

HOW TO CONTACT To query Linda Epstein: include a one-page query letter and the first 20 pages of your manuscript in the body of the e-mail. If you're sending a picture book, include the full text of the manuscript in the body of the e-mail. To query Lindsay Mealing: paste the first 5 pages of your manuscript below your query; attachments will not be opened. Accepts simultaneous submissions.

FELICIA ETH LITERARY REPRESENTATION

555 Bryant St., Suite 350, Palo Alto CA 94301-1700. **E-mail:** feliciaeth.literary@gmail.com. **Website:** ethliterary.com. **Contact:** Felicia Eth. Member of AAR.
REPRESENTS novels. **Considers these nonfiction areas:** animals, cooking, creative nonfiction, cultural interests, history, investigative, memoirs, parenting, popular culture, psychology, sociology, travel, women's issues. **Considers these fiction areas:** historical, literary, mainstream, suspense.

- This agency specializes in high-quality fiction (preferably mainstream/contemporary) and provocative, intelligent, and thoughtful nonfiction on a wide array of commercial subjects. "The agency does not represent genre fiction, including romance novels, science fiction and fantasy, westerns, anime and graphic novels, or mystery."

HOW TO CONTACT For fiction, please write a query letter introducing yourself, your book, and your writing background. Don't forget to include degrees you may have, publishing credits, awards, and endorsements. Please wait for a response before including sample pages. "We only consider material where the manuscript for which you are querying is complete, unless you have previously published." For nonfiction, a query letter is best, introducing idea and what you have written already (proposal, manuscript). "For writerly nonficiton (narratives, bio, memoir), please let us know if you have a finished manuscript. Also, it's important that you include information about yourself: your background and expertise, your platform, and your notoriety, if any. We do not ask for exclusivity in most instances but do ask that you inform us if other agents are considering the same material." Accepts simultaneous submissions.
TERMS Agent receives 15% commission on domestic sales; 20% commission on foreign and film sales.

Charges clients for photocopying and express mail services.
RECENT SALES *Bumper Sticker Philosophy*, by Jack Bowen (Random House); *Boys Adrift*, by Leonard Sax (Basic Books); *The Memory Thief*, by Emily Colin (Ballantine Books); *The World Is a Carpet*, by Anna Badkhen (Riverhead).
WRITERS CONFERENCES "Wide array—from Squaw Valley to Mills College."

MARY EVANS INC.

242 E. Fifth St., New York NY 10003. (212)979-0880. **Fax:** (212)979-5344. **E-mail:** info@maryevansinc.com. **Website:** maryevansinc.com. Member of AAR.
MEMBER AGENTS Mary Evans (progressive politics, alternative medicine, science and technology, social commentary, American history, culture); **Julia Kardon** (literary and upmarket fiction, narrative nonfiction, journalism, history); **Tom Mackay** (nonfiction that uses sport as a platform to explore other issues, playful literary fiction).
REPRESENTS nonfiction, novels. **Considers these nonfiction areas:** creative nonfiction, cultural interests, history, medicine, politics, science, technology, social commentary, journalism. **Considers these fiction areas:** literary, upmarket. No screenplays or stage plays.
HOW TO CONTACT Query by mail or e-mail. If querying by mail, include a SASE. If querying by e-mail, put "Query" in the subject line. For fiction, include the first few pages or opening chapter of your novel as a single Word attachment. For nonfiction, include your book proposal as a single Word attachment. Accepts simultaneous submissions. Responds within 4-8 weeks.

EVATOPIA, INC.

8447 Wilshire Blvd., Suite 401, Beverly Hills CA 90211. **E-mail:** submissions@evatopia.com. **Website:** www.evatopia.com. **Contact:** Margery Walshaw. Evatopia supports writers through consulting, literary management, and publishing services. Estab. 2004. Member of BAFTA, IBPA, NetGalley. Represents 15 clients.

- Prior to becoming an agent, Ms. Walshaw was a writer and publicist for the entertainment industry.

MEMBER AGENTS Mary Kay, story development; **Jamie Davis**, story editor; **Jill Jones**, story editor.

REPRESENTS nonfiction, fiction, novels, juvenile books, movie scripts, feature film, TV movie of the week. **Considers these fiction areas:** crime, detective, fantasy, juvenile, New Adult, paranormal, romance, supernatural, thriller, women's, young adult, projects aimed at women, teens, and children. **Considers these script areas:** action, contemporary issues, detective, movie scripts, romantic drama, supernatural, TV movie of the week, projects aimed at women, teens, and children. Represents screenplays and novels. Provides self-publishing support to novelists.

⌐ "All of our staff members have strong writing and entertainment backgrounds, making us sympathetic to the needs of our clients."

HOW TO CONTACT Submit via online submission form at www.evatopiaentertainment.com. Accepts simultaneous submissions. Obtains most new clients through recommendations.

TERMS Agent receives 15% commission on domestic sales; 15% commission on foreign sales. Offers written contract; 30-day notice must be given to terminate contract.

TIPS "Remember that you only have one chance to make that important first impression. Make your loglines original and your synopses concise. The secret to a screenwriter's success is creating an original story and telling it in a manner that we haven't heard before."

FAIRBANK LITERARY REPRESENTATION

P.O. Box 6, Hudson NY 12534-0006. (617)576-0030. **Fax:** (617)576-0030. **E-mail:** queries@fairbankliterary.com. **Website:** www.fairbankliterary.com. **Contact:** Sorche Fairbank. Member of AAR.

MEMBER AGENTS Sorche Fairbank (narrative nonfiction, commercial and literary fiction, memoir, food and wine); **Matthew Frederick**, matt@fairbankliterary.com (scout for sports nonfiction, architecture, design).

REPRESENTS nonfiction, novels, short story collections. **Considers these nonfiction areas:** agriculture, architecture, art, autobiography, biography, cooking, crafts, cultural interests, current affairs, decorating, diet/nutrition, design, environment, ethnic, foods, gay/lesbian, government, hobbies, horticulture, how-to, interior design, investigative, law, memoirs, photography, popular culture, politics, science, sociology, sports, technology, true crime, women's issues, women's studies. **Considers these fiction areas:** action, adventure, feminist, gay, lesbian, literary, mainstream, mystery, sports, suspense, thriller, women's, Southern voices.

⌐ "I tend to gravitate toward literary fiction and narrative nonfiction, with a strong interest in women's issues and women's voices, international voices, class and race issues, and projects that simply teach me something new about the greater world and society around us. We have a good reputation for working closely and developmentally with our authors and love what we do." Actively seeking literary fiction, international and culturally diverse voices, narrative nonfiction, topical subjects (politics, current affairs), history, sports, architecture/design and pop culture." Does not want to receive romance, poetry, science fiction, pirates, vampire, young adult, or children's works.

HOW TO CONTACT Query with SASE. Submit author bio. Accepts simultaneous submissions. Obtains most new clients through recommendations from others, solicitations, conferences, ideas generated in-house.

TERMS Agent receives 15% commission on domestic sales; 20% commission on foreign sales. Offers written contract, binding for 12 months; 45-day notice must be given to terminate contract.

RECENT SALES *When Clowns Attack*, by Chuck Sambuchino (Running Press), *101 Things I Learned in School* series, by Matthew Fredericks. All recent sales available on website.

TIPS "Be professional from the very first contact. There shouldn't be a single typo or grammatical flub in your query. Have a reason for contacting me about your project other than I was the next name listed on some website. Please do not use form query software! Believe me, we can get a dozen or so a day that look identical—we know when you are using a form. Show me that you know your audience—and your competition. Have the writing and/or proposal at the very, very best it can be before starting the querying process. Don't assume that if someone likes it enough, they'll 'fix' it. The biggest mistake new writers make is starting the querying process before they—and the work—are ready. Take your time and do it right."

DIANA FINCH LITERARY AGENCY

116 W. 23rd St., Suite 500, New York NY 10011. (917)544-4470. E-mail: diana.finch@verizon.net. E-mail: diana.finch@verizon.net or via link at the website (preferred). Website: http://dianafinchliteraryagency.blogspot.com; www.facebook.com/DianaFinchLitAg. Contact: Diana Finch. A boutique agency in Manhattan's Chelsea neighborhood. "Many of the agency's clients are journalists, and I handle book-related magazine assignments as well as book deals. I am the chair of the AAR's International Committee, attend overseas book fairs, and actively handle foreign rights to my clients' work." Estab. 2003. Member of AAR. Represents 40 clients.

○ Seeking to represent books that change lives. Prior to opening her agency in 2003, Ms. Finch worked at Ellen Levine Literary Agency for 18 years and started her publishing career in the editorial department at St. Martin's Press.

REPRESENTS nonfiction, fiction, novels, scholarly books. Considers these nonfiction areas: autobiography, biography, business, child guidance, computers, cultural interests, current affairs, dance, diet/nutrition, economics, environment, ethnic, film, government, health, history, how-to, humor, investigative, juvenile nonfiction, law, medicine, memoirs, military, money, music, parenting, photography, popular culture, politics, psychology, satire, science, self-help, sex, sports, technology, theater, translation, true crime, war, women's issues, women's studies, young adult. Considers these fiction areas: action, adventure, contemporary issues, crime, detective, ethnic, historical, literary, mainstream, New Adult, police, sports, thriller, young adult.

☞ Does not want romance, mystery, or children's picture books.

HOW TO CONTACT This agency prefers submissions via its online form. Accepts simultaneous submissions. Obtains most new clients through recommendations from others.

TERMS Agent receives 15% commission on domestic sales; 20% commission on foreign sales. Offers written contract. "I charge for overseas postage, galleys, and books purchased, and try to recoup these costs from earnings received for a client, rather than charging outright."

RECENT SALES Stealing Schooling, by Professor Noliwe Rooks (The New Press); Merchants of Men, by Loretta Napoleoni (Seven Stories Press); Beyond $15, by Jonathan Rosenblum (Beacon Press); The Age of Inequality, by the Editors of In These Times (Verso Books); Seeds of Rebellion, by Mark Schapiro (Hot Books/Skyhorse).

WRITERS CONFERENCES Florida Writers Conference; Washington Writers Conference; Writers Digest NYC Conference; CLMP/New School conference, and more.

TIPS "Do as much research as you can on agents before you query. Have someone critique your query letter before you send it. It should be only 1 page and describe your book clearly—and why you are writing it—but also demonstrate creativity and a sense of your writing style."

FINEPRINT LITERARY MANAGEMENT

207 W. 106th St., Suite 1D, New York NY 10025. (212)279-1282. Website: www.fineprintlit.com. Estab. 2007. Member of AAR.

MEMBER AGENTS Peter Rubie, CEO, peter@fineprintlit.com (nonfiction: narrative nonfiction, popular science, spirituality, history, biography, pop culture, business, technology, parenting, health, self-help, music, food; fiction: literary thriller, crime fiction, science fiction and fantasy, military fiction and literary fiction, middle-grade, boy-oriented young adult fiction); Stephany Evans, stephany@fineprintlit.com (nonfiction: health and wellness, spirituality, lifestyle, food and drink, sustainability, running and fitness, memoir, narrative nonfiction; fiction: mystery/crime, women's fiction, from literary to commercial to romance); Laura Wood, laura@fineprintlit.com (serious nonfiction:, science and nature, business, history, religion, and other areas by academics, experienced professionals, journalists; select genre fiction only: science fiction and fantasy and mystery); June Clark, june@fineprintlit.com (nonfiction: entertainment, self-help, parenting, reference/how-to books, food and wine, style/beauty, prescriptive business titles); Jacqueline Murphy, jacqueline@fineprintlit.com.

REPRESENTS nonfiction, fiction, novels, short story collections. Considers these nonfiction areas: biography, business, cooking, cultural interests, current affairs, diet/nutrition, environment, foods, health, history, how-to, humor, investigative, medicine, memoirs, music, parenting, popular culture, psychology, science, self-help, spirituality, technology, travel, wom-

NEW AGENT SPOTLIGHT

RACHEL CRAWFORD
WOLF LITERARY SERVICES

www.wolflit.com
@RachAC

ABOUT RACHEL: Rachel Crawford is a literary agent and film rights manager at Wolf Literary Services. Hailing from sunny Brisbane, Australia, Rachel moved to New York in 2011. She worked previously at Sterling Lord Literistic and as an associate at Fletcher and Company, and has a background in rights and marketing.

SHE IS SEEKING: Rachel is looking for literary and commercial fiction and young adult. She's interested in stories that defy genre conventions and play with reader expectations, and particularly enjoys dystopian, eco-fiction, and apocalyptic narratives, as well as anything with a scientist protagonist. She's also looking for international fiction, political fiction that explores big ideas through compelling narrative, and stories from traditionally underrepresented voices. She loves stories about women by women. In nonfiction she's interested in tech, futurism, psychology, environment, and science, and isn't adverse to prescriptive nonfiction from authors with a strong professional background in their topic of choice.

HOW TO CONTACT: To submit a project to Rachel, please send a detailed synopsis and the first 50 pages to queries@wolflit.com, with "For Rachel" in the e-mail subject header.

en's issues, fitness, lifestyle. **Considers these fiction areas:** commercial, crime, fantasy, historical, literary, mainstream, middle-grade, mystery, romance, science fiction, suspense, thriller, women's, young adult.
HOW TO CONTACT E-query. For fiction, send a query, synopsis, bio, and 30 pages pasted into the e-mail. No attachments. For nonfiction, send a query only; proposal requested later if the agent is interested. Accepts simultaneous submissions. Obtains most new clients through recommendations from others, solicitations.
TERMS Agent receives 15% commission on domestic sales; 20% commission on foreign sales.

JAMES FITZGERALD AGENCY
118 Waverly Place, #1B, New York NY 10011. **E-mail:** submissions@jfitzagency.com. **Website:** www.jfitzagency.com. **Contact:** James Fitzgerald. "As an agency, we primarily represent books that reflect the popular culture of today being in the forms of fiction, nonfiction, graphic, and packaged books. Please submit all information in English even if your manuscript is in another language."

Prior to his current position, Mr. Fitzgerald was an editor at St. Martin's Press and Doubleday.

MEMBER AGENTS James Fitzgerald; Alice Bauer.

REPRESENTS nonfiction, fiction, graphic novels, packaged books.

HOW TO CONTACT Query via e-mail or snail mail. This agency's online submission guidelines explain all the elements they want to see when you submit a nonfiction book proposal. Accepts simultaneous submissions.

RECENT SALES A full and diverse list of titles are on this agency's website.

FLANNERY LITERARY

1140 Wickfield Ct., Naperville IL 60563. **E-mail:** jennifer@flanneryliterary.com. **Website:** flanneryliterary.com. **Contact:** Jennifer Flannery. "Flannery Literary is a Chicago-area literary agency representing writers of books for children and young adults, because the most interesting, well-written, and time-honored books are written with young people in mind." Estab. 1992. Represents 40 clients.

REPRESENTS nonfiction, fiction, novels, juvenile books. **Considers these nonfiction areas:** young adult. **Considers these fiction areas:** juvenile, middle-grade, New Adult, picture books, young adult.

☞ This agency specializes in children's and young adult fiction and nonfiction. It also accepts picture books. 100% juvenile books.

HOW TO CONTACT Query by e-mail only. "Multiple queries are fine, but please inform us. Please, no attachments. If you're sending a query about a novel, please include in the e-mail the first 5-10 pages; if it's a picture book, please include the entire text." Accepts simultaneous submissions. Responds in 2 weeks to queries, 1 month to mss. Obtains new clients through referrals, queries.

TERMS Agent receives 15% commission on domestic sales; 20% commission on foreign sales. Offers written contract, binding for life of book in print.

TIPS "Write an engrossing, succinct query describing your work. We are always looking for a fresh new voice."

FLETCHER & CO.

78 Fifth Ave., Third Floor, New York NY 10011. **E-mail:** info@fletcherandco.com. **Website:** www.fletcherandco.com. **Contact:** Christy Fletcher. Today, Fletcher & Co. is a full-service literary management and production company dedicated to writers of upmarket nonfiction as well as commercial and literary fiction. Estab. 2003. Member of AAR.

MEMBER AGENTS Christy Fletcher (referrals only); Melissa Chinchillo (select list of her own au-

thors); **Rebecca Gradinger** (literary fiction, up-market commercial fiction, narrative nonfiction, self-help, memoir, women's studies, humor, pop culture); **Gráinne Fox** (literary fiction, quality commercial authors, award-winning journalists and food writers, American voices, international, literary crime, upmarket fiction, narrative nonfiction); **Lisa Grubka** (fiction: literary, upmarket women's, young adult; and nonfiction: narrative, food, science, and more); **Sylvie Greenberg** (literary fiction, business, sports, science, memoir, history); **Donald Lamm** (history, biography, investigative journalism, politics, current affairs, business); **Todd Sattersten** (business); **Eric Lupfer**; **Sarah Fuentes**; **Veronica Goldstein**; **Mink Choi**; **Erin McFadden**.

REPRESENTS nonfiction, novels. **Considers these nonfiction areas:** biography, business, creative nonfiction, current affairs, foods, history, humor, investigative, memoirs, popular culture, politics, science, self-help, sports, women's studies. **Considers these fiction areas:** commercial, crime, literary, women's, young adult.

HOW TO CONTACT Send queries to info@fletcherandco.com. Please do not include e-mail attachments with your initial query, as they will be deleted. Address your query to a specific agent. No snail mail queries. Accepts simultaneous submissions.

RECENT SALES *The Profiteers*, by Sally Denton; *The Longest Night*, by Andrea Williams; *Disrupted: My Misadventure in the Start-Up Bubble*, by Dan Lyons; *Free Re-Fills: A Doctor Confronts His Addiction*, by Peter Grinspoon, M.D.; *Black Man in a White Coat: A Doctor's Reflections on Race and Medicine*, by Damon Tweedy, M.D.

FOLIO LITERARY MANAGEMENT, LLC

The Film Center Building, 630 Ninth Ave., Suite 1101, New York NY 10036. (212)400-1494. **Fax:** (212)967-0977. **Website:** www.foliolit.com. Member of AAR. Represents 100+ clients.

☺ Prior to creating Folio Literary Management, Mr. Hoffman worked for several years at another agency. Mr. Kleinman was an agent at Graybill & English.

MEMBER AGENTS Claudia Cross (romance novels, commercial women's fiction, cooking and food, serious nonfiction on religious and spiritual topics); **Scott Hoffman** (literary and commercial fiction, journalistic or academic nonfiction, narrative non-

fiction, pop culture books, business, history, politics, spiritual or religious-themed fiction and nonfiction, science fiction/fantasy literary fiction, heartbreaking memoirs, humorous nonfiction); **Jeff Kleinman** (bookclub fiction [not genre commercial like mystery or romances], literary fiction, thriller and suspense novels, narrative nonfiction, memoir); **Dado Derviskadic** (nonfiction: cultural history, biography, memoir, pop science, motivational self-help, health/nutrition, pop culture, cookbooks; fiction that's gritty, introspective, or serious); **Frank Weimann** (biography, business/investing/finance, history, religious, mind/body/spirit, health, lifestyle, cookbooks, sports, African-American, science, memoir, special forces/CIA/FBI/Mafia, military, prescriptive nonfiction, humor, celebrity, adult and children's fiction); **Michael Harriot** (commercial nonfiction (both narrative and prescriptive) and fantasy/science fiction); **Erin Harris** (book club, historical fiction, literary, narrative nonfiction, psychological suspense, young adult); **Katherine Latshaw** (blogs-to-books, food/cooking, middle-grade, narrative and prescriptive nonfiction); **Annie Hwang** (literary and upmarket fiction with commercial appeal; select nonfiction: popular science, diet/health/fitness, lifestyle, narrative nonfiction, pop culture, humor); **Erin Niumata** (fiction: commercial women's fiction, romance, historical fiction, mystery, psychological thriller, suspense, humor; nonfiction: self-help, women's issues, pop culture and humor, pet care/pets, memoirs, anything blogger); **Ruth Pomerance** (narrative nonfiction and commercial fiction); **Marcy Posner** (adult: commercial women's fiction, historical fiction, mystery, biography, history, health, lifestyle, commercial novels, thriller, narrative nonfiction; children's: contemporary young adult and Middle-grade, mystery series for boys, select historical fiction, fantasy); **Jeff Silberman** (narrative nonfiction, biography, history, politics, current affairs, health, lifestyle, humor, food/cookbook, memoir, pop culture, sports, science, technology; commercial, literary, book club fiction); **Steve Troha; Emily van Beek** (YA, Middle-grade, picture books), **Melissa White** (general nonfiction, literary and commercial fiction, Middle-grade, young adult); **John Cusick** (middle-grade, picture books, young adult); **Jamie Chambliss.**
REPRESENTS nonfiction, novels. **Considers these nonfiction areas:** animals, art, biography, business,

cooking, creative nonfiction, economics, environment, foods, health, history, how-to, humor, inspirational, memoirs, military, parenting, popular culture, politics, psychology, religious, satire, science, self-help, technology, war, women's issues, women's studies. **Considers these fiction areas:** commercial, fantasy, horror, literary, middle-grade, mystery, picture books, religious, romance, thriller, women's, young adult.

No poetry, stage plays, or screenplays.
HOW TO CONTACT Query via e-mail only (no attachments). Read agent bios online for specific submission guidelines and e-mail addresses, and to check if someone is closed to queries. "All agents respond to queries as soon as possible, whether interested or not. If you haven't heard back from the individual agent within the time period specified on his or her bio page, it's possible that something has gone wrong and your query has been lost—in that case, please e-mail a follow-up."
TIPS "Please do not submit simultaneously to more than one agent at Folio. If you're not sure which of us is exactly right for your book, don't worry; we work closely as a team, and if one of our agents gets a query that might be more appropriate for someone else, we'll always pass it along. It's important that you check each agent's bio page for clear directions as to how to submit, as well as when to expect feedback."

FOUNDRY LITERARY + MEDIA
33 W. 17th St., PH, New York NY 10011. (212)929-5064. **Fax:** (212)929-5471. **Website:** www.foundrymedia.com.
MEMBER AGENTS Peter McGuigan, pmsubmissions@foundrymedia.com (smart, offbeat voices in all genres of fiction and nonfiction); **Yfat Reiss Gendell**, yrgsubmissions@foundrymedia.com (practical nonfiction: health and wellness, diet, lifestyle, how-to, parenting; narrative nonfiction: humor, memoir, history, science, pop culture, psychology, adventure/travel stories; unique commercial fiction, including young adult fiction, that touch on her nonfiction interests, including speculative fiction, thriller, historical fiction); **Chris Park**, cpsubmissions@foundrymedia.com (memoirs, narrative nonfiction, sports books, Christian nonfiction, character-driven fiction); **Hannah Brown Gordon**, hbgsubmissions@foundrymedia.com (stories and narratives that blend genres, including thriller, suspense, historical, literary, speculative, memoir, pop-science, psychol-

ogy, humor, pop culture); **Brandi Bowles**, bbsubmissions@foundrymedia.com (nonfiction: cookbooks to prescriptive books, science, pop culture, real-life inspirational stories; high-concept novels that feature strong female bonds and psychological or scientific themes); **Kirsten Neuhaus**, knsubmissions@foundrymedia.com (platform-driven narrative nonfiction: memoir, business, lifestyle [beauty/fashion/relationships], current events, history, stories with strong female voices; smart fiction that appeals to a wide market); **Jessica Regel**, jrsubmissions@foundrymedia.com (young adult and middle-grade books, as well as a select list of adult general fiction, women's fiction, adult nonfiction); **Anthony Mattero**, amsubmissions@foundrymedia.com (smart, platform-driven nonfiction: pop culture, humor, music, sports, pop-business); **Peter Steinberg**, pssubmissions@foundrymedia.com (narrative nonfiction, commercial and literary fiction, memoir, health, history, lifestyle, humor, sports, young adult); **Roger Freet**, rfsubmissions@foundrymedia.com (narrative and idea-driven nonfictio:n religion, spirituality, memoir, cultural issues by leading scholars, pastors, historians, activists and musicians); **Adriann Ranta**, arsubmissions@foundrymedia.com (accepts all genres and age groups; loves gritty, realistic, true-to-life narratives; women's fiction and nonfiction; accessible, pop nonfiction in science, history, craft; smart, fresh, genre-bending works for children).

REPRESENTS Considers these nonfiction areas: creative nonfiction, current affairs, diet/nutrition, health, history, how-to, humor, medicine, memoirs, music, parenting, popular culture, psychology, science, sports, travel. **Considers these fiction areas:** commercial, historical, humor, literary, middle-grade, suspense, thriller, women's, young adult.

HOW TO CONTACT Target one agent only. Send queries to the specific submission e-mail of the agent. For fiction, send query, synopsis, author bio, first 3 chapters—all pasted in the e-mail. For nonfiction, send query, sample chapters, TOC, author bio (all pasted). "We regret that we cannot guarantee a response to every submission we receive. If you do not receive a response within 8 weeks, your submission is not right for our lists at this time." Accepts simultaneous submissions.

TIPS "Consult website for each agent's submission instructions."

FOX LITERARY

110 W. 40th St., Suite 2305, New York NY 10018. **E-mail:** submissions@foxliterary.com. **Website:** foxliterary.com. Fox Literary is a boutique agency that represents commercial fiction, along with select works of literary fiction and nonfiction that have broad commercial appeal.

MEMBER AGENTS Diana Fox.

REPRESENTS nonfiction, fiction, graphic novels. **Considers these nonfiction areas:** biography, creative nonfiction, history, popular culture, mind/body/spirit. **Considers these fiction areas:** fantasy, historical, romance, science fiction, thriller, young adult, general.

HOW TO CONTACT E-mail query and first 5 pages in body of e-mail; e-mail queries preferred. No e-mail attachments. For snail mail queries, must include an e-mail address for response and no response means "No." Do not send SASE. Accepts simultaneous submissions.

LYNN C. FRANKLIN ASSOCIATES, LTD.

1350 Broadway, Suite 2015, New York NY 10018. (212)868-6311. **E-mail:** agency@franklinandsiegal.com. **Website:** www.publishersmarketplace.com/members/LynnCFranklin. **Contact:** Lynn Franklin, president; Claudia Nys, foreign rights.

REPRESENTS nonfiction. **Considers these nonfiction areas:** biography, current affairs, memoirs, psychology, self-help, spirituality, alternative medicine.

> Primary interest lies in nonfiction (memoir, biography, current affairs, spirituality, psychology/self-help, alternative medicine, etc.).

HOW TO CONTACT Query via e-mail to agency@franklinandsiegal.com. No unsolicited mss. No attachments. For nonfiction, send query letter with short outline and synopsis. For fiction, send query letter with short synopsis and a maximum of 10 sample pages (in the body of the e-mail). Accepts simultaneous submissions.

FRASER-BUB LITERARY, LLC

401 Park Avenue South, 10th Floor, New York NY 10016. (917)524-6982. **E-mail:** mackenzie@fraserbubliterary.com. **E-mail:** submissions@fraserbubliterary.com. **Website:** http://www.fraserbubliterary.com/. "Fraser-Bub Literary enthusiastically capitalizes on all subsidiary rights platforms, including eBook, audio, serial, performance, and translation rights. MacKenzie Fraser-Bub has a solid network of media professionals that can be called upon to assist

her in implementing her clients' goals; these include eBook experts, film and TV agents, scouts, and publicity and marketing gurus. " Estab. 2016.

○ MacKenzie Fraser-Bub began her career in publishing as a teenager reading manuscripts and writing readers reports at the Crown Publishing Group, a division of Penguin Random House. She is a veteran of the Columbia Publishing Course, having taught and worked there. She also spent several years at Simon and Schuster (Touchstone Books), in one of the industry's finest marketing departments, before becoming an agent at the venerable Trident Media Group.

MEMBER AGENTS MacKenzie Fraser-Bub; **Linda Kaplan** (subrights director);, **Kasey Poserina** (contracts director).

REPRESENTS nonfiction, fiction, novels. **Considers these nonfiction areas:** cooking, diet/nutrition, design, foods, psychology, self-help, true crime, fashion, exercise, relationships. **Considers these fiction areas:** crime, historical, mystery, New Adult, romance, thriller, women's, young adult.

○— "99.9% of the time I am not interested in science, fantasy, westerns, philosophy, sports. I am never interested in children's/picture books, middle-grade, screenplays, poetry, graphic novels/comics."

HOW TO CONTACT E-mail your query to submissions@fraserbubliterary.com. Include the word "Query" in your subject line. For fiction submissions, your query may include the first chapter in the body of the e-mail. For nonfiction submissions, your query may include the first 10 pages in the body of the e-mail. No attachments. Accepts simultaneous submissions. Responds in 1 week for queries, 6 weeks for mss.

JEANNE FREDERICKS LITERARY AGENCY, INC.

221 Benedict Hill Rd., New Canaan CT 06840. (203)972-3011. **Fax:** (203)972-3011. **E-mail:** jeanne.fredericks@gmail.com. **Website:** www.jeannefredericks.com. **Contact:** Jeanne Fredericks. "The Jeanne Fredericks Literary Agency specializes in representing quality adult nonfiction by experts in their fields. We particularly enjoy working with authors who communicate important new information that will make a positive difference in the lives of a sizable population.

We are more likely to represent authors who understand the importance of having a marketing platform and have already secured media placements and significant social media followings." Estab. 1997. Member of AAR, Authors Guild. Represents 75+ clients.

○ Prior to opening her agency in 1997, Ms. Fredericks was an agent and acting director with the Susan P. Urstadt, Inc. Agency. Previously, she was the editorial director of Ziff-Davis Books and managing editor and acquisitions editor at Macmillan Publishing Company.

REPRESENTS nonfiction. **Considers these nonfiction areas:** Americana, animals, autobiography, biography, child guidance, cooking, decorating, diet/nutrition, environment, foods, gardening, health, history, how-to, interior design, medicine, parenting, photography, psychology, self-help, women's issues.

○— This agency specializes in quality adult nonfiction by authorities in their fields. "We do not handle fiction, true crime, juvenile, textbooks, poetry, essays, screenplays, short stories, science fiction, pop culture, guides to computers and software, politics, horror, pornography, books on overly depressing or violent topics, romance, teachers manuals, or memoirs."

HOW TO CONTACT Query first by e-mail, then send outline/proposal, 1-2 sample chapters, if requested and after you have consulted the submission guidelines on the agency website. If you do send requested submission materials, include the word "Requested" in the subject line. Accepts simultaneous submissions. Responds in 3-5 weeks to queries, 2-4 months to mss. Obtains most new clients through recommendations from others, solicitations, conferences.

TERMS Agent receives 15% commission on domestic sales; 25% commission on foreign sales with co-agent. Offers written contract, binding for 9 months; 2-month notice must be given to terminate contract. Charges client for photocopying of whole proposals and mss, overseas postage, expedited mail services. Almost all submissions are made electronically so these charges rarely apply.

RECENT SALES *Yoga Therapy*, by Larry Payne, Ph.D., Terra Gold, D.O.M., and Eden Goldman, D.C. (Basic Health); *The Creativity Cure*, by Carrie Alton, M.D. and Alton Barron, M.D. (Scribner); *For Sale—*

NEW AGENT SPOTLIGHT

JENNIFER WILLS
THE SEYMOUR AGENCY

www.theseymouragency.com
@WillsWork4Books

ABOUT JENNIFER: Jennifer has five years of experience in some of the publishing industry's leading literary agencies. She worked with publishers around the world as an assistant in Trident Media Group's huge foreign rights department, and with domestic publishers as an assistant at Writers House (where, incidentally, she began her career as an intern). She joined The Seymour Agency in April 2016, where she has quickly moved up the ranks to associate agent. Jennifer has always loved helping fledgling authors become *New York Times* bestsellers and she's ready to be a relentless champion for her own clients' work. You can find her on Twitter.

SHE IS SEEKING: Jennifer is particularly interested in a wide range of picture books and cookbooks, with a soft spot for author/illustrators of sweet and wacky picture books, and cookbooks with mouth-watering recipes of the health conscious, budget friendly or celebrity chef variety. For fiction, she's also interested in middle-grade and young adult with a science fiction/fantasy, horror/suspense, or contemporary bent, and upmarket women's fiction with a sense of humor. On the nonfiction side, narrative nonfiction and memoir are also welcome. Jennifer tends to shy away from rhyming picture books, historical fiction, and high fantasy, although she's willing to make exceptions. If your manuscript has a great hook, a distinct voice, and can make her laugh out loud or ugly cry (or, even better, both), she'd love to see it.

HOW TO SUBMIT: Please submit your query letter, first five pages and synopsis in the body of an e-mail to jennifer@theseymouragency.com. You can find some helpful information on querying in general at www.theseymouragency.com/submissions. No snail mail, please.

America's Paradise, by Willie Drye (Lyons); *Lilias! Yoga,* by Lilias Folan (Skyhorse).
TIPS "Be sure to research competition for your work and be able to justify why there's a need for your book.

I enjoy building an author's career, particularly if he/she is professional, hardworking, and courteous, and actively involved in establishing a marketing platform. Aside from 25 years of agenting experience, I've had

10 years of editorial experience in adult trade book publishing that enables me to help an author polish a proposal so that it's more appealing to prospective editors. My MBA in marketing also distinguishes me from other agents."

GRACE FREEDSON'S PUBLISHING NETWORK

7600 Jericho Turnpike, Suite 300, Woodbury NY 11797. (516)931-7757. **Fax:** (516)931-7759. **E-mail:** gfreedson@gmail.com. **Contact:** Grace Freedson. The Publishing Network is a literary agency and book packager. "We consult on a number of publishing concerns including, peer evaluation, content review, ghost writing, and contracts." Estab. 2000. Member of AAR, Women's Media Group, Authors' Guild. Represents 100 clients.

○ Prior to becoming an agent, Ms. Freedson was a managing editor and director of acquisition for Barron's Educational Series.

REPRESENTS nonfiction, scholarly books. **Considers these nonfiction areas:** animals, business, child guidance, computers, cooking, crafts, creative nonfiction, current affairs, diet/nutrition, economics, education, environment, foods, gardening, health, history, hobbies, horticulture, how-to, humor, inspirational, interior design, juvenile nonfiction, language, law, medicine, memoirs, metaphysics, money, multicultural, parenting, philosophy, popular culture, psychology, recreation, regional, satire, science, self-help, sports, technology, true crime, war, women's issues, women's studies. **Considers these script areas:** test preparation.

☞ "In addition to representing many qualified authors, I work with publishers as a packager of unique projects—mostly series." Actively seeking true crime and science for the general reader. Does not want to receive fiction.

HOW TO CONTACT Query with SASE. Submit synopsis, SASE. Responds in 2-6 weeks to queries. Obtains most new clients through recommendations from others.

TERMS Agent receives 15% commission on domestic sales. Offers written contract; 30-day notice must be given to terminate contract.

RECENT SALES *If He's So Great, Why Do I Feel So Bad*, by Avery Neal (Citadel); *Southern Appalachian Cooking: New and Traditional Recipes*, by John Tullock (Countryman Press); *Mad City: The True Story of the Campus Murders that America Forgot*, by Dr. Michael Arntfield (Little A).

WRITERS CONFERENCES BookExpo of America.

TIPS "At this point, I am only reviewing proposals on nonfiction topics by credentialed authors with platforms."

SARAH JANE FREYMANN LITERARY AGENCY

(212)362-9277. **E-mail:** sarah@sarahjanefreymann.com, submissions@sarahjanefreymann.com. **Website:** www.sarahjanefreymann.com. **Contact:** Sarah Jane Freymann, Steve Schwartz.

MEMBER AGENTS Sarah Jane Freymann (nonfiction: spiritual, psychology, self-help, women/men's issues, books by health experts [conventional and alternative], cookbooks, narrative nonfiction, natural science, nature, memoirs, cutting-edge journalism, travel, multicultural issues, parenting, lifestyle, fiction: literary, mainstream young adult); **Jessica Sinsheimer**, jessica@sarahjanefreymann.com; **Steven Schwartz**, steve@sarahjanefreymann.com (popular fiction [crime, thriller, historical novels], world and national affairs, business books, self-help, psychology, humor, sports, travel).

REPRESENTS nonfiction, fiction, novels. **Considers these nonfiction areas:** business, cooking, creative nonfiction, current affairs, health, humor, memoirs, multicultural, parenting, psychology, science, self-help, spirituality, sports, travel, women's issues, men's issues, nature, journalism, lifestyle. **Considers these fiction areas:** crime, historical, literary, mainstream, thriller, young adult, popular fiction.

HOW TO CONTACT Query via e-mail. No attachments. Below the query, please paste the first 10 pages of your work. Accepts simultaneous submissions.

TERMS Charges clients for long distance, overseas postage, photocopying. 100% of business is derived from commissions on ms sales.

FREDRICA S. FRIEDMAN AND CO., INC.

857 Fifth Ave., New York NY 10065. (212)639-9455. **E-mail:** info@fredricafriedman.com, submissions@fredricafriedman.com. **Website:** www.fredricafriedman.com. **Contact:** Chandler Smith.

○ Prior to establishing her own literary management firm, Ms. Friedman was the editorial director, associate publisher and vice president of Little, Brown & Co., a division of Time Warner, and the first woman to hold those positions.

REPRESENTS nonfiction, fiction.

Does not want poetry, plays, screenplays, children's picture books, science fiction/fantasy, or horror.

HOW TO CONTACT Submit e-query, synopsis; be concise and include any pertinent author information, including relevant writing history. If you are a fiction writer, submit the first 10 pages of your manuscript. Keep all material in the body of the e-mail. Accepts simultaneous submissions. Responds in 6 weeks.

REBECCA FRIEDMAN LITERARY AGENCY

E-mail: brandie@rfliterary.com. **Website:** www.rfliterary.com. Estab. 2013. Member of AAR. Signatory of WGA.

Prior to opening her own agency in 2013, Ms. Friedman was with Sterling Lord Literistic from 2006 to 2011, then with Hill Nadell Agency.

MEMBER AGENTS Rebecca Friedman (commercial and literary fiction, with a focus on literary novels of suspense, women's fiction, contemporary romance, young adult; journalistic nonfiction and memoir); **Susan Finesman**, susan@rfliterary.com (fiction, cookbooks, lifestyle); **Abby Schulman**, abby@rfliterary.com (YA and nonfiction: health, wellness, personal development); **Brandie Coonis**, brandie@rfliterary.com (writers that defy genre).

REPRESENTS nonfiction, fiction. **Considers these nonfiction areas:** cooking, health, memoirs, journalistic nonfiction. **Considers these fiction areas:** commercial, fantasy, literary, mystery, New Adult, romance, science fiction, suspense, women's, young adult.

HOW TO CONTACT Please submit your query letter and first chapter (no more than 15 pages, double-spaced). If querying Kimberly, paste a full synopsis into the e-mail submission; no attachments. Accepts simultaneous submissions. Tries to respond in 6-8 weeks.

RECENT SALES A complete list of agency authors is available online.

THE FRIEDRICH AGENCY

19 W. 21st St., Suite 201, New York NY 10010. (212)317-8810. **E-mail:** mfriedrich@friedrichagency.com; lcarson@friedrichagency.com; kwolf@friedrichagency.com. **Website:** www.friedrichagency.

com. **Contact:** Molly Friedrich; Lucy Carson; Kent D. Wolf. Estab. 2006. Member of AAR. Signatory of WGA. Represents 50+ clients.

Prior to her current position, Ms. Friedrich was an agent at the Aaron Priest Literary Agency.

MEMBER AGENTS **Molly Friedrich**, founder and agent; **Lucy Carson**, TV/film rights director and agent; **Kent D. Wolf**, foreign rights director and agent.

REPRESENTS nonfiction, fiction, novels, short story collections. **Considers these nonfiction areas:** creative nonfiction, memoirs. **Considers these fiction areas:** commercial, literary, multicultural, suspense, women's, young adult.

HOW TO CONTACT Query by e-mail only. Please query only one agent at this agency. Accepts simultaneous submissions.

RECENT SALES *W is for Wasted*, by Sue Grafton; *Olive Kitteridge*, by Elizabeth Strout. Other clients include Frank McCourt, Jane Smiley, Esmeralda Santiago, Terry McMillan, Cathy Schine, Ruth Ozeki, Karen Joy Fowler.

FULL CIRCLE LITERARY, LLC

3268 Governor Dr. #323, San Diego CA 92122. **E-mail:** info@fullcircleliterary.com. **Website:** www.fullcircleliterary.com. **Contact:** Stefanie Von Borstel. "Full Circle Literary is a full-service literary agency, offering a full-circle approach to literary representation. Our team has diverse experience in book publishing, including editorial, marketing, publicity, legal, and rights, which we use collectively to build careers book by book. We work with both award-winning veteran and debut writers and artists, and our team has a knack for finding and developing new and diverse talent. Learn more about our agency and submission guidelines by visiting our website." This agency goes into depth about what they are seeking and submission guidelines on its website. Estab. 2005. Member of AAR, SCBWI, Authors Guild. Represents 100+ clients.

MEMBER AGENTS Stefanie Von Borstel; Adriana Dominguez; Taylor Martindale Kean (multicultural voices); **Lilly Ghahremani**.

REPRESENTS **Considers these nonfiction areas:** creative nonfiction, how-to, interior design, multicultural, women's issues, young adult. **Considers these fiction areas:** literary, middle-grade, multicultural, picture books, women's, young adult.

Actively seeking nonfiction by authors with a unique voice and strong platform, projects that offer new and diverse viewpoints, and literature with a global or multicultural perspective. "We are particularly interested in books with a Latino or Middle Eastern angle."

HOW TO CONTACT Online submissions only via submissions form online. Please complete the form and submit cover letter, author information and sample writing. For fiction, include the first 10 ms pages. For nonfiction, include a proposal with 1 sample chapter. Accepts simultaneous submissions. "Due to the high volume of submissions, please keep in mind that we are no longer able to personally respond to every submission. If you have not heard from us in 6-8 weeks, your project is not right for our agency at the current time and we wish you all the best with your writing."

TERMS Agent receives 15% commission on domestic sales; 25% commission on foreign sales. Offers written contract that outlines responsibilities of the author and the agent.

FUSE LITERARY

Foreword Literary, Inc. dba Fuse Literary, P.O. Box 258, La Honda CA 94020. **E-mail:** info@fuseliterary. com. **E-mail:** query[firstnameofagent]@fuseliterary. com. **Website:** www.fuseliterary.com. **Contact:** Contact one agent directly via e-mail. Estab. 2013. Member of RWA, SCBWI. Represents 100+ clients.

MEMBER AGENTS Laurie McLean (only accepting referral inquiries and submissions requested at conferences or online events, with the exception of unsolicited adult and children's science fiction); **Gordon Warnock**, querygordon@fuseliterary.com (fiction: high-concept commercial fiction, literary fiction [adults through young adult], graphic novels [adults through Middle-grade]; nonfiction: memoir [adult, young adult, NA, graphic], cookbooks/food narrative/food studies, illustrated/art/photography [especially graphic nonfiction], political and current events, pop science, pop culture [especially punk culture and geek culture], self-help, how-to, humor, pets, business and career); **Connor Goldsmith**, queryconnor@fuseliterary.com (fiction: science fiction/fantasy/horror, thriller, upmarket commercial fiction with a unique and memorable hook; books by and about people from marginalized perspectives, such as LGBTQ people and/or racial minorities; nonfiction [from recognized experts with established platforms]: history [particularly of the ancient world], theater, cinema, music, television, mass media, popular culture, feminism and gender studies, LGBTQ issues, race relations, the sex industry); **Michelle Richter**, querymichelle@ fuseliterary.com (primarily seeking fiction, specifically book club reads, literary fiction, mystery/suspense/thriller; for nonfiction: fashion, pop culture, science/medicine, sociology/social trends, economics); **Emily S. Keyes**, queryemily@fuseliterary.com (young adult, middle-grade, select commercial fiction, including fantasy & science fiction, women's fiction, New Adult fiction, pop culture, humor); **Tricia Skinner**, query-tricia@fuseliterary.com (Romance: science fiction, futuristic, fantasy, military/special ops, medieval historical; brand new relationships; diversity); **Jennifer Chen Tran**, queryjennifer@fuseliterary.com (literary fiction, commercial fiction, women's fiction, upmarket fiction, contemporary romance, mature young adult, New Adult, suspense/thriller, select graphic novels [adult, young adult, Middle-grade]; memoir, narrative nonfiction in the areas of adventure, biography, business, current affairs, medical, history, how-to, pop-culture, psychology, social entrepreneurism, social justice, travel, lifestyle books [home, design, fashion, food].

HOW TO CONTACT E-query an individual agent. Check the website to see if any individual agent is closed to submissions, as well each agent's individual submission preferences. (You can find these details by clicking on 'Team Fuse' and then clicking on each agent's photo.) Usually responds in 4-6 weeks, but sometimes more if an agent is exceptionally busy. Check each agent's bio/submissions page on the website. Only accepts e-mailed queries that follow online guidelines.

TERMS "We earn 15% on negotiated deals for books and with our co-agents earn between 20-30% on foreign translation deals depending on the territory; 20% on TV/movies/plays. Other multimedia deals are so new there is no established commission rate. The author has the last say, approving or not approving all deals." After the initial 90-day period, there is a 30-day termination of the agency agreement clause. No fees.

RECENT SALES Seven-figure deal for *NYT* bestseller Julie Kagawa (YA); mid-six-figure deal for Michael J. Sullivan (fantasy); quarter-million-dollar deal for Melissa D. Savage (Middle-grade); *First*

Watch, by Dale Lucas (fantasy); *Elektra's Adventures in Tragedy*, by Douglas Rees (YA); Runebinder Trilogy, by Alex Kahler (YA); *Perceptual Intelligence*, by Dr. Brian Boxler Wachler (science); *Game Programming for Artists*, by Huntley & Brady (how-to); *Pay Day*, by Kellye Garrett (mystery); *Reality Star*, by Laura Heffernan (women's fiction); *Everything We Keep, Things We Leave Behind*, by Kerry Lonsdale (women's fiction); *Maggie and Abby's Neverending Pillow Fort*, by Will Taylor (Middle-grade); *The Sky Between You and Me*, by Catherine Alene (YA).

THE G AGENCY, LLC

P.O. Box 374, Bronx NY 10471. **E-mail:** gagencyquery@gmail.com. **Website:** www.publishersmarketplace.com/members/jeffg. **Contact:** Jeff Gerecke. Estab. 2012. Member of AAR.
MEMBER AGENTS Jeff Gerecke.
REPRESENTS nonfiction, fiction. **Considers these nonfiction areas:** biography, business, computers, history, military, money, popular culture, technology. **Considers these fiction areas:** historical, mainstream, military, mystery, suspense, thriller, war.
HOW TO CONTACT E-mail submissions required. Please attach sample chapters or proposal. Enter "QUERY" along with the title in the subject line of e-mails. "I cannot guarantee replies to every submission. If you do not hear from me the first time, you may send me one reminder. I encourage you to make multiple submissions but want to know that is the case if I ask for a manuscript to read." Accepts simultaneous submissions.
RECENT SALES *The Race for Paradise*, by Paul Cobb (Oxford UP); *Barles Story*, by Else Poulsen (Greystone); *Weed Land*, by Peter Hecht (University of California Press); *Nothin' But Blue Skies*, by Edward McClelland (Bloomsbury); *Tear Down*, by Gordon Young (University of California Press).

GALLT AND ZACKER LITERARY AGENCY

273 Charlton Ave., South Orange NJ 07079. (973)761-6358. **Website:** www.galltzacker.com. **Contact:** Nancy Gallt, Marietta Zacker. "At the Gallt and Zacker Literary Agency, we represent people, not projects, and we focus solely on writers and illustrators of children's books." Estab. 2000. Represents 60 clients.

○ Ms. Gallt was subsidiary rights director of the children's book division at Morrow, Harper and Viking. Ms. Zacker started her career as a teacher, championing children's and young adult books, then worked in the children's book world, bookselling, marketing, and editing.

MEMBER AGENTS Nancy Gallt, **Marietta Zacker**.
REPRESENTS Considers these fiction areas: juvenile, middle-grade, picture books, young adult.

☛ Actively seeking author/illustrators who create books for young adults and younger readers.

HOW TO CONTACT Submit through online submission form on agency website. No e-mail queries, please. Accepts simultaneous submissions. Obtains new clients through submissions, conferences and recommendations from others.
TERMS Agent receives 15% commission on domestic sales; commission on foreign sales. Offers written contract; 30-day notice must be given to terminate contract.
RECENT SALES Rick Riordan's books (Hyperion); *This Is It*, by Daria Peoples (Harper); *Playing Possum*, by Jennifer Black Reinhardt (Clarion/HMH); *Brave Molly*, by Brooke Boynton Hughes (Chronicle); *Brown Baby Lullaby*, by Tameka Fryer Brown (Macmillan); *Fenway and Hattie Up to New Tricks*, by Victoria J. Coe (Putnam/Penguin); *Caterpillar Summer*, by Gillian McDunn (Bloomsbury); *The Kids Are Alright*, by Dana Alison Levy (Delacorte/Random House); *Namesake*, by Paige Britt (Scholastic); *The Turning*, by Emily Whitman (Harper); *Rot*, by Ben Clanton (Simon & Schuster).
TIPS "Writing and illustrations stand on their own, so submissions should tell the most compelling stories possible—whether visually, in narrative, or both."

THE GARAMOND AGENCY, INC.

1840 Columbia Rd. NW, #503, Washington DC 20009. **E-mail:** query@garamondagency.com. **Website:** www.garamondagency.com. Memberships include the Author's Guild.
MEMBER AGENTS Lisa Adams, David Miller.
REPRESENTS nonfiction. **Considers these nonfiction areas:** anthropology, archeology, biography, business, creative nonfiction, current affairs, economics, environment, government, history, law, medicine, parenting, politics, psychology, science, sociology, sports, technology, women's issues.

☛ "We work closely with our authors through each stage of the publishing process, first in developing their books and then in presenting

NEW AGENT SPOTLIGHT

ELIZABETH COPPS
MARIA CARVAINIS AGENCY

www.mariacarvainisagency.com
@escopps

ABOUT ELIZABETH: I migrated from Florida to start my career with Maria Carvainis Agency as an intern in 2010. In 2011, I signed on with the agency as a full-time assistant, and two years later I was promoted to Associate Agent. For me, the very best books are timeless, thought provoking, and discussion spurring. I want to see characters who burst off the page and elicit some sort of emotional response in their readers. There are only so many settings and themes to expound on, but every single person is different which means there are limitless combinations of character traits a writer can play with. That's pretty amazing. The King said it best regarding what it means to create a complex character: "Bad writing usually arises from a stubborn refusal to tell stories about what people actually do–to face the fact, let us say, that murderers sometimes help old ladies cross the street."

SHE IS SEEKING: I represent a wide range of genres from middle-grade and young adult, to adult contemporary and literary fiction, mystery, psychological thriller, women's fiction, historical fiction, horror, and select nonfiction projects. I'm an equal fan of hilarious stories as well as dark, gritty and sinister reads.

HOW TO SUBMIT: Please send a query letter, a synopsis of the work, first 5-10 pages, and note of any writing credentials. Please email queries to mca@mariacarvainisagency.com. All attachments must be either Word documents or PDF files.

themselves and their ideas effectively to publishers and to readers. We represent our clients throughout the world in all languages, media, and territories through an extensive network of subagents." No proposals for children's or young adult books, fiction, poetry, or memoir.
HOW TO CONTACT "Queries sent by e-mail may not make it through the spam filters on our server. Please e-mail a brief query letter only; we do not read unsolicited manuscripts submitted by e-mail

under any circumstances. See our website." Accepts simultaneous submissions.
RECENT SALES *Data Capitalism*, by Viktor Mayer-Schoenberger and Thomas Ramiddle-gradee (Basic Books); *Occupying Boston*, by Serena Zabin (Houghton Mifflin Harcourt; *A Most Elegant Equation*, by David Stipp; *$2.00 a Day*, by Kathryn Edin and H. Luke Shaefer (Houghton Mifflin Harcourt).
TIPS "Query us first if you have any questions about whether we are the right agency for your work."

MAX GARTENBERG LITERARY AGENCY

912 N. Pennsylvania Ave., young adultrdley PA
19067. (215)295-9230. **Website:** www.maxgarten-
berg.com. **Contact:** Anne Devlin (nonfiction). Estab.
1954. Represents 100 clients.
MEMBER AGENTS Anne G. Devlin (current
events, politics, true crime, women's issues, sports,
parenting, biography, environment, narrative nonfiction, health, lifestyle, celebrity).
REPRESENTS novels. **Considers these nonfiction
areas:** animals, art, biography, current affairs, film,
health, history, money, music, psychology, science,
sports, true crime.
HOW TO CONTACT Writers desirous of having
their work handled by this agency may query by
e-mail to agdevlin@aol.com. Accepts simultaneous submissions. Responds in 2 weeks to queries, 6
weeks to mss. Obtains most new clients through
recommendations from others, following up on
good query letters.
TERMS Agent receives 15% commission on domestic sales; 20% commission on foreign sales.
RECENT SALES *The Enlightened College Appli-
cant*, by Andrew Belasco (Rowman and Littlefield);
Beethoven for Kids: His Life and Music, by Helen
Bauer (Chicago Review Press); *Portrait of a Past Life
Skeptic*, by Robert L. Snow (Llewellyn Books); *What
Patients Taught Me*, by Audrey Young, MD (Sas-
quatch Books); *Unorthodox Warfare: The Chinese
Experience*, by Ralph D. Sawyer (Westview Press);
Encyclopedia of Earthquakes and Volcanoes, by Al-
exander E. Gates (Facts on File); *Starved*, by Ann
McTiernan, M.D., PhD (Central Recovery Press).
TIPS "We have recently expanded to allow more ac-
cess for new writers."

GELFMAN SCHNEIDER/ICM PARTNERS

850 Seventh Ave., Suite 903, New York NY 10019. **E-
mail:** mail@gelfmanschneider.com. **Website:** www.
gelfmanschneider.com. **Contact:** Jane Gelfman, Deborah Schneider. Member of AAR. Represents 300+
clients.
MEMBER AGENTS Deborah Schneider (all categories of literary and commercial fiction and nonfiction); **Jane Gelfman**; **Heather Mitchell** (particularly
interested in narrative nonfiction, historical fiction,
young debut authors with strong voices); **Penelope
Burns**, penelope.gsliterary@gmail.com (literary

and commercial fiction and nonfiction, a variety of
young adult and middle-grade).
REPRESENTS nonfiction, fiction, juvenile books.
Considers these nonfiction areas: creative nonfiction, popular culture. **Considers these fiction areas:** commercial, fantasy, historical, literary, mainstream, middle-grade, mystery, science fiction, suspense, women's, young adult.

"Among our diverse list of clients are novelists, journalists, playwrights, scientists, activists and humorists writing narrative nonfiction, memoir, political and current affairs,
popular science and popular culture nonfiction, as well as literary and commercial fiction, women's fiction, and historical fiction."
Does not currently accept screenplays or
scripts, poetry, or picture book queries.
HOW TO CONTACT Query. Check Submissions
page of website to see which agents are open to queries and further instructions. Accepts simultaneous
submissions.
TERMS Agent receives 15% commission on domestic
sales; 20% commission on foreign sales; 15% commission on film sales. Offers written contract. Charges clients for photocopying and messengers/couriers.

THE GERNERT COMPANY

136 E. 57th St., New York NY 10022. (212)838-7777.
E-mail: info@thegernertco.com. **Website:** www.
thegernertco.com. **Contact:** Sarah Burnes. "Our client list is as broad as the market; we represent equal
parts fiction and nonfiction." Estab. 1996.

Prior to her current position, Ms. Burnes was
with Burnes & Clegg, Inc.
MEMBER AGENTS Sarah Burnes (literary fiction and nonfiction; children's fiction); **Stephanie
Cabot** (represents a variety of genres, including
crime/thriller, commercial and literary fiction,
latte lit, nonfiction); **Chris Parris-Lam**b (nonfiction, literary fiction); **Seth Fishman** (looking
for the new voice, the original idea, the entirely
breathtaking creative angle in both fiction and
nonfiction); **Logan Garrison Savits** (young adult
fiction); **Will Roberts** (smart, original thriller with
distinctive voices, compelling backgrounds, and
fast-paced narratives); **Erika Storella** (nonfiction
projects that make an argument, narrate a history,
and/or provide a new perspective); **Anna Wor-
rall** (smart women's literary and commercial fic-

tion, psychological thriller, narrative nonfiction); **Ellen Coughtrey** (women's literary and commercial fiction, historical fiction, narrative nonfiction and smart, original thriller, well-written Southern Gothic anything); **Jack Gernert** (stories about heroes—both real and imagined); **Libby McGuire** (distinctive storytelling in both fiction and nonfiction, across a wide range of genres). At this time, **Courtney Gatewood** and **Rebecca Gardner** are closed to queries. See the website to find out the tastes of each agent.

REPRESENTS nonfiction, novels. **Considers these fiction areas:** commercial, crime, fantasy, historical, literary, middle-grade, science fiction, thriller, women's, young adult.

HOW TO CONTACT "Please send us a query letter by e-mail to info@thegernertco.com describing the work you'd like to submit, along with some information about yourself and a sample chapter, if appropriate. Please indicate in your letter which agent you are querying. Please do not send e-mails directly to individual agents. It's our policy to respond to your query only if we are interested in seeing more material, usually within 4-6 weeks." See company website for more instructions. Accepts simultaneous submissions. Obtains most new clients through recommendations from others, solicitations.

RECENT SALES *Partners*, by John Grisham; *The River Why*, by David James Duncan; *The Thin Green Line*, by Paul Sullivan; *A Fireproof Home for the Bride*, by Amy Scheibe; *The Only Girl in School*, by Natalie Standiford.

GHOSH LITERARY

E-mail: submissions@ghoshliterary.com. **Website:** www.ghoshliterary.com. **Contact:** Anna Ghosh. Member of AAR. Signatory of WGA.

○ Prior to opening her own agency, Ms. Ghosh was previously a partner at Scovil Galen Ghosh.

REPRESENTS nonfiction, fiction.

⚷ "Anna's literary interests are wide and eclectic, and she is known for discovering and developing writers. She is particularly interested in literary narratives and books that illuminate some aspect of human endeavor or the natural world. Anna does not typically represent genre fiction but is drawn to compelling storytelling in most guises."

HOW TO CONTACT E-query. Please send an e-mail briefly introducing yourself and your work. Although no specific format is required, it is helpful to know the following: your qualifications for writing your book, including any publications and recognition for your work, who you expect to buy and read your book, and similar books and authors. Accepts simultaneous submissions.

GLASS LITERARY MANAGEMENT

138 W. 25th St., Tenth Floor, New York NY 10001. (646)237-4881. **E-mail:** alex@glassliterary.com; rick@glassliterary.com. **Website:** www.glassliterary.com. **Contact:** Alex Glass, Rick Pascocello. Mr. Glass is a generalist and takes submissions for virtually all kinds of fiction and nonfiction (except children's picture books). Estab. 2014. Member of AAR. Signatory of WGA.

MEMBER AGENTS Alex Glass, Rick Pascocello.

REPRESENTS nonfiction, novels.

⚷ Represents general fiction, mystery, suspense/thriller, juvenile fiction, biography, history, mind/body/spirit, health, lifestyle, cookbooks, sports, literary fiction, memoir, narrative nonfiction, pop culture. "We do not represent picture books for children."

HOW TO CONTACT "Please send your query letter in the body of an e-mail, and if we are interested, we will respond and ask for the complete manuscript or proposal. No attachments." Accepts simultaneous submissions.

RECENT SALES *100 Days of Cake*, by Shari Goldhagen; *The Red Car*, by Marcy Dermansky; *The Overnight Solution*, by Dr. Michael Breus; *So That Happened: A Memoir*, by Jon Cryer; *Bad Kid*, by David Crabb; *Finding Mr. Brightside*, by Jay Clark; *Strange Animals*, by Chad Kultgen.

GLOBAL LION INTELLECTUAL PROPERTY MANAGEMENT

P.O. Box 669238, Pompano Beach FL 33066. **E-mail:** queriesgloballionmiddle-gradet@gmail.com. **Website:** www.globallionmanagement.com. **Contact:** Peter Miller. Estab. 2013. Member of AAR. Signatory of WGA.

○ Prior to his current position, Mr. Miller was formerly the founder of PMA Literary & Film Management Inc. of New York.

☛ "I look for cutting-edge authors of both fiction and nonfiction with global marketing and motion picture/television production potential."

HOW TO CONTACT E-query. Global Lion Intellectual Property Management. Inc. accepts exclusive submissions only. "If your work is under consideration by another agency, please do not submit it to us." Below the query, paste a 1- page synopsis, a sample of your book (20 pages is fine), a short author bio, and any impressive social media links.

BARRY GOLDBLATT LITERARY LLC

320 Seventh Ave. #266, Brooklyn NY 11215. **E-mail:** query@bgliterary.com. **Website:** www.bgliterary. com. **Contact:** Barry Goldblatt. Estab. 2000. Member of AAR. Signatory of WGA.

MEMBER AGENTS Barry Goldblatt; Jennifer Udden, query.judden@gmail.com (speculative fiction of all stripes, especially innovative science fiction or fantasy, contemporary/erotic/LGBTQ/paranormal/historical romance, contemporary or speculative young adult. select mystery, thriller, urban fantasies).

REPRESENTS fiction. **Considers these fiction areas:** fantasy, middle-grade, mystery, romance, science fiction, thriller, young adult.

☛ "Please see our website for specific submission guidelines and information on our particular tastes."

HOW TO CONTACT "E-mail queries can be sent to query@bgliterary.com and should include the word 'query' in the subject line. To query Jen Udden specifically, e-mail queries can be sent to query.judden@gmail.com. Please know that we will read and respond to every e-query that we receive, provided it is properly addressed and follows the submission guidelines below. We will not respond to e-queries that are addressed to no one, or to multiple recipients. While we do not require exclusivity, exclusive submissions will receive priority review. If your submission is exclusive to Barry Goldblatt Literary, please indicate so by including the word 'Exclusive' in the subject line of your e-mail. Your e-query should include the following within the body of the e-mail: your query letter, a synopsis of the book, and the first 5 pages of your manuscript. We will not open or respond to any e-mails that have attachments. Our response time is 4 weeks on queries, 6-8 weeks on full manuscripts. If you haven't heard from us within that time, feel free to check in via e-mail." Accepts simultaneous submissions. Obtains clients through referrals, queries, conferences.

TERMS Agent receives 15% commission on domestic sales; 20% on foreign and dramatic sales. Offers written contract; 60-day notice must be given to terminate contract.

RECENT SALES *Other Broken Things*, by C. Desir; *Masks and Shadows*, by Stephanie Burgis; *Wishing Day*, by Lauren Myracle; *Mother-Daughter Book Camp*, by Heather Vogel Frederick.

TIPS "We're a hands-on agency, focused on building an author's career, not just making an initial sale. We don't care about trends or what's hot; we just want to sign great writers."

FRANCES GOLDIN LITERARY AGENCY, INC.

214 W. 29th St., Suite 410, New York NY 10001. (212)777-0047. **Fax:** (212)228-1660. **Website:** www. goldinlit.com. Estab. 1977. Member of AAR.

MEMBER AGENTS Frances Goldin, founder/president; **Ellen Geiger**, vice president/principal (nonfiction: history, biography, progressive politics, photography, science and medicine, women, religion, serious investigative journalism; fiction: literary thriller, novels in general that provoke and challenge the status quo, historical and multicultural works. Please no New Age, romance, how-to, or right-wing politics); **Matt McGowan**, agent/rights director, mm@goldinlit.com, (literary fiction, essays, history, memoir, journalism, biography, music, popular culture and science, sports [particularly soccer], narrative nonfiction, cultural studies, literary travel, crime, food, suspense and science fiction); **Sam Stoloff**, vice president/principal, (literary fiction, memoir, history, accessible sociology and philosophy, cultural studies, serious journalism, narrative and topical nonfiction with a progressive orientation); **Ria Julien**, agent/counsel; **Nina Cochran**, literary assistant.

REPRESENTS nonfiction, novels. **Considers these nonfiction areas:** biography, creative nonfiction, cultural interests, foods, history, investigative, medicine, memoirs, music, philosophy, photography, popular culture, politics, science, sociology, sports, travel, women's issues, crime. **Considers these fiction areas:** historical, literary, mainstream, multicultural, suspense, thriller.

☛ "We are hands-on, and we work intensively with clients on proposal and manuscript development." "Please note that we do not handle screenplays, romances. or most other genre fiction, and hardly any poetry. We do not handle work that is racist, sexist, ageist, homophobic, or pornographic."

HOW TO CONTACT There is an online submission process you can find on the website. Responds in 4-6 weeks to queries.

IRENE GOODMAN LITERARY AGENCY

27 W. 24th St., Suite 700B, New York NY 10010. **E-mail:** miriam.queries@irenegoodman.com, barbara.queries@irenegoodman.com, rachel.queries@irenegoodman.com, kim.queries@irenegoodman.com, victoria.queries@irenegoodman.com, irene.queries@irenegoodman.com, submissions@irenegoodman.com. **Website:** www.irenegoodman.com. Estab. 1978. Member of AAR. Represents 150 clients.
MEMBER AGENTS Irene Goodman, Miriam Kriss, Barbara Poelle, Rachel Ekstrom, Kim Perel, Victoria Marini.
REPRESENTS nonfiction, fiction, novels, juvenile books. **Considers these nonfiction areas:** animals, autobiography, cooking, creative nonfiction, cultural interests, current affairs, decorating, diet/nutrition, design, foods, health, history, how-to, humor, interior design, juvenile nonfiction, memoirs, parenting, politics, science, self-help, women's issues, young adult, parenting, social issues, francophilia, anglophilia, Judaica, lifestyles, cooking, memoir.
Considers these fiction areas: action, crime, detective, family saga, historical, horror, middle-grade, mystery, romance, science fiction, suspense, thriller, urban fantasy, women's, young adult.

> Commercial and literary fiction and nonfiction. No screenplays, poetry, or inspirational fiction.

HOW TO CONTACT Query. Submit synopsis, first 10 pages pasted into the body of the e-mail. E-mail queries only! See the website submission page. No e-mail attachments. Query one agent only. Accepts simultaneous submissions. Responds in 2 months to queries. Consult website for each agent's submission guidelines.
TERMS Agent receives 15% commission.
TIPS "We are receiving an unprecedented amount of e-mail queries. If you find that the mailbox is full, please try again in 2 weeks. E-mail queries to our personal addresses will not be answered. E-mails to our personal inboxes will be deleted."

DOUG GRAD LITERARY AGENCY, INC.

68 Jay St., Suite N3, Brooklyn NY 11201. (718)788-6067. **E-mail:** query@dgliterary.com. **Website:** www.dgliterary.com. **Contact:** Doug Grad. Estab. 2008. Member of AAR. Signatory of WGA.

> Prior to being an agent, Doug Grad spent 22 years as an editor at imprints at four major publishing houses—Simon & Schuster, Random House, Penguin, and HarperCollins.

MEMBER AGENTS Doug Grad (narrative nonfiction, military, sports, celebrity memoir, thriller, mystery, cozies, historical fiction, music, style, business, home improvement, cookbooks, science, theater).
REPRESENTS nonfiction, fiction, novels. **Considers these nonfiction areas:** Americana, autobiography, business, cooking, creative nonfiction, current affairs, diet/nutrition, design, film, government, history, humor, military, music, popular culture, politics, science, sports, technology, theater, travel, true crime, war. **Considers these fiction areas:** action, adventure, commercial, crime, detective, historical, horror, literary, mainstream, military, mystery, police, science fiction, suspense, thriller, war, young adult.

> Does not want fantasy, young adult, or children's picture books.

HOW TO CONTACT Query by e-mail first. No sample material unless requested; no printed submissions by mail. Accepts simultaneous submissions.
RECENT SALES *The Earthend Saga*, by Gillian Anderson and Jeff Rovin (Simon451); *NBA Hall of Famer Bernard King Memoir*, by Bernard King with Jerome Preisler (Da Capo); *Bounty*, by Michael Byrnes (Bantam); Dan Morgan thriller series, by Leo Maloney (Kensington); Cajun Country cozy mystery series, by Ellen Byron (Crooked Lane); *Sports Idioms and Words*, by Josh Chetwynd (Ten Speed Press).

KATHRYN GREEN LITERARY AGENCY, LLC

157 Columbus Ave., Suite 510, New York NY 10023. (212)245-4225. **E-mail:** query@kgreenagency.com. **Website:** www.kathryngreenliteraryagency.com. **Contact:** Kathy Green. Estab. 2004. Member of Women's Media Group. Represents approximately 20 clients.

> Prior to becoming an agent, Ms. Green was a book and magazine editor.

NEW AGENT SPOTLIGHT

SERENE HAKIM
AYESHA PANDE LITERARY

www.pandeliterary.com
@serenemaria

ABOUT SERENE: Prior to joining Ayesha Pande Literary, Serene Hakim worked at Laura Gross Literary Agency in Boston. She has also interned at David Godine Publisher and Chase Literary Agency. Serene holds an M.A. in French to English translation from NYU and a B.A. in French and Women's Studies from the University of Kansas.

SHE IS SEEKING: Serene is actively seeking young adult (all genres but in particular: science fiction and fantasy with a unique hook, realistic young adult with diverse characters), upmarket women's fiction, and anything that gives voice to those whose voices are underrepresented and/or marginalized. Stories dealing with the Middle East and the variety of immigrant experiences out there will definitely catch her eye. Intriguing female characters are also a huge plus. For nonfiction, she is seeking humorous and fascinating memoirs, and is particularly interested in LGBTQ and feminist issues.

HOW TO SUBMIT: To submit a query, please use the query form on the Ayesha Pande Literary website: www.pandeliterary.com/queries.

REPRESENTS nonfiction, fiction, novels, short story collections, juvenile books. **Considers these nonfiction areas:** autobiography, biography, business, cooking, cultural interests, current affairs, diet/nutrition, foods, history, how-to, humor, inspirational, memoirs, parenting, popular culture, psychology, satire, science, spirituality, sports, true crime, women's issues, young adult. **Considers these fiction areas:** commercial, crime, detective, family saga, historical, humor, juvenile, literary, mainstream, middle-grade, multicultural, mystery, police, romance, satire, suspense, thriller, women's, young adult.

⚬— "Considers all types of fiction but particularly like historical fiction, cozy mystery, young adult and middle-grade. For nonfiction, I am interested in memoir, parenting, humor with a pop culture bent, and history. Quirky nonfiction is also a particular favorite." Does not want to receive science fiction, fantasy, children's picture books, screenplays, or poetry.

HOW TO CONTACT Query by e-mail. Send no attachments unless requested. Do not send queries via regular mail. Responds in 4 weeks. "Queries do not have to be exclusive; however, if further material is requested, please be in touch before accepting other representation." Accepts simultaneous submissions. Obtains most new clients through recommendations from others, solicitations, conferences.

TERMS Agent receives 15% commission on domestic sales; 20% commission on foreign sales.

RECENT SALES *Sit Stay Heal*, by Mel C. Miskimen; *Unholy City*, by Carrie Smith.

SANFORD J. GREENBURGER ASSOCIATES, INC.

55 Fifth Ave., New York NY 10003. (212)206-5600. **Fax:** (212)463-8718. **Website:** www.greenburger.com. Member of AAR. Represents 500 clients.
MEMBER AGENTS Matt Bialer, lribar@sjga. com (fantasy, science fiction, thriller, mystery, select group of literary writers; loves smart narrative non-fiction: current events, popular culture, biography, history, music, race, sports); **Brenda Bowen**, querybb@sjga.com (literary fiction, writers and illustrators of picture books, chapter books, middle-grade and teen fiction); **Faith Hamlin**, fhamlin@sjga.com (receives submissions by referral); **Heide Lange**, queryhl@sjga.com (receives submissions by referral); **Daniel Mandel**, querydm@sjga.com (literary and commercial fiction, memoirs and nonfiction about business, art, history, politics, sports, popular culture); **Courtney Miller-Callihan**, cmiller@ sjga.com (YA, middle-grade, women's fiction, romance, and historical novels, nonfiction projects on unusual topics, humor, pop culture, lifestyle books); **Nicholas Ellison**, nellison@sjga.com; **Chelsea Lindman**, clindman@sjga.com (playful literary fiction, upmarket crime fiction, forward thinking or boundary-pushing nonfiction); **Rachael Dillon Fried**, rfried@sjga.com (both fiction and nonfiction authors, with a keen interest in unique literary voices, women's fiction, narrative nonfiction, memoir, comedy); **Lindsay Ribar**, co-agents with Matt Bialer (young adult and middle-grade fiction); **Bethany Buck** querybbuck@sjga.com (middle-grade and chapter books, teen fiction, select list of picture book authors and illustrators); **Stephanie Delman** sdelman@sjga.com (literary/upmarket contemporary fiction, psychological thriller/suspense, atmospheric, near-historical fiction); **Ed Maxwell** emaxwell@sjga.com (expert and narrative nonfiction authors, novelists and graphic novelists, children's book authors and illustrators).
REPRESENTS nonfiction, fiction, novels, juvenile books. **Considers these nonfiction areas:** art, biography, business, creative nonfiction, current affairs, ethnic, history, humor, memoirs, music, popular culture, politics, sports. **Considers these fiction areas:** commercial, crime, family saga, fantasy, feminist, historical, literary, middle-grade, multicultural, mystery, picture books, romance, science fiction, thriller, women's, young adult.

HOW TO CONTACT E-query. "Please look at each agent's profile page for current information about what each agent is looking for and for the correct e-mail address to use for queries to that agent. Please be sure to use the correct query e-mail address for each agent." Agents may not respond to all queries, will respond within 6-8 weeks if interested. Obtains most new clients through recommendations from others.
TERMS Agent receives 15% commission on domestic sales; 20% commission on foreign sales. Charges for photocopying and books for foreign and subsidiary rights submissions.
RECENT SALES *Inferno* by Dan Brown, *Sweet Pea and Friends: A Sheepover* by John Churchman and Jennifer Churchman, *Code of Conduct* by Brad Thor.

THE GREENHOUSE LITERARY AGENCY

E-mail: submissions@greenhouseliterary.com. **Website:** www.greenhouseliterary.com. **Contact:** Sarah Davies. Estab. 2008. Member of AAR. Other memberships include SCBWI. Represents 50 clients.

Before launching Greenhouse, Sarah Davies had an editorial and management career in children's publishing spanning 25 years; for 5 years prior to launching the Greenhouse she was publishing director of Macmillan Children's Books in London, and published leading authors from both sides of the Atlantic.

MEMBER AGENTS Sarah Davies, vice president (fiction and nonfiction by North American authors, chapter books through to middle-grade, young adult); **Polly Nolan**, agent (fiction by UK, Irish, Commonwealth—including Australia, New Zealand and India—authors, plus European authors writing in English, author/illustrators (texts under 1,000 words) to young fiction series, through middle-grade, young adult).
REPRESENTS juvenile books. **Considers these nonfiction areas:** juvenile nonfiction, young adult. **Considers these fiction areas:** juvenile, young adult.

"We represent authors writing fiction and nonfiction for children and teens. The agency has offices in both the US and UK, and the agency's commission structure reflects this—taking 15% for sales to both US and UK, thus treating both as 'domestic' market." All genres of children's and young adult fiction. Very occasionally, a nonfiction proposal will be considered. Does not want to receive picture book texts (i.e., written by writers who aren't also illustrators) or short stories, educational or religious/inspirational work, pre-school/novelty material, screenplays, or writing aimed at adults. Represents novels and some nonfiction. Considers these fiction areas: juvenile, chapter book series, middle-grade, young adult.

HOW TO CONTACT Query one agent only. Put the target agent's name in the subject line. Paste the first 5 pages of your story (or your complete picture book) after the query. Accepts simultaneous submissions.

TERMS Agent receives 15% commission on domestic sales; 25% commission on foreign sales. Offers written contract. This agency occasionally charges for submission copies to film agents or foreign publishers.

RECENT SALES *Places No One Knows*, by Brenna Yovanoff (Delacorte); *Race to the Bottom of the Sea*, by Lindsay Eagar (Candlewick); *Cheerful Chick*, by Martha Brockenbrough (Scholastic); *Olive and the Backstage Ghost*, by Michelle Schusterman (Random House); *Wanted: Women Mathematicians*, by Tami Lewis Brown & Debbie Loren Dunn (Disney-Hyperion).

WRITERS CONFERENCES Bologna Children's Book Fair, ALA, SCBWI, BookExpo America.

TIPS "Before submitting material, authors should visit the Greenhouse Literary Agency website and carefully read all submission guidelines."

GREYHAUS LITERARY

3021 20th St., Pl. SW, Puyallup WA 98373. **E-mail:** scott@greyhausagency.com, submissions@greyhausagency.com. **Website:** www.greyhausagency.com. **Contact:** Scott Eagan, member RWA. Estab. 2003. Member of AAR. Signatory of WGA.

REPRESENTS novels. **Considers these fiction areas:** New Adult, romance, women's.

Greyhaus only focuses on romance and women's fiction. Please review submission information found on the website to know exactly what Greyhaus is looking for. Stories should be 75,000-120,000 words in length or meet the word count requirements for Harlequin found on its website. Does not want fantasy, single-title inspirational, young adult or middle-grade, picture books, memoirs, biography, erotica, urban fantasy, science fiction, screenplays, poetry, or authors interested in only e-publishing or self-publishing.

HOW TO CONTACT Submissions to Greyhaus can be done in one of three ways: 1) A standard query letter via e-mail. If using this method, do not attach documents or send anything else other than a query letter. 2) Use the Submission Form found on the website on the Contact page. 3) Send a query, the first 3 pages, and a synopsis of no more than 3-5 pages (and a SASE) using a snail mail submission. Accepts simultaneous submissions. Responds in up to 3 months.

JILL GRINBERG LITERARY MANAGEMENT

392 Vanderbilt Ave., Brooklyn NY 11238. (212)620-5883. **E-mail:** info@jillgrinbergliterary.com. **Website:** www.jillgrinbergliterary.com. Estab. 1999. Member of AAR.

Prior to her current position, Ms. Grinberg was at Anderson Grinberg Literary Management.

MEMBER AGENTS Jill Grinberg, Cheryl Pientka, Katelyn Detweiler, Sophia Seidner.

REPRESENTS nonfiction, fiction, novels. **Considers these nonfiction areas:** biography, creative nonfiction, current affairs, ethnic, history, language, literature, memoirs, parenting, popular culture, politics, science, sociology, spirituality, sports, travel, women's issues, young adult. **Considers these fiction areas:** fantasy, historical, juvenile, literary, mainstream, middle-grade, picture books, romance, science fiction, women's, young adult.

HOW TO CONTACT "Please send queries via e-mail to info@jillgrinbergliterary.com—include your query letter, addressed to the agent of your choice, along with the first 50 pages of your ms pasted into the body of the e-mail or attached as a .doc. or .docx file. We also accept queries via mail, though e-mail is preferred. Please send your query letter and the first 50 pages of your ms by mail, along with a SASE, to the attention of your agent of choice. Please note that unless a SASE with sufficient postage is provided, your materials will not be returned. As submissions are shared within the office, please only query one agent with your project." Accepts simultaneous submissions.

TIPS "We prefer submissions by electronic mail."

JILL GROSJEAN LITERARY AGENCY

1390 Millstone Rd., Sag Harbor NY 11963. (631)725-7419. **E-mail:** jilllit310@aol.com. **Contact:** Jill Grosjean. Estab. 1999.

Prior to becoming an agent, Ms. Grosjean managed an independent bookstore. She also worked in publishing and advertising.

REPRESENTS novels. **Considers these fiction areas:** historical, literary, mainstream, mystery, thriller, women's.

Actively seeking literary novels and mystery. Does not want serial killer, science fiction, or young adult novels.

HOW TO CONTACT E-mail queries preferred; no attachments. No cold calls, please. Accepts simultaneous submissions, though when a manuscript is requested, it requires exclusive reading time. Accepts simultaneous submissions. Responds in 1 week to queries. Obtains most new clients through recommendations, solicitations.

TERMS Agent receives 15% commission on domestic sales; 20% commission on foreign and film sales.

RECENT SALES *A Murder in Time*, by Julie McEwain (Pegasus Books); *A Twist in Time*, by Julie McEwain (Pegasus Books); *The Silver Gun*, by LA Chandlar (Kensington Books); *The Edison Effect*, by Bernadette Pajer (Poison Pen Press); *Threading the Needle*, by Marie Bostwick (Kensington Publishing); *Tim Cratchit's Christmas Carol: A Novel of Scrooge's Legacy*, by Jim Piecuch (Simon & Schuster).

WRITERS CONFERENCES Thrillerfest, Texas Writer's League, Book Passage Mystery Writer's Conference.

LAURA GROSS LITERARY AGENCY

E-mail: assistant@lg-la.com. **Website:** www.lg-la.com. Estab. 1988. Represents 30 clients.

Prior to becoming an agent, Ms. Gross was an editor and ran a reading series.

REPRESENTS nonfiction, novels.

"I represent a broad range of both fiction and nonfiction writers. I am particularly interested in history, politics, and current affairs, and also love beautifully written literary fiction and intelligent thriller."

HOW TO CONTACT Queries accepted online via online form on LGLA Submittable site. No e-mail queries. "On the submission form, please include a concise but substantive cover letter. You may include the first 6,000 words of your manuscript in the form as well. We will request further sample chapters from you at a later date, if we think your work suits our list."

There may be a delay of several weeks in responding to your query. Accepts simultaneous submissions.

TERMS Agent receives 15% commission on domestic sales; 20% commission on foreign sales. Offers written contract.

THE JOY HARRIS LITERARY AGENCY, INC.

1501 Broadway, Suite 2310, New York NY 10036. (212)924-6269. **Fax:** (212)540-5776. **E-mail:** contact@joyharrisliterary.com. **E-mail:** submissions@joyharrisliterary.com. **Website:** joyharrisliterary.com. **Contact:** Joy Harris. Estab. 1990. Member of AAR. Represents 100+ clients.

MEMBER AGENTS Joy Harris (literary fiction, strongly written commercial fiction, narrative nonfiction across a broad range of topics, memoir, biography); **Adam Reed** (literary fiction, science and technology, pop culture); **Elizabeth Trout**.

REPRESENTS nonfiction, fiction. **Considers these nonfiction areas:** art, biography, creative nonfiction, memoirs, popular culture, science, technology. **Considers these fiction areas:** commercial, literary.

"We are not accepting poetry, screenplays, genre fiction, or self-help submissions at this time."

HOW TO CONTACT Please e-mail all submissions, comprised of a query letter and an outline or sample chapter to submissions@joyharrisliterary.com. Accepts simultaneous submissions. Obtains most new clients through recommendations from clients and editors.

TERMS Agent receives 15% commission on domestic sales; 20% commission on foreign sales. Charges clients for some office expenses.

RECENT SALES *Smash Cut*, by Brad Gooch; *The Other Paris*, by Luc Sante; *The Past*, by Tessa Hadley; *In a Dark Wood*, by Joseph Luzzi.

HARTLINE LITERARY AGENCY

123 Queenston Dr., Pittsburgh PA 15235-5429. (412)829-2483. **E-mail:** joyce@hartlineliterary.com. **Website:** www.hartlineliterary.com. **Contact:** Joyce A. Hart. Many of the agents at this agency are generalists. This agency also handles inspirational and Christian works. Estab. 1992. Member of ACFW. Represents 200 clients.

Joyce Hart was the vice president of marketing at Whitaker House Publishing. Jim Hart was a production journalist for 20 years.

MEMBER AGENTS Joyce A. Hart, principal agent (no unsolicited queries); **Jim Hart,** jim@hartlineliterary.com; **Diana Flegal,** diana@hartlineliterary.com; **Linda Glaz,** linda@hartlineliterary.com; **Andy Scheer,** andy@hartlineliterary.com; **Cyle Young,** cyle@hartlineliterary.com.

REPRESENTS nonfiction, fiction, novels, novellas, juvenile books, scholarly books. **Considers these nonfiction areas:** diet/nutrition, health, history, inspirational, parenting, philosophy, popular culture, politics, psychology, recreation, religious, spirituality, women's issues. **Considers these fiction areas:** contemporary issues, family saga, humor, inspirational, New Adult, religious, romance, suspense, women's, young adult.

> ☞ "This agency specializes in the Christian bookseller market." Actively seeking adult fiction, self-help, nutritional books, Christian living, devotional, and business. Does not want to receive erotica, gay/lesbian, fantasy, horror.

HOW TO CONTACT E-query preferred, USPS to the Pittsburgh office. Target one agent only. "All e-mail submissions sent to Hartline Agents should be sent as a Word document (or in rich text file format from another word processing program) attached to an e-mail with 'submission: title, author's name, and word count' in the subject line. A proposal is a single document, not a collection of files. Place the query letter in the e-mail itself. Do not send the entire proposal in the body of the e-mail or send PDF files." Further guidelines online. Accepts simultaneous submissions. Responds in 2 months to queries, 3 months to mss. Obtains most new clients through recommendations from others, conferences.

TERMS Agent receives 15% commission on domestic sales. Offers written contract.

JOHN HAWKINS & ASSOCIATES, INC.

80 Maiden Lane, Suite 1503, New York NY 10038. (212)807-7040. **E-mail:** jha@jhalit.com. **Website:** www.jhalit.com. **Contact:** Moses Cardona, rights and translations; Annie Kronenberg, permissions; Warren Frazier, literary agent; Anne Hawkins, literary agent. Member of AAR, the Authors Guild. Represents 100+ clients.

MEMBER AGENTS Moses Cardona, moses@jhalit.com (commercial fiction, suspense, business, science, multicultural fiction); **Warren Frazier,** frazier@jhalit.com (fiction; nonfiction, specifically technology,

history, world affairs, foreign policy); **Anne Hawkins,** ahawkins@jhalit.com (thriller to literary fiction to serious nonfiction; interested in science, history, public policy, medicine, women's issues).

REPRESENTS nonfiction, fiction, novels, short story collections, novellas. **Considers these nonfiction areas:** biography, business, history, medicine, politics, science, technology, women's issues. **Considers these fiction areas:** commercial, historical, literary, multicultural, suspense, thriller.

HOW TO CONTACT Query. Include the word "Query" in the subject line. For fiction, include 1-3 chapters of your book as a single Word attachment. For nonfiction, include your proposal as a single attachment. E-mail a particular agent directly if you are targeting one. Accepts simultaneous submissions. Responds in 1 month to queries. Obtains most new clients through recommendations from others.

TERMS Agent receives 15% commission on domestic sales; 20% commission on foreign sales. Charges clients for photocopying.

RECENT SALES *Forty Rooms*, by Olga Grushin; *A Book of American Martyrs*, by Joyce Carol Oates; *City on Edge*, by Stefanie Pintoff; *Cold Earth*, by Ann Cleeves; *The Good Lieutenant*, by Whitney Terrell; *Grief Cottage*, by Gail Godwin.

✪ HELEN HELLER AGENCY INC.

4-216 Heath St. W., Toronto ON M5P 1N7 Canada. (416)489-0396. **E-mail:** info@helenhelleragency.com. **Website:** www.helenhelleragency.com. **Contact:** Helen Heller. Represents 30+ clients.

> ◑ Prior to her current position, Ms. Heller worked for Cassell & Co. (England), was an editor for Harlequin Books, a senior editor for Avon Books, and editor-in-chief for Fitzhenry & Whiteside.

MEMBER AGENTS Helen Heller, helen@helenhelleragency.com (thriller and front-list general fiction); **Sarah Heller,** sarah@helenhelleragency.com (front list commercial young adult and adult fiction, with a particular interest in high concept historical fiction); **Barbara Berson,** barbara@helenhelleragency.com (literary fiction, nonfiction, and young adult).

REPRESENTS nonfiction, novels. **Considers these fiction areas:** commercial, crime, historical, literary, mainstream, thriller, young adult.

NEW AGENT SPOTLIGHT

HANNAH FERGESEN

KT LITERARY

www.ktliterary.com
@HannahFergesen

ABOUT HANNAH: Before settling in New York City, Hannah worked and went to school in Denver, where she obtained her degree in Writing for Film and Television. Opportunities in New York presented themselves before she could run off to LA, and she course-corrected her career toward publishing, a dream of hers since childhood. After stints as a remote intern for a well-known agent, a bookseller at the famous Books of Wonder, an intern at Soho Press, a literary assistant at Trident Media Group, and a freelance editor working with well-known authors, Hannah joined KT Literary in 2016. Hannah is a proud geek and TV junkie, with an all-consuming love for Doctor Who, Harry Potter, and anything created by Joss Whedon.

SHE IS SEEKING: I'm looking for young adult and middle-grade, as well as some select adult fiction. In young adult and middle-grade, I'm looking for speculative and contemporary stories, running the gamut from fantasy, mystery, horror, and magical realism to family-oriented dramas, historical fiction, and stories dealing with contemporary issues, such as mental health or addiction. I'm also very interested in finding a good, twisty mystery or suspense. If it's historical or has a speculative bent, even better. I am into contemporaries with light science fiction elements, as well as pure science fiction with politics and an edge, or a bold reimagining of another time. I'd love to see historical fiction in both young adult and middle-grade.

In adult, I want weird and/or lyrical fantasies and speculative mysteries. I'd also love something with a good twist.

HOW TO SUBMIT: Send queries to hannahquery@ktliterary.com. The subject line of your email should include the word "Query" along with the title of your manuscript. Queries should not contain attachments. If we like your query, we'll ask for the first five chapters and a complete synopsis. For our purposes, the synopsis should include the full plot of the book, including the conclusion.

HOW TO CONTACT E-mail info@helenhelle-ragency.com. Submit a brief synopsis, publishing history, author bio, and writing sample, pasted in the body of the e-mail. No attachments with e-queries. Accepts simultaneous submissions. Responds within 3 months if interested. Accepts simultaneous submissions. Obtains most new clients through recommendations from others, solicitations.

TIPS "Whether you are an author searching for an agent, or whether an agent has approached you, it is in your best interest to first find out who the agent represents, what publishing houses has that agent sold to recently and what foreign sales have been made. You should be able to go to the bookstore, or search online and find the books the agent refers to. Many authors acknowledge their agents in the front or back or their books."

RICHARD HENSHAW GROUP

145 W. 28th St., 12th Floor, New York NY 10001. (212)414-1172. **E-mail:** submissions@henshaw.com. **Website:** www.richardhenshawgroup.com. **Contact:** Rich Henshaw. Member of AAR.

○ Prior to opening his agency, Mr. Henshaw served as an agent with Richard Curtis Associates, Inc.

REPRESENTS novels. **Considers these fiction areas:** fantasy, historical, horror, literary, mainstream, mystery, police, romance, science fiction, thriller, young adult.

⚷ "We specialize in popular fiction and nonfiction and are affiliated with a variety of writers' organizations. Our clients include *New York Times* bestsellers and recipients of major awards in fiction and nonfiction." "We only consider works between 65,000-150,000 words." "We do not represent children's books, screenplays, short fiction, poetry, textbooks, scholarly works or coffee-table books."

HOW TO CONTACT "Please feel free to submit a query letter in the form of an e-mail of fewer than 250 words to submissions@henshaw.com address." No snail mail queries. Accepts simultaneous submissions. Obtains most new clients through recommendations from others, solicitations, conferences.

TERMS Agent receives 15% commission on domestic sales; 20% commission on foreign sales. No written contract. Charges clients for photocopying and book orders.

TIPS "While we do not have any reason to believe that our submission guidelines will change in the near future, writers can find up-to-date submission policy information on our website. Always include a SASE with correct return postage."

THE JEFF HERMAN AGENCY, LLC

P.O. Box 1522, Stockbridge MA 01262. (413)298-0077. **E-mail:** jeff@jeffherman.com. **Contact:** Jeffrey H. Herman. Specializes in all areas of adult nonfiction. Estab. 1987. Represents 100 clients.

○ Prior to opening his agency, Mr. Herman served as a public relations executive.

MEMBER AGENTS Deborah Levine, vice president (nonfiction book doctor); **Jeff Herman**.

REPRESENTS nonfiction, textbooks. **Considers these nonfiction areas:** Americana, animals, biography, business, child guidance, computers, crafts, creative nonfiction, cultural interests, current affairs, diet/nutrition, economics, ethnic, government, health, history, hobbies, how-to, humor, inspirational, investigative, law, medicine, metaphysics, military, money, multicultural, New Age, parenting, popular culture, politics, psychology, regional, religious, science, self-help, sex, sociology, software, spirituality, technology, true crime, war, women's issues, women's studies, popular reference.

⚷ This agency specializes in adult nonfiction.

HOW TO CONTACT Query by e-mail. Accepts simultaneous submissions.

TERMS Agent receives 15% commission on domestic sales. Offers written contract.

RECENT SALES This agency has more than 1,000 titles.

RONNIE ANN HERMAN

350 Central Park W., Apt. 41, New York NY 10025. (212)749-4907. **E-mail:** ronnie@hermanagencyinc.com, katia.hermanagency@gmail.com. **Website:** www.hermanagencyinc.com. **Contact:** Ronnie Ann Herman. "We are a small boutique literary agency that represents authors and artists for the children's book market. We are only accepting submissions for middle-grade and young adult books at this time." Estab. 1999. Member of SCBWI. Represents 19 clients.

MEMBER AGENTS Ronnie Ann Herman, **Katia Herman**.

REPRESENTS novels, juvenile books. **Considers these nonfiction areas:** juvenile nonfiction. **Con-**

siders these **fiction areas:** juvenile, middle-grade, picture books, young adult.

- Childrens' books of all genres. Actively seeking middle-grade and young adult.

HOW TO CONTACT Submit via e-mail. Accepts simultaneous submissions.

TERMS Agent receives 15% commission.

TIPS "Check our website to see if you belong with our agency."

JULIE A. HILL AND ASSOCIATES, LLC

12997 Caminito Del Pasaje, Del Mar CA 92014. (858)259-2595. **Fax:** (858)259-2777. **E-mail:** hillagent@aol.com. **Website:** www.publishersmarketplace/members/hillagent. **Contact:** Julie Hill.

MEMBER AGENTS Julie Hill, agent and principal.

REPRESENTS nonfiction. **Considers these nonfiction areas:** architecture, art, biography, health, memoirs, New Age, self-help, technology, travel, women's issues, technology books, for professionals and laypersons..

- Specialties of the house are memoir, health, self-help, art, architecture, business/technology, and literary and reference travel. "We also do contract and sale consulting for authors who are working unagented. Consulting inquiries welcome. "

HOW TO CONTACT E-query or query via snail mail with SASE. Accepts simultaneous submissions. Responds in 4-6 weeks to queries. Obtains most new clients through recommendations from other authors, editors, and agents.

HILL NADELL LITERARY AGENCY

6442 Santa Monica Blvd., Suite 201, Los Angeles CA 90038. (310)860-9605. **E-mail:** queries@hillnadell.com. **Website:** www.hillnadell.com. Represents 100 clients.

MEMBER AGENTS Bonnie Nadell (nonfiction: current affairs, food, memoirs, narrative nonfiction; fiction: thriller, upmarket women's and literary fiction); **Dara Hyde** (literary and genre fiction, narrative nonfiction, graphic novels, memoir, the occasional young adult novel).

REPRESENTS nonfiction, novels. **Considers these nonfiction areas:** biography, current affairs, environment, government, health, history, language, literature, medicine, popular culture, politics, science, technology, biography, narrative nonfiction. **Considers these fiction areas:** literary, mainstream, thriller, women's, young adult.

HOW TO CONTACT Send a query and SASE. If you would like your materials returned, please include adequate postage. To submit electronically, send your query letter and the first 5-10 pages to queries@hillnadell.com. No attachments. Due to the high volume of submissions the agency receives, it cannot guarantee a response to all e-mailed queries. Accepts simultaneous submissions.

TERMS Agent receives 15% commission on domestic and film sales; 20% commission on foreign sales. Charges clients for photocopying and foreign mailings.

HOLLOWAY LITERARY

P.O. Box 771, Cary NC 27512. **E-mail:** submissions@hollowayliteraryagency.com. **Website:** hollowayliteraryagency.com. **Contact:** Nikki Terpilowski. A full-service boutique literary agency located in Raleigh, NC. Estab. 2011. Member of AAR, signatory of WGA, International Thriller Writers, Romance Writers of America. Represents 26 clients.

MEMBER AGENTS Nikki Terpilowski (romance, women's fiction, Southern fiction, historical fiction, cozy mystery, military/political thriller, commercial, upmarket/book club fiction, African-American fiction of all types); **Rachel Burkot** (young adult contemporary, women's fiction, upmarket/book club fiction, contemporary romance, Southern fiction, literary fiction); **Michael Caligaris** (literary fiction, autobiographical fiction, short story collections or connected stories as a novel, Americana, crime fiction, mystery/noir, dystopian fiction, civil unrest/political uprising/war novels, memoir, new journalism and/or long-form journalism, essay collections, satirical/humor writing, environmental writing).

REPRESENTS nonfiction, fiction, movie scripts, feature film. **Considers these nonfiction areas:** Americana, environment, humor, narrative nonfiction, New Journalism, essays. **Considers these fiction areas:** action, adventure, commercial, contemporary issues, crime, detective, ethnic, family saga, fantasy, glitz, historical, inspirational, literary, mainstream, metaphysical, middle-grade, military, multicultural, mystery, New Adult, New Age, regional, romance, short story collections, spiritual, suspense, thriller, urban fantasy, war, women's, young adult. **Considers these script areas:** action, adventure, biography, contemporary issues, ethnic, romantic comedy, romantic drama, teen, thriller, TV movie of the week.

- "Note to self-published authors: While we are happy to receive submissions from authors who have previously self-published novels, we do not represent self-published works. Send us your unpublished manuscripts only." Nikki is open to submissions and is selectively reviewing queries for cozy mystery with culinary, historical, or book/publishing industry themes written in the vein of Jaclyn Brady, Laura Childs, Julie Hyzy, and Lucy Arlington; women's fiction with strong magical realism similar to Meena van Praag's *The Dress Shop of Dreams*, Sarah Addison Allen's *Garden Spells*, Sarah Creech's *Season of the Dragonflies*, and Mary Robinette Kowal's Glamourist series. She would love to find a wine-themed mystery series similar to Nadia Gordon's Sunny McCoskey series or Ellen Crosby's Wine County Mystery that combine culinary themes with a lot of great Southern history. Nikki is also interested in seeing contemporary romance set in the southern US or any wine county, or featuring a culinary theme, dark, edgy historical romance, gritty military romance, or romantic suspense with sexy Alpha heroes and lots of technical detail. She is also interested in acquiring historical fiction written in the vein of Alice Hoffman, Lalita Tademy and Isabel Allende. Nikki is also interested in espionage, military, political, and artificial intelligence thriller similar to Tom Clancy, Robert Ludlum, Steve Berry, Vince Flynn, Brad Thor, and Daniel Silva. Nikki has a special interest in nonfiction subjects related to governance, politics, military strategy, and foreign relations. Does not want horror, true crime, or novellas.

HOW TO CONTACT Send query and first 15 pages of ms pasted into the body of e-mail to submissions@hollowayliteraryagency.com. In the subject header write 'Agent's Name/Title/Genre.' Holloway Literary does accept submissions via mail (query letter and first 50 pages). Expect a response time of at least 3 months. Include e-mail address, phone number, social media accounts, and mailing address on your query letter. Accepts simultaneous submissions. Responds in 4-6 weeks. If the agent is interested, he or she will respond with a request for more material.

RECENT SALES A list of recent sales is available on the website's client news page.

HORNFISCHER LITERARY MANAGEMENT

P.O. Box 50544, Austin TX 78763. **E-mail:** queries@hornfischerlit.com. **Website:** www.hornfischerlit.com. **Contact:** James D. Hornfischer, president.

- Prior to opening his agency, Mr. Hornfischer held editorial positions at HarperCollins and McGraw-Hill. "My New York editorial background is useful in this regard. In 17 years as an agent, I've handled 12 *New York Times* nonfiction bestsellers, including three No. 1s."

REPRESENTS nonfiction.

- Hornfischer Literary Management, L.P. is a literary agency with a strong track record of handling a broad range of serious and commercial nonfiction.

HOW TO CONTACT E-mail queries preferred. Responds if interested. Accepts simultaneous submissions. Responds in 5-6 weeks to mailed submissions with SASE. Obtains most new clients through referrals from clients, reading books and magazines, pursuing ideas with New York editors.

TERMS Agent receives 15% commission on domestic sales; 25% commission on foreign sales. Offers written contract.

TIPS "When you query agents and send out proposals, present yourself as someone who's in command of his material and comfortable in his own skin. Too many writers have a palpable sense of anxiety and insecurity. Take a deep breath and realize that if you're good, someone in the publishing world will want you."

HSG AGENCY

37 W. 28th St., Eighth Floor, New York NY 10001. **E-mail:** channigan@hsgagency.com, jsalky@hsgagency.com, jgetzler@hsgagency.com, tprasanna@hsgagency.com, leigh@hsgagency.com. **Website:** hsgagency.com. **Contact:** Carrie Hannigan, Jesseca Salky, Josh Getzler,Tanusri Prasanna, Leigh Eisenman. Estab. 2011. Member of AAR. Signatory of WGA.

- Prior to opening HSG Agency, Ms. Hannigan, Ms. Salky. and Mr. Getzler were agents at Russell & Volkening.

MEMBER AGENTS Carrie Hannigan; Jesseca Salky (literary and mainstream fiction); Josh Getzler (foreign and historical fiction; women's fiction, straight-ahead historical fiction, thriller, mystery); **Tanusri Prasanna** (picture books, children's, Middle-grade, young adult, select nonfiction); **Leigh Eisenman** (literary and upmarket fiction, foodie/cookbooks, health and fitness, lifestyle, select narrative nonfiction).

REPRESENTS nonfiction, fiction, novels, juvenile books. **Considers these nonfiction areas:** business, cooking, creative nonfiction, current affairs, diet/nutrition, education, environment, foods, health, history, humor, literature, memoirs, multicultural, music, parenting, photography, politics, psychology, science, self-help, sports, women's issues, women's studies, young adult. **Considers these fiction areas:** adventure, commercial, contemporary issues, crime, detective, ethnic, family saga, historical, juvenile, literary, mainstream, middle-grade, multicultural, mystery, picture books, thriller, translation, women's, young adult.

HOW TO CONTACT Electronic submissions only. Send query letter, first 5 pages of ms within e-mail to appropriate agent. Avoid submitting to multiple agents within the agency. For picture books, include entire ms. Responds in 4-6 weeks if interested.

RECENT SALES *A Spool of Blue Thread*, by Anne Tyler (Knopf); *Blue Sea Burning*, by Geoff Rodkey (Putnam); *The Partner Track*, by Helen Wan (St. Martin's Press); *The Thrill of the Haunt*, by E.J. Copperman (Berkley); *Aces Wild*, by Erica Perl (Knopf Books for Young Readers); *Steve & Wessley: The Sea Monster*, by Jennifer Morris (Scholastic); *Infinite Worlds*, by Michael Soluri (Simon & Schuster).

⊘ ICM PARTNERS

65 E. 55th St., New York NY 10022. (212)556-5600. **Website:** www.icmtalent.com. **Contact:** Literary Department. Member of AAR. Signatory of WGA. **REPRESENTS** nonfiction, fiction, novels. **HOW TO CONTACT** Accepts simultaneous submissions.

INKLINGS LITERARY AGENCY

3419 Virginia Beach Blvd., #183, Virginia Beach VA 23452. (757)340-1070. **Fax:** (904)758-5440. **E-mail:** michelle@inklingsliterary.com. **E-mail:** query@inklingsliterary.com. **Website:** www.inklingsliterary.com. Inklings Literary Agency is a full-service, hands-on literary agency seeking submissions from established authors as well as talented new authors. "We represent a broad range of commercial and literary fiction, as well as memoirs and true crime. We are not seeking short stories, poetry, screenplays, or children's picture books." Estab. 2013. Memberships include RWA, SinC, HRW.

○ "We offer our clients interactive representation for their work, as well as developmental guidance for their author platforms, working with them as they grow. "

MEMBER AGENTS Michelle Johnson, michelle@inklingsliterary.com (adult and young adult fiction, contemporary, suspense, thriller, mystery, horror, fantasy [including paranormal and supernatural elements within those genres], romance of every level, nonfiction in the areas of memoir and true crime); **Dr. Jamie Bodnar Drowley**, jamie@inklingsliterary.com (New Adult fiction in the areas of romance [all subgenres], fantasy [urban fantasy, light science fiction, steampunk], mystery and thriller, young adult [all subgenres], middle-grade stories); **Margaret Bail**, margaret@inklingsliterary.com (romance, science fiction, mystery, thriller, action adventure, historical fiction, Western, some fantasy, memoir, cookbooks, true crime); **Naomi Davis**, naomi@inklingsliterary.com (romance of any variety including paranormal, fresh urban fantasy, general fantasy, New Adult, light science fiction, young adult in any of those same genres, memoirs about living with disabilities, facing criticism, mental illness); **Whitley Abell**, whitley@inklingsliterary.com (young adult, middle-grade, select upmarket women's fiction); **Alex Barba**, alex@inklingsliterary.com (YA fiction).

REPRESENTS nonfiction, fiction, novels, juvenile books. **Considers these nonfiction areas:** cooking, creative nonfiction, diet/nutrition, gay/lesbian, memoirs, true crime, women's issues. **Considers these fiction areas:** action, adventure, commercial, contemporary issues, crime, detective, erotica, ethnic, fantasy, feminist, gay, historical, horror, juvenile, lesbian, mainstream, metaphysical, middle-grade, military, multicultural, multimedia, mystery, New Adult, New Age, occult, paranormal, police, psychic, regional, romance, science fiction, spiritual, sports, supernatural, suspense, thriller, urban fantasy, war, women's, young adult.

HOW TO CONTACT E-queries only. To query, type "Query (Agent Name)" plus the title of your novel in the subject line, then please send your query letter, short synopsis, and first 10 pages pasted into the body of the e-mail to query@inklingsliterary.com. Check the agency website to make sure that your targeted

NEW AGENT SPOTLIGHT

ED MAXWELL

SANFORD J. GREENBURGER ASSOCIATES

www.greenburger.com
@IgnatiusMaxwell

ABOUT ED: Associate agent Ed Maxwell joined Greenburger Associates in 2011. Previously, he interned in various political offices on Capitol Hill and in New York. Ed graduated from New York University with a degree in history. Starting as the assistant to Faith Hamlin, he distinguished himself as a close reader with an eclectic range. In addition to agenting on his own, he continues to co-agent certain titles and authors while assisting Faith in managing her list. Find him on Twitter.

HE IS SEEKING: Ed is seeking expert and narrative nonfiction authors, novelists and graphic novelists, and children's book authors and illustrators. His aim as a literary agent is to help authors grow their intellectual properties into compelling books. He is especially interested in working with authors who may publish across different genres and formats—scholarly and trade—over the course of their careers. Ed believes in popular media as a living cultural record and hopes to connect with authors of diverse backgrounds, perspectives, and voices.

HOW TO SUBMIT: Please email emaxwell@sjga.com with your submission under the subject line "QUERY: [Project Title]." Include a query letter in the body of the email and attach a proposal or a sample from your project (40 pages maximum).

agent is currently open to submissions. Accepts simultaneous submissions. For queries, no response in 3 months is considered a rejection. Yes
TERMS Agent receives 15% commission on domestic sales, 20% commission on subsidiary rights. Charges no fees.

INKWELL MANAGEMENT, LLC

521 Fifth Ave., Suite 2600, New York NY 10175. (212)922-3500. **Fax:** (212)922-0535. **E-mail:** info@inkwellmanagement.com. **E-mail:** submissions@

inkwellmanagement.com. **Website:** www.inkwell-management.com. Represents 500 clients.
MEMBER AGENTS Stephen Barbara (select adult fiction and nonfiction); **William Callahan** (nonfiction of all stripes, especially American history and memoir, pop culture and illustrated books; voice-driven fiction that stands out from the crowd); **Michael V. Carlisle**; **Catherine Drayton** (best-selling authors of books for children, young adults and women readers); **David Forrer** (literary, commercial, historical, and crime fiction to suspense/thriller, humor-

ous nonfiction, and popular history); **Alexis Hurley** (literary and commercial fiction, memoir, narrative nonfiction, and more); **Nathaniel Jacks** (memoir, narrative nonfiction, social sciences, health, current affairs, business,religion, popular history, as well as fiction—literary and commercial, women's, young adult, historical, short story, among others); **Jacqueline Murphy**; (fiction, children's books, graphic novels and illustrated works, compelling narrative nonfiction); **Richard Pine**; **Eliza Rothstein** (literary and commercial fiction, narrative nonfiction, memoir, popular science, food writing); **David Hale Smith**; **Kimberly Witherspoon**; **Jenny Witherell**; **Charlie Olson**; **Liz Parker** (commercial and upmarket women's fiction; narrative, practical, and platform-driven nonfiction); **George Lucas**; **Lyndsey Blessing**; **Claire Draper**; **Kate Falkoff**; **Claire Friedman**; **Michael Mungiello**; **Jessica Mileo**; **Corinne Sullivan**; **Maria Whelan**.

REPRESENTS novels. **Considers these nonfiction areas:** biography, business, cooking, creative nonfiction, current affairs, foods, health, history, humor, memoirs, popular culture, religious, science. **Considers these fiction areas:** commercial, crime, historical, literary, middle-grade, picture books, romance, short story collections, suspense, thriller, women's, young adult.

HOW TO CONTACT "In the body of your e-mail, please include a query letter and a short writing sample (1-2 chapters). We currently accept submissions in all genres, except screenplays. Due to the volume of queries we receive, our response may take up to 2 months. Feel free to put 'Query for [Agent Name]: [Your Book Title]' in the e-mail subject line." Accepts simultaneous submissions. Obtains most new clients through recommendations from others.

TERMS Agent receives 15% commission on domestic sales; 20% commission on foreign sales. Offers written contract.

TIPS "We will not read mss before receiving a letter of inquiry."

INTERNATIONAL TRANSACTIONS, INC.

P.O. Box 97, Gila NM 88038. (845)373-9696. **Fax:** (480)393-5162. **E-mail:** submission-nonfiction@intltrans.com, submission-fiction@intltrans.com. **Website:** www.intltrans.com. **Contact:** Peter Riva. Estab. 1975.

MEMBER AGENTS Peter Riva (nonfiction, fiction, illustrated; television and movie rights placement); Sandra Riva (fiction, juvenile, biography); JoAnn Collins (fiction, women's fiction, medical fiction).

REPRESENTS nonfiction, fiction, novels, short story collections, juvenile books, scholarly books, illustrated books, anthologies. **Considers these nonfiction areas:** Americana, anthropology, archeology, architecture, art, autobiography, biography, business, computers, cooking, cultural interests, current affairs, diet/nutrition, design, environment, ethnic, film, foods, gay/lesbian, government, health, history, humor, inspirational, investigative, language, law, literature, medicine, memoirs, military, multicultural, music, photography, popular culture, politics, religious, satire, science, self-help, sports, technology, translation, true crime, war, women's issues, women's studies, young adult. **Considers these fiction areas:** action, adventure, commercial, crime, detective, erotica, experimental, family saga, feminist, gay, historical, humor, inspirational, lesbian, literary, mainstream, middle-grade, military, multicultural, mystery, New Adult, police, satire, science fiction, spiritual, sports, suspense, thriller, translation, war, westerns, women's, young adult, chick lit.

HOW TO CONTACT First, e-query with an outline or synopsis. E-queries only. Put "Query: [Title]" in the e-mail subject line. Responds in 3 weeks to queries, 5 weeks to mss after request. Obtains most new clients through recommendations from others, solicitations.

TERMS Agent receives 15% (25% on illustrated books) commission on domestic sales; 20% commission on foreign sales and media rights. Offers written contract; 100-day notice must be given to terminate contract. No additional fees, ever.

RECENT SALES Averaging 20+ book placements per year.

JABBERWOCKY LITERARY AGENCY

49 W. 45th St., New York NY 10036. (917)388-3010. **Website:** www.awfulagent.com. **Contact:** Joshua Bilmes. Estab. 1990. Member of SFWA. Represents 40 clients.

MEMBER AGENTS Joshua Bilmes, Eddie Schneider, Lisa Rodgers, Sam Morgan, Brady McReynolds.

REPRESENTS nonfiction, fiction, novels, novellas, juvenile books. **Considers these nonfiction areas:** autobiography, biography, business, cooking, current affairs, economics, film, foods, gay/lesbian, government, health, history, humor, language, law, literature, medicine, money, music, popular culture, politics, satire, science, sociology, sports, technology, theater, war, women's issues, women's studies, young adult. **Considers these fiction areas:** action, adventure, contemporary issues, crime, detective, ethnic, family saga, fantasy, feminist, gay, glitz, historical, horror, humor, juvenile, lesbian, literary, mainstream, middle-grade, mystery, New Adult, paranormal, police, psychic, regional, romance, satire, science fiction, sports, supernatural, thriller, women's, young adult.

⌐ This agency represents quite a lot of genre fiction, romance, and mystery, and is actively seeking to increase the amount of nonfiction projects. It does not handle children's or picture books. Book-length material only—no poetry, articles, or short fiction.

HOW TO CONTACT "We are currently open to unsolicited queries. No e-mail, phone, or fax queries, please. Query with SASE. Please check our website, as there may be times during the year when we are not accepting queries. Query letter only; no manuscript material unless requested." Accepts simultaneous submissions. Responds in 3 weeks to queries. Obtains most new clients through solicitations, recommendation by current clients.

TERMS Agent receives 15% commission on domestic sales; 20% commission on foreign sales. Offers written contract, binding for 1 year. Charges clients for book purchases, photocopying, international book/ms mailing.

RECENT SALES 188 individual deals done in 2014: 60 domestic and 128 foreign. *Alcatraz #5*, by Brandon Sanderson; *Aurora Teagarden*, by Charlaine Harris; *The Unnoticeables*, by Robert Brockway; *Messenger's Legacy*, by Peter V. Brett; *Slotter Key*, by Elizabeth Moon. Other clients include Tanya Huff, Simon Green, Jack Campbell, Myke Cole, Marie Brennan, Daniel Jose Older, Jim Hines, Mark Hodder, Toni Kelner, Ari Marmell, Ellery Queen, Erin Tettensor, Walter Jon Williams.

JANKLOW & NESBIT ASSOCIATES

285 Madison Ave., 21st Floor, New York NY 10017. (212)421-1700. **Fax:** (212)355-1403. **E-mail:** info@janklow.com. **E-mail:** submissions@janklow.com. **Website:** www.janklowandnesbit.com. Estab. 1989. **MEMBER AGENTS** Morton L. Janklow, Anne Sibbald, Lynn Nesbit, Luke Janklow, PJ Mark (interests are eclectic, including short stories and literary novels; nonfiction: journalism, popular culture, memoir/narrative, essays, cultural criticism); **Paul Lucas** (literary and commercial fiction, focusing on literary thriller, science fiction and fantasy; also seeks narrative histories of ideas and objects, as well as biography and popular science); **Emma Parry** (nonfiction by experts, but will consider outstanding literary fiction and upmarket commercial fiction); **Kirby Kim; Marya Spence; Allison Hunter; Melissa Flashman; Stefanie Lieberman.**
REPRESENTS nonfiction, fiction.

HOW TO CONTACT Query via snail mail or e-mail. Include a cover letter, synopsis, and the first 10 pages if sending fiction (no attachments). For nonfiction, send a query and full outline. Address your submission to an individual agent. Accepts simultaneous submissions. Responds in 8 weeks to queries/mss. Obtains most new clients through recommendations from others.

THE CAROLYN JENKS AGENCY

30 Cambridge Park Dr., Cambridge MA 02140. (617)354-5099. **E-mail:** queries@carolynjenksagency.com. **Website:** www.carolynjenksagency.com. **Contact:** Carolyn Jenks. "This is a boutique agency, which means we give special attention to all of our clients. We act as a mentor to young professionals and students who are entering the profession, in addition to representing established writers." Estab. 1987. Signatory of WGA.
MEMBER AGENTS Carolyn Jenks; see agency website for a list of junior agents.
REPRESENTS nonfiction, fiction, novels, juvenile books. **Considers these nonfiction areas:** animals, autobiography, biography, gay/lesbian, history, juvenile nonfiction, literature, memoirs, theater, true crime, women's issues, women's studies, young adult. **Considers these fiction areas:** action, adventure, contemporary issues, crime, ethnic, experimental, family saga, feminist, gay, historical, horror, juvenile, lesbian, literary, mainstream, mystery, New Adult, science fiction, thriller, women's, young adult. **Considers these script areas:** biography, contemporary issues, ethnic, experimental, family saga, feminist, frontier, historical, inspirational, mainstream, mystery, romantic drama, science fiction, supernatural, suspense, thriller.

HOW TO CONTACT Please submit a 1-page query including a brief bio via the form on the agency website. "Due to the high volume of queries we receive, we are unable to respond to everyone. Queries are reviewed on a rolling basis, and we will follow up directly with the author if there is interest in a full manuscript. Queries should not be addressed to specific agents. All queries go directly to the director for distribution." Obtains new clients by recommendations from others, queries/submissions, agency outreach.

TERMS Offers written contract, binding for 1-3 years, depending on the project; 60-day notice msut be given before terminating contract. No fees.

RECENT SALES *Snafu*, by Miryam Sivan (Cuidano Press); *The Land of Forgotten Girls*, by Erin Kelly (Harper Collins); *The Christos Mosaic*, by Vincent Czyz (Blank Slate Press); *A Tale of Two Maidens*, by Anne Echols (Bagwyn Books); *Esther*, by Rebecca Kanner (Simon and Schuster); *Magnolia City*, by Duncan Alderson (Kensington Books).

TIPS "Do not make cold calls to the agency. E-mail contact only. Do not query for more than one property at a time. If possible, have a professional photograph of yourself ready to submit with your query, as it is important to be media-genic in today's marketplace. Be ready to discuss platform."

JERNIGAN LITERARY AGENCY

P.O. Box 741624, Dallas TX 75374. (972)722-4838. E-mail: jerniganliterary@gmail.com. **Contact:** Barry Jernigan. Estab. 2010. Represents 45 clients.

MEMBER AGENTS Barry Jernigan (eclectic tastes in nonfiction and fiction; nonfiction: women's issues, gay/lesbian, ethnic/cultural, memoirs, true crime; fiction: mystery, suspense, thriller).

REPRESENTS nonfiction, fiction, novels, movie scripts, feature films. **Considers these nonfiction areas:** biography, business, child guidance, current affairs, education, ethnic, health, history, how-to, memoirs, military, psychology, self-help, true crime. **Considers these fiction areas:** historical, mainstream, mystery, romance, thriller.

HOW TO CONTACT E-mail your query with a synopsis, brief bio and the first few pages embedded; no attachments. "We do not accept unsolicited manuscripts. We accept submissions via e-mail only. No snail mail accepted." Accepts simultaneous submissions. Responds in 2 weeks to queries, 6 weeks to mss. Obtains new clients through conferences, word of mouth.

TERMS Agent receives 15% commission.

JET LITERARY ASSOCIATES

941 Calle Mejia, #507, Santa Fe NM 87501. (505)780-0721. **E-mail:** etp@jetliterary.com. **Website:** www.jetliterary.wordpress.com. **Contact:** Liz Trupin-Pulli. Estab. 1975.

MEMBER AGENTS Liz Trupin-Pulli (adult fiction and nonfiction; romance, mystery, parenting); **Jim Trupin** (adult fiction and nonfiction, military history, pop culture).

REPRESENTS nonfiction, fiction, novels, short story collections.

> "JET was founded in New York in 1975, so we bring a wealth of knowledge and contacts, as well as quite a bit of expertise, to our representation of writers." JET represents the full range of adult fiction and nonfiction. Does not want to receive young adult, science fiction, fantasy, horror, poetry, children's, how-to, or religious books.

HOW TO CONTACT Only an e-query should be sent at first. Accepts simultaneous submissions. Responds in 1 week to queries, 8-12 weeks to mss. Obtains most new clients through recommendations from others, solicitations, conferences.

TERMS Agent receives 15% commission on domestic sales; 10% commission on foreign sales, while foreign agent receives 10%. Offers written agency contract, binding for 3 years. This agency charges for reimbursement of mailing and any photocopying.

TIPS "Do not write cute queries, stick to a straightforward message that includes the title and what your book is about, why you are suited to write this particular book, and what you have written in the past (if anything), along with a bit of a bio."

KELLER MEDIA INC.

578 Washington Blvd., No. 745, Marina del Rey CA 90292. (800)278-8706. **Website:** www.kellermedia.com. **Contact:** Wendy Keller, senior agent (nonfiction); Megan Close Zavala, literary agent (nonfiction, fiction); Elise Howard, query manager. Keller Media has made more than 1,200 deals; has 16 *New York Times* bestsellers and 6 international bestsellers. Estab. 1989. Member of the National Speakers Association.

> Prior to becoming an agent, Ms. Keller was an award-winning journalist and worked for PR Newswire. Prior to her agenting career, Ms.

Close Zavala read, reviewed, edited, rejected, and selected thousands of book and script projects for agencies, film companies, and publishing companies. She uses her background in entertainment and legal affairs in negotiating the best deals for her clients and in helping them think outside the box.

REPRESENTS nonfiction, fiction. **Considers these nonfiction areas:** archeology, autobiography, biography, business, crafts, creative nonfiction, current affairs, diet/nutrition, economics, environment, foods, gardening, health, history, hobbies, how-to, literature, money, parenting, popular culture, politics, psychology, science, self-help, sociology, true crime, women's issues. **Considers these fiction areas:** action, adventure, commercial, family saga, historical, literary, multicultural, mystery, New Adult, police, regional, romance, suspense, thriller, women's.

❧ "All of our authors are highly credible experts who have or want to create a significant platform in media, academia, politics, paid professional speaking, syndicated columns, and/or regular appearances on radio/TV. For fiction submissions, we are interested in working with authors who have strong, fresh voices and who have unique stories especially in the mystery/thriller/suspense, and literary fiction genres." Does not want (and absolutely will not respond to) scripts, teleplays, screenplays, poetry, juvenile, science fiction, fantasy, anything religious or overtly political, picture books, illustrated books, young adult, science fiction, fantasy, first-person stories of mental or physical illness, wrongful incarceration, abduction by aliens, books channeled by aliens, demons, or dead celebrities ("we wish we were kidding!").

HOW TO CONTACT To query, please review current screening criteria on website: http://www.kellermedia.com/our-screening-criteria. "Please do not mail us anything unless requested to do so by a staff member." Accepts simultaneous submissions. Responds in 7 days or less. Obtains most new clients through referrals.

TERMS Agent receives 15% commission on domestic sales; 20% commission on foreign, dramatic, sponsorship, appearance fees, audio, and merchandising deals; 30% on speaking engagements booked for the author.

RECENT SALES Check online for latest sales.

TIPS "Don't send a query to any agent (including us) unless you're certain they handle the type of book you're writing. Have your proposal in order before you query. Never make apologies for 'bad writing' or sloppy content. Please just get it right before you waste your one shot with us. Have something new, different, or interesting to say, and be ready to dedicate your whole heart to marketing it. Marketing is everything in publishing these days. If you are submitting fiction to us, please make sure that the story hasn't been told 1,000 times over and that your unique voice shines through!"

⊘ NATASHA KERN LITERARY AGENCY

White Salmon WA 98672. **E-mail:** via website. **Website:** www.natashakern.com. **Contact:** Natasha Kern. Estab. 1986. Memberships include RWA, MWA, SinC, the Authors Guild, ASJA. Represents 40 clients.

○ Prior to opening her agency, Ms. Kern worked in publishing in New York. This agency has sold more than 1,500 books.

REPRESENTS fiction, novels. **Considers these nonfiction areas:** investigative journalism. **Considers these fiction areas:** commercial, historical, inspirational, mainstream, multicultural, mystery, romance, suspense, women's, only inspirational fiction in these genres..

❧ This agency specializes in inspirational fiction in a broad range of genres, including suspense and mystery, historicals, romance, and contemporary novels. By referral only. Does not represent horror, true crime, erotica, children's books, short stories or novellas, poetry, screenplays, technical, photography or art/craft books, cookbooks, travel, or sports books. No nonfiction.

HOW TO CONTACT This agency is currently closed to unsolicited fiction and nonfiction submissions. Submissions only via referral. Obtains new clients by referral only.

TERMS Agent receives 15% commission on domestic sales; 20% commission on foreign sales; 15% commission on film sales.

TIPS "Your chances of being accepted for representation will be greatly enhanced by going to our website first. Our idea of a dream client is someone who participates in a mutually respectful business relationship, is clear about needs and goals, and communicates about career planning. If we know what you need and want, we can help you achieve it. A dream

NEW AGENT SPOTLIGHT

RICK PASCOCELLO

GLASS LITERARY

www.glassliterary.com

ABOUT RICK: Rick Pascocello has spent his entire career marketing books, including 23 years with Penguin Random House, where he was vice president, executive director of marketing. While there, he was given the rare opportunity to work closely with a wonderfully diverse collection of writers, including some of fiction's premier authors like Harlan Coben, Patricia Cornwell, Ken Follett, Charlaine Harris, Khaled Hosseini, Nora Roberts, Patrick Rothfuss, and JR Ward, as well as nonfiction bestsellers such as Stephen Johnson, Jen Lancaster, James McBride, Dan Pink, and Joan Rivers. Rick oversaw the marketing campaigns for thousands of *New York Times* bestsellers and spearheaded innovative marketing strategies in social media, retail partnerships, and cause-related marketing, such as 'Read Pink' to benefit the Breast Cancer Research Foundation and the *Kite Runner* campaign that built a school in Afghanistan. Since 2015, he has provided independent marketing support to authors, corporations, and nonprofit organizations. He brings a vast and diverse range of experience and relationships to his role as a literary agent, and he will continue to leverage his broad insider knowledge of book publishing and media to advocate for his clients.

HE IS SEEKING: Rick is interested in working with nonfiction authors who bring a unique perspective to memoir, biography, business, history, narrative nonfiction, sports, popular culture, social commentary, and other thought-provoking ideas, as well as mainstream and literary fiction writers whose voices ring true on every page.

HOW TO SUBMIT: Rick accepts queries by email only. Please send your query to rick@glassliterary.com. Please send your query letter in the body of an email; do not include attachments. If Rick is interested, he will respond and ask for the complete manuscript or proposal. He prefers queries that describe your book concisely, are well written and typo-free, show an understanding of the marketplace and where your book would fit into it, and show why you are the best person to be writing the book you're proposing.

client has a storytelling gift, a commitment to a writing career, a desire to learn and grow, and a passion for excellence. We want clients who are expressing their own unique voice and truly have something of their own to communicate. This client understands that many people have to work together for a book to succeed and that everything in publishing takes far longer than one imagines. Trust and communication are truly essential."

HARVEY KLINGER, INC.

300 W. 55th St., Suite 11V, New York NY 10019. (212)581-7068. **E-mail:** queries@harveyklinger.com. **Website:** www.harveyklinger.com. **Contact:** Harvey Klinger. Always interested in considering new clients, both published and unpublished. Estab. 1977. Member of AAR, PEN. Represents 100 clients.

MEMBER AGENTS Harvey Klinger; David Dunton (popular culture, music-related books, literary fiction, young adult, fiction, memoirs); **Andrea Somberg** (literary fiction, commercial fiction, romance, science fiction/fantasy, mystery/thriller, young adult, middle-grade, quality narrative nonfiction, popular culture, how-to, self-help, humor, interior design, cookbooks, health/fitness); **Wendy Levinson** (literary and commercial fiction, occasional children's young adult or Middle-grade, wide variety of nonfiction); **Rachel Ridout** (Middle-grade and young adult).

REPRESENTS nonfiction, fiction, novels, juvenile books. **Considers these nonfiction areas:** autobiography, biography, business, child guidance, cooking, crafts, creative nonfiction, cultural interests, current affairs, diet/nutrition, foods, gay/lesbian, health, history, how-to, investigative, literature, medicine, memoirs, money, music, popular culture, psychology, science, self-help, sociology, spirituality, sports, technology, true crime, women's issues, women's studies, young adult. **Considers these fiction areas:** action, adventure, commercial, contemporary issues, crime, detective, erotica, family saga, fantasy, gay, glitz, historical, horror, juvenile, lesbian, literary, mainstream, middle-grade, mystery, New Adult, police, romance, suspense, thriller, women's, young adult.

⚷ This agency specializes in big, mainstream, contemporary fiction and nonfiction.

HOW TO CONTACT Use online e-mail submission form on the website, or query with SASE via snail mail. No phone or fax queries. Don't send unsolicited mss or e-mail attachments. Make submission letter to the point and as brief as possible. Accepts simultaneous submissions. Responds in 2-4 weeks to queries, if interested. Obtains most new clients through recommendations from others.

TERMS Agent receives 15% commission on domestic sales; 25% commission on foreign sales. Offers written contract. Charges for photocopying mss and overseas postage for mss.

RECENT SALES *Land of the Afternoon Sun*, by Barbara Wood; *I Am Not a Serial Killer*, by Dan Wells; *Me, Myself and Us*, by Brian Little; *The Secret of Magic*, by Deborah Johnson; *Children of the Mist*, by Paula Quinn.

THE KNIGHT AGENCY

232 W. Washington St., Madison GA 30650. **E-mail:** deidre.knight@knightagency.net, submissions@knightagency.net. **Website:** http://knightagency.net/. **Contact:** Deidre Knight. Estab. 1996. Member of AAR, SCWBI, WFA, SFWA, RWA. Represents 200+ clients.

MEMBER AGENTS Deidre Knight (romance, women's fiction, erotica, commercial fiction, inspirational, fiction, memoir, nonfiction narrative, personal finance, true crime, business, popular culture, self-help, religion, health); **Pamela Harty** (romance, women's fiction, young adult, business, motivational, diet and health, memoir, parenting, pop culture, true crime); **Elaine Spencer** (romance [single title and category], women's fiction, commercial "book-club" fiction, cozy mystery, young adult and middle-grade material); **Lucienne Diver** (fantasy, science fiction, romance, suspense, young adult); **Nephele Tempest** (literary/commercial fiction, women's fiction, fantasy, science fiction, romantic suspense, paranormal romance, contemporary romance, historical fiction, young adult, middle-grade fiction); **Melissa Jeglinski** (romance [contemporary, category, historical, inspirational], young adult, middle-grade, women's fiction, mystery); **Kristy Hunter** (romance, women's fiction, commercial fiction, young adult, middle-grade material), **Travis Pennington** (young adult, middle-grade, mystery, thriller, commercial fiction, romance [nothing paranormal/fantasy in any genre for now]).

REPRESENTS nonfiction, fiction, novels. **Considers these nonfiction areas:** autobiography, business, creative nonfiction, cultural interests, current affairs, diet/nutrition, design, economics, ethnic, film, foods, gay/lesbian, health, history, how-to, inspirational, interior design, investigative, juvenile nonfiction, literature, memoirs, military, money, multicultural, parenting, popular culture, politics, psychology, self-help, sociology, technology, travel, true crime, women's issues, young adult. **Considers these fiction areas:** commercial, crime, erotica, fantasy, gay, historical, juvenile, lesbian, literary, mainstream, middle-grade, multicultural, mystery, New Adult, paranormal, psychic, romance, science fiction, thriller, urban fantasy, women's, young adult.

⊶ Actively seeking romance in all subgenres, including romantic suspense, paranormal romance, historical romance (a particular love of mine), LGBTQ, contemporary, and also category romance. Does not want to receive screenplays, short stories, poetry, essays, or children's picture books.

HOW TO CONTACT E-queries only. "Your submission should include a 1-page query letter and the first 5 pages of your manuscript. All text must be contained in the body of your e-mail. Attachments will not be opened nor included in the consideration of your work. Queries must be addressed to a specific agent. Please do not query multiple agents." Accepts simultaneous submissions. Responds in 1-2 weeks on queries, 6-8 weeks on submissions.

TERMS 15% simple agency agreement with open-ended commitment. Agent receives 15% commission on all domestic sales; 20% on foreign and film sales.

LINDA KONNER LITERARY AGENCY

10 W. 15th St., Suite 1918, New York NY 10011. **E-mail:** ldkonner@cs.com. **Website:** www.lindakonnerliteraryagency.com. **Contact:** Linda Konner. Represents approximately 75 authors of adult nonfiction. Estab. 1996. Member of AAR, ASJA. Represents 75 clients.

REPRESENTS nonfiction. **Considers these nonfiction areas:** business, cooking, diet/nutrition, foods, health, medicine, money, popular culture, psychology, science, self-help, women's issues, biography (celebrity), African-American and Latino issues, relationships, popular science.

⊶ This agency specializes in health, self-help, and how-to books. Authors/co-authors must be top experts in their field with a substantial

media platform. Does not want fiction, children's, young adult, illustrated books.

HOW TO CONTACT Query by e-mail (or snail mail with SASE) with synopsis and author bio, including size of social media following, size of website following, appearances in traditional media (print/TV/radio), and frequency/size of speaking engagements. Prefers to read materials exclusively for 2 weeks. Accepts simultaneous submissions. Responds within 2 weeks. Obtains most new clients through recommendations from others, occasional solicitation among established authors/journalists.

TERMS Agent receives 15% commission on domestic sales; 25% commission on foreign sales. Offers written contract. Charges one-time fee for domestic expenses; additional expenses may be incurred for foreign sales.

RECENT SALES *Iron Cowboy*, by James Lawrence with Matt Fitzgerald (Regan Arts); *Relation-Shifts*, by Helen Riess, M.D., with Liz Neporent (Sounds True); *What to Feed Your Baby & Toddler*, by Nicole Avena, PhD (Ten Speed Press); *The Reducetarian Solution*, by Brian Kateman (Tarcher-Perigee/PRH).

STUART KRICHEVSKY LITERARY AGENCY, INC.

6 E. 39th St., Suite 500, New York NY 10016. (212)725-5288. **Fax:** (212)725-5275. **Website:** www.skagency.com. Member of AAR.

MEMBER AGENTS Stuart Krichevsky, query@skagency.com (emphasis on narrative nonfiction, literary journalism, literary and commercial fiction); **Ross Harris**, rhquery@skagency.com (voice-driven humor and memoir, books on popular culture and our society, narrative nonfiction and literary fiction); **David Patterson**, dpquery@skagency.com (writers of upmarket narrative nonfiction and literary fiction, historians, journalists, and thought leaders); **Mackenzie Brady Watson**, mbwquery@skagency.com (narrative nonfiction, science, history, sociology, investigative journalism, food, business, memoir, and select upmarket and literary young adult fiction); **Hannah Schwartz**, hsquery@skagency.com; **Laura Usselman**, luquery@skagency.com.

REPRESENTS nonfiction, novels. **Considers these nonfiction areas:** business, creative nonfiction, foods, history, humor, investigative, memoirs, popular culture, science, sociology, memoir. **Considers these fiction areas:** commercial, contemporary issues, literary, young adult.

HOW TO CONTACT Please send a query letter and the first few (up to 10) pages of your ms or proposal in the body of an e-mail (not an attachment) to one of the e-mail addresses. No attachments. Responds if interested. Accepts simultaneous submissions. Obtains most new clients through recommendations from others, solicitations.

EDITE KROLL LITERARY AGENCY, INC.

20 Cross St., Saco ME 04072. (207)283-8797. **Fax:** (207)283-8799. **E-mail:** ekroll@maine.rr.com. **Contact:** Edite Kroll. Represents 45 clients.

○ Prior to opening her agency, Ms. Kroll served as a book editor and translator.

REPRESENTS nonfiction, fiction, juvenile books. **Considers these nonfiction areas:** cultural interests, humor, women's issues, young adult. **Considers these fiction areas:** feminist, juvenile, mainstream, picture books.

➳ "We represent writers and writer-artists of adult and children's books. We have a special focus on international feminist writers, women writers of nonfiction, and artists who write their own children's and humor books." Does not represent genre fiction (mystery, thriller, diet, cookery, etc.), photography books, coffee table books, romance, or commercial fiction.

HOW TO CONTACT Query by e-mail. Only submit—on request—proposals, including 1-2 sample chapters; first 50 pages of fiction; complete text and PDFs of picture books. No telephone queries. Accepts simultaneous submissions. Responds in 2-4 weeks to queries, 4-8 weeks to mss. Obtains most new clients through recommendations from others. Presently adding only a few new clients.

TERMS Agent receives 15% commission on domestic sales; 20% commission on foreign sales. Offers written contract; 30-day notice must be given to terminate contract. Charges clients for photocopying and legal fees with prior approval from clients.

RECENT SALES Sold 12 domestic/ and 5 foreign titles in the last year. Clients include Shel Silverstein and Charlotte Zolotow estates.

TIPS "Please do your research so you won't send me books/proposals I specifically excluded."

KT LITERARY, LLC

9249 S. Broadway, #200-543, Highlands Ranch CO 80129. **E-mail:** contact@ktliterary.com. **E-mail:** kate-query@ktliterary.com, saraquery@ktliterary.com, reneequery@ktliterary.com, hannahquery@ktliterary.com. **Website:** www.ktliterary.com. **Contact:** Kate Schafer Testerman, Sara Megibow, Renee Nyen, Hannah Fergesen, Hilary Harwell. Estab. 2008. Member of AAR, SCBWI, young adultLSA, ALA, SFWA, RWA. Represents 75 clients.

MEMBER AGENTS Kate Testerman (middle-grade, young adult), **Renee Nyen** (middle-grade, young adult), **Sara Megibow** (middle-grade, young adult, romance, erotica, science fiction, fantasy), **Hannah Fergesen** (middle-grade, young adult, speculative fiction). Always LGBTQ and diversity friendly.

REPRESENTS fiction. **Considers these fiction areas:** erotica, fantasy, middle-grade, romance, science fiction, young adult.

➳ Kate is looking only at young adult and middle-grade fiction and selective nonfiction. Sara seeks authors in middle-grade, young adult, and adult romance, erotica, science fiction, and fantasy. Renee is looking for young adult and middle-grade fiction only. Hannah is interested in speculative fiction in young adult, middle-grade, and adult. "We're thrilled to be actively seeking new clients with great writing, unique stories, and complex characters, for middle-grade, young adult, and adult fiction. We are especially interested in diverse voices." Does not want adult mystery, thriller, or adult literary fiction.

HOW TO CONTACT "To query us, please select one of the agents at KT Literary at a time. If we pass, you can feel free to submit to another. Please e-mail your query letter and the first 3 pages of your manuscript in the body of the e-mail. The subject line of your e-mail should include the word 'Query' along with the title of your manuscript. Queries should not contain attachments. Attachments will not be read, and queries containing attachments will be deleted unread. We aim to reply to all queries within 2 weeks of receipt." Accepts simultaneous submissions. Responds in 2-4 weeks to queries, 2 months to mss. Obtains most new clients through query slush pile.

TERMS Agent receives 15% commission on domestic sales; 20% commission on foreign sales. Offers written contract; 30-day notice must be given to terminate contract.

RECENT SALES *On the Wall*, by Carrie Harris; *A Red Peace*, by Spencer Ellsworth; *The Odds of Loving Grover Cleveland*, by Rebekah Crane; *Trail of Lightning*, by Rebecca Roanhorse; *Future Lost*, by Elizabeth Briggs; *Full Court Press*, by Maggie Wells; *An Enchantment of Ravens*, by Margaret Rogerson; *The Summer of Jordi Perez*, by Amy Spalding; *What Goes Up*, by Wen Baragrey.

THE LA LITERARY AGENCY

P.O. Box 46370, Los Angeles CA 90046. (323)654-5288. **E-mail:** ann@laliteraryagency.com; maureen@laliteraryagency.com. **Website:** www.laliteraryagency.com. **Contact:** Ann Cashman.

Prior to becoming an agent, Eric Lasher worked in broadcasting and publishing in New York and Los Angeles. Prior to opening the agency, Maureen Lasher worked in New York at Prentice-Hall, Liveright, and Random House. Please visit the agency website (www.laliteraryagency.com) for more information.

MEMBER AGENTS Ann Cashman, Eric Lasher, Maureen Lasher.

REPRESENTS nonfiction, fiction, novels. **Considers these nonfiction areas:** Americana, animals, anthropology, archeology, art, autobiography, biography, business, child guidance, cooking, crafts, creative nonfiction, cultural interests, current affairs, education, government, health, history, investigative, literature, memoirs, multicultural, music, parenting, popular culture, politics, psychology, recreation, science, sports, technology, true crime. **Considers these fiction areas:** action, adventure, commercial, contemporary issues, crime, detective, family saga, feminist, historical, literary, mainstream, mystery, suspense, thriller, women's.

HOW TO CONTACT Nonfiction: query letter and book proposal. Fiction: query letter and full ms as an attachment. Accepts simultaneous submissions.

RECENT SALES *The Fourth Trimester*, by Susan Brink (University of California Press); *Rebels in Paradise*, by Hunter Drohojowska-Philp (Holt); *La Cucina Mexicana*, by Marilyn Tausend (UC Press); *The Orpheus Clock*, by Simon Goodman (Scribner). Please visit the agency website for more information.

PETER LAMPACK AGENCY, INC.

The Empire State Building, 350 Fifth Ave., Suite 5300, New York NY 10118. (212)687-9106. **Fax:** (212)687-9109. **E-mail:** andrew@peterlampackagency.com. **Website:** www.peterlampackagency.com. **Contact:** Andrew Lampack. "The Peter Lampack Agency specializes in both commercial and literary fiction as well as nonfiction by recognized experts in a given field."

REPRESENTS nonfiction, fiction, novels. **Considers these fiction areas:** action, adventure, commercial, crime, detective, literary, mainstream, mystery, police, suspense, thriller.

"This agency specializes in commercial fiction, and nonfiction by recognized experts." Actively seeking literary and commercial fiction in the following categories: adventure, action, thriller, mystery, suspense, and psychological thriller. Does not want to receive horror, romance, science fiction, westerns, historical literary fiction, or academic material.

HOW TO CONTACT The Peter Lampack Agency no longer accepts material through conventional mail. E-queries only. When submitting, you should include a cover letter, author biography and a 1- or 2-page synopsis. Please do not send more than 1 sample chapter of your manuscript at a time. "Due to the extremely high volume of submissions,we ask that you allow 4-6 weeks for a response." Accepts simultaneous submissions. Obtains most new clients through referrals made by clients.

TERMS Agent receives 15% commission on domestic sales; 20% commission on foreign sales.

RECENT SALES *Built to Thrill*, by Clive Cussler; *Frozen Fire*, by Clive Cussler and Graham Brown; *Odessa Sea*, by Clive Cussler and Dirk Cussler; *The Oregon Files*, by Clive Cussler and Boyd Morrison; *Police State: How America's Cops Get Away with Murder*, by Gerry Spence; *The Cutthroat*, by Clive Cussler and Justin Scott; *The Pirate*, by Clive Cussler and Robin Burcell; *The Schooldays of Jesus*, by J.M. Coetzee.

TIPS "Submit only your best work for consideration. Have a very specific agenda of goals you wish your prospective agent to accomplish for you. Provide the agent with a comprehensive statement of your credentials—educational and professional accomplishments."

THE STEVE LAUBE AGENCY

24 W. Camelback Rd., A-635, Phoenix AZ 85013. (602)336-8910. **E-mail:** krichards@stevelaube.com. **Website:** www.stevelaube.com. The Steve Laube Agency is committed to providing top-quality guid-

NEW AGENT SPOTLIGHT

SHANA KELLY
EINSTEIN LITERARY

www.einsteinliterary.com

ABOUT SHANA: Shana started her publishing career in the literary department of the William Morris Agency, where she worked for ten years. She began in foreign rights in the New York office and later worked out of the London office for two years. Shana was the signing agent for many successful authors, including *New York Times* bestseller Curtis Sittenfeld, author of *Prep* and *Eligible*. For the past eight years, Shana has worked as a freelance editor and publishing consultant.

SHE IS SEEKING: Shana is looking for novels with great writing and surprising plots; her favorite books fall between commercial and literary. She has a soft spot for well written thrillers and psychological suspense.

HOW TO SUBMIT: Please submit a query letter and the first ten double-spaced pages of your manuscript in the body of the e-mail (no attachments) to submissions@einsteinliterary.com. Please put Shana's name in the subject line of your e-mail.

---

ance to authors and speakers. "Our years of experience and success bring a unique service to our clients. We focus primarily in the Christian marketplace and have put together an outstanding gallery of authors and speakers whose books continue to make an impact throughout the world." Estab. 2004. Memberships include CBA, RWA, the Author's Guild. Represents 250+ clients.

○ Prior to becoming an agent, Mr. Laube worked over a decade as a Christian bookseller (named bookstore of the year in 1989) and 11 years as editorial director of nonfiction with Bethany House Publishers (named editor of the year by AWSA). Mrs. Murray was an accomplished novelist and agent for 15 years. Mrs. Ball was an executive editor with Tyndale, Multnomah, Zondervan, and B&H

Publishing. Mr. Balow was marketing director for the "Left Behind" series at Tyndale.

MEMBER AGENTS Steve Laube (president), **Tamela Hancock Murray**, **Karen Ball**, **Dan Balow**. **REPRESENTS** nonfiction, fiction, novels. **Considers these nonfiction areas:** inspirational, religious, spirituality. **Considers these fiction areas:** fantasy, inspirational, religious, science fiction.

○ Primarily serves the Christian market (CBA). Actively seeking Christian fiction and Christian nonfiction. Does not want to receive children's picture books, poetry, or cookbooks.

HOW TO CONTACT Submit proposal package, outline, 3 sample chapters, SASE. For e-mail submissions, attach as Word doc or PDF. Consult website for guidelines, because queries are sent to assistants, and the assistants' e-mail addresses may change. Accepts simultaneous submissions. Responds in 6-8 weeks to queries. Obtains most new clients through recommendations from others, solicitations, conferences.

TERMS Agent receives 15% commission on domestic sales; 20% commission on foreign sales. Offers written contract; 30-day notice must be given to terminate contract.

RECENT SALES Average closing on a new book deal every two business days, often for multiple titles in a contract. Clients include Susan May Warren, Lisa Bergren, Lynette Eason, Deborah Raney, Allison Bottke, H. Norman Wright, Ellie Kay, Karol Ladd, Stephen M. Miller, Judith Pella, Nancy Pearcey, William Lane Craig, Elizabeth Goddard, Pamela Tracy, Kim Vogel Sawyer, Mesu Andrews, Mary Hunt, Hugh Ross, Timothy Smith, Roseanna White, Bill & Pam Farrel, Ronie Kendig.

LAUNCHBOOKS LITERARY AGENCY

E-mail: david@launchbooks.com. **Website:** www.launchbooks.com. **Contact:** David Fugate. Represents 45 clients.

○ Mr. Fugate has been an agent for over 25 years and has successfully represented more than 1,000 book titles. He left another agency to found LaunchBooks in 2005.

REPRESENTS nonfiction, fiction, novels. **Considers these nonfiction areas:** animals, anthropology, autobiography, biography, business, computers, creative nonfiction, current affairs, diet/nutrition, economics, environment, film, health, history, how-to, humor, investigative, language, literature, medicine, memoirs, money, music, parenting, popular culture, politics, psychology, recreation, science, self-help, sex, sociology, sports, technology, travel. **Considers these fiction areas:** action, adventure, commercial, crime, fantasy, horror, humor, mainstream, military, paranormal, satire, science fiction, sports, suspense, thriller, urban fantasy, war, westerns, young adult.

☛ "We're looking for genre-breaking fiction. Do you have the next *The Martian*? Or maybe the next *Red Rising, Ready Player One, Ancillary Sword,* or *The Bone Clocks*? We're on the lookout for fun, engaging, contemporary novels that appeal to a broad audience. In nonfiction, we're interested in a broad range of topics. Check www.launchbooks.com/submissions for a complete list."

HOW TO CONTACT Query via e-mail. Accepts simultaneous submissions. Responds in 1 week to queries, 4 weeks to mss. Obtains most new clients through recommendations from others, solicitations.

TERMS Agent receives 15% commission on domestic sales; 25% commission on foreign sales. Offers written contract; 30-day notice to terminate contract. Charges occur very seldom. This agency's agreement limits any charges to $50 unless the author gives a written consent.

RECENT SALES *The Martian*, by Andy Weir (Random House); *The Remaining: Allegiance*, by DJ Molles (Orbit); *The Fold*, by Peter Clines (Crown); *Faster, Higher, Stronger*, by Mark McClusky (Hudson Street Press); *Fluent in Three Months*, by Benny Lewis (HarperOne).

⊘ SARAH LAZIN BOOKS

19 W. 21st St., Suite 501, New York NY 10010. (212)989-5757. **Fax:** (212)989-1393. **E-mail:** julia@lazinbooks.com. **Website:** www.lazinbooks.com. **Contact:** Julia Conrad. Estab. 1984. Member of AAR.

MEMBER AGENTS Sarah Lazin, Julia Conrad.

REPRESENTS nonfiction. **Considers these nonfiction areas:** autobiography, biography, business, current affairs, environment, history, investigative, memoirs, music, parenting, photography, popular culture, politics, women's studies. **Considers these fiction areas:** commercial, literary, short story collections.

HOW TO CONTACT As of 2017: "We accept submissions through referral only. We do not accept fiction submissions." Only accepts queries on referral.

TERMS Agent receives 15% commission on domestic sales; 20% commission on foreign sales.

⊘ THE NED LEAVITT AGENCY

70 Wooster St., Suite 4F, New York NY 10012. (212)334-0999. **Website:** www.nedleavittagency.com. **Contact:** Ned Leavitt, Jillian Sweeney. Member of AAR. Represents 40+ clients.

MEMBER AGENTS Ned Leavitt, founder and agent; **Britta Alexander**, agent; **Jillian Sweeney**, agent.

REPRESENTS novels.

☛ "We are small in size, but intensely dedicated to our authors and to supporting excellent and unique writing."

HOW TO CONTACT This agency now only takes queries/submissions through referred clients. Do not cold query. Accepts simultaneous submissions.

TIPS "Look online for this agency's recently changed submission guidelines."

ROBERT LECKER AGENCY

4055 Melrose Ave., Montreal QC H4A 2S5 Canada. **E-mail:** robert.lecker@gmail.com. **Website:** www.leckeragency.com. **Contact:** Robert Lecker. Represents 20 clients.

○ Prior to becoming an agent, Mr. Lecker was the cofounder and publisher of ECW Press and professor of English literature at McGill University. He has 30 years of experience in book and magazine publishing.

MEMBER AGENTS Robert Lecker (popular culture, music); **Mary Williams** (travel, food, popular science).

REPRESENTS nonfiction, novels, syndicated material. **Considers these nonfiction areas:** autobiography, biography, cooking, cultural interests, dance, diet/nutrition, ethnic, film, foods, how-to, language, literature, music, popular culture, science, technology, theater. **Considers these fiction areas:** action, adventure, crime, detective, erotica, literary, mainstream, mystery, police, suspense, thriller.

⌐ RLA specializes in books about popular culture, popular science, music, entertainment, food, and travel. The agency responds to articulate, innovative proposals within 2 weeks. Does not represent children's literature, screenplays, poetry, self-help books, or spiritual guides.

HOW TO CONTACT E-query. In the subject line, write: "New Submission QUERY." Accepts simultaneous submissions. Responds in 2 weeks to queries. Responds in 1 month to mss. Obtains most new clients through recommendations from others, conferences, interest in website.

TERMS Agent receives 15% commission on domestic sales; 15-20% commission on foreign sales. Offers written contract, binding for 1 year; 6-month notice must be given to terminate contract.

THE LESHNE AGENCY

New York NY **E-mail:** info@leshneagency.com. **E-mail:** submissions@leshneagency.com. **Website:** www.leshneagency.com. **Contact:** Lisa Leshne, agent and owner. "We are a full-service literary and talent management agency committed to the success of our clients over the course of their careers. We represent a select and growing number of writers, artists, and entertainers interested in building their brands, audience platforms, and developing long-term relationships via all forms of traditional and social media. We take a deeply personal approach by working closely with our clients to develop their best ideas for maximum impact and reach across print, digital, and other formats, providing hands-on guidance and networking for lasting success." Estab. 2011. Member of AAR, Women's Media Group.

MEMBER AGENTS Lisa Leshne, agent and owner; **Sandy Hodgman**, director of foreign rights.

REPRESENTS nonfiction, fiction, novels. **Considers these nonfiction areas:** business, creative nonfiction, cultural interests, health, how-to, humor, inspirational, memoirs, parenting, politics, science, self-help, sports, women's issues. **Considers these fiction areas:** commercial, middle-grade, young adult.

HOW TO CONTACT The Leshne Agency is seeking new and existing authors across all genres. "We are especially interested in narrative, memoir, prescriptive nonfiction, with a particular interest in sports, health, wellness, business, political, and parenting topics;,and truly terrific commercial fiction, young adult, and middle-grade books. We are not interested in screenplays, scripts, poetry, and picture books. If your submission is in a genre not specifically listed here, we are still open to considering it, but if your submission is for a genre we've mentioned as not being interested in, please don't bother sending it to us. All submissions should be made through the Authors.me portal by clicking on the link at: https://app.authors.me/#submit/the-leshne-agency." Accepts simultaneous submissions.

LEVINE GREENBERG ROSTAN LITERARY AGENCY, INC.

307 Seventh Ave., Suite 2407, New York NY 10001. (212)337-0934. **Fax:** (212)337-0948. **E-mail:** submit@lgrliterary.com. **Website:** www.lgrliterary.com. Member of AAR. Represents 250 clients.

○ Prior to opening his agency, Mr. Levine served as vice president of the Bank Street College of Education.

MEMBER AGENTS Jim Levine (nonfiction, including business, science, narrative nonfiction, social and political issues, psychology, health, spirituality, parenting); **Stephanie Rostan** (adult and young adult fiction; nonfiction, including parenting, health and wellness, sports, memoir); **Melissa Rowland**; **Daniel Greenberg** (nonfiction: popular culture, narrative nonfiction, memoir, humor; literary fiction); **Victoria Skurnick**; **Danielle Svetcov** (nonfiction); **Lindsay Edgecombe** (narrative nonfiction, memoir, lifestyle and health, illustrated books, as well as literary fiction); **Monika Verma** (nonfiction: humor, pop culture, memoir, narrative nonfiction, style and fashion; some young adult fiction [paranormal, historical, contemporary]); **Kerry Sparks** (young adult and middle-grade; select adult fiction, occasional nonfiction); **Tim Wojcik** (nonfiction, including food narratives, humor, pop culture, popular history, science; literary fiction); **Arielle Eckstut** (no queries); **Sarah Bedingfield** (literary and upmarket commercial fiction, epic family dramas, literary novels with notes of magical realism, darkly gothic stories, psychological suspense).

REPRESENTS nonfiction, novels. **Considers these nonfiction areas:** business, creative nonfiction, health, history, humor, memoirs, parenting, popular culture, science, spirituality, sports. **Considers these fiction areas:** commercial, literary, mainstream, middle-grade, suspense, young adult.

HOW TO CONTACT E-query to submit@lgrliterary.com, or online submission form. "If you would like to direct your query to one of our agents specifically, please feel free to name the agent in the online form or in the e-mail you send." Cannot respond to submissions by mail. Do not attach more than 50 pages. "Due to the volume of submissions we receive, we are unable to respond to each individually. If we would like more information about your project, we'll contact you within 3 weeks (though we do get backed up on occasion!)." Accepts simultaneous submissions. Obtains most new clients through recommendations from others.

TERMS Agent receives 15% commission on domestic sales; 20% commission on foreign sales. Offers written contract. Charges clients for out-of-pocket expenses—telephone, fax, postage, photocopying—directly connected to the project.

RECENT SALES *Notorious RBG*, by Irin Carmon and Shana Knizhnik; *Pogue's Basics: Life*, by David Pogue; In*visible City*, by Julia Dahl; *Gumption*, by Nick Offerman; *All the Bright Places*, by Jennifer Niven.

TIPS "We focus on editorial development, business representation, and publicity and marketing strategy."

PAUL S. LEVINE LITERARY AGENCY

1054 Superba Ave., Venice CA 90291. (310)450-6711. **Fax:** (310)450-0181. **E-mail:** paul@paulslevinelit.com. **Website:** www.paulslevinelit.com. **Contact:** Paul S. Levine. Estab. 1992. Member of the State Bar of California. Represents over 100 clients.

MEMBER AGENTS Paul S. Levine (children's and young adult fiction and nonfiction, adult fiction and nonfiction except science fiction, fantasy, and horror); **Loren R. Grossman** (archeology, art/photography, architecture, child guidance/parenting, coffee table books, gardening, education/academics, health/medicine/science/technology, law, religion, memoirs, sociology).

REPRESENTS nonfiction, fiction, novels, TV movie of the week, episodic drama, sitcom, animation, documentary, miniseries, syndicated material, variety show, comic books, graphic novels. **Considers these nonfiction areas:** architecture, art, autobiography, biography, business, child guidance, cooking, crafts, creative nonfiction, current affairs, decorating, diet/nutrition, design, education, foods, gardening, gay/lesbian, health, history, how-to, humor, inspirational, interior design, investigative, juvenile nonfiction, law, medicine, memoirs, money, music, New Age, parenting, philosophy, photography, popular culture, politics, psychology, recreation, religious, satire, science, self-help, sex, sociology, spirituality, sports, technology, travel, true crime, women's issues, women's studies, young adult. **Considers these fiction areas:** adventure, ethnic, mainstream, mystery, romance, thriller, young adult.

HOW TO CONTACT E-mail preferred; snail mail with SASE is also acceptable. Send a 1-page, single-spaced query letter. In your query letter, note your target market, with a summary of specifics on how your work differs from other authors' previously published work. Accepts simultaneous submissions. Responds in 1 day to queries, 6-8 weeks to mss. Obtains most new clients through conferences, referrals, listings on various websites, directories.

TERMS Agent receives 15% commission on domestic sales. Offers written contract. Charges for postage and actual, out-of-pocket costs only.

TIPS "Write good, sellable books."

LIPPINCOTT MASSIE MCQUILKIN

27 West 20th Street, Suite 305, New York NY 10011. **E-mail:** info@lmqlit.com. **Website:** www.lmqlit.com. **MEMBER AGENTS** Laney Katz Becker, laney@lmqlit.com (book club fiction, upmarket women's fiction, suspense, thriller, memoir); **Ethan Bassoff**, ethan@lmqlit.com (literary fiction, crime fiction, and narrative nonfiction: history, sports writing, journalism, science writing, pop culture, humor, food writing); **Jason Anthony**, jason@lmqlit.com (commercial fiction of all types, including young adult, and nonfiction: memoir, pop culture, true crime, general psychology and sociology); **Will Lippincott**, will@lmqlit.com (narrative nonfiction and nonfiction: politics, history, biography, foreign affairs, health); **Rob McQuilkin**, rob@lmqlit.com (literary fiction; narrative nonfiction and nonfiction: memoir, history, biography, art history, cultural criticism, popular sociology and psychology; **Rayhane Sanders**, rayhane@lmqlit.com (literary fiction, historical fiction, upmarket commercial fiction [including select young adult], narrative nonfiction [including essays], select memoir); **Stephanie Abou** (literary and upmarket commercial fiction [including select young adult and middle-grade], crime fiction, memoir, narrative nonfiction); **Julie Stevenson** (literary and upmarket fiction, narrative nonfiction, young adult, children's books).

REPRESENTS nonfiction, novels. **Considers these nonfiction areas:** art, biography, cultural interests, foods, health, history, humor, memoirs, popular culture, politics, psychology, science, sociology, sports, true crime, narrative nonfiction. **Considers these fiction areas:** commercial, contemporary issues, crime, literary, mainstream, middle-grade, suspense, thriller, women's, young adult.

➞ "Lippincott Massie McQuilkin is a full-service literary agency that focuses on bringing fiction and nonfiction of quality to the largest possible audience."

HOW TO CONTACT E-query preferred. Include the word "Query" in the subject line of your e-mail. Review the agency's online page of agent bios (lmqlit.com/contact.html), as some agents want sample pages with their submissions and some do not. If you have not heard back from the agency in 4 weeks, assume they are not interested in seeing more. Accepts simultaneous submissions. Obtains most new clients through recommendations from others, solicitations, conferences.

TERMS Agent receives 15% commission on domestic sales; 20% commission on foreign sales. Offers written contract; 30-day notice must be given to terminate contract. Only charges for reasonable business expenses upon successful sale.

RECENT SALES Clients include Peter Ho Davies, Kim Addonizio, Natasha Trethewey, David Sirota, Katie Crouch, Uwen Akpan, Lydia Millet, Tom Perrotta, Jonathan Lopez, Chris Hayes, Caroline Weber.

⊘ LITERARY AND CREATIVE ARTISTS, INC.

3543 Albemarle St., NW, Washington DC 20008-4213. (202)362-4688. **Fax:** (202)362-8875. **E-mail:** lca9643@lcadc.com. **Website:** www.lcadc.com. **Contact:** Muriel Nellis. Member of AAR, the Authors Guild, American Bar Association, American Booksellers Association.

MEMBER AGENTS Prior to becoming an agent, Mr. Powell was in sales and contract negotiation.

REPRESENTS **Considers these nonfiction areas:** autobiography, biography, business, cooking, economics, foods, government, health, how-to, law, medicine, memoirs, philosophy, politics.

➞ "Actively seeking quality projects by authors with a vision of where they want to be in 10 years and a plan of how to get there." We do not handle poetry or purely academic/technical work.

HOW TO CONTACT Query via e-mail first and include a synopsis. No attachments. We do not accept unsolicited mss, faxed mss, mss sent by e-mail, or mss on computer disk. Accepts simultaneous submissions. Responds in 3 weeks to queries, 1 week to mss. Obtains new clients through recommendations from others.

TERMS Agent receives 15% commission on domestic sales; 25% commission on foreign sales. Offers written contract. Charges clients for long-distance phone/fax, photocopying, shipping.

TIPS "If you are an unpublished author, join a writers group, even if it is on the Internet. You need good, honest feedback. Don't send a manuscript that has not been read by at least five people. Don't send a manuscript cold to any agent without first asking if they want it. Try to meet the agent face to face before signing. Make sure the fit is right."

NEW AGENT SPOTLIGHT

AIMEE ASHCRAFT
BROWER LITERARY & MANAGEMENT

www.browerliterary.com
@AimeeAshcraft

ABOUT AIMEE: Aimee has always loved books. She loved them so much that as a child, she was often caught sneakily reading Roald Dahl and Harry Potter under her desk at school. As an adult, she's thankfully managed to make reading part of her job and is busy seeking out novels that feature engrossing worlds as well as compelling and complex female characters. She loves stories that are told from an original point of view and are as addictive as a good Netflix binge. After earning her BA from Transylvania University, Aimee moved to New York and received her Master's from NYU. She is based in New York City and is thrilled to be a part of Brower Literary and Management.

SHE IS SEEKING: Aimee is specifically interested in literary and upmarket fiction, historical and women's fiction, and young adult fiction (all genres).

HOW TO SUBMIT: Queries should be emailed to aimee@browerliterary.com with the subject line: QUERY [Manuscript/Project Title] and include a query letter, full synopsis, and the first chapter pasted directly in the e-mail.

LITERARY MANAGEMENT GROUP, INC.

P.O. Box 41004, Nashville TN 37204. (615)812-4445. **E-mail:** brucebarbour@literarymanagementgroup. com. **Website:** literarymanagementgroup.com. **Contact:** Bruce R. Barbour. Literary Management Group provides intellectual property development and management consulting, literary representation and book packaging services to publishers, authors, and clients. Specializes in adult nonfiction content with a distinctive Christian worldview; specifically from the Evangelical perspective. Estab. 1996. Represents 100+ clients.

○ Prior to becoming an agent, Mr. Barbour held executive positions at several publishing houses, including Revell, Barbour Books, Thomas Nelson, and Random House.

REPRESENTS nonfiction. **Considers these nonfiction areas:** biography, business, child guidance, current affairs, diet/nutrition, health, history, how-to, inspirational, money, parenting, psychology, religious, self-help, spirituality, Christian living, spiritual growth, women's and men's issues, prayer, devotional, meditational, Bible study, marriage, business, family/parenting.

☛ Does not want to receive gift books, poetry, children's books, short stories, or juvenile/ young adult fiction. No unsolicited mss or proposals from unpublished authors.

HOW TO CONTACT E-mail proposal as an attachment. Consult website for submission guidelines. Accepts simultaneous submissions. "We acknowledge receipt and review proposals within 4 weeks."

TERMS Agent receives 15% commission on domestic sales.

LITERARY SERVICES, INC.

P.O. Box 888, Barnegat NJ 08005. **E-mail:** jwlitagent@msn.com;. **E-mail:** john@literaryservicesinc.com. **Website:** www.literaryservicesinc.com. **Contact:** John Willig. Estab. 1991. Members of the Author's Guild. Represents 90 clients.

MEMBER AGENTS John Willig (business, personal growth, history, health and lifestyle, science and technology, politics, psychology, current events, food and travel, reference and gift books, true crime, humor, historical fiction).

REPRESENTS nonfiction. **Considers these nonfiction areas:** Americana, architecture, art, autobiography, biography, business, child guidance, cooking, crafts, creative nonfiction, current affairs, decorating, diet/nutrition, design, economics, environment, foods, gardening, health, history, hobbies, how-to, humor, inspirational, interior design, language, literature, medicine, military, money, parenting, popular culture, politics, psychology, recreation, regional, science, self-help, sex, sociology, spirituality, sports, technology, travel, true crime, war, women's issues. **Considers these fiction areas:** historical, literary, mystery, translation.

☞ Works primarily with nonfiction and historical crime fiction authors. "Our publishing experience and 'inside' knowledge of how companies and editors really work set us apart from many agencies; our specialties are noted above, but we are open to unique research, creative and contrarian approaches, and fresh presentations with expert advice in all nonfiction topic areas." Actively seeking science, history, current events, health, lifestyle topics, psychology, business, food and travel, and story-and research-driven narratives. Does not want to receive fiction (except historical crime fiction), children's books, science fiction, religion, or memoirs.

HOW TO CONTACT Query with SASE. For starters, a 1-page outline sent via e-mail is acceptable. See our website and our Submissions section to learn more about our questions. Do not send a ms unless requested. Accepts simultaneous submissions. Obtains most new clients through recommendations from others, solicitations, writers conferences.

TERMS Agent receives 15% commission on domestic sales; 15% commission on foreign sales. Offers written contract. This agency charges an administrative fee for copying, postage, etc.

RECENT SALES Sold 25 titles in the last year including *Winning the Brain*, by Matthew May; *The Amazing Cell*, by Josh Rappaport; *John Lennon vs. The U.S.A.*, by Leon Wildes; *Life After the Diagnosis*, by Steven Pantilant; *The Future Workplace Experience*, by Jeanne Meister; *Amazing Stories of the Space Age*, by Rod Pyle.

TIPS "Be focused. In all likelihood, your work is not going to be of interest to 'a very broad audience' or 'every parent,' so I appreciate when writers research and do some homework; i.e., positioning, special features, and benefits of your work. Be a marketer. How have you tested your ideas and writing (beyond your inner circle of family and friends)? Have you received any key awards for your work or endorsements from influential persons in your field? What steps, especially social media and speaking, have you taken to increase your presence in the market?"

⊘ LIVING WORD LITERARY AGENCY

P.O. Box 40974, Eugene OR 97404. **E-mail:** livingwordliterary@gmail.com. **Website:** livingwordliterary.wordpress.com. **Contact:** Kimberly Shumate, agent. Estab. 2009. Member of Evangelical Christian Publishers Association, American Christian Fiction Writers, Willamette Writers.

💬 Ms. Shumate began her employment in the sales department with Harvest House Publishers in 1997. In 2001, she transferred into the editorial department as the manuscript coordinator. She is currently an expert advisor for George Fox University.

REPRESENTS nonfiction, fiction, novels. **Considers these nonfiction areas:** relationships. **Considers these fiction areas:** adult fiction, Christian living.

☞ This agency is not accepting new clients at this time and does not want to receive young adult fiction, cookbooks, children's books, science fiction or fantasy, memoirs, screenplays, or poetry.

LKG AGENCY

465 West End Ave., 2A, New York NY 10024. **E-mail:** query@lkgagency.com. **E-mail:** For middle-grade or young adult: middle-gradeya@lkgagency.com. For nonfiction: nonfiction@lkgagency.com.

Website: lkgagency.com. **Contact:** Lauren Galit, Caitlen Rubino-Bradway. The LKG Agency was founded in 2005 and is based on the Upper West Side of Manhattan. "We are a boutique literary agency that specializes in middle-grade and young adult fiction, as well as nonfiction, both practical and narrative, with a particular interest in women-focused how-to. We invest a great deal of care and personal attention in each of our authors with the aim of developing long-term relationships that last well beyond the sale of a single book." Estab. 2005.

MEMBER AGENTS Lauren Galit (nonfiction, middle-grade, young adult); **Caitlen Rubino-Bradway** (middle-grade and young adult, some nonfiction).

REPRESENTS nonfiction, juvenile books. **Considers these nonfiction areas:** animals, child guidance, creative nonfiction, diet/nutrition, design, health, how-to, humor, juvenile nonfiction, memoirs, parenting, popular culture, psychology, women's issues, young adult. **Considers these fiction areas:** middle-grade, young adult.

☛ Actively seeking parenting, beauty, celebrity, dating and relationships, entertainment, fashion, health, diet and fitness, home and design, lifestyle, memoir, narrative, pets, psychology, women's, middle-grade and young adult fiction. Does not want history, biography, true crime, religion, picture books, spirituality, screenplays, poetry, any fiction other than middle-grade or young adult.

HOW TO CONTACT For nonfiction submissions, please send a query letter to nonfiction@lkgagency.com, along with a TOC and 2 sample chapters. The TOC should be fairly detailed, with a paragraph or two overview of the content of each chapter. Please also make sure to mention any publicity you have at your disposal. For middle-grade and young adult submissions, please send a query, synopsis, and 3 chapters, and address all submissions to middlegradeya@lkgagency.com. On a side note, while both Lauren and Caitlen consider young adult and middle-grade, Lauren tends to look more for middle-grade, while Caitlen deals more with young adult fiction. Please note: due to the high volume of submissions, we are unable to reply to every one. If you do not receive a reply, please consider that a rejection. Accepts simultaneous submissions.

STERLING LORD LITERISTIC, INC.

115 Broadway, New York NY 10006. (212)780-6050. **Fax:** (212)780-6095. **E-mail:** info@sll.com. **Website:** www.sll.com. Estab. 1987. Member of AAR. Signatory of WGA.

MEMBER AGENTS Philippa Brophy (represents journalists, nonfiction writers, and novelists, and is most interested in current events, memoir, science, politics, biography, women's issues); **Laurie Liss** (represents authors of commercial and literary fiction and nonfiction whose perspectives are well developed and unique); **Sterling Lord**; **Peter Matson** (abiding interest in storytelling, whether in the service of history, fiction, the sciences); **Douglas Stewart** (primarily fiction for all ages, from the innovatively literary to the unabashedly commercial); **Neeti Madan** (memoir, journalism, popular culture, lifestyle, women's issues, multicultural books, virtually any intelligent writing on intriguing topics); **Robert Guinsler** (literary and commercial fiction [including young adult], journalism, narrative nonfiction with an emphasis on pop culture, science and current events, memoirs, biography); **Jim Rutman**; **Celeste Fine** (expert, celebrity, corporate clients with strong national and international platforms, particularly in the health, science, self-help, food, business, lifestyle fields); **Martha Millard** (fiction and nonfiction, including well-written science fiction and young adult); **Mary Krienke** (literary fiction, memoir, narrative nonfiction [psychology, popular science, cultural commentary]); **Jenny Stephens** (nonfiction: cookbooks, practical lifestyle projects, transportive travel and nature writing, creative nonfiction; fiction: contemporary literary narratives strongly rooted in place); **Alison MacKeen** (idea-driven research books: social scientific, scientific, historical, relationships/parenting, learning and education, sexuality, technology, the life-cycle, health, the environment, politics, economics, psychology, geography, culture; literary fiction, literary nonfiction, memoirs, essays, travel writing); **John Maas** (serious nonfiction, specifically business, personal development, science, self-help, health, fitness, lifestyle); **Sarah Passick** (commercial nonfiction in the celebrity, food, blogger, lifestyle, health, diet, fitness, fashion categories).

REPRESENTS nonfiction, fiction. **Considers these nonfiction areas:** biography, business, cooking, creative nonfiction, current affairs, economics, education, foods, gay/lesbian, history, humor, memoirs, multicultural, parenting, popular culture, politics, psychology, science, technology, travel, women's issues, fitness. **Considers these fiction areas:** commercial, juvenile, literary, middle-grade, picture books, science fiction, young adult.

HOW TO CONTACT Query via snail mail. "Please submit a query letter, a synopsis of the work, a brief proposal or the first 3 chapters of the manuscript, a brief bio or resume, and SASE for reply. Original artwork is not accepted. Enclose sufficient postage if you wish to have your materials returned to you. We do not respond to unsolicited e-mail inquiries." Accepts simultaneous submissions.

TERMS Agent receives 15% commission on domestic sales; 20% commission on foreign sales. Offers written contract.

LOWENSTEIN ASSOCIATES INC.

115 E. 23rd St., Fourth Floor, New York NY 10010. (212)206-1630. **E-mail:** assistant@bookhaven.com. **Website:** www.lowensteinassociates.com. **Contact:** Barbara Lowenstein. Member of AAR.

MEMBER AGENTS Barbara Lowenstein, president (nonfiction: narrative nonfiction, health, money, finance, travel, multicultural, popular culture, memoir; fiction: literary fiction and women's fiction); Mary South (literary fiction, nonfiction: neuroscience, bioengineering, women's rights, design, digital humanities, investigative journalism, essays, memoir).

REPRESENTS nonfiction, fiction, novels, short story collections. **Considers these nonfiction areas:** autobiography, biography, business, creative nonfiction, cultural interests, health, humor, literature, memoirs, money, multicultural, popular culture, science, technology, travel, women's issues. **Considers these fiction areas:** commercial, literary, middle-grade, science fiction, women's, young adult.

⌖ Barbara Lowenstein is currently looking for writers who have a platform and are leading experts in their field, including business, women's issues, psychology, health, science, and social issues, and is particularly interested in strong new voices in fiction and narrative nonfiction. Does not want westerns, textbooks, children's picture books, and books in need of translation.

HOW TO CONTACT "For fiction, please send us a 1-page query letter, along with the first 10 pages pasted in the body of the message by e-mail to assistant@bookhaven.com. If nonfiction, please send a 1-page query letter, a table of contents, and, if available, a proposal pasted into the body of the e-mail. Please put the word 'QUERY' and the title of your project in the subject field of your e-mail and address it to the agent of your choice. Please do not send an attachment, as the message will be deleted without being read and no reply will be sent." Accepts simultaneous submissions. Responds in 6 weeks to queries. Obtains most new clients through recommendations from others, solicitations, conferences.

TERMS Agent receives 15% commission on domestic sales; 20% commission on foreign sales. Offers written contract. Charges for large photocopy batches, messenger service, international postage.

TIPS "Know the genre you are working in and read!"

DONALD MAASS LITERARY AGENCY

1000 Dean St., Suite 252, Brooklyn NY 11238. (212)727-8383. **Website:** www.maassagency.com. Estab. 1980. Member of AAR, SFWA, MWA, RWA. Represents more than 100 clients.

MEMBER AGENTS Donald Maass (mainstream, literary, mystery/suspense, science fiction, romance); Jennifer Jackson (science fiction and fantasy for both adult and young adult markets, thriller that mine popular and controversial issues, young adult that challenges traditional thinking); Cameron McClure (literary, mystery/suspense, urban, fantasy, narrative nonfiction, and projects with multicultural, international, and environmental themes, gay/lesbian); Amy Boggs (fantasy and science fiction, young adult/Middle-grade, historical fiction about eras that aren't well known); Katie Shea Boutillier (women's fiction/book club, edgy/dark, realistic/contemporary young adult, commercial-scale literary fiction, celebrity memoir); Michael Curry (science fiction and fantasy, near-future thriller); Caitlin McDonald (science fiction and fantasy [young adult/middle-grade/adult], genre-bending/cross-genre fiction, diversity).

REPRESENTS nonfiction, fiction, novels, juvenile books. **Considers these nonfiction areas:** creative nonfiction, memoirs, popular culture. **Considers these fiction areas:** contemporary issues, crime, detective, ethnic, fantasy, feminist, gay, historical, horror, juvenile, lesbian, literary, mainstream, middle-grade, multicultural, mystery, paranormal, police, regional, romance, science fiction, supernatural, suspense, thriller, urban fantasy, westerns, women's, young adult.

⚷ This agency specializes in commercial fiction, especially science fiction, fantasy, thriller, suspense, and women's fiction, for both the adult and young adult markets. Does not want poetry, screenplays, or picture books.

HOW TO CONTACT Query via e-mail only. All the agents have different submission addresses and instructions. See the website and each agent's online profile for exact submission instructions. Accepts simultaneous submissions.

TERMS Agency receives 15% commission on domestic sales; 20% commission on foreign sales.

RECENT SALES *The Aeronaut's Windlass*, by Jim Butcher (Penguin Random House); *City of Blades*, by Robert Jackson Bennett (Crown); *I Am Princess X*, by Cherie Priest (Scholastic); *Treachery at Lancaster Gate*, by Anne Perry (Random House); *Marked in Flesh*, by Anne Bishop (Penguin Random House); *We Are the Ants*, by Shaun David Hutchinson (Simon & Schuster); *The Book of Phoenix*, by Nnedi Okorafor (DAW); *Ninefox Gambit*, by Yoon Ha Lee (Solaris); *The Far End of Happy*, by Kathryn Craft (Sourcebooks); *The Traitor Baru Cormorant*, by Seth Dickinson (Tor).

TIPS "We are fiction specialists, also noted for our innovative approach to career planning. We are always open to submissions from new writers." Works with subagents in all principal foreign countries and for film and television.

GINA MACCOBY LITERARY AGENCY

P.O. Box 60, Chappaqua NY 10514. (914)238-5630. **E-mail:** query@maccobylit.com. **Website:** www.publishersmarketplace.com/members/ginamaccoby. **Contact:** Gina Maccoby. Estab. 1986. Member of AAR, AAR Board of Directors, Royalties and Ethics and Contracts subcommittees, Authors Guild, SCBWI.

REPRESENTS nonfiction, fiction, novels, juvenile books. **Considers these nonfiction areas:** autobiography, biography, cultural interests, current affairs, ethnic, history, juvenile nonfiction, literature, popular culture, women's issues, women's studies, young adult. **Considers these fiction areas:** crime, detective, family saga, juvenile, literary, mainstream,

middle-grade, multicultural, mystery, New Adult, thriller, women's, young adult.

HOW TO CONTACT Query by e-mail only. Accepts simultaneous submissions. Owing to volume of submissions, may not respond to queries unless interested. Obtains most new clients through recommendations.

TERMS Agent receives 15% commission on domestic sales; 20-25% commission on foreign sales, which includes subagent's commissions. May recover certain costs, such as purchasing books, shipping books overseas by airmail, legal fees for vetting motion picture contracts, bank fees for electronic funds transfers, overnight delivery services.

⊘ MACGREGOR LITERARY INC.

P.O. Box 1316, Manzanita OR 97130. **E-mail:** submissions@macgregorliterary.com. **Website:** www.macgregorliterary.com. **Contact:** Chip MacGregor. Estab. 2006. Member of AAR, signatory of WGA. Represents 80 clients.

🖸 Prior to his current position, Mr. MacGregor was the senior agent with Alive Communications, an agency in Colorado. Most recently, he was an associate publisher with the Time-Warner Book Group (now Hachette Book Group) and helped put together its Center Street imprint.

MEMBER AGENTS Chip MacGregor (general nonfiction and memoir, select fiction); Amanda Luedeke (nonfiction, literary fiction, romance, twenty-something/post-college-aged hip lit); Brian Tibbetts (literary fiction, New Adult titles, science fiction, fantasy, horror, art and music memoirs, natural foods, alternative healing, sustainability issues).

REPRESENTS nonfiction, fiction. **Considers these nonfiction areas:** business, creative nonfiction, cultural interests, current affairs, history, inspirational, memoirs, parenting, popular culture, politics, religious, self-help, spirituality, sports, true crime, women's issues. **Considers these fiction areas:** action, commercial, crime, detective, family saga, humor, inspirational, literary, mainstream, mystery, New Adult, police, religious, romance, suspense, thriller, women's.

⚷ "My specialty has been in career planning with authors—finding commercial ideas, then helping authors bring them to market, and in the midst of that, assisting the authors as they get

NEW AGENT SPOTLIGHT

AMANDA AYERS BARNETT

DONAGHY LITERARY GROUP

www.donaghyliterary.com
@amandaabarnett

ABOUT AMANDA: Amanda began her publishing career 20 years ago, fresh out of Middlebury College and the Radcliffe Publishing Course. She has worn many hats—publicity assistant at Random House, associate editor at Pocket Books, acquisitions editor at Re.ad Publishing, freelance book editor for New York Book Editors—all of which have given her extensive and valuable experience. She is thrilled to add literary agent to these titles, and to join the Donaghy Literary Group.

SHE IS SEEKING: Amanda especially loves mystery/thrillers and middle-grade, young adult, new adult and women's fiction. She enjoys coming of age novels and precocious main characters. But more than anything, she loves an intriguing and well-written story.

HOW TO SUBMIT: Visit Amanda's page at the Donaghy Literary site and click on the "Submit a Query" button underneath her picture. Fill out the Query Submission form to submit.

firmly established in their writing careers. I'm probably best known for my work with spirituality books and memoir over the years, but I've done a fair amount of general nonfiction as well." Nonfiction from authors with a proven platform. Significant literary and thriller fiction. Does not want screenplays, westerns, erotica, paranormal fiction, children's books, young adult fiction, art books, poetry.

HOW TO CONTACT MacGregor Literary is not currently accepting submissions except through referrals. Please do not query this agency without an invitation or referral. Accepts simultaneous submissions. Responds in 4-6 weeks to queries. Obtains most new clients through recommendations from others. Not looking to add unpublished authors except through referrals from current clients.

TERMS Agent receives 15% commission on domestic sales; 10% commission on foreign sales. Offers written contract.

WRITERS CONFERENCES BEA, RWA, Thriller-Fest, Left Coast Crime, several West-Coast writing conferences.

TIPS "Seriously consider attending a good writers conference. It will give you the chance to be face-to-face with people in the industry. Also, if you're a novelist, consider joining one of the national writers organizations. RWA, ACFW, and MWA, ITW are wonderful groups for new and established writers and will help you make connections and become a better writer."

CAROL MANN AGENCY

55 Fifth Ave., New York NY 10003. (212)206-5635. **Fax:** (212)675-4809. **E-mail:** submissions@carolmannagency.com. **Website:** www.carolmannagency.

com. **Contact:** Isabella Ruggiero. Member of AAR. Represents roughly 200 clients.

MEMBER AGENTS Carol Mann (health/medical, religion, spirituality, self-help, parenting, narrative nonfiction, current affairs); **Laura Yorke**; **Gareth Esersky**; **Myrsini Stephanides** (nonfiction: pop culture and music, humor, narrative nonfiction and memoir, cookbooks; fiction: offbeat literary fiction, graphic works, edgy young adult fiction); **Joanne Wyckoff** (nonfiction: memoir, narrative nonfiction,personal narrative, psychology, women's issues, education, health and wellness, parenting, serious self-help, natural history; also accepts fiction); **Lydia Shamah** (edgy, modern fiction and timely nonfiction in the areas of business, self-improvement, relationship and gift books, particularly interested in female voices and experiences); **Tom Miller** (narrative nonfiction, self-help/psychology, popular culture, body-mind-spirit, wellness, business, literary fiction).

REPRESENTS novels. **Considers these nonfiction areas:** anthropology, archeology, architecture, art, autobiography, biography, business, child guidance, cultural interests, current affairs, design, ethnic, government, health, history, law, medicine, money, music, parenting, popular culture, politics, psychology, self-help, sociology, sports, women's issues, women's studies. **Considers these fiction areas:** commercial, literary, young adult, graphic works.

☛ Does not want to receive genre fiction (romance, mystery, etc.).

HOW TO CONTACT Please see website for submission guidelines. Accepts simultaneous submissions. Responds in 4 weeks to queries.

TERMS Agent receives 15% commission on domestic sales; 20% commission on foreign sales. Offers written contract.

MANSION STREET LITERARY MANAGEMENT

E-mail: querymansionstreet@gmail.com, querymichelle@mansionstreet.com. **Website:** mansionstreet.com. **Contact:** Jean Sagendorph, Michelle Witte. Member of AAR. Signatory of WGA.

MEMBER AGENTS Jean Sagendorph, querymansionstreet@gmail.com (pop culture, gift books, cookbooks, general nonfiction, lifestyle, design, brand extensions); **Michelle Witte**, querymichelle@mansionstreet.com (young adult, middle-grade,

early readers, picture books [especially from author/illustrators], juvenile nonfiction).

REPRESENTS nonfiction, novels. **Considers these nonfiction areas:** cooking, design, popular culture. **Considers these fiction areas:** juvenile, middle-grade, young adult.

☛ Ms. Sagendorph is not interested in memoirs or medical/reference. Typically sports and self-help are not a good fit; also does not represent travel books. Ms. Witte is not interested in fiction or nonfiction for adults.

HOW TO CONTACT Send a query letter and no more than the first 10 pages of your ms in the body of an e-mail. Query one specific agent at this agency. No attachments. You must list the genre in the subject line. If the genre is not in the subject line, your query will be deleted. Accepts simultaneous submissions. Responds in up to 6 weeks.

RECENT SALES *Shake and Fetch*, by Carli Davidson; *Bleed, Blister, Puke and Purge*, by J. Marin Younker; *Spectrum*, by Ginger Johnson; *I Left You a Present* and *Movie Night Trivia*, by Robb Pearlman; *Open Sesame!*, by Ashley Evanson; *Fox Hunt*, by Nilah Magruder; *ABC Now You See Me*, by Kim Siebold.

MANUS & ASSOCIATES LITERARY AGENCY, INC.

425 Sherman Ave., Suite 200, Palo Alto CA 94306. NYC address: 444 Madison Ave., 39th Floor, New York NY 10022. Member of AAR. (650)470-5151. **Fax:** (650)470-5159. **E-mail:** manuslit@manuslit.com. **Website:** www.manuslit.com. **Contact:** Jillian Manus, Jandy Nelson, Penny Nelson.

💬 Prior to becoming an agent, Ms. Manus was associate publisher of two national magazines and director of development at Warner Bros. and Universal Studios; she has been a literary agent for 20 years.

MEMBER AGENTS Jandy Nelson (currently not taking on new clients); **Jillian Manus**, jillian@manuslit.com (political, memoirs, self-help, history, sports, women's issues, thriller); **Penny Nelson**, penny@manuslit.com (memoirs, self-help, sports, nonfiction).

REPRESENTS nonfiction, novels. **Considers these nonfiction areas:** cooking, history, inspirational, memoirs, politics, psychology, religious, self-help, sports, women's issues. **Considers these fiction areas:** thriller.

"Our agency is unique in the way that we not only sell the material, but edit, develop concepts, and participate in the marketing effort. We specialize in large, conceptual fiction and nonfiction, and always value a project that can be sold in the TV/feature film market." Actively seeking high-concept thriller, commercial literary fiction, women's fiction, celebrity biography, memoirs, multicultural fiction, popular health, women's empowerment, and mystery. No horror, romance, science fiction, fantasy, western, young adult, children's, poetry, cookbooks, or magazine articles.

HOW TO CONTACT Snail mail submissions welcome. E-queries also accepted. For nonfiction, send a full proposal via snail mail. For fiction, send a query letter and 30 pages (unbound) if submitting via snail mail. Send only an e-query if submitting fiction via e-mail. If querying by e-mail, submit directly to one of the agents. Accepts simultaneous submissions. Responds in 3 months. Obtains most new clients through recommendations from others, solicitations, conferences.

TERMS Agent receives 15% commission on domestic sales; 20-25% commission on foreign sales. Offers written contract, binding for 2 years; 60-day notice must be given to terminate contract. Charges for photocopying and postage/UPS.

RECENT SALES *Nothing Down for the 2000s* and *Multiple Streams of Income for the 2000s*, by Robert Allen; *Missed Fortune 101*, by Doug Andrew; *Cracking the Millionaire Code*, by Mark Victor Hansen and Robert Allen; *Stress Free for Good*, by Dr. Fred Luskin and Dr. Ken Pelletier; *The Mercy of Thin Air*, by Ronlyn Domangue; *The Fine Art of Small Talk*, by Debra Fine; *Bone Men of Bonares*, by Terry Tamoff.

DENISE MARCIL LITERARY AGENCY, LLC

483 Westover Rd., Stamford CT 06902. (203)327-9970. **E-mail:** dmla@denisemarcilagency.com, annemarie@denisemarcilagency.com, dmla@denisemarcilagency.com. **Website:** www.denisemarcilagency.com. **Contact:** Denise Marcil, Anne Marie O'Farrell. Address for Anne Marie O'Farrell: 86 Dennis St., Manhasset, NY 11030. Estab. 1977. Member of AAR, Women's Media Group.

Prior to opening her agency, Ms. Marcil served as an editorial assistant with Avon Books and as an assistant editor with Simon & Schuster.

MEMBER AGENTS Denise Marcil (self-help and popular reference books: wellness, health, women's issues, self-help, popular reference); Anne Marie O'Farrell (books that convey and promote innovative, practical, and cutting-edge information and ideas that help people increase their self-awareness and fulfillment and maximize their potential in whatever area they choose; she is dying to represent a great basketball book).

REPRESENTS nonfiction. **Considers these nonfiction areas:** business, cooking, diet/nutrition, education, health, how-to, New Age, psychology, self-help, spirituality, women's issues. **Considers these fiction areas:** commercial, suspense, thriller, women's.

"In nonfiction, we are looking for self-help, personal growth, popular psychology, how-to, business, and popular reference; we want to represent books that help people's lives." Does not want fiction.

HOW TO CONTACT E-query. Accepts simultaneous submissions.

TERMS Agent receives 15% commission on domestic sales; 20% commission on foreign sales and film sales. Offers written contract, binding for 2 years.

RECENT SALES *Willow Brook Road*, by Sherryl Woods; *Dr. Knox*, by Peter Spiegelman; *The Baby Book*, by William Sears, M.D. and Martha Sears, R.N.; *The Allergy Book*, by Robert W. Sears, M.D. and William Sears, M.D.

MARSAL LYON LITERARY AGENCY, LLC

PMB 121, 665 San Rodolfo Dr. 124, Solana Beach CA 92075. **E-mail:** kevan@marsallyonliteraryagency.com. **Website:** www.marsallyonliteraryagency.com. **Contact:** Kevan Lyon, Jill Marsal. Query e-mails: jill@marsallyonliteraryagency.com, kevan@marsallyonliteraryagency.com, deborah@marsallyonliteraryagency.com, shannon@marsallyonliteraryagency.com, patricia@marsallyonliteraryagency.com. Estab. 2009. Member of RWA

MEMBER AGENTS Kevan Lyon (women's fiction with an emphasis on commercial women's fiction, young adult fiction, all genres of romance); Jill Marsal (all types of women's fiction and all types of romance; mystery, cozies, suspense, thriller; nonfiction: current

events, business, health, self-help, relationships, psychology, parenting, history, science, narrative nonfiction); **Patricia Nelson** (literary fiction and commercial fiction, all types of women's fiction, contemporary and historical romance, young adult and middle-grade fiction, LGBTQ fiction for both young adult and adult); **Deborah Ritchkin** (lifestyle books: food, design, entertaining; pop culture; women's issues; biography; current events; her niche interest is projects about France, including fiction); **Shannon Hassan** (literary and commercial fiction, young adult and middle-grade fiction, select nonfiction).
REPRESENTS nonfiction, fiction, novels, juvenile books. **Considers these nonfiction areas:** animals, biography, business, cooking, creative nonfiction, current affairs, diet/nutrition, history, investigative, memoirs, parenting, popular culture, politics, psychology, science, self-help, sports, women's issues, women's studies. **Considers these fiction areas:** commercial, juvenile, literary, mainstream, middle-grade, multicultural, mystery, paranormal, romance, suspense, thriller, women's, young adult.
HOW TO CONTACT Query by e-mail. Query only one agent at this agency at a time. "Please visit our website to determine who is best suited for your work. Write 'query' in the subject line of your e-mail. Please allow up to several weeks to hear back on your query." Accepts simultaneous submissions.
TIPS "Our agency's mission is to help writers achieve their publishing dreams. We want to work with authors not just for a book but for a career; we are dedicated to building long-term relationships with our authors and publishing partners. Our goal is to help find homes for books that engage, entertain, and make a difference."

THE EVAN MARSHALL AGENCY

1 Pacio Court, Roseland NJ 07068-1121. (973)287-6216. **Fax:** (973)488-7910. **E-mail:** evan@evanmarshallagency.com. **Website:** www.evanmarshallagency.com. **Contact:** Evan Marshall. Founded in 1987, the Evan Marshall Agency is a leading literary management firm specializing in adult and young adult fiction. "We handle a wide-ranging roster of writers in numerous genres, from romance to mystery and thriller to literary fiction. We take pride in providing careful career guidance and strategizing to our clients. As a result, a number of our authors have been with us for nearly three decades, and our titles regularly hit national

bestseller lists including Amazon, *USA Today*, Barnes & Noble, *Publishers Weekly* and the *New York Times*." Estab. 1987. Member of AAR, Novelists, Inc. Represents 50+ clients.

○ Prior to becoming an agent, Evan Marshall held senior editorial positions at Houghton Mifflin, Ariel Books, New American Library, Everest House and Dodd, Mead, where he acquired national and international bestsellers.

REPRESENTS fiction, novels. **Considers these fiction areas:** action, adventure, crime, detective, erotica, ethnic, family saga, fantasy, feminist, frontier, gay, glitz, historical, horror, humor, inspirational, lesbian, literary, mainstream, military, multicultural, multimedia, mystery, New Adult, New Age, occult, paranormal, police, psychic, regional, religious, romance, satire, science fiction, spiritual, sports, supernatural, suspense, thriller, translation, urban fantasy, war, westerns, women's, young adult, romance (contemporary, gothic, historical, regency).

☛ "We represent all genres of adult and young adult full-length fiction." Actively seeking high-quality adult and young adult fiction in all genres. Does not want articles, children's books, essays, memoirs, nonfiction, novellas, poetry, screenplays, short stories, stage plays.

HOW TO CONTACT Actively seeking new clients. E-mail query letter, synopsis, and first 3 chapters of novel within body of e-mail. Accepts simultaneous submissions. Responds in 1 week to queries, 1 month to mss. Obtains new clients through queries and through recommendations from editors and current clients.
TERMS Agent receives 15% commission on domestic sales; 20% commission on foreign sales. Offers written contract.
RECENT SALES *No Place I'd Rather Be*, by Cathy Lamb (Kensington); *A Beau for Katie*, by Emma Miller (Love Inspired); *The Bloody Black Flag*, by Steve Goble (Seventh Street); *Fortune's Secret Husband*, by Karen Rose Smith (Harlequin); *Windigo Moon*, by Robert Downes (Blank Slate Press).

THE MARTELL AGENCY

1350 Avenue of the Americas, Suite 1205, New York NY 10019. **Fax:** (212)317-2676. **E-mail:** submissions@themartellagency.com. **Website:** www.themartellagency.com. **Contact:** Alice Martell.

REPRESENTS nonfiction, novels. **Considers these nonfiction areas:** "big idea" books, business, current affairs, economics, health/diet, history, medicine, memoirs, multicultural, politics, personal finance, psychology, science for the general reader, self-help, women's issues.

•— Seeks the following subjects in fiction: literary and commercial, including mystery, suspense, and thriller. Does not want to receive romance, genre mystery, genre historical fiction, or children's books.

HOW TO CONTACT E-query Alice Martell. This should include a summary of the project and a short biography and any information, if appropriate, as to why you are qualified to write on the subject of your book, including any publishing credits. Accepts simultaneous submissions.

MARTIN LITERARY AND MEDIA MANAGEMENT

914 164th St. SE, Suite B12, #307, Mill Creek WA 98012. **E-mail:** sharlene@martinliterarymanagement.com. **Website:** www.martinlit.com. **Contact:** Sharlene Martin. Estab. 2002.

💬 Prior to becoming an agent, Ms. Martin worked in film/TV production and acquisitions.

MEMBER AGENTS Sharlene Martin (nonfiction); Clelia Gore (children's, middle-grade, young adult); Adria Goetz (Christian books, Lifestyle books).
REPRESENTS nonfiction. **Considers these nonfiction areas:** autobiography, biography, business, child guidance, creative nonfiction, current affairs, economics, health, history, how-to, humor, inspirational, investigative, medicine, memoirs, parenting, popular culture, psychology, satire, self-help, true crime, war, women's issues, women's studies. **Considers these fiction areas:** juvenile, middle-grade, young adult.

•— This agency has strong ties to film/TV. Actively seeking nonfiction that is highly commercial and that can be adapted to film. "We are being inundated with queries and submissions that are wrongfully being submitted to us, which only results in more frustration for the writers."

HOW TO CONTACT Query via e-mail . No attachments on queries, place letter in body of e-mail. Accepts simultaneous submissions. Responds in 2 weeks to queries, 3-4 weeks to mss. Obtains most new clients through recommendations from others.

TERMS Agent receives 15% commission on domestic sales. Offers written contract, binding for 1 year; 1-month notice must be given to terminate contract.
RECENT SALES *Taking My Life Back*, by Rebekah Gregory with Anthony Flacco; *Maximum Harm*, by Michele McPhee; *Breakthrough*, by Jack Andraka; *In the Matter of Nikola Tesla: A Romance of the Mind*, by Anthony Flacco; *Honor Bound: My Journey to Hell and Back with Amanda Knox*, by Raffaele Sollecito.

TIPS "Have a strong platform for nonfiction. Please don't call. (I can't tell how well you write by the sound of your voice.) I welcome e-mail. I'm very responsive when I'm interested in a query and work hard to get my clients' materials in the best possible shape before submissions. Do your homework prior to submission and only submit your best efforts. Please review our website carefully to make sure we're a good match for your work. If you read my book, *Publish Your Nonfiction Book: Strategies for Learning the Industry, Selling Your Book and Building a Successful Career* (Writer's Digest Books), you'll know exactly how to charm me."

MARGRET MCBRIDE LITERARY AGENCY

P.O. Box 9128, La Jolla CA 92038. (858)454-1550. **E-mail:** staff@mcbridelit.com. **Website:** www.mcbrideliterary.com. Estab. 1981. Member of AAR, the Authors Guild.

💬 Prior to opening her agency, Ms. McBride worked at Random House and Ballantine Books. Later, she became the director of publicity at Warner Books, and director of publicity, promotions and advertising for Pinnacle Books.

MEMBER AGENTS Margret McBride, Faye Atchison.
REPRESENTS nonfiction, fiction, novels. **Considers these nonfiction areas:** autobiography, biography, business, cooking, creative nonfiction, cultural interests, current affairs, diet/nutrition, ethnic, foods, gay/lesbian, health, history, hobbies, how-to, inspirational, investigative, juvenile nonfiction, medicine, memoirs, money, multicultural, music, popular culture, psychology, science, self-help, sex, sociology, theater, travel, true crime, women's issues, young adult. **Considers these fiction areas:** action, adventure, comic books, commercial, confession, contemporary issues, crime, detective, family saga, feminist, historical, horror, juvenile, mainstream, multicultural, multimedia, mys-

NEW AGENT SPOTLIGHT

JUSTIN WELLS
CORVISIERO LITERARY AGENCY

www.corvisieroagency.com
@Justin_941

ABOUT JUSTIN: Justin started his journey six years ago when he began his young adult literature blog. If you had asked him then, he would have never imagined just how much his journey over the course of those early years would impact his future. Starting as an intern with the Corvisiero Literary Agency in May of 2016 quickly turned into a position as a Literary Agent Apprentice, under the guidance of Marisa Corvisiero. Being a literary agent is something that Justin has fallen in love with, and is eager to continue for years to come.

Justin is going into his senior year of college, and will be graduating with a B.S. in Mass Communications with a focus in Public Relations. He loves being able to utilize his skills in public relations to assist the agency and his own clients through his work as a literary agent.

HE IS SEEKING: Justin is looking to represent middle grade, young adult, new adult, and adult novels. For middle grade, he is actively seeking fantasy, science fiction, paranormal, adventure, and historical fiction. In young adult, he is seeking fantasy, science fiction, paranormal, adventure, historical fiction, contemporary, and dystopian fiction. For new adult, he is seeking fantasy, contemporary romance, and science fiction. And, lastly, for adult, he is seeking fantasy, science fiction, and historical fiction. He would really like to see submissions for all categories and genres that have diverse main characters.

HOW TO SUBMIT: To submit a query to Justin, e-mail query@corvisieroagency.com with the subject line "Query – ATTN: Justin Wells, [insert name of manuscript]". When submitting your query, please make sure that you are making it as strong as it can be. Please include a one to two page synopsis, and also the first ten pages of your manuscript within the body of your query, at the bottom (no attachments will be accepted.

tery, New Adult, paranormal, police, psychic, regional, supernatural, suspense, thriller, young adult.

☛ This agency specializes in mainstream nonfiction and some commercial fiction. Actively seeking commercial nonfiction, business, health, self-help. Does not want screenplays, romance, poetry, or children's.

HOW TO CONTACT "Please check our website, as instructions are subject to change. Only e-mail queries are accepted: staff@mcbridelit.com. In your query letter, provide a brief synopsis of your work, as well as any pertinent information about yourself. We recommend that authors look at book jacket copy of professionally published books to get an idea of the style and content that should be included in a query letter. Essentially, you are marketing yourself and your work to us, so that we can determine whether we feel we can market you and your work to publishers. There are detailed nonfiction proposal guidelines on our website." Accepts simultaneous submissions. Responds within 8 weeks to queries, 6-8 weeks to requested mss. "You are welcome to follow up by phone or e-mail after 8 weeks if you have not yet received a response."

TERMS Agent receives 15% commission on domestic sales; 25% commission on translation rights sales (15% to agency, 10% to sub-agent). Charges for overnight delivery and photocopying.

RECENT SALES *Nimble*, by Baba Prasad (Perigee/Penguin Random House—US and World rights excluding India); *Carefrontation*, by Dr. Arlene Drake (Regan Arts/Phaidon); *There Are No Overachievers*, by Brian Biro (Crown Business/Penguin Random House); *Cheech Is Not My Real Name*, by Richard Marin (Grand Central Books/Hachette); *Killing It!*, by Sheryl O'Loughlin (Harper Business/HarperCollins); *Scrappy*, by Terri Sjodin (Portfolio/Penguin Random House).

E.J. MCCARTHY AGENCY

(415)383-6639. **E-mail:** ejmagency@gmail.com. **Website:** http://www.publishersmarketplace.com/members/ejmccarthy/. Signatory of WGA.

○ Prior to his current position, Mr. McCarthy was a former executive editor with more than 20 years book publishing experience (Bantam Doubleday Dell, Presidio Press, Ballantine/Random House).

REPRESENTS Considers these nonfiction areas: biography, history, memoirs, military, sports.

☛ This agency specializes in nonfiction.

HOW TO CONTACT Query first by e-mail. Accepts simultaneous submissions.

RECENT SALES *One Bullet Away*, by Nathaniel Fick; *The Unforgiving Minute*, by Craig Mullaney; *The Sling and the Stone*, by Thomas X. Hammes; *The Heart and the First*, by Eric Greitens; *When Books Went to War*, by Molly Guptill Manning.

SEAN MCCARTHY LITERARY AGENCY

E-mail: submissions@mccarthylit.com. **Website:** www.mccarthylit.com. **Contact:** Sean McCarthy. Estab. 2013.

○ Sean McCarthy began his publishing career as an editorial intern at Overlook Press and then moved over to the Sheldon Fogelman Agency prior to his current position.

REPRESENTS Considers these nonfiction areas: juvenile nonfiction, young adult. **Considers these fiction areas:** juvenile, middle-grade, picture books, young adult.

☛ Sean is drawn to flawed, multifaceted characters with devastatingly concise writing in young adult, and boy-friendly mystery or adventures in Middle-grade. In picture books, he looks more for unforgettable characters, off-beat humor, and especially clever endings. He is not currently interested in high fantasy, message-driven stories, or query letters that pose too many questions.

HOW TO CONTACT E-query. "Please include a brief description of your book, your biography, and any literary or relevant professional credits in your query letter. If you are a novelist: Please submit the first 3 chapters of your manuscript (or roughly 25 pages) and a 1-page synopsis in the body of the e-mail or as a Word or PDF attachment. If you are a picture book author: Please submit the complete text of your manuscript. We are not currently accepting picture book manuscripts over 1,000 words. If you are an illustrator: Please attach up to 3 JPEGs or PDFs of your work, along with a link to your website." Accepts simultaneous submissions.

MCCORMICK LITERARY

37 W. 20th St., New York NY 10011. (212)691-9726. **E-mail:** queries@mccormicklit.com. **Website:** mccormicklit.com. "McCormick Literary is an inde-

pendent literary agency specializing in literary and commercial fiction and quality nonfiction, including memoir, history, narrative, biography, lifestyle, sports, self-help, and pop culture." Member of AAR. Signatory of WGA.

MEMBER AGENTS David McCormick; **Pilar Queen** (narrative nonfiction, practical nonfiction, and commercial women's fiction); **Bridget McCarthy** (literary and commercial fiction, narrative nonfiction, memoir, and cookbooks); **Alia Hanna Habib** (literary fiction, narrative nonfiction, memoir and cookbooks); **Edward Orlof**f (literary fiction and narrative nonfiction, especially cultural history, politics, biography, and the arts); **Daniel Menaker**; **Leslie Falk**; **Emma Borges-Scott**.

REPRESENTS nonfiction, novels. **Considers these nonfiction areas:** biography, cooking, history, memoirs, politics. **Considers these fiction areas:** literary, women's.

HOW TO CONTACT Snail mail queries only. Send an SASE. Accepts simultaneous submissions.

✪⊘ ANNE MCDERMID & ASSOCIATES, LTD

320 Front St. W., Suite 1105, Toronto ON M5V 3B6 Canada. (647)788-4016. **Fax:** (416)324-8870. **E-mail:** admin@mcdermidagency.com. **E-mail:** info@mcdermidagency.com. **Website:** www.mcdermidagency.com. **Contact:** Anne McDermid. Estab. 1996.

MEMBER AGENTS Anne McDermid, Martha Webb, Monica Pacheco, Chris Bucci.

REPRESENTS novels.

☛ The agency represents literary novelists and commercial novelists of high quality, and also writers of nonfiction in the areas of memoir, biography, history, literary travel, narrative science, and investigative journalism. "We also represent a certain number of children's and young adult writers and writers in the fields of science fiction and fantasy."

HOW TO CONTACT Query via e-mail or mail with a brief bio, description, and first 5 pages of project only. Accepts simultaneous submissions. *No unsolicited manuscripts.* Obtains most new clients through recommendations from others.

MCINTOSH & OTIS, INC.

353 Lexington Ave., New York NY 10016. (212)687-7400. **Fax:** (212)687-6894. **E-mail:** info@mcintoshandotis.com. **Website:** www.mcintoshandotis.

com. **Contact:** Eugene H. Winick, Esq.. McIntosh & Otis has a long history of representing authors of adult and children's books. The children's department is a separate division. Estab. 1928. Member of AAR. Signatory of WGA. SCBWI

MEMBER AGENTS Elizabeth Winick Rubinstein, ewrquery@mcintoshandotis.com (literary fiction, women's fiction, historical fiction, mystery/suspense, along with narrative nonfiction, spiritual/self-help, history and current affairs); **Shira Hoffman**, shquery@mcintoshandotis.com (young adult, Middle-grade, mainstream commercial fiction, mystery, literary fiction, women's fiction, romance, urban fantasy, fantasy, science fiction, horror, dystopian); **Christa Heschke**, CHquery@mcintoshandotis.com (picture books, middle-grade, young adult New Adult projects); **Adam Muhlig**, AMquery@mcintoshandotis.com (music—from jazz to classical to punk—popular culture, natural history, travel and adventure, sports); **Eugene Winick**.

REPRESENTS Considers these nonfiction areas: creative nonfiction, current affairs, history, popular culture, self-help, spirituality, sports, travel. **Considers these fiction areas:** fantasy, historical, horror, literary, middle-grade, mystery, New Adult, paranormal, picture books, romance, science fiction, suspense, urban fantasy, women's, young adult.

☛ Actively seeking "books with memorable characters, distinctive voices, and great plots."

HOW TO CONTACT E-mail submissions only. All agents have their own e-mail address for subs. For fiction, please send a query letter, synopsis, author bio, and the first 3 consecutive chapters (no more than 30 pages) of your novel. For nonfiction, please send a query letter, proposal, outline, author bio, and 3 sample chapters (no more than 30 pages) of the ms. For children's & young adult: Please send a query letter, synopsis and the first 3 consecutive chapters (not to exceed 25 pages) of the ms. Accepts simultaneous submissions. Obtains clients through recommendations from others, editors, conferences and queries.

TERMS Agent receives 15% commission on domestic sales; 20% on foreign sales.

MENDEL MEDIA GROUP, LLC

115 W. 30th St., Suite 800, New York NY 10001. (646)239-9896. **Fax:** (212)685-4717. **Website:** www.mendelmedia.com. Member of AAR. Represents 40-60 clients.

Prior to becoming an agent, Mr. Mendel was an academic. "I taught American literature, Yiddish, Jewish studies, and literary theory at the University of Chicago and the University of Illinois at Chicago while working on my PhD in English. I also worked as a freelance technical writer and as the managing editor of a healthcare magazine. In 1998, I began working for the late Jane Jordan Browne, a longtime agent in the book publishing world."

REPRESENTS novels. **Considers these nonfiction areas:** Americana, animals, anthropology, architecture, art, biography, business, child guidance, cooking, current affairs, dance, education, environment, ethnic, foods, gardening, gay/lesbian, government, health, history, how-to, humor, investigative, language, medicine, memoirs, military, money, multicultural, music, parenting, philosophy, popular culture, psychology, recreation, regional, religious, science, self-help, sex, sociology, software, spirituality, sports, true crime, war, women's issues, women's studies, Jewish topics, creative nonfiction. **Considers these fiction areas:** action, adventure, contemporary issues, crime, detective, erotica, ethnic, feminist, gay, glitz, historical, humor, inspirational, juvenile, lesbian, literary, mainstream, mystery, picture books, police, religious, romance, satire, sports, thriller, young adult, Jewish fiction.

"I am interested in major works of history, current affairs, biography, business, politics, economics, science, major memoirs, narrative nonfiction, and other sorts of general nonfiction." Actively seeking new, major or definitive work on a subject of broad interest, or a controversial, but authoritative, new book on a subject that affects many people's lives. "I also represent more light-hearted nonfiction projects, such as gift or novelty books, when they suit the market particularly well." Does not want "queries about projects written years ago that were unsuccessfully shopped to a long list of trade publishers by either the author or another agent. I am specifically not interested in reading short, category romances (regency, time travel, paranormal, etc.), horror novels, supernatural stories, poetry, original plays, or film scripts."

HOW TO CONTACT Query with SASE. Do not e-mail or fax queries. For nonfiction, include a complete, fully edited book proposal with sample chapters. For fiction, include a complete synopsis and no more than 20 pages of sample text. Responds in 2 weeks to queries, 4-6 weeks to mss. Obtains most new clients through recommendations from others.
TERMS Agent receives 15% commission on domestic sales; 20% commission on foreign sales.
TIPS "While I am not interested in being flattered by a prospective client, it does matter to me that she knows why she is writing to me in the first place. Is one of my clients a colleague of hers? Has she read a book by one of my clients that led her to believe I might be interested in her work? Authors of descriptive nonfiction should have real credentials and expertise in their subject areas, either as academics, journalists, or policy experts, and authors of prescriptive nonfiction should have legitimate expertise and considerable experience communicating their ideas in seminars and workshops, in a successful business, through the media, etc."

SCOTT MEREDITH LITERARY AGENCY

One Exchange Plaza, Suite 2002, 55 Broadway, New York NY 10006. (646)274-1970. **Fax:** (212)977-5997. **E-mail:** info@scottmeredith.com. **Website:** www.scottmeredith.com. **Contact:** Arthur Klebanoff, CEO. Adheres to the AAR canon of ethics. Represents 20 clients.

Prior to becoming an agent, Mr. Klebanoff was a lawyer.

REPRESENTS textbooks.

This agency's specialty lies in category nonfiction publishing programs. Actively seeking category leading nonfiction. Does not want to receive first fiction projects.

HOW TO CONTACT Query with SASE. Submit proposal package, author bio. Accepts simultaneous submissions. Responds in 2 weeks to queries, 4 weeks to mss. Obtains most new clients through recommendations from others.
TERMS Agent receives 15% commission on domestic sales. Offers written contract.

ROBIN MIZELL LTD.

1600 Burnside St., Suite 205, Beaufort SC 29902. (614)774-7405. **E-mail:** mail@robinmizell.com. **Website:** www.robinmizell.com. **Contact:** Robin Mizell. This agency represents a limited number of authors. Estab. 2008.

REPRESENTS nonfiction, fiction, novels. **Considers these nonfiction areas:** creative nonfiction, cultural interests, history, how-to, humor, popular culture, psychology, sociology, women's issues, young adult. **Considers these fiction areas:** action, adventure, contemporary issues, crime, ethnic, family saga, feminist, frontier, gay, historical, humor, lesbian, literary, mainstream, military, multicultural, mystery, New Adult, police, suspense, thriller, translation, war, young adult.

⚬— This agency specializes in prescriptive nonfiction, long-form narrative journalism, neuroscience, psychology, sociology, pop culture, literary and upmarket commercial fiction, and young adult (not children's or middle-grade) fiction and nonfiction. Actively seeking psychological suspense.

HOW TO CONTACT E-query with the first 5 pages of your work pasted below in the e-mail. More specific submission instructions can be found on the agency website. Accepts simultaneous submissions. You should receive a response to your e-mail query within 30 days.

HOWARD MORHAIM LITERARY AGENCY

30 Pierrepont St., Brooklyn NY 11201. (718)222-8400. **Fax:** (718)222-5056. **E-mail:** info@morhaim-literary.com. **Website:** www.morhaimliterary.com. Member of AAR.

MEMBER AGENTS Howard Morhaim, howard@morhaimliterary.com, **Kate McKean**, kmckean@morhaimliterary.com, **DongWon Song**, dongwon@morhaimliterary.com, **Kim-Mei Kirtland**, kimmei@morhaimliterary.com.

REPRESENTS Considers these nonfiction areas: biography, business, cooking, crafts, creative nonfiction, design, economics, foods, health, humor, memoirs, parenting, self-help, sports. **Considers these fiction areas:** fantasy, historical, literary, middle-grade, New Adult, romance, science fiction, women's, young adult, LGBTQ young adult, magical realism, e high fantasy, historical fiction no earlier than the 20th century..

⚬— Kate McKean is open to many subgenres and categories of young adult and Middle-grade fiction. Check the website for the most details. Actively seeking fiction, nonfiction, and young adult novels.

HOW TO CONTACT Query via e-mail with cover letter and 3 sample chapters. See each agent's listing for specifics. Accepts simultaneous submissions.

MOVEABLE TYPE MANAGEMENT

244 Madison Ave., Suite 334, New York NY 10016. **E-mail:** achromy@movabletm.com. **Website:** www.movabletm.com. **Contact:** Adam Chromy. Estab. 2002.

REPRESENTS nonfiction, fiction, novels. **Considers these nonfiction areas:** Americana, business, creative nonfiction, current affairs, film, foods, history, how-to, humor, literature, memoirs, military, money, music, popular culture, politics, psychology, satire, science, self-help, sex, sports, technology, theater, true crime, war, women's issues, women's studies. **Considers these fiction areas:** action, commercial, crime, detective, erotica, hi-lo, historical, literary, mainstream, mystery, romance, satire, science fiction, sports, suspense, thriller, women's.

⚬— Mr. Chromy is a generalist, meaning that he accepts fiction submissions of virtually any kind (except juvenile books aimed for middle-grade and younger) as well as nonfiction. He has sold books in the following categories: New Adult, women's, romance, memoir, pop culture, young adult, lifestyle, horror, how-to, general fiction, and more.

HOW TO CONTACT E-queries only. Responds if interested. For nonfiction: Send a query letter in the body of an e-mail that precisely introduces your topic and approach, and includes a descriptive bio. For journalists and academics, please also feel free to include a CV. Fiction: Send your query letter and the first 10 pages of your novel in the body of an e-mail. Your subject line needs to contain the word "Query" or your message will not reach the agency. No attachments and no snail mail. Accepts simultaneous submissions.

RECENT SALES *The Wedding Sisters*, by Jamie Brenner (St. Martin's Press); *Sons Of Zeus*, by Noble Smith (Thomas Dunne Books); *World Made by Hand and Too Much Magic*, by James Howard Kunstler (Grove/Atlantic Press); *Dirty Rocker Boys*, by Bobbie Brown (Gallery/S&S).

DEE MURA LITERARY

P.O. Box 131, Massapequa NY 11762. (516)795-1616. **E-mail:** info@deemuraliterary.com. **E-mail:** query@deemuraliterary.com. **Website:** www.deemuraliterary.com. **Contact:** Dee Mura. "We focus on de-

NEW AGENT SPOTLIGHT

DAMIAN MCNICHOLL

JENNIFER DE CHIARA LITERARY AGENCY

www.jdlit.com
@DamianMcN

ABOUT DAMIAN: Damian McNicholl grew up in Northern Ireland and moved to the US in the early nineties. A former attorney, he is also an author whose latest novel, *The Moment of Truth*, will be published by Pegasus Books in June 2017. His critically acclaimed novel *A Son Called Gabriel* will be republished by Pegasus in Fall 2017. Damian regards himself as an agent who likes to edit and help polish a client's work before submission.

HE IS SEEKING: Great nonfiction and fiction that appeals to a wide audience and makes people think, laugh and sob. In fiction, his interests are compelling novels that hit the sweet spot between literary and commercial, historical and select offbeat/quirky. Nonfiction interests include memoir, biography, investigative journalism and current events, especially cultural, legal and LGBT issues that can help lead to meaningful change in society. To see the types of books he likes, please visit Damian's agent page.

HOW TO SUBMIT: For fiction and memoir, please email a succinct query to damianmcnichollvarney@gmail.com with a subject line of QUERY. Include a short synopsis of the plot (think dust jacket copy), concise bio setting forth any publishing credits and the first 15 pages in the body of the email. For all other nonfiction, please attach a proposal as a Word document that includes the first chapter and your author platform.

veloping our client's' careers from day one through to publication and beyond by providing personalized editorial feedback, social media and platform marketing, and thorough rights management. Both new and experienced authors are welcome to submit." Signatory of WGA. Member of Women's National Book Association, GrubStreet

○ Prior to opening her agency, Mura was a public relations executive with a roster of film and entertainment clients. She is the president and CEO of both Dee Mura Literary and Dee Mura Entertainment.

MEMBER AGENTS Dee Mura, Kimiko Nakamura, Kaylee Davis.

REPRESENTS nonfiction, fiction, novels, short story collections, juvenile books. **Considers these nonfiction areas:** agriculture, Americana, animals, anthropology, archeology, architecture, art, autobiography, biography, business, child guidance, cooking, crafts, creative nonfiction, cultural interests, current affairs, dance, decorating, diet/nutrition, design, economics, education, environment, ethnic, film, foods, gardening, gay/lesbian, government, health, history, hobbies, horticulture, how-to, humor, inspirational, interior design, investigative, juvenile nonfiction, language, law, literature, medicine, memoirs, metaphysics, military, money, multicultural, music, New Age, parenting, photography, popular culture, politics, psychology, recreation, religious, science, self-help, sex, sociology, spirituality, sports, technology, travel, true crime, war, women's issues, women's studies, young adult, Judaism. **Considers these fiction areas:** action, adventure, comic books, commercial, contemporary issues, crime, detective, erotica, ethnic, family saga, fantasy, feminist, frontier, gay, glitz, historical, horror, humor, inspirational, juvenile, lesbian, literary, mainstream, metaphysical, middle-grade, military, multicultural, multimedia, mystery, New Adult, New Age, occult, paranormal, police, psychic, regional, religious, romance, satire, science fiction, short story collections, spiritual, sports, supernatural, suspense, thriller, translation, urban fantasy, war, westerns, women's, young adult, espionage, magical realism, speculative fiction, crossover.

➤ No screenplays, poetry, or children's picture books.

HOW TO CONTACT Query with SASE or e-mail query@deemuraliterary.com (e-mail queries are preferred). Please include the first 25 pages in the body of the e-mail as well as a short author bio and synopsis of the work. Responds to queries in 4-5 weeks. Responds to mss in approximately 8 weeks. Obtains new clients through recommendations, queries, and conferences. Accepts simultaneous submissions. Responds to queries in 3-4 weeks. Responds to mss in approximately 8 weeks. Obtains new clients through recommendations, queries, and conferences.

TERMS Agent receives 15% commission on domestic sales; 20% commission on foreign sales. Offers written contract.

RECENT SALES *An Infinite Number of Parallel Universes*, by Randy Ribay; *The Number 7*, by Jessica Lidh.

⊘ ERIN MURPHY LITERARY AGENCY

824 Roosevelt Trail, #290, Windham ME 04062. **Website:** emliterary.com. **Contact:** Erin Murphy, president; Ammi-Joan Paquette, senior agent; Tricia Lawrence, agent; Tara Gonzalez, associate agent. Estab. 1999.

REPRESENTS Considers these fiction areas: middle-grade, picture books, young adult.

➤ Specializes in children's books only.

HOW TO CONTACT Accepts simultaneous submissions.

TERMS Agent receives 15% commission on domestic sales; 20-30% on foreign sales. Offers written contract; 30-days notice must be given to terminate contract.

JEAN V. NAGGAR LITERARY AGENCY, INC.

JVNLA, Inc., 216 E. 75th St., Suite 1E, New York NY 10021. (212)794-1082. **Website:** www.jvnla.com. **Contact:** Jennifer Weltz. Estab. 1978. Member of AAR, Women's Media Group, SCBWI, Pace University's Masters in Publishing Board Member. Represents 450 clients.

MEMBER AGENTS Jennifer Weltz (well researched and original historicals, thriller with a unique voice, wry dark humor, magical realism; enthralling narrative nonfiction; voice driven young adult, middle-grade); **Alice Tasman** (literary, commercial, young adult, middle-grade, nonfiction: narrative, biography, music, pop culture); **Laura Biagi** (literary fiction, magical realism, psychological thriller, young adult, middle-grade, picture books).

REPRESENTS nonfiction, fiction, novels, short story collections, novellas, juvenile books, scholarly books, poetry books.

➤ This agency specializes in mainstream fiction and nonfiction and literary fiction with commercial potential as well as young adult, middle-grade, and picture books. Does not want to receive screenplays.

HOW TO CONTACT "Visit our website to send submissions and see what our individual agents are looking for. No snail mail submissions please!" Accepts simultaneous submissions. Depends on the agent. No responses for queries unless the agent is interested.

TERMS Agent receives 15% commission on domestic sales; 20% commission on foreign sales.

RECENT SALES *Mort(e)*, by Robert Repino; *The Paying Guests*, by Sarah Waters; *Violent Crimes*, by Phillip Margolin; *An Unseemly Wife*, by E.B. Moore; *The Man Who Walked Away*, by Maud Casey; *Dietland*, by Sarai Walker; *In the Land of Armadillos*, by Helen Maryles Shankman; *Not If I See You First*, by Eric Lindstrom.

TIPS "We recommend courage, fortitude, and patience: the courage to be true to your own vision, the fortitude to finish a novel and polish it again and again before sending it out, and the patience to accept rejection gracefully and wait for the stars to align themselves appropriately for success."

NELSON LITERARY AGENCY

1732 Wazee St., Suite 207, Denver CO 80202. (303)292-2805. **E-mail:** query@nelsonagency.com. **E-mail:** querykristin@nelsonagency.com. **Website:** www.nelsonagency.com. **Contact:** Kristin Nelson, President. Kristin Nelson established Nelson Literary Agency, LLC in 2002 and over the last decade of her career, has represented over 35 *New York Times* bestselling titles and many *USA Today* bestsellers. Estab. 2002. Member of AAR, RWA, SCBWI, SFWA. Represents 37 clients.

REPRESENTS fiction, novels, young adult, middle-grade, literary commercial, upmarket women's fiction, single-title romance, science fiction, fantasy. **Considers these fiction areas:** commercial, fantasy, historical, horror, literary, mainstream, middle-grade, romance, science fiction, suspense, thriller, urban fantasy, women's, young adult.

- NLA specializes in representing commercial fiction and high-caliber literary fiction. "We represent many popular genre categories, including historical romance, steampunk, and all subgenres of young adult." Regardless of genre, "we are actively seeking good stories well told." Does not want nonfiction, memoir, stage plays, screenplays, short story collections, poetry, children's picture books, early reader chapter books, or material for the Christian/inspirational market.

HOW TO CONTACT "Please visit our website and carefully read our submission guidelines. We do not accept any queries on Facebook or Twitter. Query by e-mail only. Write the word 'Query' in the e-mail subject line along with the title of your novel. Send no attachments, but please paste the first 10 pages of your novel in the body of the e-mail beneath your query letter." Accepts simultaneous submissions. Makes best efforts to respond to all queries within 10 business day. Response to full mss requested can take up to 3 months.

NEW LEAF LITERARY & MEDIA, INC.

110 W. 40th St., Suite 2201, New York NY 10018. (646)248-7989. **Fax:** (646)861-4654. **E-mail:** query@newleafliterary.com. **Website:** www.newleafliterary.com. Estab. 2012. Member of AAR.

MEMBER AGENTS Joanna Volpe (women's fiction, thriller, horror, speculative fiction, literary fiction and historical fiction, young adult, middle-grade, art-focused picture books); **Kathleen Ortiz**, Director of Subsidiary Rights and literary agent (new voices in young adult and animator/illustrator talent); **Suzie Townsend** (New Adult, young adult, middle-grade, romance [all subgenres], fantasy [urban fantasy, science fiction, steampunk, epic fantasy] and crime fiction [mystery, thriller]); **Pouya Shahbazian**, Director of Film and Television (no unsolicited queries); **Janet Reid**, janet@newleafliterary.com; **Jaida Temperly** (all fiction: magical realism, historical fiction; literary fiction; stories that are quirky and fantastical; nonfiction: niche, offbeat, a bit strange; middle-grade); **JL Stermer** (nonfiction, smart pop culture, comedy/satire, fashion, health and wellness, self-help, memoir).

REPRESENTS nonfiction, fiction, novels, novellas, juvenile books, poetry books. **Considers these nonfiction areas:** cooking, crafts, creative nonfiction, science, technology, women's issues, young adult. **Considers these fiction areas:** crime, fantasy, historical, horror, literary, mainstream, middle-grade, mystery, New Adult, paranormal, picture books, romance, thriller, women's, young adult.

HOW TO CONTACT Send query via e-mail. Please do not query via phone. The word "Query" must be in the subject line, plus the agent's name—Subject: Query, Suzie Townsend. You may include up to 5 double-spaced sample pages within the body of the e-mail. No attachments, unless specifically requested. Include all necessary contact information. You will receive an auto-response confirming receipt of your query. "We only respond if we are interested in seeing your work." Responds only if interested. All queries read within 1 month.

RECENT SALES *Carve the Mark*, by Veronica Roth (HarperCollins); *Red Queen*, by Victoria Aveyard (HarperCollins); *Lobster Is the Best Medicine*, by Liz Climo (Running Press); *Ninth House*, by Leigh Bardugo (Henry Holt); *A Snicker of Magic*, by Natalie Lloyd (Scholastic).

DANA NEWMAN LITERARY

9720 Wilshire Blvd., Fifth Floor, Beverly Hills CA 90212. **E-mail:** dananewmanliterary@gmail.com. **Website:** dananewman.com. **Contact:** Dana Newman. Dana Newman Literary, LLC is a boutique literary agency in Los Angeles. Estab. 2009. Member of AAR, California State Bar. Represents 28 clients.

○ Prior to becoming an agent, Ms. Newman was an attorney in the entertainment industry for 14 years.

MEMBER AGENTS Dana Newman (narrative nonfiction, business, lifestyle, current affairs, parenting, memoir, pop culture, sports, health, literary, upmarket fiction).

REPRESENTS nonfiction, novels, short story collections. **Considers these nonfiction areas:** architecture, art, autobiography, biography, business, child guidance, cooking, creative nonfiction, cultural interests, current affairs, diet/nutrition, design, education, ethnic, film, foods, gay/lesbian, government, health, history, how-to, inspirational, investigative, language, law, literature, medicine, memoirs, money, multicultural, music, New Age, parenting, popular culture, politics, psychology, science, self-help, sociology, sports, technology, theater, travel, true crime, women's issues, women's studies. **Considers these fiction areas:** commercial, contemporary issues, family saga, feminist, historical, literary, multicultural, sports, women's.

⌐ Ms. Newman has a background as an attorney in contracts, licensing, and intellectual property law. She is experienced in digital content creation and distribution. "We are interested in practical nonfiction (business, health and wellness, psychology, parenting, technology) by authors with smart, unique perspectives and established platforms who are committed to actively marketing and promoting their books. We love compelling, inspiring narrative nonfiction in the areas of memoir, biography, history, pop culture, current affairs/women's interest, sports, and social trends. On the fiction side, we consider a very selective amount of literary fiction and women's upmarket fiction." Does not want religious, children's, poetry, horror, mystery, thriller, romance, or science fiction.

HOW TO CONTACT E-mail queries only. For both nonfiction and fiction, please submit a query letter, including a description of your project and a brief biography. "If we are interested in your project, we will contact you and request a full book proposal (nonfiction) or a synopsis and the first 25 pages (fiction). If we have requested your materials after receiving your query, we usually respond within 4 weeks." Accepts simultaneous submissions. Obtains new clients through recommendations from others, queries, submissions.

TERMS Obtains 15% commission on domestic sales; 20% on foreign sales. Offers 1 year written contract. Notice must be given 1 month prior to terminate a contract.

RECENT SALES *Into the Abyss*, by Ginger Lerner-Wren (Beacon Press); *Native Advertising*, by Mike Smith (McGraw-Hill); *Breakthrough: The Making of America's First Woman President*, by Nancy L. Cohen (Counterpoint); *Just Add Water*, by Clay Marzo and Robert Yehling (Houghton Mifflin Harcourt).

ALLEN O'SHEA LITERARY AGENCY

615 Westover Rd., Stamford CT 06902. (203)359-9965. **Fax:** (203)357-9909. **E-mail:** marilyn@allen-oshea.com, coleen@allenoshea.com. **Website:** www.allenoshea.com. **Contact:** Marilyn Allen, Coleen O'Shea.

○ Prior to becoming agents, both Ms. Allen and Ms. O'Shea held senior positions in publishing.

MEMBER AGENTS Marilyn Allen, Coleen O'Shea.

REPRESENTS nonfiction. **Considers these nonfiction areas:** autobiography, biography, business, cooking, crafts, creative nonfiction, current affairs, decorating, diet/nutrition, design, environment, film, foods, gardening, health, history, how-to, humor, inspirational, interior design, medicine, memoirs, military, money, New Age, parenting, popular culture, psychology, regional, science, self-help, true crime.

⌐ This agency specializes in practical nonfiction, including health, cooking and cocktails, business, and pop culture. Looks for passionate clients with strong marketing platforms and new ideas coupled with writing talent. Actively seeking narrative nonfiction, health, popular science, cookbooks, and history writers; very interested in writers who have large media platforms and interesting topics.

Does not want to receive fiction, poetry, text-books, or children's books.

HOW TO CONTACT Query via e-mail or mail with SASE. Submit book proposal with sample chapters, competitive analysis, outline, author bio, and marketing page. No phone or fax queries. Accepts simultaneous submissions. Obtains most new clients through recommendations from others, conferences.

TERMS Agent receives 15% commission on domestic sales. Offers written contract, binding for 2 years; one-month notice must be given to terminate contract.

TIPS "Prepare a strong overview, with competition, marketing, and bio. We will consider your project when your proposal is ready."

HAROLD OBER ASSOCIATES

425 Madison Ave., New York NY 10017. (212)759-8600. **Fax:** (212)759-9428. **Website:** www.haroldober.com. **Contact:** Appropriate agent. Member of AAR. Represents 250 clients.

MEMBER AGENTS Phyllis Westberg; **Craig Tenney** (few new clients; mostly Ober backlist and foreign rights).

HOW TO CONTACT Submit concise query letter addressed to a specific agent with the first 5 pages of the ms or proposal and SASE. No fax or e-mail. Does not handle filmscripts or plays. Responds as promptly as possible. Obtains most new clients through recommendations from others.

TERMS Agent receives 15% commission on domestic sales; 20% commission on foreign sales. Charges clients for express mail/package services.

PARK LITERARY GROUP, LLC

270 Lafayette St., Suite 1504, New York NY 10012. (212)691-3500. **Fax:** (212)691-3540. **E-mail:** info@parkliterary.com. **E-mail:** queries@parkliterary.com. **Website:** www.parkliterary.com. Estab. 2005.

MEMBER AGENTS Theresa Park (plot-driven fiction, serious nonfiction); **Abigail Koons** (popular science, history, politics, current affairs, art, women's fiction); **Peter Knapp** (children's, young adult).

REPRESENTS nonfiction, novels. **Considers these nonfiction areas:** art, current affairs, history, politics, science. **Considers these fiction areas:** juvenile, middle-grade, suspense, thriller, women's, young adult.

The Park Literary Group represents fiction and nonfiction with a boutique approach: an emphasis on servicing a relatively small number of clients, with the highest professional standards and focused personal attention. Does not want to receive poetry or screenplays.

HOW TO CONTACT Please specify the first and last name of the agent to whom you are submitting in the subject line of the e-mail. All materials must be in the body of the e-mail. Responds if interested. For fiction submissions, please include a query letter with short synopsis and the first 3 chapters of your work. Accepts simultaneous submissions.

RECENT SALES This agency's client list is on its website. It includes bestsellers Nicholas Sparks, Soman Chainani, Emily Giffin, Debbie Macomber.

L. PERKINS AGENCY

5800 Arlington Ave., Riverdale NY 10471. (718)543-5344. **E-mail:** submissions@lperkinsagency.com. **Website:** lperkinsagency.com. Estab. 1987. Member of AAR. Represents 150 clients.

Ms. Perkins has been an agent for 25 years. She is also the author of *The Insider's Guide to Getting an Agent* (Writer's Digest Books), as well as 3 other nonfiction books. She has edited 25 erotic anthologies, and is also the founder and publisher of Riverdale Avenue Books, an award-winning hybrid publisher with 9 imprints.

MEMBER AGENTS Tish Beaty, ePub agent (erotic romance, including paranormal, historical, gay/lesbian/bisexual, light-BDSM fiction; New Adult, young adult); **Sandy Lu**, sandy@lperkinsagency.com (fiction: dark literary and commercial fiction, mystery, thriller, psychological horror, paranormal/urban fantasy, historical fiction, young adult, historical thriller or mystery set in Victorian times; nonfiction: narrative nonfiction, history, biography, pop science, pop psychology, pop culture [music/theatre/film], humor, food writing); **Lori Perkins** (not currently taking new clients); **Leon Husock** (science fiction and fantasy, young adult and middle-grade); **Rachel Brooks** (picture books, all genres of young adult and New Adult fiction, adult romance—especially romantic suspense [NOTE: Rachel is currently closed to unsolicited submissions]); **Maximilian Ximinez** (fiction: science fiction, fantasy, horror, thrill-

NEW AGENT SPOTLIGHT

KAITLYN JOHNSON
CORVISIERO LITERARY AGENCY

www.corvisieroagency.com
@kaitylynne13

ABOUT KAITLYN: After receiving a BA in Writing, Publishing, and Literature from Emerson College, Kaitlyn refused to leave the concept of nightly homework behind. Centering her life around everything literary, she started her own freelance editing company, K. Johnson Editorial, as soon as her diploma came in the mail. Holding two years of literary magazine editing experience, Kaitlyn is proud to be on staff for the increasingly popular Muse and the Marketplace Conference held in Boston every April/May through GrubStreet. She currently works as both the Muse Conference Assistant and the Donor Communications Assistant at GrubStreet.

SHE IS SEEKING: Young adult, New Adult, and adult. Lots of fantasy (yes, that very much includes urban!), time travel, select dystopian, romance (erotic elements OK), and historical fiction if it is anything other than Henry VIII. Contemporary with unique concept and good execution. No overplayed tropes/characters. Same goes for upper middle-grade. LGBT (as well as characters questioning their sexuality) welcome in all genres accepted above. Fairytale retellings but *only* if it's from an unexpected point of view.

HOW TO SUBMIT: Please follow the submission guidelines on the "Submissions" page of Corvisiero Literary Agency and send to query@corvisieroagency.com with the subject title: "Query: Kaitlyn Johnson, [name of manuscript]" Also include a strong query, 5-page sample, and 1-2 page synopsis.

er; nonfiction: popular science, true crime, arts, trends in developing fields and cultures).
REPRESENTS nonfiction, fiction, novels, short story collections. **Considers these nonfiction areas:** autobiography, biography, business, creative nonfiction, cultural interests, current affairs, film, foods, gay/lesbian, history, how-to, humor, literature, memoirs, music, popular culture, psychology, science, sex, theater, true crime, women's issues, women's studies, young adult. **Considers these fiction areas:** commercial, crime, detective, erotica, fantasy, feminist, gay, historical, horror, lesbian, literary, middle-grade, mystery, New Adult, paranormal, picture books, romance, science fiction, short story collections, supernatural, thriller, urban fantasy, women's, young adult.
HOW TO CONTACT E-queries only. Include your query, a 1-page synopsis, and the first 5 pages from your novel pasted into the e-mail, or your proposal. No attachments. Submit to only 1 agent at the

agency. No snail mail queries. "If you are submitting to one of our agents, please be sure to check the submission status of the agent by visiting our social media accounts listed [on the agency website]." Accepts simultaneous submissions. Obtains most new clients through recommendations from others, solicitations, conferences.

TERMS Agent receives 15% commission on domestic sales; 20% commission on foreign sales. No written contract. Charges clients for photocopying.

RECENT SALES *Arena*, by Holly Jennings; *Taking the Lead*, by Cecilia Tan; *The Girl with Ghost Eyes*, by M. H. Boroson; *Silent Attraction*, by Lauren Brown.

RUBIN PFEFFER CONTENT

648 Hammond St., Chestnut Hill MA 02467. **E-mail:** info@rpcontent.com. **Website:** www.rpcontent.com. **Contact:** Rubin Pfeffer. Rubin Pfeffer Content is a literary agency exclusively representing children's and young adult literature, as well as content that will serve educational publishers and digital developers. Working closely with authors and illustrators, RPC is devoted to producing long-lasting children's literature: work that exemplifies outstanding writing, innovative creativity, and artistic excellence. Estab. 2014. Member of AAR. Signatory of WGA.

- Rubin has previously worked as the vice-president and publisher of Simon & Schuster Children's Books and as an independent agent at East West Literary Agency.

REPRESENTS Considers these fiction areas: juvenile, middle-grade, picture books, young adult.

HOW TO CONTACT Note: This agent accepts submissions by referral only. Specify the contact information of your reference when submitting. Authors/illustrators should send a query and a 1-3 chapter ms via e-mail (no postal submissions). The query, placed in the body of the e-mail, should include a synopsis of the piece, as well as any relevant information regarding previous publications, referrals, websites, and biography. The ms may be attached as a .doc or a .pdf file. Specifically for illustrators, attach a PDF of the dummy or artwork to the e-mail. If you would like to query Melissa Nasson with your picture book, middle-grade, or young adult ms, query with the first 50 pages to melissa@

rpcontent.com. Accepts simultaneous submissions. Responds within 6-8 weeks.

PIPPIN PROPERTIES, INC.

110 W. 40th St., Suite 1704, New York NY 10018. (212)338-9310. **Fax:** (212)338-9579. **E-mail:** info@pippinproperties.com. **Website:** www.pippinproperties.com. **Contact:** Holly McGhee. "Pippin Properties, Inc. opened its doors in 1998, and for the past 17 years we have been privileged to help build careers for authors and artists whose work stands the test of time, many of whom have become household names in their own right, such as Peter H. Reynolds, Kate DiCamillo, Sujean Rim, Doreen Cronin, Renata Liwska, Sarah Weeks, Harry Bliss, Kate and Jim McMullan, Katherine Applegate, David Small, and Kathi Appelt. We also love to launch new careers for amazing authors and artists such as Jason Reynolds, Anna Kang and Chris Weyant, and Jandy Nelson."Estab. 1998.

- Prior to becoming an agent, Ms. McGhee was an editor for 7 years and in book marketing for 4 years.

MEMBER AGENTS Holly McGhee, Elena Giovinazzo, Heather Alexander, Sara Crowe. Although each of the agents take children's books, you can find in-depth preferences for each agent on the Pippin website.

REPRESENTS juvenile books. **Considers these fiction areas:** middle-grade, picture books, young adult.

- "We are strictly a children's literary agency devoted to the management of authors and artists in all media. We are small and discerning in choosing our clientele."

HOW TO CONTACT If you are a writer who is interested in submitting a ms, please query us via e-mail, and within the body of that e-mail please include the first chapter of your novel with a short synopsis of the work or the entire picture book ms. For illustrators interested in submitting their work, please send a query letter detailing your background in illustration and include links to website with a dummy or other examples of your work. Direct all queries to the agent whom you wish to query and please do not query more than one. No attachments, please. Accepts simultaneous submissions. Obtains most new clients through recommendations from others.

TERMS Agent receives 15% commission on domestic sales; 25% commission on foreign sales. Offers written contract; 30-day notice must be given to terminate contract.

AARON M. PRIEST LITERARY AGENCY

200 W. 41st St., 21st Floor, New York NY 10036. (212)818-0344. **Fax:** (212)573-9417. **E-mail:** info@aaronpriest.com. **Website:** www.aaronpriest.com. Estab. 1974. Member of AAR.

MEMBER AGENTS Aaron Priest, querypriest@aaronpriest.com (thriller, commercial fiction, biography); **Lisa Erbach Vance**, queryvance@aaronpriest.com (contemporary fiction, thriller/suspense, international fiction, narrative nonfiction); **Lucy Childs**, querychilds@aaronpriest.com (literary and commercial fiction, memoir, edgy women's fiction); **Mitch Hoffman**, queryhoffman@aaronpriest.com (thriller, suspense, crime fiction, literary fiction, narrative nonfiction, politics, popular science, history, memoir, current events, pop culture).

REPRESENTS Considers these nonfiction areas: biography, current affairs, history, memoirs, popular culture, politics, science. **Considers these fiction areas:** commercial, contemporary issues, crime, literary, middle-grade, suspense, thriller, women's, young adult.

☛ Does not want to receive poetry, screenplays, horror or science fiction.

HOW TO CONTACT Query one of the agents using the appropriate e-mail listed on the website. "Please do not submit to more than 1 agent at this agency. We urge you to check our website and consider each agent's emphasis before submitting. Your query letter should be about 1-page long and describe your work as well as your background. You may also paste the first chapter of your work in the body of the e-mail. Do not send attachments." Accepts simultaneous submissions. Responds in 4 weeks, only if interested.

TERMS Agent receives 15% commission on domestic sales.

PROSPECT AGENCY

551 Valley Rd., PMB 377, Upper Montclair NJ 07043. (718)788-3217. **Fax:** (718)360-9582. **Website:** www.prospectagency.com. Estab. 2005. Member of AAR. Signatory of WGA. Represents 130+ clients.

MEMBER AGENTS Emily Sylvan Kim, esk@prospectagency.com (romance, women's, commercial, young adult, New Adult); **Rachel Orr**, rko@prospectagency.com (picture books, illustrators, middle-grade, young adult); **Becca Stumpf**, becca@prospectagency.com (young adult and middle-grade [all genres, including fantasy/science fiction, literary, mystery, contemporary, historical, horror/suspense], especially middle-grade and young adult novels featuring diverse protagonists and life circumstances. Adult science fiction and fantasy novels with broad appeal, upmarket women's fiction, smart, spicy romance novels); **Carrie Pestritto**, carrie@prospectagency.com (narrative nonfiction, general nonfiction, biography, memoir; commercial fiction with a literary twist, women's fiction, romance, upmarket, historical fiction, high-concept young adult, upper middle-grade); **Linda Camacho**, linda@prospectagency.com (middle-grade, young adult, adult fiction across all genres, especially women's fiction/romance, horror, fantasy/science fiction, graphic novels, contemporary; select literary fiction; fiction featuring diverse/marginalized groups); **Kirsten Carleton**, kcarleton@prospectagency.com (upmarket speculative, thriller, literary fiction for adult and young adult).

REPRESENTS nonfiction, fiction, novels, novellas, juvenile books, scholarly books, textbooks. **Considers these nonfiction areas:** biography, memoirs, popular culture, psychology. **Considers these fiction areas:** commercial, contemporary issues, crime, ethnic, family saga, fantasy, feminist, gay, historical, horror, humor, juvenile, lesbian, literary, mainstream, middle-grade, multicultural, mystery, New Adult, picture books, romance, science fiction, suspense, thriller, urban fantasy, women's, young adult.

☛ "We're looking for strong, unique voices and unforgettable stories and characters."

HOW TO CONTACT All submissions are electronic and must be submitted through the portal at prospectagency.com/submissions. We do not accept any submissions through snail mail. Accepts simultaneous submissions. Obtains new clients through conferences, recommendations, queries, and some scouting.

TERMS Agent receives 15% on domestic sales; 20% on foreign sales sold directly; 25% on sales using a subagent. Offers written contract.

P.S LITERARY AGENCY

2010 Winston Park Dr., Second Floor, Oakville ON L6H 5R7 Canada. **E-mail:** query@psliterary.com. **Website:** www.psliterary.com. **Contact:** Curtis Russell, principal agent; Carly Watters, senior agent; Maria Vicente, associate agent; Kurestin Armada, associate agent; Eric Smith; associate agent. Estab. 2005.

MEMBER AGENTS Curtis Russell (literary/commercial fiction, mystery, thriller, suspense, romance, young adult, middle-grade, picture books, business, history, politics, current affairs, memoirs, health/wellness, sports, humor, pop culture, pop science, pop psychology); **Carly Watters** (upmarket/commercial fiction, women's fiction, book club fiction, literary thriller, cookbooks, health/wellness, memoirs, humor, pop science, pop psychology); **Maria Vicente** (young adult, middle-grade, illustrated picture books, pop culture, science, lifestyle, design); **Kurestin Armada** (magic realism, science fiction, fantasy, illustrated picture books, middle-grade, young adult, graphic novels, romance, design, cookbooks, pop psychology, photography, nature, science); **Eric Smith** (young adult, New Adult, literary/commercial fiction, cookbooks, pop culture, humor, essay collections).

REPRESENTS nonfiction, novels, juvenile books. **Considers these nonfiction areas:** art, autobiography, biography, business, cooking, crafts, creative nonfiction, cultural interests, current affairs, decorating, diet/nutrition, design, economics, environment, film, foods, gardening, gay/lesbian, government, health, history, hobbies, how-to, humor, interior design, juvenile nonfiction, literature, memoirs, military, money, music, New Age, photography, popular culture, politics, psychology, science, self-help, sports, technology, true crime, war, women's issues, women's studies, young adult. **Considers these fiction areas:** action, adventure, detective, erotica, ethnic, experimental, family saga, fantasy, feminist, gay, historical, horror, humor, juvenile, lesbian, literary, mainstream, middle-grade, multicultural, mystery, New Adult, picture books, romance, science fiction, sports, thriller, urban fantasy, women's, young adult.

- Actively seeking both fiction and nonfiction. Seeking both new and established writers. Does not want to receive poetry or screenplays.

HOW TO CONTACT Query letters should be directed to query@psliterary.com. PSLA does not accept or respond to phone, paper, or social media queries. Responds in 4-6 weeks to queries/proposals. Obtains most new clients through solicitations.

TERMS Agent receives 15% commission on domestic sales; 25% commission on foreign sales. "We offer a written contract, with 30-days notice terminate."

THE PURCELL AGENCY

E-mail: tpaqueries@gmail.com. **Website:** www.thepurcellagency.com. **Contact:** Tina P. Schwartz. This is an agency for authors of children's and teen literature. Estab. 2012. Member of SCBWI Represents 32 clients.

MEMBER AGENTS Tina P. Schwartz, **Kim Blair McCollum**.

REPRESENTS nonfiction, novels, juvenile books. **Considers these nonfiction areas:** biography, child guidance, creative nonfiction, gay/lesbian, juvenile nonfiction, multicultural, parenting, young adult. **Considers these fiction areas:** juvenile, middle-grade, young adult.

- This agency also takes juvenile nonfiction for Middle-grade and young adult markets. At this point, the agency is not considering fantasy, science fiction, or picture book submissions.

HOW TO CONTACT Check the website to see if agency is open to submissions and for submission guidelines. Accepts simultaneous submissions.

RECENT SALES *A Kind of Justice,* by Renee James; *Adventures at Hound Hotel,* by Shelley Swanson Sateren; *Adventures at Tabby Towers,* by Shelley Swanson Sateren; *Keys to Freedom,* by Karen Meade.

QUEEN LITERARY AGENCY

30 E. 60th St., Suite 1004, New York NY 10022. (212)974-8333. **Fax:** (212)974-8347. **E-mail:** submissions@queenliterary.com. **Website:** www.queenliterary.com. **Contact:** Lisa Queen.

- Prior to her current position, Ms. Queen was a former publishing executive and most recently head of IMG Worldwide's literary division.

REPRESENTS novels. **Considers these nonfiction areas:** business, foods, psychology, science, sports. **Considers these fiction areas:** commercial, historical, literary, mystery, thriller.

☞ "While our agency represents a wide range of nonfiction titles, we have a particular interest in business books, food writing, science and popular psychology, as well as books by well-known chefs, radio and television personalities, and sports figures."

HOW TO CONTACT E-query. Accepts simultaneous submissions.

RECENT SALES A full list of this agency's clients and sales is available on their website.

SUSAN RABINER LITERARY AGENCY, INC., THE

Website: www.rabinerlit.com. **Contact:** Susan Rabiner.

○ Prior to becoming an agent, Ms. Rabiner was editorial director of Basic Books. She is also the co-author of *Thinking Like Your Editor: How to Write Great Serious Nonfiction and Get it Published* (W.W. Norton).

MEMBER AGENTS Susan Rabiner, susan@rabiner.net (well-researched, topical books written by fully credentialed academics, journalists, and recognized public intellectuals with the power to stimulate public debate on a broad range of issues including the state of our economy, political discourse, history, science, arts); **Sydelle Kramer**, sydellek@rabiner.net, (represents a diverse group of academics, journalists, sportswriters, memoirists); **Holly Bemiss**, hollyb@rabiner.net (clients include graphic novelists, journalists, memoirists, comedians, crafters, entertainment writers).

☞ "Representing narrative nonfiction and big-idea books by scholars, public intellectuals, and established journalists—work that illuminates the past and the present in current affairs, history, the sciences, and the arts."

HOW TO CONTACT Please send all queries by e-mail. Note: "Because of the number of queries we receive, we cannot respond to every one. If your project fits the profile of the agency, we will be in touch within two weeks." Accepts simultaneous submissions. Responds in 2 weeks if your project fits the profile of the agency. Obtains most new clients through recommendations from others.

TERMS Agent receives 15% commission on domestic sales; 20% commission on foreign sales. Offers written contract; 1-month notice must be given to terminate contract.

RED SOFA LITERARY

P.O. Box 40482, St. Paul MN 55104. (651)224-6670. **E-mail:** dawn@redsofaliterary.com, jennie@redsofaliterary.com, laura@redsofaliterary.com, bree@redsofaliterary.com, amanda@redsofaliterary.com, stacey@redsofaliterary.com, erik@redsofaliterary.com. **Website:** www.redsofaliterary.com. Estab. 2008. Member of the Authors Guild, the MN Publishers Round Table. Represents 125 clients.

MEMBER AGENTS Jennie Goloboy, Laura Zats, Bree Ogden, Amanda Rutter, Stacey Graham, Erik Hane.

REPRESENTS nonfiction, fiction, novels, juvenile books. **Considers these nonfiction areas:** Americana, animals, anthropology, archeology, crafts, creative nonfiction, cultural interests, current affairs, dance, environment, film, gay/lesbian, government, health, history, hobbies, humor, investigative, juvenile nonfiction, multicultural, popular culture, politics, recreation, satire, science, sociology, true crime, war, women's issues, women's studies, young adult, extreme sports. **Considers these fiction areas:** action, adventure, commercial, detective, erotica, ethnic, fantasy, feminist, gay, humor, juvenile, lesbian, literary, mainstream, middle-grade, mystery, picture books, romance, science fiction, suspense, thriller, urban fantasy, young adult.

HOW TO CONTACT Query by e-mail or mail with SASE. No attachments, please. Submit full proposal (for nonfiction especially, for fiction it would be nice) plus 3 sample chapters (or first 50 pages) and any other pertinent writing samples upon request by the specific agent. Do not send within or attached to the query letter. Accepts simultaneous submissions. Obtains new clients through queries, also through recommendations from others, solicitations.

TERMS Agent receives 15% commission on domestic sales; 20% commission on foreign sales. Offers written contract.

RECENT SALES *Semiosis*, Sue Burke (Tor, 2017); *Welcome Home*, edited/by Eric Smith (Jolly Fish Press, 2017); *Body Horror: Essays on Misogyny and Capitalism*, by Anne Elizabeth Moore (Curbside Splendor, 2017); *Dr. Potter's Medicine Show*, by Eric Scott Fischl (Angry Robot Books, 2017); *Play Like a Girl: How a Soccer School in Kenya's Slums Started a Revolution*, by Ellie Roscher (Viva Editions, 2017);

NEW AGENT SPOTLIGHT

JOANNA MACKENZIE
NELSON LITERARY AGENCY

www.nelsonagency.com
@joannamackenzie

ABOUT JOANNA: Joanna joined the Nelson Literary Agency at the start of 2017 following a tenure at a Chicago-based literary agency where she successfully placed numerous manuscripts that have gone on to become critically acclaimed, award-winning, and bestselling novels. She represents a wide-range of writers, from YA (Kristen Simmons) and romance (Shana Galen) to mysteries and thrillers (John Galligan). Joanna loves working with authors who embrace the full publishing process (read: love revisions) and is committed to the stories her clients want to tell both with the words they put on paper, as well as with the careers the build. At the Nelson Literary Agency, Joanna is looking to expand her list in both adult and YA.

SHE IS SEEKING: Joanna is looking for literary-leaning projects with commercial potential and epic reads that beat with a universal heart (think *The Secret History* or *The Namesake* or *Geek Love*). In particular, she's drawn to smart and timely women's fiction as well as absorbing, character-driven mysteries and thrillers –Tana French is a particular favorite. She has a weird obsession with, what she calls, "child in jeopardy lit" and can't get enough kick-ass mom heroines—she'd love to find the next Heather Gudenkauff. On the YA side, she's interested in coming of age stories that possess a confident voice and characters she can't stop thinking about (Morgan Matson is on her forever shelf).

HOW TO SUBMIT: Send a query via email to queryjoanna@nelsonagency.com. In the *subject line*, write QUERY and the title of your project. This will help ensure that your query isn't accidentally deleted or caught in our spam filter. In the *body of your email*, include a *one-page query letter* and the *first ten pages* of your manuscript. *No attachments!* Because of virus concerns, emails with attachments are deleted unread.

Not Now, Not Ever, by Lily Anderson (St. Martin's 2018).

TIPS "Always remember the benefits of building an author platform, and the accessibility of accomplishing this task in today's industry. Most importantly, research the agents queried. Avoid contacting every literary agent about a book idea. Due to the large volume of queries received, the process of reading queries for unrepresented categories (by the agency) becomes quite the arduous task. Investigate online directories, printed guides (like *Writer's Market*), individual agent websites, and more, before beginning the query process. It's good to remember that each agent has a vision of what he or shee wants to represent and will communicate this information accordingly. We're simply waiting for those specific book ideas to come in our direction."

REES LITERARY AGENCY

14 Beacon St., Suite 710, Boston MA 02108. (617)227-9014. **E-mail:** lorin@reesagency.com. **Website:** reesagency.com. Estab. 1983. Member of AAR. Represents more than 100 clients.

MEMBER AGENTS Ann Collette, agent10702@aol.com (fiction: literary, upscale commercial women's, crime [including mystery, thriller, psychological suspense], upscale western, historical, military and war, horror; nonfiction: narrative, military and war, books on race and class, works set in Southeast Asia, biography, pop culture, books on film and opera, humor, memoir); **Lorin Rees**, lorin@reesagency.com (literary fiction, memoirs, business books, self-help, science, history, psychology, narrative nonfiction); **Rebecca Podos**, rebecca@reesagency.com (young adult and middle-grade fiction, particularly books about complex female relationships, beautifully written contemporary, genre novels with a strong focus on character, romance with more at stake than "will they/won't they," LGBTQ books across all genres).

REPRESENTS novels. **Considers these nonfiction areas:** biography, business, film, history, humor, memoirs, military, popular culture, psychology, science, war. **Considers these fiction areas:** commercial, crime, historical, horror, literary, middle-grade, mystery, suspense, thriller, westerns, women's, young adult.

HOW TO CONTACT Consult website for each agent's submission guidelines and e-mail address, as they differ. Accepts simultaneous submissions. Obtains most new clients through recommendations from others, conferences, submissions.

TERMS Agent receives 15% commission on domestic sales; 20% commission on foreign sales.

REGAL HOFFMANN & ASSOCIATES LLC

242 W. 38th St., Second Floor, New York NY 10018. (212)684-7900. **Fax:** (212)684-7906. **E-mail:** submissions@rhaliterary.com. **Website:** www.rhaliterary.com. Estab. 2002. Member of AAR. Represents 70 clients.

MEMBER AGENTS Claire Anderson-Wheeler (nonfiction: memoirs, biography, narrative histories, popular science, popular psychology; adult fiction: primarily character-driven literary fiction, but open to genre fiction, high-concept fiction; all genres of young adult and middle-grade fiction); **Markus Hoffmann** (international and literary fiction, crime, [pop] cultural studies, current affairs, economics, history, music, popular science, travel literature); **Joseph Regal** (literary fiction, international thriller, history, science, photography, music, culture, whimsy); **Stephanie Steiker** (serious and narrative nonfiction, literary fiction, graphic novels, history, philosophy, current affairs, cultural studies, biography, music, international writing); **Grace Ross** (literary fiction, historical fiction, international narratives, narrative nonfiction, popular science, biography, cultural theory, memoir).

REPRESENTS Considers these nonfiction areas: biography, creative nonfiction, current affairs, economics, history, memoirs, music, psychology, science, travel. **Considers these fiction areas:** literary, mainstream, middle-grade, thriller, young adult.

☛ "We represent works in a wide range of categories, with an emphasis on literary fiction, outstanding thriller and crime fiction, and serious narrative nonfiction." Actively seeking literary fiction and narrative nonfiction. Does not want romance, science fiction, poetry, or screenplays.

HOW TO CONTACT Query with SASE or via e-mail to submissions@rhaliterary.com. No phone calls. Submissions should consist of a 1-page query letter detailing the book in question, as well as the qualifications of the author. For fiction, submissions may also include the first 10 pages of the novel or 1 short story from a collection. Accepts simultaneous submissions. Responds in 4-8 weeks if interested.

TERMS Agent receives 15% commission on domestic sales; 20% commission on foreign sales. "We charge no reading fees."

RECENT SALES *Wily Snare*, by Adam Jay Epstein; *Perfectly Undone*, by Jamie Raintree; *A Sister in My House*, by Linda Olsson; *This Is How It Really Sounds*, by Stuart Archer Cohen; *Autofocus*, by Lauren Gibaldi; *We've Already Gone This Far*, by Patrick Dacey; *A Fierce and Subtle Poison*, by Samantha Mabry; *The Life of the World to Come*, by Dan Cluchey; *Willful Disregard*, by Lena Andersson; *The Sweetheart*, by Angelina Mirabella.

TIPS "We are deeply committed to every aspect of our clients' careers, and are engaged in everything from the editorial work of developing a great book proposal or line-editing a fiction manuscript to negotiating state-of-the-art book deals and working to promote and publicize the book when it's published."

🚫 THE AMY RENNERT AGENCY

1550 Tiburon Blvd., #302, Tiburon CA 94920. **E-mail:** queries@amyrennert.com. **Website:** www.publishersmarketplace.com/members/amyrennert/. **Contact:** Amy Rennert.

REPRESENTS nonfiction, novels. **Considers these nonfiction areas:** biography, business, creative nonfiction, health, history, memoirs, money, sports. **Considers these fiction areas:** literary, mainstream, mystery.

> ⚷ "The Amy Rennert Agency specializes in books that matter. We provide career management for established and first-time authors, and our breadth of experience in many genres enables us to meet the needs of a diverse clientele."

HOW TO CONTACT Amy Rennert is not currently accepting unsolicited submissions. Accepts simultaneous submissions.

TIPS "Due to the high volume of submissions, it is not possible to respond to each and every one. Please understand that we are only able to respond to queries that we feel may be a good fit with our agency."

☯ THE RIGHTS FACTORY

P.O. Box 499, Station C, Toronto ON M6J 3P6 Canada. (416)966-5367. **Website:** www.therightsfactory.com. "The Rights Factory is an international literary agency." Estab. 2004. Represents about 150 clients.

MEMBER AGENTS Sam Hiyate (President; fiction, nonfiction, graphic novel); **Kelvin Kong** (Rights Manager; clients by referral only); **Ali McDonald** (Kidlit Agent; young adult, children's literature of all kinds); **Olga Filina** (Associate Agent; commercial and historical fiction, great genre fiction in the area of romance and mystery, nonfiction in the fields of business, wellness, lifestyle, memoir, and young adult and middle-grade novels with memorable characters); **Cassandra Rogers** (Associate Agent; adult literary and commercial women's fiction, historical fiction, nonfiction on politics, history, science, and finance, humorous, heartbreaking, and inspiring memoir); **Lydia Moed** (Associate Agent; science fiction and fantasy, historical fiction, diverse voices; narrative nonfiction on a wide variety of topics, including history, popular science, biography, travel); **Natalie Kimber** (Associate Agent; literary and commercial fiction and creative nonfiction in categories such as memoir, cooking, popculture, spirituality, sustainability); **Harry Endrulat** (Associate Agent; children's literature, especially author/illustrators and Canadian voices); **Haskell Nussbaum** (Associate Agent; literature of all kinds).

REPRESENTS nonfiction, fiction, novels, short story collections, novellas, juvenile books. **Considers these nonfiction areas:** biography, business, cooking, environment, foods, gardening, health, history, inspirational, juvenile nonfiction, memoirs, money, music, popular culture, politics, science, travel, women's issues, young adult. **Considers these fiction areas:** commercial, crime, family saga, fantasy, gay, hi-lo, historical, horror, juvenile, lesbian, literary, mainstream, middle-grade, multicultural, mystery, New Adult, paranormal, picture books, romance, science fiction, short story collections, suspense, thriller, urban fantasy, women's, young adult.

> ⚷ Plays, screenplays, textbooks.

HOW TO CONTACT There is a submission form on this agency's website. Accepts simultaneous submissions. Responds in 3-6 weeks.

ANGELA RINALDI LITERARY AGENCY

P.O. Box 7875, Beverly Hills CA 90212-7875. (310)842-7665. **Fax:** (310)837-8143. **E-mail:** info@rinaldiliterary.com. **Website:** www.rinaldiliterary.com. **Contact:** Angela Rinaldi. Member of AAR.

Prior to opening her agency, Ms. Rinaldi was an editor at NAL/Signet, Pocket Books and Bantam, and the manager of book development for *The Los Angeles Times*.

REPRESENTS nonfiction, novels, TV, and motion picture rights (for clients only). **Considers these nonfiction areas:** biography, business, cooking, current affairs, health, memoirs, parenting, psychology, self-help, women's issues, women's studies, narrative nonfiction, food narratives, wine, lifestyle, relationships, wellness, personal finance. **Considers these fiction areas:** commercial, historical, literary, mainstream, mystery, suspense, thriller, women's, contemporary, gothic, women's book club fiction.

Actively seeking commercial and literary fiction, as well as nonfiction. For fiction, we do not want to receive humor, CIA espionage, drug thriller, techno thriller, category romances, science fiction, fantasy, horror/occult/paranormal, poetry, film scripts, magazine articles or religion. For nonfiction, please do not send us magazine articles, celebrity bios, or tell-alls.

HOW TO CONTACT E-queries only. Include the word "Query" in the subject line. For fiction, please send a brief synopsis and paste the first 10 pages into an e-mail. Nonfiction queries should include a detailed cover letter, your credentials and platform information, as well as any publishing history. Tell us if you have a completed proposal. Accepts simultaneous submissions. Responds in 2-4 weeks.

TERMS Agent receives 15% commission on domestic sales; 25% commission on foreign sales. Offers written contract.

ANN RITTENBERG LITERARY AGENCY, INC.

15 Maiden Lane, Suite 206, New York NY 10038. (212)684-6936. **E-mail:** info@rittlit.com. **Website:** www.rittlit.com. **Contact:** Ann Rittenberg, president. Member of AAR.

REPRESENTS nonfiction, novels, juvenile books.

Does not want to receive screenplays, poetry, or self-help.

HOW TO CONTACT Query via e-mail or postal mail (with SASE). Submit query letter with 3 sample chapters pasted in the body of the e-mail. "If you query by e-mail, we will only respond if interested." Accepts simultaneous submissions. Obtains most

new clients through referrals from established writers and editors.

TERMS Agent receives 15% commission on domestic sales; 20% commission on foreign sales. Offers written contract. This agency charges clients for photocopying only.

RECENT SALES *Since We Fell* by Dennis Lehane, *A Wretched and Precarious Situation* by David Welky, *Knife Creek* by Paul Doiron.

RLR ASSOCIATES, LTD.

420 Lexington Ave., Suite 2532, New York NY 10170. (212)541-8641. **E-mail:** website.info@rlrassociates.net. **Website:** www.rlrassociates.net. **Contact:** Scott Gould. Member of AAR. Represents 50 clients.

REPRESENTS nonfiction, novels. **Considers these nonfiction areas:** biography, creative nonfiction, foods, history, humor, popular culture, sports. **Considers these fiction areas:** commercial, literary, mainstream, middle-grade, picture books, romance, women's, young adult, genre.

"We provide a lot of editorial assistance to our clients and have connections." Does not want to receive screenplays.

HOW TO CONTACT Query by snail mail. For fiction, send a query and 1-3 chapters (pasted). For nonfiction, send query or proposal. Accepts simultaneous submissions. "If you do not hear from us within 3 months, please assume that your work is out of active consideration." Obtains most new clients through recommendations from others.

TERMS Agent receives 15% commission on domestic sales; 20% commission on foreign sales. Offers written contract.

RECENT SALES Clients include Shelby Foote, The Grief Recovery Institute, Don Wade, David Plowden, Nina Planck, Karyn Bosnak, Gerald Carbone, Jason Lethcoe, Andy Crouch.

TIPS "Please check out our website for more details on our agency."

B.J. ROBBINS LITERARY AGENCY

5130 Bellaire Ave., North Hollywood CA 91607-2908. **E-mail:** robbinsliterary@gmail.com. **Website:** www.publishersmarketplace.com/members/bjrobbins. **Contact:** B.J. Robbins. Estab. 1992. Member of AAR.

Prior to becoming an agent, Ms. Robbins spent 15 years in publishing, starting in publicity at Simon & Schuster and later as Marketing Director and Senior Editor at Harcourt.

REPRESENTS nonfiction, fiction. **Considers these nonfiction areas:** autobiography, biography, cultural interests, current affairs, ethnic, film, health, history, investigative, medicine, memoirs, multicultural, music, popular culture, psychology, science, sociology, sports, theater, travel, true crime, women's issues, women's studies. **Considers these fiction areas:** contemporary issues, crime, detective, ethnic, historical, literary, mainstream, multicultural, mystery, sports, suspense, thriller, women's.

> "We do not represent screenplays, plays, poetry, science fiction, horror, westerns, romance, techno-thriller, religious tracts, dating books, or anything with the word 'unicorn' in the title."

HOW TO CONTACT E-query with no attachments. For fiction, okay to include first 10 pages in body of e-mail. Accepts simultaneous submissions. Only responds to projects if interested. Obtains most new clients through conferences, referrals.
TERMS Agent receives 15% commission on domestic sales; 20% commission on foreign sales. Offers written contract. No fees.
RECENT SALES *Shoot for the Moon: The Perilous Voyage of Apollo 11*, by James Donovan (Little, Brown); *I Was Told There'd Be Sexbots: Travels Through the Future*, by J. Maarten Troost (Holt); *Mongrels*, by Stephen Graham Jones (William Morrow); *Blood Brothers: The Story of the Strange Friendship Between Sitting Bull and Buffalo Bill*, by Deanne Stillman (Simon & Schuster); *Reliance, Illinois*, by Mary Volmer (Soho Press).

RODEEN LITERARY MANAGEMENT

3501 N. Southport #497, Chicago IL 60657. **E-mail:** info@rodeenliterary.com. **E-mail:** submissions@rodeenliterary.com. **Website:** www.rodeenliterary.com. **Contact:** Paul Rodeen. Estab. 2009. Member of AAR. Signatory of WGA.

> Paul Rodeen established Rodeen Literary Management in 2009 after 7 years of experience with the literary agency Sterling Lord Literistic, Inc.

REPRESENTS nonfiction, novels, juvenile books, illustrations, graphic novels. **Considers these fiction areas:** juvenile, middle-grade, picture books, young adult, graphic novels, comics.

> Actively seeking "writers and illustrators of all genres of children's literature including picture books, early readers, middle-grade fiction and nonfiction, graphic novels and comic books, as well as young adult fiction and nonfiction." This is primarily an agency devoted to children's books.

HOW TO CONTACT Unsolicited submissions are accepted by e-mail only. Cover letters with synopsis and contact information should be included in the body of your e-mail. An initial submission of 50 pages from a novel or a longer work of nonfiction will suffice and should be pasted into the body of your e-mail. Accepts simultaneous submissions.

LINDA ROGHAAR LITERARY AGENCY, LLC

P.O. Box 3561, Amherst MA 01004. **E-mail:** contact@lindaroghaar.com. **Website:** www.lindaroghaar.com. **Contact:** Linda L. Roghaar. Member of AAR.

> Prior to opening her agency, Ms. Roghaar worked in retail bookselling for 5 years and as a publisher's sales rep for 15 years.

REPRESENTS nonfiction.

> The Linda Roghaar Literary Agency represents authors with substantial messages and specializes in nonfiction. We sell to major, independent, and university presses. We are generalists, but we do not handle romance, horror, or science fiction.

HOW TO CONTACT "We prefer e-queries. Please mention 'query' in the subject line, and do not include attachments." For fiction, paste the first 5 pages of your ms below the query. For queries by mail, please include a SASE. Accepts simultaneous submissions. Responds within 12 weeks if interested.
TERMS Agent receives 15% commission on domestic sales; negotiable commission on foreign sales. Offers written contract.

THE ROSENBERG GROUP

23 Lincoln Ave., Marblehead MA 01945. (781)990-1341. **Fax:** (781)990-1344. **Website:** www.rosenberggroup.com. **Contact:** Barbara Collins Rosenberg. Estab. 1998. Member of AAR, RWA. Represents 25 clients.

> Prior to becoming an agent, Ms. Rosenberg was a senior editor for Harcourt.

SARAH BEDINGFIELD

LEVINE, GREENBERG, ROSTAN LITERARY AGENCY

www.lgrliterary.com
@SBedingfield_NY

ABOUT SARAH: Prior to joining LGR in 2016, Sarah began her publishing career in trade fiction editorial at Crown and Hogarth. There, she worked with a range of bestselling and award-winning novels, including *The Barrowfields* by Phillip Lewis, Han Kang's *Human Acts* and Man Booker International Prize winning debut *The Vegetarian*, as well as the *New York Times* bestselling novel *The Little Paris Bookshop* by Nina George. Sarah hails from North Carolina, where she graduated from UNC Chapel Hill with a double major in Psychology and English. Her favorite authors include Sarah Waters, Shirley Jackson, Matthew Thomas, Maria Semple, Emily St. John Mandel, Erin Morgenstern, and Victor Hugo.

SHE IS SEEKING: Sarah is seeking most types of literary and upmarket commercial fiction, especially novels that show powerful imagination, compulsive plotting, and unique voices. Epic family dramas, cross-genre narratives with notes of magical realism, darkly Gothic stories that may lead to nightmares, and twisty psychological suspense are among her favorite things to read. A southerner at heart, she can't help but love books set in the south, but she's a die-hard for any world immersive enough to make her miss her stop on the train, cry in public, or desperately seek help.

HOW TO SUBMIT: Please send queries to sbedingfield@lgrliterary.com. Query should include a brief synopsis and bio, as well as the first fifty pages of your novel.

REPRESENTS nonfiction, novels, textbooks, college textbooks only. **Considers these nonfiction areas:** biography, current affairs, foods, music, popular culture, psychology, science, self-help, sports, women's issues, women's studies, women's health, wine/beverages. **Considers these fiction areas:** romance, women's, chick lit.

Ms. Rosenberg is well-versed in the romance market (both category and single title). She is a frequent speaker at romance conferences. The Rosenberg Group is accepting new clients working in romance fiction (please see my Areas of Interest for specific romance subgenres), women's fiction, and chick lit.

Does not want to receive inspirational, time travel, futuristic, or paranormal.

HOW TO CONTACT Query via snail mail. Your query letter should not exceed 1 page in length. It should include the title of your work, the genre and/or subgenre, the manuscript's word count, and a brief description of the work. If you are writing category romance, please be certain to let her know the line for which your work is intended. Accepts simultaneous submissions. Obtains most new clients through recommendations from others, solicitations, conferences.

TERMS Agent receives 15% commission on domestic and foreign sales. Offers written contract; 1-month notice must be given to terminate contract. Charges maximum of $350/year for postage and photocopying.

RECENT SALES Sold 27 titles in the last year.

WRITERS CONFERENCES RWA National Conference, BookExpo America.

RITA ROSENKRANZ LITERARY AGENCY

440 West End Ave., #15D, New York NY 10024. (212)873-6333. **Website:** www.ritarosenkranzliteraryagency.com. **Contact:** Rita Rosenkranz. Member of AAR. Represents 35 clients.

○ Prior to opening her agency, Ms. Rosenkranz worked as an editor at major New York publishing houses.

REPRESENTS nonfiction. **Considers these nonfiction areas:** Americana, animals, anthropology, architecture, art, autobiography, biography, business, child guidance, computers, cooking, crafts, creative nonfiction, cultural interests, current affairs, dance, decorating, diet/nutrition, design, economics, education, environment, ethnic, film, government, health, history, hobbies, how-to, humor, inspirational, interior design, investigative, language, law, literature, medicine, military, money, music, New Age, parenting, photography, popular culture, politics, psychology, regional, religious, satire, science, self-help, sports, technology, theater, true crime, war, women's issues, women's studies.

➥ "This agency focuses on adult nonfiction, stresses strong editorial development and refinement before submitting to publishers, and brainstorms ideas with authors." Actively seeks authors who are well paired with

their subject, either for professional or personal reasons.

HOW TO CONTACT Send query letter only (no proposal) via regular mail or e-mail. Submit proposal package with SASE only on request. No fax queries. Accepts simultaneous submissions. Responds in 2 weeks to queries. Obtains most new clients through directory listings, solicitations, conferences, word of mouth.

TERMS Agent receives 15% commission on domestic sales; 20% commission on foreign sales. Offers written contract, binding for 3 years; 3-month written notice must be given to terminate contract. Charges clients for photocopying. Makes referrals to editing services.

RECENT SALES *Mindshift: How Ordinary and Extraordinary People Have Transformed Their Lives Through Learning—And You Can Too*, by Barbara A. Oakley (Tarcher); *On the Verge: Experience the Stillness of Presence, the Pulse of Potential, and the Power of Being Fully Alive*, by Cara Bradley (New World Library); *Lost Science*, by Kitty Ferguson (Sterling); *Power to the Poet*, by Diane Luby Lane (Beyond Words/Atria).

TIPS "Identify the current competition for your project to make sure the project is valid. A strong cover letter is very important."

ANDY ROSS LITERARY AGENCY

767 Santa Ray Ave., Oakland CA 94610. (510)238-8965. **E-mail:** andyrossagency@hotmail.com. **Website:** www.andyrossagency.com. **Contact:** Andy Ross. Estab. 2008. Member of AAR.

REPRESENTS nonfiction, fiction, novels, juvenile books, scholarly books. **Considers these nonfiction areas:** anthropology, autobiography, biography, child guidance, cooking, creative nonfiction, cultural interests, current affairs, economics, education, environment, ethnic, gay/lesbian, government, history, investigative, juvenile nonfiction, language, law, literature, memoirs, military, parenting, philosophy, popular culture, politics, psychology, science, sociology, technology, war, women's issues, women's studies, young adult. **Considers these fiction areas:** commercial, contemporary issues, historical, juvenile, literary, middle-grade, picture books, young adult.

➥ "This agency specializes in general nonfiction, politics and current events, history, biography, journalism, and contemporary culture as well as literary, commercial, and young adult fiction." Does not want to receive poetry.

HOW TO CONTACT Queries should be less than half-page. Please put the word "query" in the title header of the e-mail. In the first sentence, state the category of the project. Give a short description of the book and your qualifications for writing. Accepts simultaneous submissions. Responds in 1 week to queries.

TERMS Agent receives 15% commission on domestic sales; 20% commission on foreign sales or other deals made through a subagent. Offers written contract.

⊙ ROSS YOON AGENCY

1666 Connecticut Ave. NW, Suite 500, Washington DC 20009. (202)328-3282. **E-mail:** submissions@rossyoon.com. **Website:** http://rossyoon.com. **Contact:** Jennifer Manguera. Member of AAR.

MEMBER AGENTS Gail Ross, gail@rossyoon.com (represents important commercial nonfiction in a variety of areas; new projects must meet two criteria: it must make her daughters proud and offset their college educations); **Howard Yoon**, howard@rossyoon.com (specializes in narrative nonfiction, memoir, current events, history, science, cookbooks, and popular culture); **Anna Sproul-Latimer**, anna@rossyoon.com (nonfiction of all kinds, particularly working with clients who are driven by curiosity: exploring new worlds, uncovering hidden communities, and creating new connections with enthusiasm so infectious that national audiences have already begun to pay attention).

REPRESENTS nonfiction.

⊶ "We are a Washington, D.C.-based literary agency specializing in serious nonfiction on a variety of topics: everything from memoir and history and biography to popular science, business, and psychology. Our clients include CEOs, Pulitzer Prize-winning journalists, academics, politicos, and radio and television personalities." Does not represent fiction, screenplays, poetry, young adult, or children's titles.

HOW TO CONTACT E-query submissions@rossyoon.com with a query letter briefly explaining your idea, media platform, and qualifications for writing on this topic; or send a complete book proposal featuring an overview of your idea, author bio, media and marketing strategy, chapter outline, and 1-3 sample chapters. Please send these as attachments in .doc or .docx format. Accepts simultaneous submissions. Attempts to respond in 4-6 weeks to queries, but cannot guarantee a reply. Obtains most new clients through referrals from current clients.

TERMS Agent receives 15% commission on domestic sales; 20% commission on foreign sales. Reserves the right to bill clients for office expenses.

JANE ROTROSEN AGENCY LLC

85 Broad St., 28th Floor, New York NY 10004. (212)593-4330. **Fax:** (212)935-6985. **Website:** www.janerotrosen.com. Estab. 1974. Member of AAR, the Authors Guild. Represents more than 100 clients.

MEMBER AGENTS Jane Rotrosen Berkey (not taking on clients); **Andrea Cirillo**, acirillo@janerotrosen.com (general fiction, suspense, women's fiction); **Annelise Robey**, arobey@janerotrosen.com (women's fiction, suspense, mystery, literary fiction, select nonfiction); **Meg Ruley**, mruley@janerotrosen.com (commercial fiction, including suspense, mystery, romance, general fiction); **Christina Hogrebe**, chogrebe@janerotrosen.com (young adult, New Adult, book club fiction, romantic comedies, mystery, suspense); **Amy Tannenbaum**, atannenbaum@janerotrosen.com (contemporary romance, psychological suspense, thriller, New Adult, as well as women's fiction that falls into that sweet spot between literary and commercial; memoir, narrative and prescriptive nonfiction: health, business, pop culture, humor, popular psychology); **Rebecca Scherer** rscherer@janerotrosen.com (women's fiction, mystery, suspense, thriller, romance, upmarket/literary-leaning fiction); **Jessica Errera** (assistant to Christina and Rebecca).

REPRESENTS nonfiction, novels. **Considers these nonfiction areas:** business, health, humor, memoirs, popular culture, psychology, narrative nonfiction. **Considers these fiction areas:** commercial, literary, mainstream, mystery, New Adult, romance, suspense, thriller, women's, young adult.

⊶ Jane Rotrosen Agency is best known for representing writers of commercial fiction: thriller, mystery, suspense, women's fiction, romance, historical novels, mainstream fiction, young adult, etc. We also work with authors of memoirs and narrative and prescriptive nonfiction.

HOW TO CONTACT Check website for guidelines. Accepts simultaneous submissions. Obtains most new clients through recommendations from others.

TERMS Agent receives 15% commission on domestic sales; 20% commission on foreign sales. Offers written contract, binding for 3 years; 2-month notice must be given to terminate contract. Charges clients for photocopying, express mail, overseas postage, book purchase.

THE RUDY AGENCY

825 Wildlife Lane, Estes Park CO 80517. (970)577-8500. E-mail: mak@rudyagency.com; fred@rudyagency.com; claggett@rudyagency.com. **Website:** www.rudyagency.com. **Contact:** Maryann Karinch. Estab. 2004. Adheres to AAR canon of ethics. Represents 24 clients.

○ Ms. Karinch is also an author of nonfiction books—covering the subjects of health/medicine and human behavior. Prior to that, she was in public relations and marketing: areas of expertise she also applies in her practice as an agent.

MEMBER AGENTS Maryann Karinch, Fred Tribuzzo (fiction: thriller, historical), and **Hilary Claggett** (selected nonfiction).

REPRESENTS nonfiction, fiction, novels, short story collections, scholarly books, textbooks, theatrical stage play, stage plays. **Considers these nonfiction areas:** Americana, anthropology, archeology, architecture, autobiography, biography, business, child guidance, computers, cooking, creative nonfiction, cultural interests, current affairs, diet/nutrition, design, economics, education, environment, gay/lesbian, government, health, history, how-to, inspirational, investigative, literature, medicine, memoirs, military, money, music, parenting, popular culture, politics, psychology, science, self-help, sex, sociology, sports, technology, theater, true crime, war, women's issues, women's studies. **Considers these fiction areas:** action, adventure, commercial, crime, erotica, historical, literary, New Adult, sports, thriller.

⌁ "We support authors from the proposal stage through promotion of the published work.

We work in partnership with publishers to promote the published work and coach authors in their role in the marketing and public relations campaigns for the book." Actively seeking projects with social value, projects that open minds to new ideas and interesting lives, and projects that entertain through good storytelling. Does not want to receive poetry, screenplays, novellas, religion books, children's lit, and joke books.

HOW TO CONTACT "Query us. If we like the query, we will invite a complete proposal (or complete ms if writing fiction). No phone queries, please. We won't hang up on you, but it makes it easier if you send us a note first." Accepts simultaneous submissions. Responds in 8 weeks to mss. Obtains most new clients through recommendations from others, solicitations.

TERMS Agent receives 15% commission on domestic sales. Offers written contract, binding for 1 year.

RECENT SALES *Shakespeare's Ear*, by Tim Rayborn (Skyhorse); *Science for Fiction*, by David Siegel Bernstein (Prometheus); *Sex and Cancer*, by Saketh R. Guntupalli (Rowman & Littlefield).

TIPS "Present yourself professionally. I tell people all the time: 'Subscribe to *Writer's Digest*, because you will get good advice about how to approach an agent.'"

VICTORIA SANDERS & ASSOCIATES

440 Buck Rd., Stone Ridge NY 12484. (212)633-8811. E-mail: queriesvsa@gmail.com. **Website:** www.victoriasanders.com. **Contact:** Victoria Sanders. Estab. 1992. Member of AAR, signatory of WGA. Represents 135 clients.

MEMBER AGENTS Victoria Sanders, Chris Kepner, Bernadette Baker-Baughman.

REPRESENTS nonfiction, fiction, novels, juvenile books. **Considers these nonfiction areas:** autobiography, biography, cultural interests, current affairs, ethnic, film, gay/lesbian, government, history, humor, law, literature, music, popular culture, politics, psychology, satire, theater, translation, women's issues, women's studies. **Considers these fiction areas:** action, adventure, cartoon, comic books, contemporary issues, crime, detective, ethnic, family saga, feminist, gay, historical, humor, inspirational, juvenile, lesbian, literary, mainstream, middle-grade, multicultural, multimedia, mystery, New Adult, picture books, thriller, women's, young adult.

HOW TO CONTACT Authors who wish to contact us regarding potential representation should send a query letter with the first 3 chapters (or about 25 pages) pasted into the body of the message to queriesvsa@gmail.com. "We will only accept queries via e-mail. Query letters should describe the project and the author in the body of a single, 1-page e-mail that does not contain any attached files. Accepts simultaneous submissions. Responds in 1-4 weeks, although occasionally it will take longer. "We will not respond to e-mails with attachments or attached files."

TERMS Agent receives 15% commission on domestic sales; 20% commission on foreign and film sales. Offers written contract.

RECENT SALES Sold 20+ titles in the last year.

TIPS "Limit query to letter (no calls) and give it your best shot. A good query is going to get a good response."

SCHIAVONE LITERARY AGENCY, INC.

236 Trails End, West Palm Beach FL 33413-2135. (561)966-9294. **Fax:** (561)966-9294. **E-mail:** profschia@aol.com. **Website:** www.publishersmarketplace.com/members/profschia, www.schiavoneliteraryagencyinc.blogspot.com. **Contact:** Dr. James Schiavone, CEO, corporate offices in Florida; Jennifer DuVall, president, New York office. Estab. 1996. Member of National Education Association. Represents 40+ clients.

○ Prior to opening his agency, Dr. Schiavone was a full professor of developmental skills at the City University of New York and author of 5 trade books and 3 textbooks. Jennifer DuVall has many years of combined experience in office management and agenting.

MEMBER AGENTS James Schiavone, profschia@aol.com; **Jennifer DuVall**, jendu77@aol.com.

REPRESENTS nonfiction, fiction, novels, scholarly books. We specialize in celebrity memoirs. **Considers these nonfiction areas:** biography, business, cooking, health, history, politics, science, sports, true crime. **Considers these fiction areas:** literary, mainstream, mystery, romance, suspense, thriller, young adult.

⌀ This agency specializes in celebrity biography and autobiography and memoirs. Actively seeking celebrity memoirs. Does not want to receive poetry.

HOW TO CONTACT "One-page e-mail queries only. Absolutely no attachments. Postal queries are not accepted. No phone calls. We do not consider poetry, short stories, anthologies or children's books. Celebrity memoirs only. No scripts or screen plays. We handle dramatic, film and TV rights, options, and screenplays for books we have agented. We are not interested in work previously published in any format (e.g., self-published, online, e-books, Print On Demand). E-mail queries may be addressed to any of the agency's agents." Accepts simultaneous submissions. Responds in 2 weeks to queries; 6 weeks to mss. Obtains most new clients through referrals.

TERMS Agent receives 15% commission on domestic sales; 20% commission on foreign sales. Offers written contract. No fees.

RECENT SALES Check website.

WRITERS CONFERENCES Key West Literary Seminar, South Florida Writers Conference, Tallahassee Writers Conference, Million Dollar Writers Conference, Alaska Writers Conference, Utah writers conference.

TIPS "We prefer to work with established authors published by major houses in New York. We will consider marketable proposals from new/previously unpublished writers."

WENDY SCHMALZ AGENCY

402 Union St., #831, Hudson NY 12534. (518)672-7697. **E-mail:** wendy@schmalzagency.com. **Website:** www.schmalzagency.com. **Contact:** Wendy Schmalz. Estab. 2002. Member of AAR.

REPRESENTS nonfiction, fiction, novels, juvenile books. **Considers these nonfiction areas:** biography, cultural interests, history, popular culture, young adult. Many nonfiction subjects are of interest to this agency. **Considers these fiction areas:** literary, mainstream, middle-grade, young adult.

⌀ Not looking for picture books, science fiction, or fantasy.

HOW TO CONTACT Accepts only e-mail queries. Paste synopsis into the e-mail. Do not attach the ms, sample chapters, or synopsis. Replies to queries only if they want to read the ms. If you do not hear from this agency within 2 weeks, consider that a no. Accepts simultaneous submissions. Obtains clients through recommendations from others.

NEW AGENT SPOTLIGHT

GABRIELLE PIRAINO
DEFIORE AND COMPANY

www.defliterary.com
@ggpiraino

ABOUT GABRIELLE: Gabrielle is a graduate of St. Bonaventure University with a dual-B.A. in Honors Classical Languages and English. After graduation, Gabbie earned her Masters of Science in Publishing at Pace University in Manhattan. She has previously worked for both major commercial publishing houses and literary agencies alike, including Farrar, Strauss & Giroux and AGI Vigliano. Gabbie joined DeFiore and Company in the summer of 2016.

SHE IS SEEKING: Gabbie is actively seeking imaginative sci-fi/fantasy, horror, thrillers, and up-market chick lit for adults and young adults alike. For children's and middle-grade, she is looking for stories that introduce curious young readers to new concepts with compelling characters and an engaging voice (fiction and nonfiction). Further, she'd happily review projects form author-illustrators in the comic/graphic novel arena. An avid personal baker/cook, Gabbie is pleased to accept queries for cookbook and crafty lifestyle projects, too.

Overall, Gabbie is searching for unique narrative voices (OwnVoices, when possible!), strong world-building, and spunky, stubborn characters that never do exactly what you'd expect.

HOW TO SUBMIT: Please query her at gabrielle@defliterary.com with "QUERY" in the subject line, as well as: a brief summary of your book (no more than two paragraphs); a brief, relevant bio; for fiction, please include the first 50 pages of your manuscript in the body of your email; for illustrators, please include your website or online portfolio; no attachments.

TERMS Agent receives 15% commission on domestic sales; 20% on foreign sales; 25% for Asian sales.

SUSAN SCHULMAN LITERARY AGENCY LLC

454 W. 44th St., New York NY 10036. (212)713-1633. **E-mail:** susan@schulmanagency.com. **E-mail:** queries@schulmanagency.com. **Website:** www.publishersmarketplace.com/members/schulman/. **Contact:** Susan Schulman. Estab. 1980. Member of AAR. Signatory of WGA. Other memberships include Dramatists Guild, Writers Guild of America, East, New York Women in Film, Women's Media Group, Agents' Roundtable, League of New York Theater Women.

REPRESENTS nonfiction, fiction, novels, juvenile books, feature film, TV scripts, theatrical stage plays. **Considers these nonfiction areas:** anthropology, archeology, architecture, art, biography, business, child guidance, cooking, creative nonfiction, current affairs, economics, ethnic, government, health, history, juvenile nonfiction, law, money, popular culture, politics, psychology, religious, science, spirituality, women's issues, women's studies, young adult. **Considers these fiction areas:** commercial, contemporary issues, juvenile, literary, mainstream, New Adult, religious, women's, young adult. **Considers these script areas:** theatrical stage play.

⇘ "We specialize in books for, by, and about women and women's issues including nonfiction self-help books, fiction, and theater projects. We also handle the film, television, and allied rights for several agencies, as well as foreign rights for several publishing houses." Actively seeking new nonfiction. Considers plays. Does not want to receive poetry, television scripts, or concepts for television.

HOW TO CONTACT "For fiction: query letter with outline and 3 sample chapters, resume and SASE. For nonfiction: query letter with complete description of subject, at least 1 chapter, resume, and SASE. Queries may be sent via regular mail or e-mail. Please do not submit queries via UPS or Federal Express. Please do not send attachments with e-mail queries. Please incorporate the chapters into the body of the e-mail." Accepts simultaneous submissions. Responds in less than 1 week generally to a full query; 6 weeks to a full ms. Obtains most new clients through recommendations from others, solicitations, conferences.

TERMS Agent receives 15% commission on domestic sales; 20% commission on foreign sales. Offers written contract; 30-day notice must be given to terminate contract.

LYNN SELIGMAN, LITERARY AGENT

400 Highland Ave., Upper Montclair NJ 07043. (973)783-3631. **E-mail:** seliglit@aol.com. **Contact:** Lynn Seligman. Estab. 1986. Member of Women's Media Group. Represents 35 clients.

⏻ Prior to opening her agency, Ms. Seligman worked in the subsidiary rights department of Doubleday and Simon & Schuster, and served as an agent with Julian Bach Literary Agency (which became IMiddle-grade Literary Agency). Foreign rights are represented by Books Crossing Borders, Inc.

REPRESENTS nonfiction, fiction, novels. **Considers these nonfiction areas:** anthropology, art, biography, business, child guidance, cooking, creative nonfiction, cultural interests, current affairs, diet/nutrition, education, ethnic, film, foods, government, health, history, how-to, humor, language, medicine, memoirs, money, music, parenting, photography, popular culture, psychology, science, self-help, sociology, true crime, women's issues, young adult. **Considers these fiction areas:** commercial, ethnic, fantasy, feminist, historical, horror, humor, literary, mainstream, mystery, New Adult, romance, science fiction, women's, young adult.

⇘ "This agency specializes in general nonfiction and fiction. I also do illustrated and photography books and have represented several photographers for books."

HOW TO CONTACT Query with SASE or via e-mail with no attachments. Prefers to read materials exclusively but if not, please inform. Answers written queries, but does not respond to e-mail queries if not appropriate for the agency. Accepts simultaneous submissions. Responds in 2 weeks to queries, 2 months to mss. Obtains new clients through referrals from other writers and editors as well as unsolicited queries.

TERMS Agent receives 15% commission on domestic sales; 25% commission on foreign sales. Charges clients for photocopying, unusual postage, express mail, telephone expenses (checks with author first).

RECENT SALES Sold 10 titles in 2016 including novels by Dee Ernst, Alexandra Hawkins, Terra Little.

SERENDIPITY LITERARY AGENCY, LLC

305 Gates Ave., Brooklyn NY 11216. **E-mail:** rbrooks@serendipitylit.com; info@serendipitylit.com. **Website:** www.serendipitylit.com; facebook.com/serendipitylit. **Contact:** Regina Brooks. Estab. 2000. Member of AAR. Signatory of WGA. Represents 150 clients.

⏻ Prior to becoming an agent, Ms. Brooks was an acquisitions editor for John Wiley & Sons, Inc. and McGraw-Hill Companies.

MEMBER AGENTS Regina Brooks; Dawn Michelle Hardy (nonfiction, including sports, pop culture, blog and trend, music, lifestyle, social science);

Folade Bell (literary and commercial women's fiction, young adult, literary mystery and thriller, historical fiction, African-American issues, gay/lesbian, Christian fiction, humor, books that deeply explore other cultures; nonfiction that reads like fiction, including blog-to-book or pop culture); **Nadeen Gayle** (romance, memoir, pop culture, inspirational/religious, women's fiction, parenting, young adult, mystery, political thriller, all forms of nonfiction); **Rebecca Bugger** (narrative nonfiction, investigative journalism, memoir, inspirational self-help, religion/spirituality, international, popular culture, current affairs; literary and commercial fiction); **Christina Morgan** (literary fiction, crime fiction, narrative nonfiction in the categories of pop culture, sports, current events, memoir); **Jocquelle Caiby** (literary fiction, horror, middle-grade fiction, children's books by authors who have been published in the adult market, athletes, actors, journalists, politicians, musicians).

REPRESENTS nonfiction, fiction, novels. **Considers these nonfiction areas:** Americana, anthropology, architecture, art, autobiography, biography, business, cooking, creative nonfiction, cultural interests, current affairs, inspirational, interior design, memoirs, metaphysics, music, parenting, popular culture, religious, self-help, spirituality, sports, travel, true crime, women's issues, women's studies, young adult. **Considers these fiction areas:** commercial, gay, historical, lesbian, literary, middle-grade, mystery, romance, thriller, women's, young adult, Christian.

HOW TO CONTACT Check the website, as there are online submission forms for fiction, nonfiction and juvenile. Website will also state if they are temporarily closed to submissions to any areas. Accepts simultaneous submissions. Obtains most new clients through conferences, referrals.

TERMS Agent receives 15% commission on domestic sales; 20% commission on foreign sales. Offers written contract; 2-month notice must be given to terminate contract. Charges clients for office fees, which are taken from any advance.

⊘ SEVENTH AVENUE LITERARY AGENCY

2052-124th St., South Surrey BC Canada. (604)538-7252. **Fax:** (604)538-7252. **E-mail:** info@seventhavenuelit.com. **Website:** www.seventhavenuelit.com. **Contact:** Robert Mackwood, director.
REPRESENTS nonfiction. **Considers these nonfiction areas:** autobiography, biography, business, computers, economics, health, history, medicine, science, sports, technology, travel.

☛ Seventh Avenue Literary Agency is both a literary agency and personal management agency. (The agency was originally called Contemporary Management.) "We also own and operate a self-publishing business imprint, Brilliant Idea Books, designed to help entrepreneurs and business owners develop their own '$20 business card' to further enhance their brand."

HOW TO CONTACT Query with SASE. Submit outline, synopsis, 1 sample chapter (nonfiction), publishing history, author bio, table of contents with proposal or query. Provide full contact information. Let them know the submission history. No fiction. Accepts simultaneous submissions. Obtains most new clients through recommendations from others, some solicitations. Does not add many new clients.

TIPS "If you want your material returned, please include a SASE with adequate postage; otherwise, material will be recycled. (US stamps are not adequate; they do not work in Canada.)"

THE SEYMOUR AGENCY

475 Miner St., Canton NY 13617. (315)386-1831. **E-mail:** nicole@theseymouragency.com; julie@theseymouragency.com. **Website:** www.theseymouragency.com. Member of AAR, signatory of WGA, RWA, Authors Guild, HWA.
MEMBER AGENTS Nicole Rescinti, nicole@theseymouragency.com; **Julie Gwinn**, julie@theseymouragency.com; **Tina Wainscott**, tina@theseymouragency.com; **Jennifer Wills**, jennifer@theseymouragency.com.

REPRESENTS nonfiction, novels. **Considers these nonfiction areas:** business, health, how-to, Christian books; cookbooks; any well-written nonfiction that includes a proposal in standard format and 1 sample chapter.. **Considers these fiction areas:** action, fantasy, inspirational, middle-grade, mystery, New Adult, religious, romance, science fiction, suspense, thriller, young adult.

HOW TO CONTACT Accepts e-mail queries. Check online for guidelines. Accepts simultaneous submissions. Responds in 1 month to queries; 3 months to mss.

TERMS Agent receives 12-15% commission on domestic sales.

DENISE SHANNON LITERARY AGENCY, INC.

20 W. 22nd St., Suite 1603, New York NY 10010. **E-mail:** info@deniseshannonagency.com. **E-mail:** submissions@deniseshannonagency.com. **Website:** www.deniseshannonagency.com. **Contact:** Denise Shannon. Estab. 2002. Member of AAR.

○ Prior to opening her agency, Ms. Shannon worked for 16 years with Georges Borchardt and International Creative Management.

REPRESENTS nonfiction, novels. **Considers these nonfiction areas:** biography, business, health, narrative nonfiction, politics, journalism, social history. **Considers these fiction areas:** literary.

☛ "We are a boutique agency with a distinguished list of fiction and nonfiction authors."

HOW TO CONTACT "Queries may be submitted by post, accompanied by a SASE, or by e-mail to submissions@deniseshannonagency.com. Please include a description of the available book project and a brief bio including details of any prior publications. We will reply and request more material if we are interested. We request that you inform us if you are submitting material simultaneously to other agencies." Accepts simultaneous submissions.

RECENT SALES *Mister Monkey*, by Francine Prose (Harper); *Hotel Solitaire*, by Gary Shteyngart (Random House); *White Flights*, by Jess Row (Graywolf Press); *The Underworld*, by Kevin Canty (Norton).

⊘ KEN SHERMAN & ASSOCIATES

1275 N. Hayworth, Suite 103, Los Angeles CA 90046. (310)273-8840. **Fax:** (310)271-2875. **Website:** www.kenshermanassociates.com. **Contact:** Ken Sherman.

○ Prior to opening his agency, Mr. Sherman was with The William Morris Agency, The Lantz Office and Paul Kohner, Inc. He has taught The Business of Writing For Film and Television and The Book Worlds at UCLA and USC. He also lectures extensively at writer's conferences and film festivals around the U.S.He is currently a Commissioner of Arts and Cultural Affairs in the City of West Hollywood, and is on the International Advisory Board of the Christopher Isherwood Foundation.

REPRESENTS nonfiction, novels, teleplays, life rights, film/TV rights to books, and life rights. **Considers these nonfiction areas:** agriculture, Americana, animals, anthropology, art, biography, business, child guidance, computers, cooking, crafts, current affairs, education, ethnic, film, gardening, gay/lesbian, government, health, history, horticulture, how-to, humor, interior design, language, memoirs, military, money, multicultural, music, New Age, philosophy, photography, popular culture, psychology, recreation, regional, religious, science, self-help, sex, sociology, software, spirituality, sports, translation, travel, true crime, women's issues, young adult, creative nonfiction. **Considers these fiction areas:** action, adventure, commercial, crime, detective, family saga, gay, literary, mainstream, middle-grade, mystery, police, romance, science fiction, suspense, thriller, women's, young adult.

HOW TO CONTACT Contact by referral only. Reports in approximately 1 month to mss. Obtains most new clients through recommendations from others.

WENDY SHERMAN ASSOCIATES, INC.

138 W. 25th St., Suite 1018, New York NY 10001. (212)279-9027. **E-mail:** submissions@wsherman.com. **Website:** www.wsherman.com. **Contact:** Wendy Sherman. Estab. 1999. Member of AAR.

○ Prior to opening the agency, Ms. Sherman held positions as vice president, executive director, associate publisher, subsidiary rights director, and sales and marketing director for major publishers including Simon & Schuster and Henry Holt.

MEMBER AGENTS Wendy Sherman (women's fiction that hits that sweet spot between literary and mainstream, Southern voices, historical dramas, suspense with a well-developed protagonist, writing that illuminates the multicultural experience, anything related to food, dogs, mothers and daughters).

REPRESENTS nonfiction, fiction, novels. **Considers these nonfiction areas:** creative nonfiction, foods, humor, memoirs, parenting, popular culture, psychology, self-help, narrative nonfiction. **Considers these fiction areas:** mainstream, mainstream fiction that hits the sweet spot between literary and commercial.

☛ "We specialize in developing new writers, as well as working with more established writers. My experience as a publisher has proven to be a great asset to my clients."

HOW TO CONTACT Query via e-mail only. "We ask that you include your last name, title, and the name of the agent you are submitting to in the subject line. For fiction, please include a query letter and your first 10 pages copied and pasted in the body of the e-mail. We will not open attachments unless they have been requested. For nonfiction, please include your query letter and author bio. Due to the large number of e-mail submissions that we receive, we only reply to e-mail queries in the affirmative. We respectfully ask that you do not send queries to our individual e-mail addresses." Accepts simultaneous submissions. Obtains most new clients through recommendations from other writers. **TERMS** Agent receives standard 15% commission. Offers written contract.

RECENT SALES *All is Not Forgotten*, by Wendy Walker; *Z, A Novel of Zelda Fitzgerald*, by Therese Anne Fowler; *The Charm Bracelet*, by Viola Shipman; *The Silence of Bonaventure Arrow*, by Rita Leganski; *Together Tea*, by Marjan Kamali; *A Long Long Time Ago and Essentially True*, by Brigid Pasulka; *Lunch in Paris*, by Elizabeth Bard; *The Rules of Inheritance*, by Claire Bidwell Smith; *Eight Flavors*, by Sarah Lohman; *How to Live a Good Life*, by Jonathan Fields.

TIPS "The bottom line is: Do your homework. Be as well prepared as possible. Read the books that will help you present yourself and your work with polish. You want your submission to stand out."

BEVERLEY SLOPEN LITERARY AGENCY

131 Bloor St. W., Suite 711, Toronto ON M5S 1S3 Canada. (416)964-9598. **E-mail:** beverly@slopenagency.ca. **Website:** www.slopenagency.ca. **Contact:** Beverley Slopen. Represents 70 clients.

Prior to opening her agency, Ms. Slopen worked in publishing and as a journalist.

REPRESENTS novels. **Considers these nonfiction areas:** anthropology, archeology, autobiography, biography, business, creative nonfiction, current affairs, economics, investigative, psychology, sociology, true crime. **Considers these fiction areas:** commercial, literary, mystery, suspense.

"This agency has a strong bent toward Canadian writers." Actively seeking serious nonfiction that is accessible and appealing to the general reader. Does not want to receive fantasy, science fiction, or children's books.

HOW TO CONTACT Query by e-mail. Returns materials only with SASE (Canadian postage only). To submit a work for consideration, e-mail a short query letter and a few sample pages. Submit only one work at a time. "If we want to see more, we will contact the writer by phone or e-mail." Accepts simultaneous submissions. Responds in 1 month to queries only if interested.

TERMS Agent receives 15% commission on domestic sales; 10% commission on foreign sales. Offers written contract, binding for 2 years; 3-month notice must be given to terminate contract.

TIPS "Please, no unsolicited manuscripts."

MICHAEL SNELL LITERARY AGENCY

H. Michael Snell, Inc., P.O. Box 1206, Truro MA 02666-1206. (508)349-3718. **E-mail:** query@michaelsnellagency.com. **Website:** michaelsnellagency.com. **Contact:** Patricia Snell, Michael Snell. 32 Bridge Road (for UPS, FedEx only). Estab. 1977. Represents 300 clients.

Prior to opening his agency in 1978, Mr. Snell served as an editor at Wadsworth and Addison-Wesley for 13 years.

MEMBER AGENTS Michael Snell (business, leadership, entrepreneurship, pets, sports); **Patricia Snell** (business, business communications, parenting, relationships, health).

REPRESENTS nonfiction. **Considers these nonfiction areas:** animals, business, creative nonfiction, health, how-to, parenting, psychology, science, self-help, women's issues, women's studies, fitness.

This agency specializes in how-to, self-help, and all types of business, business leadership, and entrepreneurship titles, as well as books for small-business owners. "We place a wide range of topics, from low-level how-to to professional and reference. We are especially interested in business management, communication, strategy, culture building, performance enhancement, marketing and sales, finance and investment, career development, executive skills, leadership, and organization development." Actively seeking strong book proposals in any area of business where a clear need exists for a new book. Does not want to receive fiction, children's books, or complete mss (considers proposals only).

HOW TO CONTACT Query by mail with SASE, or e-mail. Visit the agency's website for proposal guidelines. "We only consider new clients on an exclusive basis." Responds in 1 week to queries, 2 weeks to mss. Obtains most new clients through unsolicited mss, word of mouth, Literary Market Place, *Guide to Literary Agents*.

NEW AGENT SPOTLIGHT

BLAIR WILSON
PARK LITERARY & MEDIA

www.parkliterary.com
@blair_e_wilson

ABOUT BLAIR: Since graduating from Wesleyan University with a focus on literature and theory, Blair has fallen in love with the voices of new and emerging authors. Blair is actively building her client list in the areas of middle grade and young adult fiction, as well as kids and adult non-fiction with a focus on D.I.Y., lifestyle, pop culture, pets, and books dealing with issues of sexuality, identity, and culture. In her spare time, Blair can be found teaching embroidery classes at the American Folk Art Museum, testing out a new cookbook, or settling in for a night of Hammer horror movies.

SHE IS SEEKING: Blair is actively looking for middle grade and young adult fiction, as well as middle-grade, young adult, and adult nonfiction. In nonfiction, Blair is interested in narrative nonfiction, crafting/instructional, true crime, pop culture, lifestyle, sexuality & identity, design, and STEM topics.

HOW TO SUBMIT: Send your query and accompanying materials to queries@ parkliterary.com. Put "Blair Wilson" as well as the category and genre of your book (i.e. "Blair Wilson – YA Fantasy") in the subject line of the email. All materials must be in the body of the email. For all fiction submissions, include a query letter and the first chapter or approximately the first ten pages of your work. For non-fiction submission, send a query letter, proposal, and one sample chapter or approximately ten pages.

TERMS Agent receives 15% commission on domestic and foreign sales.
RECENT SALES *Lead Right for Your Company Type*, by William Schneider (AMACOM); *Excuse me: The Survival Guide to Modern Business Etiquette*, by Rosanne Thomas (AMACOM); *Finding Peace When Your Heart is in Pieces*, by Paul Coleman (Adams Media).
TIPS "Visit the agency's website to view recent sales and publications and to review guidelines for writing a book proposal. Prospective authors can also download model

book proposals at the website. The agency only considers new clients on an exclusive basis. Simultaneous queries are OK; multiple submissions are not."

SPECTRUM LITERARY AGENCY
320 Central Park W., Suite 1-D, New York NY 10025. (212)362-4323. **Fax:** (212)362-4562. **Website:** www. spectrumliteraryagency.com. **Contact:** Eleanor Wood, president. Estab. 1976. SFWA Represents 90 clients.
MEMBER AGENTS Eleanor Wood (referrals only; commercial fiction: science fiction, fantasy,

suspense, select nonfiction); **Justin Bell** (science fiction, mystery, select nonfiction).

REPRESENTS novels. **Considers these fiction areas:** commercial, fantasy, mystery, science fiction, suspense.

HOW TO CONTACT Unsolicited mss are not accepted. Send snail mail query with SASE. "The letter should describe your book briefly and include publishing credits and background information or qualifications relating to your work, and the first 10 pages of your work. Our response time is generally 2-3 months." Obtains most new clients through recommendations from authors.

TERMS Agent receives 15% commission on domestic sales. Deducts for photocopying and book orders.

TIPS "Spectrum's policy is to read only book-length manuscripts that we have specifically asked to see. Unsolicited manuscripts are not accepted. The letter should describe your book briefly and include publishing credits and background information or qualifications relating to your work, if any."

SPEILBURG LITERARY AGENCY

E-mail: info@speilburgliterary.com. **E-mail:** speilburgliterary@gmail.com. **Website:** speilburgliterary.com. **Contact:** Alice Speilburg. Estab. 2012. Member of SCBWI, MWA, RWA.

○ Alice Speilburg previously held publishing positions at John Wiley & Sons and Howard Morhaim Literary Agency.

REPRESENTS nonfiction, fiction, novels. **Considers these nonfiction areas:** biography, cultural interests, environment, foods, health, history, investigative, music, popular culture, psychology, science, sports, travel, women's issues, women's studies, young adult. **Considers these fiction areas:** adventure, commercial, detective, fantasy, feminist, historical, horror, mainstream, middle-grade, mystery, police, science fiction, suspense, urban fantasy, westerns, women's, young adult.

➤ Does not want picture books, screenplays, poetry, romance.

HOW TO CONTACT If you are interested in submitting your manuscript or proposal for consideration, please e-mail a query letter along with either 3 sample chapters for fiction or a TOC and proposal for nonfiction. Accepts simultaneous submissions.

SPENCERHILL ASSOCIATES

8131 Lakewood Main St., Building M, Suite 205, Lakewood Ranch FL 34202. (941)907-3700. **E-mail:** submission@spencerhillassociates.com. **Website:** www.spencerhillassociates.com. **Contact:** Karen Solem, Nalini Akolekar, Amanda Leuck, Sandy Harding. Member of AAR.

○ Prior to becoming an agent, Ms. Solem was editor-in-chief at HarperCollins and an associate publisher.

MEMBER AGENTS Karen Solem, Nalini Akolekar, Amanda Leuck, Sandy Harding.

REPRESENTS fiction. **Considers these fiction areas:** commercial, crime, erotica, family saga, gay, historical, inspirational, literary, mainstream, multicultural, mystery, New Adult, paranormal, police, romance, thriller, women's, young adult.

➤ "We handle mostly commercial women's fiction, historical novels, romance (historical, contemporary, paranormal, urban fantasy), thriller, and mystery. We also represent Christian fiction only—no nonfiction." No nonfiction, poetry, science fiction, children's picture books, or scripts.

HOW TO CONTACT "We accept electronic submissions and are no longer accepting paper queries. Please send us a query letter in the body of an e-mail, pitch us your project and tell us about yourself: Do you have prior publishing credits? Attach the first 3 chapters and synopsis preferably in .doc, .rtf or .txt format to your e-mail. Send all queries to submission@spencerhillassociates.com. We do not have a preference for exclusive submissions, but do appreciate knowing if the submission is simultaneous. We receive thousands of submissions a year and each query receives our attention. Unfortunately, we are unable to respond to each query individually. If we are interested in your work, we will contact you within 12 weeks." Accepts simultaneous submissions.

TERMS Agent receives 15% commission on domestic sales; 20% commission on foreign sales. Offers written contract; 3-month notice must be given to terminate contract.

RECENT SALES A full list of sales and clients is available on the agency website.

THE SPIELER AGENCY

27 W. 20 St., Suite 302, New York NY 10011. (212)757-4439, ext. 1. **Fax:** (212)333-2019. **Website:** thespieleragency.com. **Contact:** Joe Spieler. Represents 160 clients.

Prior to opening his agency, Mr. Spieler was a magazine editor.

MEMBER AGENTS Victoria Shoemaker, victoria@thespieleragency.com (environment and natural history, popular culture, memoir, photography and film, literary fiction and poetry, food and cooking); **John Thornton**, john@thespieleragency.com (nonfiction); **Joe Spieler**, joe@thespieleragency.com (nonfiction and fiction, books for children and young adults); **Helen Sweetland**, helen@thespieleragency.com (children's from board books through young adult fiction; adult general-interest nonfiction including nature, green living, gardening, architecture, interior design, health, popular science).

REPRESENTS nonfiction, novels, juvenile books. **Considers these nonfiction areas:** architecture, biography, cooking, environment, film, foods, gardening, health, history, memoirs, photography, popular culture, science, sociology, spirituality. **Considers these fiction areas:** literary, middle-grade, New Age, picture books, thriller, young adult.

HOW TO CONTACT "Before submitting projects to the Spieler Agency, check the listings of our individual agents and see if any particular agent shows a general interest in your subject (e.g., history, memoir, young adult). Please send all queries either by e-mail or regular mail. If you query us by regular mail, we can only reply to you if you include a SASE." Accepts simultaneous submissions. Cannot guarantee a personal response to all queries. Obtains most new clients through recommendations, listing in *Guide to Literary Agents*.

TERMS Agent receives 15% commission on domestic sales. Charges clients for messenger bills, photocopying, postage.

PHILIP G. SPITZER LITERARY AGENCY, INC

50 Talmage Farm Lane, East Hampton NY 11937. (631)329-3650. **Fax:** (631)329-3651. **E-mail:** lukas.ortiz@spitzeragency.com; spitzer516@aol.com. **E-mail:** kim.lombardini@spitzeragency.com. **Website:** www.spitzeragency.com. **Contact:** Lukas Ortiz. Estab. 1969. Member of AAR.

Prior to opening his agency, Mr. Spitzer served at New York University Press, McGraw-Hill, and the John Cushman Associates Literary Agency.

MEMBER AGENTS Philip G. Spitzer, Lukas Ortiz.

REPRESENTS novels. **Considers these nonfiction areas:** biography, current affairs, history, politics, sports, travel. **Considers these fiction areas:** juvenile, literary, mainstream, suspense, thriller.

This agency specializes in mystery, suspense, literary fiction, sports, and general nonfiction (no how-to).

HOW TO CONTACT E-mail query containing synopsis of work, brief biography, and a sample chapter (pasted into the e-mail). Be aware that this agency openly says its client list is quite full. Accepts simultaneous submissions. Obtains most new clients through recommendations from others.

TERMS Agent receives 15% commission on domestic sales; 20% commission on foreign sales. Charges clients for photocopying.

RECENT SALES *The Jealous Kind*, by James Lee Burke (Simon & Schuster); *The Ex*, by Alafair Burke (HarperCollins); *Townie*, by Andre Dubus III (Norton); *The Wrong Side of Goodbye*, by Michael Connelly (Little, Brown & Co); *The Emerald Lie*, Ken Bruen (Mysterious Press/Grove-Atlantic).

NANCY STAUFFER ASSOCIATES

P.O. Box 1203, Darien CT 06820. (203)202-2500. **E-mail:** nancy@staufferliterary.com. **Website:** www.publishersmarketplace.com/members/nstauffer. **Contact:** Nancy Stauffer Cahoon. Nancy Stauffer Associates is a boutique agency representing a small, select group of authors of the highest quality literary fiction and literary narrative nonfiction. Member of the Authors Guild.

"Over the course of my more than 20 year career, I've held positions in the editorial, marketing, business, and rights departments of *The New York Times*, McGraw-Hill, and Doubleday."

REPRESENTS Considers these fiction areas: literary.

Mystery, romance, action adventure, historical fiction.

HOW TO CONTACT Accepts simultaneous submissions. Obtains most new clients through referrals from existing clients.

TERMS Agent receives 15% commission on domestic sales; 20% commission on foreign sales.

RECENT SALES *You Don't Have To Say You Love Me*, by Sherman Alexie; *Our Souls At Night*, by Kent Haruf; *Bone Fire*, by Mark Spragg.

STIMOLA LITERARY STUDIO

308 Livingston Court, Edgewater NJ 07020. **E-mail:** info@stimolaliterarystudio.com. **E-mail:** see submission page on website. **Website:** www.stimolaliterarystudio.com. **Contact:** Rosemary B. Stimola. Estab. 1997. Member of AAR, PEN, Authors Guild, ALA. Represents 50 clients.

○ Prior to opening her agency, Rosemary Stimola was an independent children's bookseller. Erica Rand Silverman, Senior Agent, was a high school teacher and former senior agent at Sterling Lord Literistic.

MEMBER AGENTS Rosemary B. Stimola; Erica Rand Silverman.

REPRESENTS juvenile books. **Considers these nonfiction areas:** cooking. **Considers these fiction areas:** young adult.

➤ Actively seeking remarkable middle-grade, young adult fiction, and debut picture book author/illustrators. No institutional books.

HOW TO CONTACT Query via e-mail as per submission guidelines on website. Author/illustrators of picture books may attach text and sample art. A PDF dummy is preferred. Accepts simultaneous submissions. Responds in 3 weeks to queries "we wish to pursue further;" 2 months to requested mss. While unsolicited queries are welcome, most clients come through editor, agent, client referrals.

TERMS Agent receives 15% commission on domestic sales; 20% (if subagents are employed) commission on foreign sales. Offers written contract, binding for all children's projects; a 60-days notice must be given to terminate contract.

TIPS Agent is hands-on, no-nonsense. May request revisions. Does not line edit but may offer suggestions for improvement before submission. Well-respected by clients and editors. "A firm but reasonable deal negotiator."

STONESONG

270 W. 39th St. #201, New York NY 10018. (212)929-4600. **E-mail:** editors@stonesong.com. **E-mail:** submissions@stonesong.com. **Website:** stonesong.com. Member of AAR. Signatory of WGA.

MEMBER AGENTS Alison Fargis; Ellen Scordato; Judy Linden; Emmanuelle Morgen; Leila Campoli (business, science, technology, self improvement); **Maria Ribas** (cookbooks, self-help, health, diet, home, parenting, humor, all from authors with demonstrable platforms; she's also interested in nar-

rative nonfiction and select memoir); **Melissa Edwards** (children's fiction and adult commercial fiction, select pop-culture nonfiction); **Alyssa Jennette** (children's and adult fiction, picture books, humor and pop culture nonfiction); **Madelyn Burt** (adult and children's fiction, select historical nonfiction).

REPRESENTS nonfiction, fiction, novels, juvenile books. **Considers these nonfiction areas:** architecture, art, biography, business, cooking, crafts, creative nonfiction, cultural interests, current affairs, dance, decorating, diet/nutrition, design, economics, foods, gay/lesbian, health, history, hobbies, how-to, humor, interior design, investigative, literature, memoirs, money, music, New Age, parenting, photography, popular culture, politics, psychology, science, self-help, sociology, spirituality, sports, technology, women's issues, young adult. **Considers these fiction areas:** action, adventure, commercial, confession, contemporary issues, ethnic, experimental, family saga, fantasy, feminist, gay, historical, horror, humor, juvenile, lesbian, literary, mainstream, middle-grade, military, multicultural, mystery, New Adult, New Age, occult, paranormal, regional, romance, satire, science fiction, supernatural, suspense, thriller, urban fantasy, women's, young adult.

➤ Does not represent plays, screenplays, picture books, or poetry.

HOW TO CONTACT Accepts electronic queries for fiction and nonfiction. Submit query addressed to a specific agent. Include first chapter or first 10 pages of ms. Accepts simultaneous submissions.

RECENT SALES *Sweet Laurel*, by Laurel Gallucci and Claire Thomas; *Terrain: A Seasonal Guide to Nature at Home*, by Terrain; *The Prince's Bane*, by Alexandra Christo; *Deep Listening*, by Jillian Pransky; *Change Resilience*, by Lior Arussy; *A Thousand Words*, by Brigit Young.

ROBIN STRAUS AGENCY, INC.

Wallace Literary Agency, 229 E. 79th St., Suite 5A, New York NY 10075. (212)472-3282. **Fax:** (212)472-3833. **E-mail:** info@robinstrausagency.com. **Website:** www.robinstrausagency.com. **Contact:** Ms. Robin Straus. Estab. 1983. Member of AAR.

○ Prior to becoming an agent, Robin Straus served as a subsidiary rights manager at Random House and Doubleday. She began her career in the editorial department of Little, Brown.

REPRESENTS **Considers these nonfiction areas:** biography, cooking, creative nonfiction, current affairs, environment, foods, health, history, memoirs, multicultural, music, parenting, popular culture, psychology, science, travel, women's issues, mainstream science. **Considers these fiction areas:** commercial, contemporary issues, literary, mainstream, women's.

➥ Does not represent juvenile, young adult, horror, romance, westerns, poetry, or screenplays.

HOW TO CONTACT E-query or query via snail mail with SASE. "Send us a query letter with contact information, an autobiographical summary, a brief synopsis or description of your book project, submission history, and information on competition. If you wish, you may also include the opening chapter of your manuscript (pasted). While we do our best to reply to all queries, you can assume that if you haven't heard from us after 6 weeks, we are not interested." Accepts simultaneous submissions.

TERMS Agent receives 15% commission on domestic sales; 20% commission on foreign sales. Offers written contract.

THE STRINGER LITERARY AGENCY LLC

P.O. Box 770365, Naples FL 34107. **E-mail:** mstringer@stringerlit.com. **Website:** www.stringerlit.com. **Contact:** Marlene Stringer. This agency focuses on commercial fiction for adults and teens. Estab. 2008. Member of AAR, signatory of WGA, RWA, MWA, ITW, SBCWI. Represents 50 clients.

REPRESENTS fiction, novels. **Considers these fiction areas:** commercial, crime, detective, fantasy, historical, horror, mainstream, multicultural, mystery, New Adult, paranormal, police, romance, science fiction, suspense, thriller, urban fantasy, women's, young adult, No space opera science fiction.

➥ This agency specializes in fiction. "We are an editorial agency, and work with clients to make their manuscripts the best they can be in preparation for submission. We focus on career planning, and help our clients reach their publishing goals. We advise clients on marketing and promotional strategies to help them reach their target readership. Because we are so hands-on, we limit the size of our list; however, we are always looking for exceptional voices and stories that demand we read to the end. You never know where the next great story is coming from." This agency is seeking thriller, crime fiction (not true crime), mystery, women's fiction, single

title and category romance, fantasy (all subgenres), earth-based science fiction (no space opera, aliens, etc.), and young adult/teen. Does not want to receive picture books, Middle-grade, plays, short stories, or poetry. This is not the agency for inspirational romance or erotica. No space opera. The agency is not seeking nonfiction as of this time (2016).

HOW TO CONTACT Electronic submissions through website submission form only. Please make sure your ms is as good as it can be before you submit. Agents are not first readers. For specific information on what we like to see in query letters, refer to the information at www.stringerlit.com under the heading "Learn." Accepts simultaneous submissions. "We strive to respond quickly, but current clients' work always comes first." Obtains new clients through referrals, submissions, conferences.

TERMS Standard commission. "We do not charge fees."

RECENT SALES *The Conqueror's Wife*, by Stephanie Thornton; *When I'm Gone*, by Emily Bleeker; *Magic Bitter, Magic Sweet*, by Charlie N. Holmberg; *Belle Chasse*, by Suzanne Johnson; *Chapel of Ease*, by Alex Bledsoe; *Wilds of the Bayou*, by Susannah Sandlin; *Summit Lake*, by Charlie Donlea.

TIPS "If your ms falls between categories, or you are not sure of the category, query and we'll let you know if we'd like to take a look. We strive to respond as quickly as possible. If you have not received a response in the time period indicated on website, please re-query."

THE STROTHMAN AGENCY, LLC

63 E. 9th St., 10X, New York NY 10003. **E-mail:** info@strothmanagency.com. **E-mail:** strothmanagency@gmail.com. **Website:** www.strothmanagency.com. **Contact:** Wendy Strothman, Lauren MacLeod. Member of AAR, the Authors' Guild. Represents 50 clients.

🗩 Prior to becoming an agent, Ms. Strothman was head of Beacon Press (1983-1995) and executive vice president of Houghton Mifflin's Trade & Reference Division (1996-2002).

MEMBER AGENTS Wendy Strothman (history, narrative nonfiction, narrative journalism, science and nature, current affairs); **Lauren MacLeod** (young adult fiction and nonfiction, middle-grade novels, highly polished literary fiction and narrative nonfiction, particularly food writing, science, pop culture, history).

NEW AGENT SPOTLIGHT

DANIELLE BURBY
NELSON LITERARY AGENCY

www.nelsonagency.com
@DanielleBurby

ABOUT DANIELLE: Based in New York City, Danielle became an agent at Nelson Literary Agency (NLA) in January 2017. Previously, she was an agent at a NYC-based firm where she managed foreign rights in addition to building her client roster. She also interned at several top agencies and publishers before graduating from Hamilton College with a dual degree in creative writing and women's studies.

SHE IS SEEKING: Danielle represents all genres of young adult and middle-grade along with select passion projects on the adult side in women's fiction, science fiction and fantasy, and mystery. She particularly enjoys complex female characters, quirky adventures, narratives that ask readers to think deeply, girls with swords, and seaside novels. Danielle also looks for a strong narrative voice and characters she wants to spend time with. For more information about her wishlist, check out NLA's Submission Guidelines. You can find details about her recent sales on Publishers Marketplace.

HOW TO SUBMIT: Send queries to querydanielle@nelsonagency.com. Paste the first 10 pages of your manuscript in the body of the email.

REPRESENTS nonfiction, novels, juvenile books. **Considers these nonfiction areas:** business, current affairs, economics, environment, foods, history, language, popular culture, science. **Considers these fiction areas:** literary, middle-grade, young adult.

⚷ "The Strothman Agency seeks out scholars, journalists, and other acknowledged and emerging experts in their fields. We specialize in history, science, narrative journalism, nature and the environment, current affairs, narrative nonfiction, business and economics, young adult fiction and nonfiction, middle-grade fiction and nonfiction. We are not signing up projects in romance, science fiction, picture books, or poetry."

HOW TO CONTACT Accepts queries only via e-mail. See submission guidelines online. Accepts simultaneous submissions. "All e-mails received will be responded to with an auto-reply. If we have not replied to your query within 6 weeks, we do not feel that it is right for us." Accepts simultaneous submissions. Obtains most new clients through recommendations from others.

TERMS Agent receives 15% commission on domestic sales; 20% commission on foreign sales. Offers written contract; 30-day notice must be given to terminate contract.

THE STUART AGENCY

260 W. 52 St., #25C, New York NY 10019. (212)586-2711. **E-mail:** andrew@stuartagency.com. **Website:** stuartagency.com. **Contact:** Andrew Stuart. The Stuart Agency is a full-service literary agency representing a wide range of high-quality nonfiction and fiction, from Pulitzer Prize winners and entertainment figures to journalists, public intellectuals, academics, and novelists. Estab. 2002.

○ Prior to his current position, Mr. Stuart was an agent with Literary Group International for five years. Prior to becoming an agent, he was an editor at Random House and Simon & Schuster.

MEMBER AGENTS Andrew Stuart (history, science, narrative nonfiction, business, current events, memoir, psychology, sports, literary fiction); **Christopher Rhodes**, christopher@stuartagency.com (literary and upmarket fiction [including thriller and horror]; connected stories/essays [humorous and serious]; memoir; creative/narrative nonfiction; history; religion; pop culture; art and design); **Rob Kirkpatrick**, rob@stuartagency.com (memoir, biography, sports, music, pop culture, current events, history, and pop science).

REPRESENTS nonfiction, novels. **Considers these nonfiction areas:** art, business, creative nonfiction, current affairs, history, memoirs, popular culture, psychology, religious, science, sports. **Considers these fiction areas:** horror, literary, thriller.

HOW TO CONTACT Query via online submission form on the agency website. Accepts simultaneous submissions.

EMMA SWEENEY AGENCY, LLC

245 E 80th St., Suite 7E, New York NY 10075. **E-mail:** queries@emmasweeneyagency.com. **Website:** www.emmasweeneyagency.com. Estab. 2006. Member of AAR, Women's Media Group. Represents 80 clients.

○ Prior to becoming an agent, Ms. Sweeney was director of subsidiary rights at Grove Press. Since 1990, she has been a literary agent. Ms. Sutherland Brown was an associate editor at St. Martin's Press/Thomas Dunne Books and a freelance editor. Ms. Watson attended Hunter College where she earned a BA in English (with a focus on Creative Writing) and a BA in Russian Language & Culture.

MEMBER AGENTS Emma Sweeney, president; **Margaret Sutherland Brown** (commercial and literary fiction, mystery and thriller, narrative nonfiction, lifestyle, cookbooks); **Kira Watson** (children's literature).

REPRESENTS nonfiction, fiction, novels, juvenile books. **Considers these nonfiction areas:** biography, cooking, creative nonfiction, cultural interests, decorating, diet/nutrition, design, foods, gardening, history, how-to, interior design, juvenile nonfiction, literature, memoirs, popular culture, psychology, religious, science, sex, sociology, young adult. **Considers these fiction areas:** commercial, contemporary issues, crime, historical, juvenile, literary, mainstream, middle-grade, mystery, New Adult, suspense, thriller, women's, young adult.

⚷ Does not want erotica.

HOW TO CONTACT "We accept only electronic queries, and ask that all queries be sent to queries@emmasweeneyagency.com rather than to any agent directly. Please begin your query with a succinct (and hopefully catchy) description of your plot or proposal. Always include a brief cover letter telling us how you heard about ESA, your previous writing credits, and a few lines about yourself. We cannot open any attachments unless specifically requested, and ask that you paste the first 10 pages of your proposal or novel into the text of your e-mail." Accepts simultaneous submissions.

STEPHANIE TADE LITERARY AGENCY

P.O. Box 235, Durham PA 18039. (610)346-8667. **E-mail:** submissions@stephanietadeagency.com. **Website:** stephanietadeagency.com. **Contact:** Stephanie Tade.

○ Prior to becoming an agent, Ms. Tade was an executive editor at Rodale Press. She was also an agent with the Jane Rotrosen Agency.

MEMBER AGENTS Stephanie Tade, president and principal agent; **Colleen Martell**, editorial director and associate agent (cmartell@stadeagency.com).

REPRESENTS nonfiction, fiction.

⚷ Seeks prescriptive and narrative nonfiction, specializing in physical, emotional, psychological, and spiritual wellness, as well as select commercial fiction.

HOW TO CONTACT Query by e-mail or mail with SASE. "When you write to the agency, please include information about your proposed book, your publishing history, and any media or online platform you have developed." Accepts simultaneous submissions.

TALCOTT NOTCH LITERARY

31 Cherry St., Suite 104, Milford CT 06460. (203)876-4959. **Fax:** (203)876-9517. **E-mail:** editorial@talcottnotch.net. **Website:** www.talcottnotch.net. **Contact:** Gina Panettieri, president. Represents 150 clients.

○ Prior to becoming an agent, Ms. Panettieri was a freelance writer and editor. Ms. Munier was Director of Acquisitions for Adams Media Corporation and had previously worked for Disney. Ms. Sulaiman holds degrees from Wellesley and the University of Chicago and had completed an internship with Sourcebooks prior to joining Talcott Notch. Mr. Shalabi holds an MS in Neuroscience and had completed internships with Folio and Veritas, agencies as well as with Talcott Notch, before joining Talcott Notch as a Junior Agent in late 2016.

MEMBER AGENTS Gina Panettieri, gpanettieri@talcottnotch.net (history, business, self-help, science, gardening, cookbooks, crafts, parenting, memoir, true crime, travel, young adult, Middle-grade, women's fiction, paranormal, urban fantasy, horror, science fiction, historical, mystery, thriller and suspense); **Paula Munier**, pmunier@talcottnotch.net (mystery/thriller, SF/fantasy, romance, young adult, memoir, humor, pop culture, health & wellness, cooking, self-help, pop psych, New Age, inspirational, technology, science, writing); **Saba Sulaiman**, ssulaiman@talcottnotch.net (upmarket literary and commercial fiction, romance [all subgenres except paranormal], character-driven psychological thriller, cozy mystery, memoir, young adult [except paranormal and science fiction], middle-grade, nonfiction humor); **Mohamed Shalabi**, mshalabi@talcottnotch (upmarket literary and commercial fiction, psychological thriller, young adult [and subgenres except romance and paranormal], Middle-grade, adult nonfiction).

REPRESENTS nonfiction, fiction, novels, short story collections, novellas, juvenile books. **Considers these nonfiction areas:** biography, business, cooking, crafts, cultural interests, current affairs, diet/nutrition, ethnic, foods, gardening, gay/lesbian, government, health, history, how-to, humor, inspirational, juvenile nonfiction, literature, memoirs, military, multicultural, parenting, popular culture, politics, psychology, science, self-help, sex, sociology, spirituality, technology, travel, true crime, women's issues, women's studies, young adult. **Considers these fiction areas:** action, adventure, commercial, contemporary issues, crime, ethnic, fantasy, feminist, gay, hi-lo, historical, horror, juvenile, lesbian, literary, mainstream, middle-grade, multicultural, multimedia, mystery, New Adult, New Age, paranormal, police, romance, science fiction, short story collections, suspense, thriller, urban fantasy, women's, young adult.

☞ "We are most actively seeking projects featuring diverse characters and stories that expand the reader's understanding of our society and the wider world we live in."

HOW TO CONTACT Query via e-mail (preferred) with first 10 pages of the ms pasted within the body of the e-mail, not as an attachment. Accepts simultaneous submissions. Responds in 2 weeks to queries, 6-10 weeks to mss.

TERMS Agent receives 15% commission on domestic sales; 20% commission on foreign sales. Offers written contract, binding for 1 year.

RECENT SALES Agency sold 65 titles in the last year, including *The Widower's Wife*, by Cate Holahan (Crooked Lane Books); *Tier One*, by Brian Andrews and Jeffrey Wilson (Thomas & Mercer) and *Beijing Red*, written as Alex Ryan (Crooked Lane Books); *Firestorm*, by Nancy Holzner (Berkley Ace Science Fiction).

TIPS "Know your market and how to reach them. A strong platform is essential in your book proposal. Can you effectively use social media? Are you a strong networker? Are you familiar with the book bloggers in your genre? Are you involved with the interest-specific groups that can help you? What can you do to break through the 'noise' and help present your book to your readers? Check our website for more tips and information on this topic."

THOMPSON LITERARY AGENCY

115 W. 29th St., Third Floor, New York NY 10001. (347)281-7685. **E-mail:** submissions@thompsonliterary.com. **Website:** thompsonliterary.com. **Contact:** Meg Thompson, founder. Estab. 2014. Member of AAR. Signatory of WGA.

○ Before her current position, Ms. Thompson was with LJK Literary and the Einstein Thompson Agency.

MEMBER AGENTS Cindy Uh, senior agent; **John Thorn**, affiliate agent; **Sandy Hodgman**, director of foreign rights.

REPRESENTS nonfiction, fiction, novels, juvenile books. **Considers these nonfiction areas:** autobiography, biography, business, cooking, crafts, creative nonfiction, current affairs, diet/nutrition, design, education, foods, health, history, how-to, humor, inspirational, interior design, juvenile nonfiction, memoirs, multicultural, popular culture, politics, science, self-help, sociology, sports, travel, women's issues, women's studies, young adult. **Considers these fiction areas:** commercial, contemporary issues, fantasy, historical, juvenile, literary, middle-grade, multicultural, picture books, women's, young adult.

➤ The agency is always on the lookout for both commercial and literary fiction, as well as young adult and children's books. "Nonfiction, however, is our specialty, and our interests include biography, memoir, music, popular science, politics, blog-to-book projects, cookbooks, sports, health and wellness, fashion, art, and popular culture. Please note that we do not accept submissions for poetry collections or screenplays, and we only consider picture books by established illustrators."

HOW TO CONTACT "For fiction: Please send a query letter, including any salient biographical information or previous publications, and attach the first 25 pages of your manuscript. For nonfiction: Please send a query letter and a full proposal, including biographical information, previous publications, credentials that qualify you to write your book, marketing information, and sample material. You should address your query to whichever agent you think is best suited for your project." Accepts simultaneous submissions. Responds in 6 weeks if interested.

THREE SEAS LITERARY AGENCY

P.O. Box 444, Sun Prairie WI 53590. (608)834-9317. **E-mail:** queries@threeseaslit.com. **Website:** threeseasagency.com. **Contact:** Michelle Grajkowski, Cori Deyoe. Estab. 2000. Member of AAR, RWA, SCBWI. Represents 55 clients.

○ Since its inception, 3 Seas has sold more than 500 titles worldwide. Ms. Grajkowski's authors have appeared on all the major lists including *The New York Times, USA Today,* and *Publishers Weekly.* Prior to joining the agency

in 2006, Ms. Deyoe was a multi-published author. She represents a wide range of authors and has sold many projects at auction.

MEMBER AGENTS Michelle Grajkowski (romance, women's fiction, young adult and middle-grade fiction, select nonfiction projects); **Cori Deyoe** (all sub-genres of romance, women's fiction, young adult, middle-grade, picture books, thriller, mystery select nonfiction); **Linda Scalissi** (women's fiction, thriller, young adult, mystery, romance).

REPRESENTS nonfiction, novels. **Considers these fiction areas:** middle-grade, mystery, picture books, romance, thriller, women's, young adult.

➤ "We represent more than 50 authors who write romance, women's fiction, science fiction/fantasy, thriller, and young adult and middle-grade fiction, as well as select nonfiction titles. Currently, we are looking for fantastic authors with a voice of their own." 3 Seas does not represent poetry or screenplays.

HOW TO CONTACT E-mail queries only; no attachments, unless requested by agents. For fiction, please e-mail the first chapter and synopsis along with a cover letter. Also, be sure to include the genre and the number of words in your manuscript, as well as pertinent writing experience in your query letter. For nonfiction, e-mail a complete proposal, including a query letter and your first chapter. For picture books, query with complete text. Accepts simultaneous submissions. Obtains most new clients through recommendations from others, conferences.

TERMS Agent receives 15% commission on domestic sales; 20% commission on foreign sales. Offers written contract.

RECENT SALES Represents best-selling authors, including Jennifer Brown, Katie MacAlister, Kerrelyn Sparks, C.L. Wilson.

THE TOBIAS AGENCY

New York NY **E-mail:** query@thetobiasagency.com. **Website:** http://www.thetobiasagency.com. "The Tobias Literary Agency is a full-service literary agency that represents both established and debut authors. We take pride in supporting not just our clients' work, but also their long-lasting careers. " Estab. 2016. Member of AAR, RWA. Represents 14 clients.

MEMBER AGENTS Albert Tobias, Lane Heymont.

REPRESENTS nonfiction, fiction, novels. **Considers these nonfiction areas:** true crime. **Considers these fiction areas:** fantasy, romance, science fiction.

⊶ "We represent a broad range of commercial fiction including all romance, all its subgenres, fantasy, science fiction, nonfiction and true crime."

HOW TO CONTACT To query, type "Query - The Title of Your Manuscript" in the subject line, then please paste the first 5 pages of your manuscript into the body of the e-mail to query@thetobiasagency.com. Please remember to include in your query: your manuscript's title, word count, and genre; your pitch (remember your GMC—goal, motivation, and conflict); and your bio including any publishing credits. Accepts simultaneous submissions.

RECENT SALES *Bedding The Highlande*r by Sabrina York, *The Vicar's Daughter* by Josi S. Kilpack, and the Christmas Mystery Series by Danica Winters.

✪ TRANSATLANTIC LITERARY AGENCY

2 Bloor St. E., Suite 3500, Toronto ON M4W 1A8 Canada. (416)488-9214. **E-mail:** info@transatlanticagency.com. **Website:** transatlanticagency.com. The Transatlantic Agency represents adult and children's authors of all genres, including illustrators. We do not handle stage plays, musicals or screenplays. Please review the agency website and guidelines carefully before making any inquiries, as each agent has particular submission guidelines.

MEMBER AGENTS Trena White (upmarket, accessible nonfiction: current affairs, business, culture, politics, technology, the environment); Amy Tompkins (adult: literary fiction, historical fiction, women's fiction including smart romance, narrative nonfiction, quirky or original how-to books; children's: early readers, middle-grade, young adult, New Adult); Stephanie Sinclair (literary fiction, upmarket women's and commercial fiction, literary thriller and suspense, young adult crossover; narrative nonfiction, memoir, investigative journalism, true crime); Samantha Haywood (literary fiction and upmarket commercial fiction, specifically literary thriller and upmarket mystery, historical fiction, smart contemporary fiction, upmarket women's fiction and cross-over novels; narrative nonfiction, including investigative journalism, politics, women's issues, memoirs, environmental issues, historical narratives, sexuality, true crime; graphic novels [fiction and nonfiction]: preferably full length graphic novels, story collections considered, memoirs, biography, travel narratives); Jesse Finkelstein (nonfiction: current affairs, business, culture, politics, technology, religion, the environment); Marie Campbell (middle-grade fiction); Shaun Bradley (referrals only; adult literary fiction and narrative nonfiction, primarily science and investigative journalism); Sandra Bishop (fiction; nonfiction: biography, memoir, positive or humorous how-to books on advice/relationships, mind/body/spirit, religion, healthy living, finances, life-hacks, traveling, living a better life); Fiona Kenshole (children's and young adult; only accepting submissions from referrals or conferences she attends as faculty); Lynn Bennett (not accepting submissions or new clients); David Bennett (children's, young adult, adult).

REPRESENTS nonfiction, novels, juvenile books.

⊶ "In both children's and adult literature, we market directly into the US, the UK, and Canada." Represents adult and children's authors of all genres, including illustrators. Does not want to receive picture books, musicals, screenplays or stage plays.

HOW TO CONTACT Always refer to the website, as guidelines will change, and only various agents are open to new clients at any given time. Obtains most new clients through recommendations from others.

TERMS Agent receives 15% commission on domestic sales; 20% commission on foreign sales. Offers written contract; 45-day notice must be given to terminate contract. This agency charges for photocopying and postage when it exceeds $100.

RECENT SALES Sold 250 titles in the last year.

TRIADA US

P.O. Box 561, Sewickley PA 15143. (412)401-3376. **E-mail:** uwe@triadaus.com, brent@triadaus.com. laura@triadaus.com. mallory@triadaus.com. lauren@triadaus.com. **Website:** www.triadaus.com. **Contact:** Dr. Uwe Stender, President. Triada US was founded by Dr. Uwe Stender over 12 years ago. Since then, the agency has built a high-quality list of fiction and nonfiction for kids, teens, and adults. Triada US titles are consistently critically acclaimed and translated into multiple languages. Estab. 2004. Member of AAR.

MEMBER AGENTS Uwe Stender, Brent Taylor, Laura Crockett, Mallory Brown, Lauren Spieller. **REPRESENTS** nonfiction, fiction, novels, juvenile books. **Considers these nonfiction areas:** biography, business, cooking, crafts, creative nonfiction, cultural interests, current affairs, diet/nutrition, economics, education, environment, ethnic, foods, gardening, health, history, how-to, juvenile nonfiction, literature, memoirs, music, parenting, popular culture, politics, science, self-help, sports, true crime, women's issues, young adult. **Considers these fiction areas:** action, adventure, comic books, commercial, contemporary issues, crime, detective, ethnic, family saga, fantasy, gay, historical, horror, juvenile, lesbian, literary, mainstream, middle-grade, multicultural, mystery, New Adult, occult, picture books, police, suspense, thriller, urban fantasy, women's, young adult.

➻ Actively seeking fiction and nonfiction across a broad range of categories of all age levels.

HOW TO CONTACT E-mail queries preferred. Please paste your query letter and the first 10 pages of your ms into the body of a message e-mailed to the agent of your choice. Please note: a rejection from one Triada US agent is a rejection from all. Triada US agents personally respond to all queries and requested material and pride themselves on having some of the fastest response times in the industry. Obtains most new clients through submission inbox (query letters and requested mss), client referrals, and conferences.

TERMS Agent receives 15% commission on domestic sales; 20% commission on foreign and translation sales. Offers written contract; 30-day notice must be given prior to termination.

RECENT SALES *Plants You Can't Kill*, by Stacy Tornio (Skyhorse); *Gettysburg Rebels*, by Tom McMillan (Regnery); *The Smart Girl's Guide to Polyamory*, by Dedeker Winston (Skyhorse); *Raised By Animals*, by Jennifer Verdolin (The Experiment); *The Hemingway Thief*, by Shaun Harris (Seventh Street); *The Perfect Fit*, by Summer Heacock (Mira); *Not Perfect*, by Elizabeth LaBan (Lake Union).

TRIDENT MEDIA GROUP

41 Madison Ave., 36th Floor, New York NY 10010. (212)333-1511. **Website:** www.tridentmediagroup.com. **Contact:** Ellen Levine. Member of AAR.

MEMBER AGENTS Kimberly Whalen, ws.assistant@tridentmediagroup (commercial fiction and nonfiction including women's fiction, romance, suspense, paranormal, pop culture); **Alyssa Eisner Henkin** (picture books through young adult fiction, including mystery, period pieces, contemporary school-settings, issues of social justice, family sagas, eerie magical realism, retellings of classics; children's/YA nonfiction: history, STEM/STEAM themes, memoir) **Scott Miller**, smiller@tridentmediagroup.com (commercial fiction including thriller, crime fiction, women's, book club fiction, middle-grade, young adult; nonfiction including military, celebrity, pop culture, narrative, sports, prescriptive, current events); **Melissa Flashman**, mflashman@tridentmediagroup.com (nonfiction: pop culture, memoir, wellness, popular science, business and economics, technology; fiction: adult and young adult, literary and commercial); **Don Fehr**, dfehr@tridentmediagroup.com (literary and commercial fiction, young adult fiction, narrative nonfiction, memoirs, travel, science, health); **John Silbersack**, silbersack.assistant@tridentmediagroup.com (fiction: literary fiction, crime fiction, science fiction and fantasy, children's, thriller/suspense; nonfiction: narrative nonfiction, science, history, biography, current events, memoirs, finance, pop culture); **Erica Spellman-Silverman**; **Ellen Levine**, levine.assistant@tridentmediagroup.com (popular commercial fiction and compelling nonfiction, including memoir, popular culture, narrative nonfiction, history, politics, biography, science, the odd quirky book); **Mark Gottlieb** (fiction: science fiction, fantasy, young adult, graphic novels, historical, middle-grade, mystery, romance, suspense, thriller; nonfiction: business, finance, history, religious, health, cookbooks, sports, African-American, biography, memoir, travel, mind/body/spirit, narrative nonfiction, science, technology); **Alexander Slater**, aslater@tridentmdiagroup.com (children's, middle-grade, young adult fiction); **Amanda O'Connor**, aoconnor@tridentmediagroup.com; **Tara Carberry**, tcarberry@tridentmediagroup.com (women's commercial fiction, romance, New Adult, young adult, select nonfiction); **Alexa Stark**, astark@tridentmediagroup.com (literary fiction, upmarket commercial fiction, young adult, memoir, narrative nonfiction, popular science, cultural criticism, women's issues).

REPRESENTS Considers these nonfiction areas: biography, business, cooking, creative nonfiction, current affairs, economics, health, history, memoirs, military, popular culture, politics, religious, science, sports, technology, travel, women's issues, young adult, middle-grade. **Considers these fiction areas:** commercial, crime, fantasy, historical, juvenile, literary, middle-grade, mystery, New Adult, paranormal, picture books, romance, science fiction, suspense, thriller, women's, young adult.

☞ Actively seeking new or established authors in a variety of fiction and nonfiction genres.

HOW TO CONTACT Submit through the agency's online submission form on the agency website. Query only one agent at a time. If you e-query, include no attachments. Accepts simultaneous submissions.

TIPS "If you have any questions, please check FAQ page before e-mailing us."

UNION LITERARY

30 Vandam St., Suite 5A, New York NY 10013. (212)255-2112. **E-mail:** info@unionliterary.com. **E-mail:** submissions@unionliterary.com. **Website:** http://unionliterary.com. Member of AAR, signatory of WGA.

○ "Prior to becoming an agent, Trena Keating was editor-in-chief of Dutton and associate publisher of Plume, both imprints of Penguin, senior editor at HarperCollins, and humanities assistant at Stanford University Press.

MEMBER AGENTS Trena Keating, tk@unionliterary.com (fiction and nonfiction, specifically a literary novel with an exotic setting, a young adult/middle-grade journey or transformation novel, a distinctly modern novel with a female protagonist, a creepy page-turner, a quest memoir that addresses larger issues, nonfiction based on primary research or a unique niche, a great essayist, a voicy writer who is a great storyteller or makes her laugh); **Sally Wofford-Girand**, swg@unionliterary.com (history, memoir, women's issues, cultural studies, gripping literary fiction); **Jenni Ferrari-Adler**, jenni@unionliterary.com (fiction, cookbook/food, young adult and middle-grade, narrative nonfiction); **Christina Clifford**, christina@unionliterary.com (literary fiction, international fiction, narrative nonfiction, specifically historical biography, memoir, business, science); **Shaun Dolan**, sd@unionliterary.com (muscular and lyrical literary fiction, narrative nonfiction, memoir, pop culture, sports narratives).

☞ "Union Literary is a full-service boutique agency specializing in literary fiction, popular fiction, narrative nonfiction, memoir, social history, business and general big idea books, popular science, cookbooks and food writing." The agency does not represent romance, poetry, science fiction or illustrated books.

HOW TO CONTACT Nonfiction submissions: include a query letter, a proposal and a sample chapter. Fiction submissions: should include a query letter, synopsis, and either sample pages or full ms. "Due to the high volume of submissions we receive, we will only be in contact regarding projects that feel like a match for the respective agent." Accepts simultaneous submissions. Responds in 1 month.

RECENT SALES *The Sunlit Night*, by Rebecca Dinerstein; *Dept. of Speculation*, by Jenny Offill; *Mrs. Houdini*, by Victoria Kelly.

◉ UNITED TALENT AGENCY

142 W. 57th St., 6th Floor, New York NY 10019. (212)581-3100. **Website:** www.theagencygroup.com. **Contact:** Marc Gerald.

○ Prior to becoming an agent, Mr. Gerald owned and ran an independent publishing and entertainment agency.

MEMBER AGENTS Marc Gerald (no queries); **Juliet Mushens**, UK Literary division, juliet.mushens@unitedtalent.com (high-concept novels, thriller, young adult, historical fiction, literary fiction, psychological suspense, reading group fiction, science fiction, fantasy); **Sasha Raskin**, sasah.raskin@unitedtalent.com (popular science, business books, historical narrative nonfiction, narrative and/or literary nonfiction, historical fiction, genre fiction like science fiction but when it fits the crossover space and isn't strictly confined to its genre); **Sarah Manning**, sarah.manning@unitedtalent.com (crime, thriller, historical fiction, commercial women's fiction, accessible literary fiction, fantasy, young adult); **Diana Beaumont**, UK Literary division, diana.beaumont@unitedtalent.com (accessible literary fiction with a strong hook, historical fiction, crime, thriller, women's commercial fiction that isn't too marshmallowy, cookery, lifestyle, celebrity books, memoir with a distinctive voice).

REPRESENTS nonfiction, novels. **Considers these nonfiction areas:** business, cooking, history, memoirs, popular science, narrative nonfiction, literary nonfiction, lifestyle, celebrity. **Considers these fiction areas:** commercial, crime, fantasy, historical, literary, science fiction, suspense, thriller, women's, young adult.

HOW TO CONTACT To query Juliet: Please send your cover letter, first 3 chapters and synopsis by e-mail. Juliet replies to all submissions, and aims to respond within 8-12 weeks of receipt of e-mail. To query Sasha: e-query. To query Sarah: Please send you cover letter in the body of your e-mail with synopsis and first 3 chapters by e-mail. She responds to all submissions within 8-12 weeks. Accepts simultaneous submissions.

THE UNTER AGENCY

23 W. 73rd St., Suite 100, New York NY 10023. (212)401-4068. **E-mail:** jennifer@theunteragency.com. **Website:** www.theunteragency.com. **Contact:** Jennifer Unter. Estab. 2008. Member of AAR, Women Media Group.

◯ Ms. Unter began her book publishing career in the editorial department at Henry Holt & Co. She later worked at the Karpfinger Agency while she attended law school. She then became an associate at the entertainment firm of Cowan, DeBaets, Abrahams & Sheppard LLP where she practiced primarily in the areas of publishing and copyright law.

REPRESENTS nonfiction, fiction, novels, short story collections, juvenile books. **Considers these nonfiction areas:** animals, art, autobiography, biography, cooking, creative nonfiction, current affairs, diet/nutrition, environment, foods, health, history, how-to, humor, juvenile nonfiction, law, memoirs, popular culture, politics, spirituality, sports, travel, true crime, women's issues, young adult, nature subjects. **Considers these fiction areas:** action, adventure, cartoon, commercial, family saga, inspirational, juvenile, mainstream, middle-grade, mystery, paranormal, picture books, thriller, women's, young adult.

⚬━ This agency specializes in children's, nonfiction, and quality fiction.

HOW TO CONTACT Send an e-query. There is also an online submission form. If you do not hear back from this agency within 3 months, consider that a no. Accepts simultaneous submissions. Responds in 3 months.

RECENT SALES A full list of recent sales/titles is available on the agency website.

UPSTART CROW LITERARY

244 Fifth Avenue, 11th Floor, New York NY 10001. **E-mail:** danielle.submission@gmail.com. **Website:** www.upstartcrowliterary.com. **Contact:** Danielle Chiotti, Alexandra Penfold. Estab. 2009. Member of AAR. Signatory of WGA.

MEMBER AGENTS Michael Stearns (not accepting submissions); **Danielle Chiotti** (all genres of young adult and middle-grade fiction; adult up-market commercial fiction [not considering romance, mystery/suspense/thriller, science fiction, horror, or erotica]; nonfiction in the areas of narrative/memoir, lifestyle, relationships, humor, current events, food, wine, and cooking); **Ted Malawer** (not accepting submissions); **Alexandra Penfold** (not accepting submissions); **Susan Hawk** (books for children and teens only).

REPRESENTS **Considers these nonfiction areas:** cooking, current affairs, foods, humor, memoirs. **Considers these fiction areas:** commercial, mainstream, middle-grade, picture books, young adult.

HOW TO CONTACT Submit a query and 20 pages pasted into an e-mail. Accepts simultaneous submissions.

VERITAS LITERARY AGENCY

601 Van Ness Ave., Opera Plaza, Suite E, San Francisco CA 94102. (415)647-6964. **Fax:** (415)647-6965. **E-mail:** submissions@veritasliterary.com. **Website:** www.veritasliterary.com. **Contact:** Katherine Boyle. Member of AAR, the Author's Guild, SCBWI.

MEMBER AGENTS Katherine Boyle, kboyle@veritasliterary.com (literary fiction, middle-grade, young adult, narrative nonfiction/memoir, historical fiction, crime/suspense, history, pop culture, popular science, business/career); **Michael Carr**, michael@veritasliterary.com (historical fiction, women's fiction, science fiction and fantasy, nonfiction).

REPRESENTS nonfiction, novels. **Considers these nonfiction areas:** business, history, memoirs, popular culture, women's issues. **Considers these fiction areas:** commercial, crime, fantasy, historical, literary, middle-grade, New Adult, science fiction, suspense, women's, young adult.

HOW TO CONTACT This agency accepts short queries or proposals via e-mail only. "Fiction: Please include a cover letter listing previously published work, a 1-page summary and the first 5 pages in the body of the e-mail (not as an attachment). Nonfiction: If you are sending a proposal, please include an author biography, an overview, a chapter-by-chapter summary, and an analysis of competitive titles. We do our best to review all queries within 4-6 weeks; however, if you have not heard from us in 12 weeks, consider that a no." Accepts simultaneous submissions.

WALES LITERARY AGENCY, INC.

1508 10th Ave. E. #401, Seattle WA 98102. (206)284-7114. **E-mail:** waleslit@waleslit.com. **Website:** www.waleslit.com. **Contact:** Elizabeth Wales; Neal Swain. Estab. 1990. Member of AAR, the Authors Guild.

○ Prior to becoming an agent, Ms. Wales worked at Oxford University Press and Viking Penguin.

MEMBER AGENTS Elizabeth Wales; Neal Swain. **REPRESENTS** nonfiction, fiction, novels.

⊶ This agency specializes in quality mainstream fiction and narrative nonfiction. "We're looking for more narrative nonfiction writing about nature, science, and animals." Does not handle screenplays, children's picture books, genre fiction, or most category nonfiction, such as self-help or how-to books.

HOW TO CONTACT E-query with no attachments. Submission guidelines can be found at the agency website along with a list of current clients and titles. Accepts simultaneous submissions. Responds in 2 weeks to queries, 2 months to mss.

TERMS Agent receives 15% commission on domestic sales; 20% commission on foreign sales.

RECENT SALES *Mozart's Starling*, by Lyanda Lynn Haupt (Little, Brown); *The Witness Tree*, by Lynda Mapes (Bloomsbury USA); *Growing a Revolution*, by David Montgomery (W.W. Norton); *Victory Parade*, by Leela Corman (Grand Central Publishing); *Find the Good*, by Heather Lende (Algonquin).

TIPS "We are especially interested in work that espouses a progressive cultural or political view, projects a new voice, or simply shares an important, compelling story. We also encourage writers living in the Pacific Northwest, West Coast, Alaska, and Pacific Rim countries, and writers from historically underrepresented groups, such as gay and lesbian writers and writers of color, to submit work (but do not discourage writers outside these areas). Most important,

whether in fiction or nonfiction, the agency is looking for talented storytellers."

WAXMAN LEAVELL LITERARY AGENCY, INC.

443 Park Ave. S, Suite 1004, New York NY 10016. (212)675-5556. **Fax:** (212)675-1381. **Website:** www.waxmanleavell.com.

MEMBER AGENTS Scott Waxman (nonfiction: history, biography, health and science, adventure, business, inspirational sports); Byrd Leavell (narrative nonfiction, sports, humor, select commercial fiction); Larry Kirschbaum (fiction and nonfiction; select self-published breakout books); Rachel Vogel (nonfiction: subject-driven narratives, memoirs and biography, journalism, popular culture, the occasional humor and gift book; selective fiction); Cassie Hanjian (New Adult novels, plot-driven commercial and upmarket women's fiction, historical fiction, psychological suspense, cozy mystery, contemporary romance; for nonfiction, mind/body/spirit, self-help, health and wellness, inspirational memoir, food/wine (narrative and prescriptive), a limited number of accessible cookbooks); Fleetwood Robbins (fantasy and speculative fiction—all subgenres); Molly O'Neill (middle-grade and young adult fiction and picture book author/illustrators, and—more selectively—narrative nonfiction [including children's/YA/Middle-grade, pop science/pop culture, lifestyle/food/travel/cookbook projects by authors with well-established platforms]).

REPRESENTS nonfiction, novels. **Considers these nonfiction areas:** biography, business, foods, health, history, humor, inspirational, memoirs, popular culture, science, sports, adventure. **Considers these fiction areas:** fantasy, historical, literary, mainstream, middle-grade, mystery, paranormal, romance, science fiction, suspense, thriller, urban fantasy, women's, young adult.

HOW TO CONTACT To submit a project, please send a query letter only via e-mail to one of the addresses included on the website. Do not send attachments, though for fiction you may include 5-10 pages of your manuscript in the body of your e-mail. "Due to the high volume of submissions, agents will reach out to you directly if interested. The typical time range for consideration is 6-8 weeks." "Please do not query more than 1 agent at our agency simultaneously." (To see the types of projects each agent is looking for, refer to the Agent Biography page on website.) Use these e-mails: scottsubmit@waxmanleavell.com, byrdsubmit@waxmanleavell.com, rachelsubmit@waxmanleavell.com, larrysubmit@waxmanleavell.com, cassiesubmit@waxmanleavell.com, mollysubmit@waxmanleavell.com. Accepts simultaneous submissions.

TERMS Agent receives 15% commission on domestic sales; 10% commission on foreign sales. Offers written contract; 2-month notice must be given to terminate contract.

THE WEINGEL-FIDEL AGENCY

310 E. 46th St., 21E, New York NY 10017. (212)599-2959. **Contact:** Loretta Weingel-Fidel.

○ Prior to opening her agency, Ms. Weingel-Fidel was a psychoeducational diagnostician.

REPRESENTS novels. **Considers these nonfiction areas:** art, autobiography, biography, dance, memoirs, music, psychology, science, sociology, technology, women's issues, women's studies, investigative journalism. **Considers these fiction areas:** literary, mainstream.

➤ This agency specializes in commercial and literary fiction and nonfiction. Does not want to receive childrens books, self-help, science fiction, or fantasy.

HOW TO CONTACT Accepts writers by referral only. *No unsolicited mss.* Accepts simultaneous submissions.

TERMS Agent receives 15% commission on domestic sales; 20% commission on foreign sales. Offers written contract, binding for 1 year with automatic renewal.

TIPS "A very small, selective list enables me to work very closely with my clients to develop and nurture talent. I only take on projects and writers about which I am extremely enthusiastic."

WELLS ARMS LITERARY

New York NY **E-mail:** info@wellsarms.com. **Website:** www.wellsarms.com. Wells Arms Literary represents children's book authors and illustrators to the trade children's book market. Estab. 2013. Member of AAR, SCBWI, Society of Illustrators. Represents 25 clients.

○ Victoria's career began as an editor at Dial Books for Young Readers, then G. P. Putnam's Sons and then as the founding editorial director and Associate Publisher of Bloomsbury USA's Children's Division. She opened the agency in 2013.

REPRESENTS nonfiction, fiction, novels, juvenile books, children's book illustrators. **Considers these nonfiction areas:** juvenile nonfiction, young adult. **Considers these fiction areas:** juvenile, middle-grade, New Adult, picture books, young adult.

➤ "We focus on books for young readers of all ages: board books, picture books, readers, chapter books, middle-grade, and young adult fiction." Actively seeking middle-grade, young adult, magical realism, contemporary, romance, fantasy. "We do not represent to the textbook, magazine, adult romance or fine art markets."

HOW TO CONTACT E-query. Put "query" and your title in your e-mail subject line addressed to info@wellsarms.com. Accepts simultaneous submissions. Tries to respond in a month's time. If no response, assume it's a no.

WERNICK & PRATT AGENCY

E-mail: submissions@wernickpratt.com. **Website:** www.wernickpratt.com. **Contact:** Marcia Wernick, Linda Pratt, Emily Mitchell. Member of AAR, signatory of WGA, SCBWI

○ Prior to co-founding Wernick & Pratt Agency, Ms. Wernick worked at the Sheldon Fogelman Agency, in subsidiary rights, advancing to director of subsidiary rights. Ms. Pratt also worked at the Sheldon Fogelman Agency. Emily Mitchell began her publishing career at Sheldon Fogelman Agency and then spent eleven years as an editor at Charlesbridge Publishing.

MEMBER AGENTS Marcia Wernick, Linda Pratt, Emily Mitchell.

REPRESENTS juvenile books. **Considers these fiction areas:** middle-grade, young adult.

➤ "Wernick & Pratt Agency specializes in children's books of all genres, from picture books through young adult literature and everything in between. We represent both authors and illustrators. We do not represent authors of adult books." Wants people who both write and illustrate in the picture book genre; humorous young chapter books with strong voice, and which are unique and compelling; middle-grade/YA novels, both literary and commercial. No picture book mss of more than 750 words, or mood pieces; work specifically targeted to the educational market; fiction about the American Revolution, Civil War, or World War II unless it is told from a very unique perspective.

HOW TO CONTACT Submit via e-mail only to submissions@wernickpratt.com. "Please indicate to which agent you are submitting." Detailed submission guidelines available on website. "Submissions will only be responded to further if we are interested in them. If you do not hear from us within 6 weeks of your submission, it should be considered declined." Accepts simultaneous submissions. Responds in 6 weeks.

✪ WESTWOOD CREATIVE ARTISTS, LTD.

94 Harbord St., Toronto ON M5S 1G6 Canada. (416)964-3302. **E-mail:** wca_office@wcaltd.com. **Website:** www.wcaltd.com. Represents 350+ clients. **MEMBER AGENTS** Jack Babad; Lix Culotti (foreign contracts and permissions); **Carolyn Ford** (literary fiction, commerical, women's/literary crossover, thriller, serious narrative nonfiction, pop culture); **Jackie Kaiser** (president and CEO); **Michael A. Levine**; **Linda McKnight**; **Hilary McMahon** (fiction, nonfiction, children's); **John Pearce** (fiction, nonfiction); **Meg Tobin-O'Drowsky**; **Bruce Westwood**. **REPRESENTS** nonfiction, fiction, novels. **Considers these nonfiction areas:** biography, current affairs, history, parenting, science, journalism, practical nonfiction. **Considers these fiction areas:** commercial, juvenile, literary, thriller, women's, young adult.

> ☛ "We take on children's and young adult writers very selectively. The agents bring their diverse interests to their client lists, but are generally looking for authors with a mastery of language, a passionate, expert or original perspective on their subject, and a gift for storytelling. Please note that WCA does not represent screenwriters, and our agents are not currently seeking poetry or children's picture book submissions."

HOW TO CONTACT E-query only. Include credentials, synopsis, and no more than 10 pages. No attachments. Accepts simultaneous submissions. **RECENT SALES** *Ellen in Pieces*, by Caroline Adderson (HarperCollins); *Paper Swan*, by Ann Y.K. Choi (Simon & Schuster); *Hope Makes Love*, by Trevor Cole (Cormorant). **TIPS** "We will reject outright complete, unsolicited manuscripts, or projects that are presented poorly in the query letter. We prefer to receive exclusive submissions and request that you do not query more than one agent at the agency simultaneously. It's often best if you approach WCA after you have accumulated some publishing credits."

WHIMSY LITERARY AGENCY, LLC

49 N. 8th St., 6G, Brooklyn NY 11249. (212)674-7162. **E-mail:** whimsynyc@aol.com. **Website:** whimsyliteraryagency.com. **Contact:** Jackie Meyer. Whimsy Literary Agency LLC, specializes in nonfiction books and authors that educate, entertain, and inspire people. Represents 30 clients.

> ☿ Prior to becoming an agent, Ms. Meyer was a VP at Warner Books (now Grand Central/Hachette) for 20 years.

MEMBER AGENTS Jackie Meyer; Lenore Skomal (literary fiction accepted). **REPRESENTS** nonfiction, fiction. **Considers these nonfiction areas:** art, autobiography, biography, business, child guidance, cooking, design, education, foods, health, history, how-to, humor, inspirational, interior design, literature, memoirs, money, New Age, photography, popular culture, psychology, self-help, software, spirituality, women's issues. **Considers these fiction areas:** commercial, glitz, inspirational, literary, mainstream, metaphysical, New Age, paranormal, psychic. **HOW TO CONTACT** Send your proposal via e-mail to whimsynyc@aol.com (include your media platform, table of contents with full description of each chapter). First-time authors: "We appreciate proposals that are professional and complete. Please consult the many fine books available on writing book proposals. We are not considering poetry, or screenplays. Please Note: Due to the volume of queries and submissions, we are unable to respond unless they are of interest to us." Accepts simultaneous submissions. Responds "quickly, but only if interested" to queries. *Does not accept unsolicited mss.* Obtains most new clients through recommendations from others, solicitations. **TERMS** Agent receives 15% commission on domestic sales; 20% commission on foreign sales. Offers written contract.

WOLF LITERARY SERVICES, LLC

E-mail: queries@wolflit.com. **Website:** wolflit.com. "Wolf Literary Services LLC is a full-service literary agency specializing in dynamic, quirky books written for all ages. As an agency, we have a deep respect for the place where 'low' art meets high art; we like a good story, regardless of genre." Estab. 2008. Member of AAR. Signatory of WGA.

MEMBER AGENTS Kirsten Wolf (no queries); **Kate Johnson** (literary fiction, particularly character-driven stories, psychological investigations, modern-day fables, international tales, magical realism, historical fiction; nonfiction: food, feminism, parenting, art, travel and the environment, loves working with journalists); **Allison Devereux** (literary and upmarket commercial fiction; nonfiction, including examinations of contemporary culture, pop science, modern feminist perspectives; humor and blog-to-book; illustrated novels or memoir; narrative nonfiction that uses a particular niche topic to explore larger truths about our culture).

REPRESENTS Considers these nonfiction areas: art, creative nonfiction, environment, foods, history, humor, memoirs, parenting, science, travel, women's issues. **Considers these fiction areas:** commercial, historical, literary, magical realism.

HOW TO CONTACT To submit a project, please send a query letter along with a 50-page writing sample (for fiction) or a detailed proposal (for nonfiction) to queries@wolflit.com. Samples may be submitted as an attachment or embedded in the body of the e-mail. Accepts simultaneous submissions.

RECENT SALES *A Criminal Magic*, by Lee Kelly (Saga Press/Simon & Schuster); *Shallow Graves*, by Kali Wallace (Katherine Tegen Books/HarperCollins); *A Hard and Heavy Thing*, by Matthew J. Hefti (Tyrus Books); *What Was Mine*, by Helen Klein Ross (S&S/Gallery); *The Extra Woman*, by Joanna Scutts (Liveright/Norton); *For the Record*, by Charlotte Huang (Delacorte).

WOLFSON LITERARY AGENCY

P.O. Box 266, New York NY 10276. **E-mail:** query@wolfsonliterary.com. **Website:** www.wolfsonliterary.com. **Contact:** Michelle Wolfson. Estab. 2007. Adheres to AAR canon of ethics.

○   Prior to forming her own agency in December 2007, Ms. Wolfson spent 2 years with Artists & Artisans, Inc. and 2 years with Ralph Vicinanza, Ltd.

REPRESENTS nonfiction, fiction. **Considers these fiction areas:** commercial, mainstream, New Adult, romance, thriller, women's, young adult.

⟿   Actively seeking commercial fiction: young adult, mainstream, women's fiction, romance. "I am not taking on new nonfiction clients at this time."

HOW TO CONTACT E-queries only. Accepts simultaneous submissions. Responds only if interested. Positive response is generally given within 2-4 weeks. Responds in 3 months to mss. Obtains most new clients through queries or recommendations from others.

TERMS Agent receives 15% commission on domestic sales; 25% commission on foreign sales. Offers written contract; 30-day notice must be given to terminate contract.

TIPS "Be persistent."

WORDSERVE LITERARY GROUP

7061 S. University Blvd., Suite 307, Centennial CO 80122. **E-mail:** admin@wordserveliterary.com. **Website:** www.wordserveliterary.com. **Contact:** Greg Johnson. WordServe Literary Group was founded in 2003 by veteran literary agent Greg Johnson. Represents 100 clients.

○   Prior to becoming an agent in 1994, Mr. Johnson was a magazine editor and freelance writer of more than 20 books and 200 articles.

MEMBER AGENTS Greg Johnson, Nick Harrison, Sarah Freese.

REPRESENTS nonfiction, fiction, novels. **Considers these nonfiction areas:** biography, business, current affairs, diet/nutrition, history, inspirational, literature, memoirs, military, parenting, religious, self-help, sports, war, women's issues. **Considers these fiction areas:** historical, inspirational, literary, mainstream, religious, spiritual, suspense, thriller, women's, young adult.

⟿   Materials with a faith-based angle. No gift books, poetry, short stories, screenplays, graphic novels, children's picture books, science fiction or fantasy. Please do not send mss that are more than 120,000 words.

HOW TO CONTACT E-query admin@wordserveliterary.com. In the subject line, include the word "query." All queries should include the following three elements: a pitch for the book, information about you and your platform (for nonfiction) or writing background (for fiction), and the first 5 (or so) pages of the manuscript pasted into the e-mail. Please view our website for full guidelines: http://

www.wordserveliterary.com/submission-guidlines/. Accepts simultaneous submissions. Response within 60 days. Obtains most new clients through recommendations from others.

TERMS Agent receives 15% commission on domestic sales; 10-15% commission on foreign sales. Offers written contract; up to 60-day notice must be given to terminate contract.

TIPS "We are looking for good proposals, great writing and authors willing to market their books. We specialize in projects with a faith element bent. See the website before submitting."

WRITERS HOUSE

21 W. 26th St., New York NY 10010. (212)685-2400. **Fax:** (212)685-1781. **Website:** www.writershouse. com. Estab. 1973. Member of AAR.

MEMBER AGENTS Amy Berkower, Stephen Barr, Susan Cohen, Dan Conaway, Lisa DiMona, Susan Ginsburg, Susan Golomb, Merrilee Heifetz, Brianne Johnson, Daniel Lazar, Simon Lipskar, Steven Malk, Jodi Reamer, Esq., Robin Rue, Rebecca Sherman, Geri Thoma, Albert Zuckerman, Alec Shane, Stacy Testa, Victoria Doherty-Munro, Beth Miller, Andrea Morrison. Soumeya Roberts.

REPRESENTS nonfiction, novels. **Considers these nonfiction areas:** biography, business, cooking, economics, history, how-to, juvenile nonfiction, memoirs, parenting, psychology, science, self-help. **Considers these fiction areas:** commercial, fantasy, juvenile, literary, mainstream, middle-grade, picture books, science fiction, women's, young adult.

- This agency specializes in all types of popular fiction and nonfiction, for both adult and juvenile books as well as illustrators. Does not want to receive scholarly, professional, poetry, plays, or screenplays.

HOW TO CONTACT Individual agent e-mail addresses are available on the website. "Please e-mail us a query letter, which includes your credentials, an explanation of what makes your book unique and special, and a synopsis. Some agents within our agency have different requirements. Please consult their individual Publisher's Marketplace (PM) profile for details. We respond to all queries, generally within 6-8 weeks." If you prefer to submit by mail, address it to an individual agent, and please include SASE for our reply. (If submitting to Steven Malk: Writers House, 7660 Fay Ave., #338H, La Jolla, CA

92037.) Accepts simultaneous submissions. "We respond to all queries, generally within 6-8 weeks." Obtains most new clients through recommendations from authors and editors.

TERMS Agent receives 15% commission on domestic sales; 20% commission on foreign sales. Offers written contract, binding for 1 year. Agency charges fees for copying mss/proposals and overseas airmail of books.

TIPS "Do not send mss. Write a compelling letter. If you do, we'll ask to see your work. Follow submission guidelines and please do not simultaneously submit your work to more than one Writers House agent."

WRITERS' REPRESENTATIVES, LLC

116 W. 14th St., 11th Floor, New York NY 10011-7305. **E-mail:** transom@writersreps.com. **Website:** www.writersreps.com. **Contact:** Glen Hartley. Estab. 1985. Represents 100 clients.

- Prior to becoming an agent, Ms. Chu was a lawyer. Mr. Hartley worked at Simon & Schuster, Harper & Row, and Cornell University Press.

MEMBER AGENTS Lynn Chu, Glen Hartley.

REPRESENTS nonfiction, fiction.

- Serious nonfiction and quality fiction. No motion picture or television screenplays. "We generally will not consider science fiction or children's or young adult fiction unless it aspires to serious literature."

HOW TO CONTACT Query with SASE or by e-mail. Send ms, full CV, list of previously published works, and a table of contents. Advise on submission if the projects has been sent to other agents and if it was previously submitted to publishers. Accepts simultaneous submissions.

TERMS Agents receive 15% on domestic sales; 10% for screenwriting or other consulting services. No reading fee. "We may charge clients the costs of out-of-house photocopying or for buying books or galleys for manuscript or proposal submissions, messengers, long-distance telephone and long-distance courier services such as FedEx. Any other expenses must be approved by the author. We do our best to minimize all expenses."

JASON YARN LITERARY AGENCY

3544 Broadway, No. 68, New York NY 10031. **E-mail:** jason@jasonyarnliteraryagency.com. **Website:** www.jasonyarnliteraryagency.com. Member of AAR. Signatory of WGA.

REPRESENTS nonfiction, fiction. **Considers these nonfiction areas:** creative nonfiction, current affairs, foods, history, science. **Considers these fiction areas:** commercial, fantasy, literary, middle-grade, science fiction, suspense, thriller, young adult, graphic novels, comics.

HOW TO CONTACT Please e-mail your query to jason@jasonyarnliteraryagency.com with the word "Query" in the subject line, and please paste the first 10 pages of your manuscript or proposal into the text of your e-mail. Do not send any attachments. "Visit the About page for information on what we are interested in, and please note that JYLA does not accept queries for film, TV, or stage scripts." Accepts simultaneous submissions.

KAREN GANTZ ZAHLER LITERARY MANAGEMENT AND ATTORNEY AT LAW

(212)734-3619. **E-mail:** karen@karengantzlit.com. **Website:** www.karengantzlit.com. **Contact:** Karen Gantz.

○ Prior to her current position, Ms. Gantz practiced law at two law firms, wrote two cookbooks, *Taste of New York* (Addison-Wesley) and *Superchefs* (John Wiley & Sons). She also participated in a Presidential Advisory Committee on Intellectual Property, U.S. Department of Commerce.

REPRESENTS nonfiction.

⌖ Actively seeking nonfiction.

HOW TO CONTACT Accepting queries and summaries by e-mail only. Check the website for complete submission information, because it is intricate and specific. Accepts simultaneous submissions. Responds in 4-8 weeks to queries.

RECENT SALES *Nevertheless,* by Alec Baldwin (Harper); *The Magic of Math: Solving for X and Figuring Out Why,* by Arthur Benjamin (Basic Books); *The Nixon Effect: How His Presidency has Changed American Politics,* by Douglas Schoen (Encounter Books).

HELEN ZIMMERMANN LITERARY AGENCY

E-mail: submit@zimmagency.com. **Website:** www.zimmermannliterary.com. **Contact:** Helen Zimmermann. Estab. 2003.

○ Prior to opening her agency, Ms. Zimmermann was the director of advertising and promotion at Random House and the events coordinator at an independent bookstore.

REPRESENTS nonfiction, fiction. **Considers these nonfiction areas:** diet and nutrition, health, memoirs, music, sports, women's issues, relationships. **Considers these fiction areas:** literary, mainstream.

⌖ "I am currently concentrating my nonfiction efforts in health and wellness, relationships, popular culture, women's issues, lifestyle, sports, and music. I am also drawn to memoirs that speak to a larger social or historical circumstance, or introduce me to a new phenomenon. And I am always looking for a work of fiction that will keep me up at night!"

HOW TO CONTACT Accepts e-mail queries only. "For nonfiction queries, initial contact should just be a pitch letter. For fiction queries, I prefer a summary, your bio, and the first chapter as text in the e-mail (not as an attachment). If I express interest I will need to see a full proposal for nonfiction and the remainder of the manuscript for fiction." Accepts simultaneous submissions. Responds in 2 weeks to queries, only if interested. Obtains most new clients through recommendations from others, solicitations.

TERMS Agent receives 15% commission on domestic sales. Offers written contract; 30-day notice must be given to terminate contract.

WRITERS CONFERENCES Washington Independent Review of Books Writers Conference, young adultle Writers Conference, American Society of Journalists and Authors Conference, Writer's Digest Conference, LaJolla Writer's Conference, Gulf Coast Writers Conference, Kansas Writers Association Conference, New York Writers Workshop, Self Publishing Book Expo, Burlington Writers Conference, Southern Expressions Writers Conference, Literary Writers Conference, NYC.

WRITERS CONFERENCES

Attending a writers conference that includes agents gives you the opportunity to learn more about what agents do and to show an agent your work. Ideally, a conference should include a panel or two with a number of agents to give writers a sense of the variety of personalities and tastes of different agents.

Not all agents are alike: Some are more personable, and sometimes you simply click better with one agent versus another. When only one agent attends a conference, there is a tendency for every writer at that conference to think, "Ah, this is the agent I've been looking for!" When the number of agents attending is larger, you have a wider group from which to choose, and you may have less competition for the agent's time.

Besides including panels of agents discussing what representation means and how to go about securing it, many of these gatherings also include time—either scheduled or impromptu—to meet briefly with an agent to discuss your work.

If they're impressed with what they see and hear about your work, they will invite you to submit a query, a proposal, a few sample chapters, or possibly your entire manuscript. Some conferences even arrange for agents to review manuscripts in advance and schedule one-on-one sessions during which you can receive specific feedback or advice regarding your work. Such meetings often cost a small fee, but the input you receive is usually worth the price.

Ask writers who attend conferences and they'll tell you that, at the very least, you'll walk away with new knowledge about the industry. At the very best, you'll receive an invitation to send an agent your material!

Many writers try to make it to at least one conference a year, but cost and location can count as much as subject matter when determining which one to attend. There are conferences in almost every state and province that can provide answers to your questions about writing and the publishing industry. Conferences also connect you with a community of other writers. Such connections help you learn about the pros and cons of different agents, and they can also give you a renewed sense of purpose and direction in your own writing.

SUBHEADS

Each listing is divided into subheads to make locating specific information easier. In the first section, you'll find contact information for conference contacts. You'll also learn conference dates, specific focus, and the average number of attendees. Finally, names of agents who will be speaking or have spoken in the past are listed along with details about their availability during the conference. Calling or e-mailing a conference director to verify the names of agents in attendance is always a good idea.

COSTS: Looking at the price of events, plus room and board, may help writers on a tight budget narrow their choices.

ACCOMMODATIONS: Here conferences list overnight accommodations and travel information. Often conferences held in hotels will reserve rooms at a discount rate and may provide a shuttle bus to and from the local airport.

ADDITIONAL INFORMATION: This section includes information on conference-sponsored contests, individual meetings, the availability of brochures, and more.

AGENTS & EDITORS CONFERENCE, WRITERS LEAGUE OF TEXAS

Writers' League of Texas, 611 S. Congress Ave., Suite 200 A-3, Austin TX 78704. (512)499-8914. **E-mail:** michael@writersleague.org. **E-mail:** michael@writersleague.org. **Website:** www.writersleague.org/38/conference. **Contact:** Michael Noll, program director. Estab. 1982. Annual conference held in summer. 2017 dates: June 30-July 2. "This standout conference gives each attendee the opportunity to become a publishing insider. Meet more than 25 top agents, editors, and industry professionals through one-on-one consultations and receptions. Get tips and strategies for revising and improving your manuscript from keynote speakers and presenters (including award-winning and best-selling writers)."

COSTS Registration for the 2017 conference opens January 3. Early bird registration: $399 for members and $459 for non-members. After April 30, 2017: $439 for members and $499 for non-members.

ACCOMMODATIONS Discounted rates are available at the conference hotel.

ADDITIONAL INFORMATION Register before March 15 to receive a free consultation with an agent or editor.

ALASKA WRITERS CONFERENCE

Alaska Writers Guild, P.O. Box 670014, Chugiak AK 99567. **E-mail:** alaskawritersguild.awg@gmail.com. **Website:** alaskawritersguild.com. Annual event held in the fall—usually September. Duration: 2 days. There are many workshops and instructional tracks. Sometimes teams up with SCBWI and Alaska Pacific University to offer courses at the event. Literary agents are in attendance each year to hear pitches and meet writers.

ALGONKIAN FIVE DAY NOVEL CAMP

2020 Pennsylvania Ave. NW, Suite 443, Washington DC 20006. **E-mail:** info@algonkianconferences.com. **Website:** algonkianconferences.com. Conference duration: 5 days. Attendance: 12 students maximum per workshop. "During more than 45 hours of actual workshop time, students will engage in those rigorous narrative and complication/plot exercises necessary to produce a publishable manuscript. Genres we work with include general commercial fiction, literary fiction, serious and light women's fiction, mystery/cozy/thriller, science fiction/fantasy, young adult, and memoir/narrative nonfiction. The

three areas of workshop emphasis will be premise, platform, and execution.

AMERICAN CHRISTIAN WRITERS CONFERENCES

P.O. Box 110390, Nashville TN 37222. (800)219-7483 or (615)331-8668. **E-mail:** acwriters@aol.com. **Website:** www.acwriters.com. **Contact:** Reg Forder, director. Estab. 1981. ACW hosts a dozen annual two-day writers conferences and mentoring retreats across America taught by editors and professional freelance writers. These events provide excellent instruction, networking opportunities, and valuable one-on-one time with editors. Open to all forms of Christian writing (fiction, nonfiction, and scriptwriting). Conferences are held between March and November during each year.

COSTS Costs vary and may depend on type of event (conference or mentoring retreat).

ACCOMMODATIONS Special rates are available at the host hotel (usually a major chain like Holiday Inn).

ADDITIONAL INFORMATION E-mail or call for conference brochures.

ANTIOCH WRITERS' WORKSHOP

Antioch Writers' Workshop, c/o Antioch University Midwest, 900 Dayton St., Yellow Springs OH 45387. (937)769-1803. **E-mail:** info@antiochwritersworkshop.com. **Website:** www.antiochwritersworkshop.com. **Contact:** Sharon Short, director. Estab. 1986. Programs are offered year-round; annual conference held in summer. Average attendance: 80. Workshop concentrations: fiction, poetry, personal essay, and memoir. Site: Antioch University Midwest in the Village of Yellow Springs. Literary agents attend. Writers of all levels (beginner to advanced) are warmly welcomed to discover their next steps on their writing paths—whether that's developing craft or preparing to submit for publication. An agent and an editor will be speaking and available for meetings with attendees.

ACCOMMODATIONS Accommodations are available at local hotels and bed-and-breakfasts.

ADDITIONAL INFORMATION The easiest way to contact this event is through the website's contact form.

ASJA ANNUAL WRITERS CONFERENCE

American Society of Journalists and Authors, 355 Lexington Ave., 15th Floor, New York NY 10017 USA. (212)997-0947. **E-mail:** asjaoffice@asja.org, director@asja.org. **Website:** www.asjaconferences.org. **Contact:** Alexandra Owens, executive director. Estab. 1971. Annual conference held in New York each spring. Duration: 2 or 3 days. Average attendance: 600. Covers nonfiction. Site: Roosevelt Hotel in New York. Speakers have included Kitty Kelley, Jennifer Finney Boylan, Daniel Jones, D.T. Max, and more.

COSTS Approximately $300/day, depending on when you sign up. Check website for details.

ACCOMMODATIONS Venue hotel has a block of rooms at discounted conference rate.

ADDITIONAL INFORMATION Conference program available online mid-January. Registration is online only. Sign up for e-mail updates online.

ATLANTA WRITERS CONFERENCE

Atlanta Writers Club, Westin Atlanta Airport Hotel, 4736 Best Road, Atlanta GA 30337. **E-mail:** awconference@gmail.com. **Website:** www.atlantawritersconference.com/about. **Contact:** George Weinstein. Estab. 2008. Annual conference held in spring. 2017 dates: May 12-13. Literary agents and editors are in attendance to take pitches and critique ms samples and query letters. Conference offers a self-editing workshop, instructional sessions with local authors, and separate question-and-answer panels with the agents and editors. Site: Westin Airport Atlanta Hotel.

COSTS Ms critiques are $160 each (2 spots/waitlists maximum). Pitches are $60 each (2 spots/waitlists maximum). There's no charge for waitlists unless a spot opens. Query letter critiques are $60 (1 spot maximum). Other workshops and panels may also cost extra; see website. The "all activities" option is $560 and includes 2 ms critiques, 2 pitches, and 1 of each remaining activity.

ACCOMMODATIONS A block of rooms is reserved at the conference hotel. Booking instructions will be sent in the registration confirmation e-mail.

ADDITIONAL INFORMATION A free shuttle runs between the airport and the hotel.

BALTIMORE WRITERS' CONFERENCE

English Department, Liberal Arts Bldg., Towson University, 8000 York Road, Towson MD 21252. (410)704-5196. **E-mail:** prwr@towson.edu. **Website:** baltimorewritersconference.org. Estab. 1994. Annual conference held in November at Towson University. Conference duration: 1 day. Average attendance: 150-200. Covers all areas of writing and getting published. Held at Towson University. Session topics include fiction, nonfiction, poetry, magazines and journals, and agents and publishers. Sign up the

day of the conference for quick critiques to improve your stories, essays, and poems.

ACCOMMODATIONS Hotels are close by, if required.

ADDITIONAL INFORMATION Writers may register through the website. Send inquiries via e-mail.

BAY TO OCEAN WRITERS CONFERENCE

P.O. Box 1773, Easton MD 21601. (410)482-6337. **E-mail:** info@baytoocean.com. **Website:** www.baytoocean.com. Estab. 1998. Annual conference held the second Saturday in March. Average attendance: 200. Approximately 30 speakers conduct workshops on publishing, agents, editing, marketing, craft, the Internet, poetry, fiction, nonfiction, and freelance writing. Site: Chesapeake College, Rt. 213 and Rt. 50, Wye Mills, on Maryland's historic Eastern Shore. Accessible to individuals with disabilities.

COSTS Adults: $100-120. Students: $55. A paid ms review is also available; details on website. Includes continental breakfast and networking lunch.

ADDITIONAL INFORMATION Registration is on website. Preregistration is required; no registration at door. Conference usually sells out 1 month in advance. Conference is for all levels of writers.

BIG SUR WRITING WORKSHOP

Henry Miller Library, Hwy. 1, Big Sur CA 93920. (831)667-2574. **E-mail:** writing@henrymiller.org. **Website:** bigsurwriting.wordpress.com. Annual workshop focusing on children's writing (picture books, middle-grade, and young adult). Held every spring in Big Sur Lodge in Pfeiffer State Park. Cost of workshop includes meals, lodging, workshop, and Saturday evening reception. This event is helmed by the literary agents of the Andrea Brown Literary Agency. All attendees meet with at least 2 faculty members to have their work critiqued.

BLUE RIDGE MOUNTAINS CHRISTIAN WRITERS CONFERENCE

(800)588-7222. **Website:** www.blueridgeconference.com. **Contact:** Edie Melson, director. Annual retreat held in May at Ridgecrest/LifeWay Conference Center near Asheville, North Carolina. 2017 dates: May 21-25. Duration: Sunday through lunch on Thursday. Average attendance: 350. The conference is a training and networking event for both seasoned and aspiring writers that allows attendees to interact with editors, agents, professional writers, and readers. Workshops and continuing classes in a variety of creative categories are offered.

COSTS $325 for the conference; meal package is $145 per person (12 meals beginning with dinner Sunday and ending with lunch on Thursday). $350 conference fee for those not staying on campus. Room rates vary from $60-$70 per night.

ADDITIONAL INFORMATION For a PDF of the complete schedule (typically posted in April), visit the website.

BOOKS-IN-PROGRESS CONFERENCE

Carnegie Center for Literacy and Learning, 251 W. Second St., Lexington KY 40507. (859)254-4175. **E-mail:** ccll1@carnegiecenterlex.org. **Website:** carnegiecenterlex.org. **Contact:** Laura Whitaker, program director. Estab. 2010. This is an annual writing conference at the Carnegie Center for Literacy and Learning in Lexington, Kentucky. It typically happens in June. "Each conference will offer writing and publishing workshops and includes a keynote presentation." Literary agents are flown in to meet with writers and hear pitches. Website is updated several months prior to each annual event.

ACCOMMODATIONS See website for list of area hotels.

BREAD LOAF ORION ENVIRONMENTAL WRITERS' CONFERENCE

Middlebury College, Middlebury College, Middlebury VT 05753. (802)443-5286. **Fax:** (802)443-2087. **E-mail:** blorion@middlebury.edu. **Website:** www.middlebury. edu/bread-loaf-conferences/blorion. Estab. 2014. Annual specialized conference held in June. Duration: 7 days. Offers workshops for fiction, nonfiction, and poetry. Agents and editors will be in attendance. 2017 dates: June 3-9. Average attendance: 70.

COSTS $2205 for full participants and $1875 for auditors. Both options include room and board.

ACCOMMODATIONS Mountain campus of Middlebury College in Vermont.

ADDITIONAL INFORMATION The event is designed to hone the skills of people interested in producing literary writing about the environment and the natural world. The conference is co-sponsored by the Bread Loaf Writers' Conference, Orion magazine, and Middlebury College's Environmental Studies Program. Application deadline for 2017 conference: February 15. Rolling admissions. Space is limited.

BREAD LOAF IN SICILY WRITERS' CONFERENCE

Middlebury College, Middlebury VT 05753. (802)443-5286. **Fax:** (802)443-2087. **E-mail:** blsicily@middlebury.edu. **Website:** www.middlebury. edu/bread-loaf-conferences/blsicily. Estab. 2011. Annual conference held in September in Erice, Sicily (western coast of the island). Duration: 7 days. Offers workshops for fiction, nonfiction, and poetry. 2017 dates: September 17-23. Average attendance: 32.

COSTS $3,020. Includes the conference program, transfer to and from Palermo Airport, 6 nights of lodging, 3 meals daily (except for Wednesday), wine reception at the readings, and an excursion to the ancient ruins of Segesta. The charge for an additional person is $1,750. There is a $15 application fee and a $300 deposit.

ACCOMMODATIONS Accommodations are single rooms with private bath. Breakfast and lunch are served at the hotel, and dinner is available at select Erice restaurants. A double room is possible for those who would like to be accompanied by a spouse or significant other.

ADDITIONAL INFORMATION Application deadline for 2017 conference: April 15. Rolling admissions. Space is limited.

BREAD LOAF WRITERS' CONFERENCE

Middlebury College, Middlebury VT 05753. (802)443-5286. **Fax:** (802)443-2087. **E-mail:** blwc@ middlebury.edu. **Website:** www.middlebury.edu/ bread-loaf-conferences/bl_writers. Estab. 1926. Annual conference held in late August. 2017 dates: August 16-26. Duration: 10 days. Average attendance: 230. Offers workshops for fiction, nonfiction, and poetry. Agents and editors attend.

COSTS $3,265 for general contributors and $3,130 for auditors. Both options include room and board.

ACCOMMODATIONS Bread Loaf campus of Middlebury College in Ripton, Vermont.

ADDITIONAL INFORMATION The application deadline for the 2017 event is February 15; there is a $15 application fee.

CALIFORNIA CRIME WRITERS CONFERENCE

Sisters in Crime Los Angeles and Southern California Mystery Writers of America, DoubleTree by Hilton Los Angeles-Westside, 6161 W. Centinela Ave., Culver City CA 90230. **E-mail:** ccwconference@gmail.com. **E-mail:** ccwconference@gmail.

com. **Website:** www.ccwconference.org. **Contact:** Rochelle Staab and Sue Ann Jaffarian, 2017 co-chairs. Estab. 1995. Biennial conference usually held in early June. 2017 dates: June 10-11. Average attendance: 200. Two-day conference on mystery and crime writing. Offers craft, forensic, industry news, marketing, and career-building sessions; 2 keynote speakers; author, editor, and agent panels; ms critiques (additional fee); and book signings. 2017 keynote speakers are William Kent Krueger and Hallie Ephron. Breakfast and lunch included both days.

COSTS Early bird registration through January 31: $265. Registration February 1-April 30: $300. Registration May 1-31: $335. Onsite registration: $350.

CAMPBELL CONFERENCE

University of Kansas Gunn Center for the Study of Science Fiction, Wesoce Hall, 1445 Jayhawk Blvd., Lawrence KS 66045. (785)864-2508. **E-mail:** cmckit@ku.edu, cssf@ku.edu. **Website:** www.sfcenter.ku.edu/campbell-conference.htm. Estab. 1985. Annual conference for science fiction, generally held at the University of Kansas. Established in 1985 by James Gunn and currently led by Christopher McKitterick. Writer and editor instructors have included Lou Anders, Bradley Denton, James Gunn, Kij Johnson, John Ordover, Frederik Pohl, Pamela Sargent, and George Zebrowski, and each year the winners of the Campbell and Sturgeon Memorial Awards participate as guests of honor.

ACCOMMODATIONS Housing information is available. Several airport shuttle services offer reasonable transportation from the Kansas City International Airport to Lawrence.

ADDITIONAL INFORMATION Admission to the workshop is by submission of an acceptable story. Two additional stories are submitted by the middle of June. These 3 stories are distributed to other participants for critiquing and are the basis for the first week of the workshop. One story is rewritten for the second week, when students also work with guest authors. See website for guidelines. This workshop is intended for writers who have just started to sell their work or need that extra bit of understanding or skill to become a published writer.

CAPE COD WRITERS CENTER ANNUAL CONFERENCE

P.O. Box 408, Osterville MA 02655. **E-mail:** writers@capecodwriterscenter.org. **Website:** www.capecodwriterscenter.org. **Contact:** Nancy Rubin Stuart, ex-ecutive director. Annual conference held in Hyannis, Massachusetts. 2017 dates: August 3-6. Offers workshops in fiction, commercial fiction, creative nonfiction, poetry, memoir, mystery, thrillers, writing for children, social media, screenwriting, promotion, and pitches and queries, as well as agent meetings and ms mentorship with agents and faculty.

COSTS Costs vary, depending on the number of courses selected, beginning at $150. Several scholarships are available.

ACCOMMODATIONS Resort and Conference Center of Hyannis, Massachusetts.

CELEBRATION OF SOUTHERN LITERATURE

Southern Lit Alliance, 301 E. 11th St., Suite 301, Chattanooga TN 37403. (423)267-1218. **Fax:** (866)483-6831. **Website:** www.southernlitalliance.org. Biennial conference held in odd-numbered years. "The Celebration of Southern Literature stands out because of its unique collaboration with the Fellowship of Southern Writers, an organization founded by towering literary figures like Eudora Welty, Cleanth Brooks, Walker Percy, and Robert Penn Warren to recognize and encourage literature in the South. The Fellowship awards 11 literary prizes and inducts new members, making this event the place to discover up-and-coming voices in Southern literature. The Southern Lit Alliance's Celebration of Southern Literature attracts more than 1,000 readers and writers from all over the United States. It strives to maintain an informal atmosphere where conversations will thrive, inspired by a common passion for the written word. The Southern Lit Alliance (formerly the Arts & Education Council) started as one of 12 pilot agencies founded by a Ford Foundation grant in 1952. The Alliance is the only organization of the 12 still in existence. The Southern Lit Alliance celebrates Southern writers and readers through community education and innovative literary arts experiences."

CHICAGO WRITERS CONFERENCE

E-mail: mare@chicagowritersconference.org. **Website:** chicagowritersconference.org. **Contact:** Mare Swallow. Estab. 2011. Annual conference held in fall (typically September or October). The event brings together a variety of publishing professionals (agents, editors, and authors) and several Chicago literary, writing, and bookselling groups. Often sells out. Past speakers have included *New York Times* best-selling author Sara Paretsky, children's author Allan Woodrow, young adult author Erica O'Rourke, novelist Eric Charles May, and novelist Loretta Nyhan.

CHRISTOPHER NEWPORT UNIVERSITY WRITERS' CONFERENCE & WRITING CONTEST

(757)269-4368. **E-mail:** eleanor.taylor@cnu.edu. **Website:** writers.cnu.edu. Estab. 1981. Annual conference held in spring. This is a working conference. Presentations made by editors, agents, fiction writers, poets, and more. Breakout sessions in fiction, nonfiction, poetry, juvenile fiction, and publishing. Previous panels have included publishing, proposal writing, and Internet research.

ACCOMMODATIONS Provides list of area hotels.

CLARION WEST WRITERS WORKSHOP

P.O. Box 31264, Seattle WA 98103. (206)322-9083. **E-mail:** info@clarionwest.org. **Website:** www.clarionwest.org. **Contact:** Nelle Graham, workshop director. Clarion West is an intensive 6-week workshop for writers preparing for professional careers in science fiction and fantasy held annually in Seattle, usually from mid-June through the end of July. Average attendance: 18. Held near the University of Washington. Deadline for applications is March 1. Instructors are well-known writers and editors in the field.

COSTS $4,200 (for tuition, housing, and most meals). Limited scholarships are available based on financial need. Students can apply by mail or e-mail and must submit 20-30 pages of ms with 4-page biography and $60 fee ($35 if received by February 10).

ACCOMMODATIONS Students stay on-site in workshop housing at one of the University of Washington's sorority houses.

ADDITIONAL INFORMATION Conference information available in fall. For brochure/guidelines, send SASE, visit website, e-mail, or call.

CLARKSVILLE WRITERS CONFERENCE

1123 Madison St., Clarksville TN 37040. (931)551-8870. **E-mail:** artsandheritage@cdelightband.net. **Website:** www.artsandheritage.us/writers. **Contact:** Ellen Kanervo. Annual conference held in the summer at Austin Peay State University. Features a variety of presentations on fiction, nonfiction, and more. Past presenting authors include Tom Franklin, Frye Gaillard, William Gay, Susan Gregg Gilmore, Will Campbell, John Seigenthaler Sr., Alice Randall, George Singleton, Alanna Nash, and Robert Hicks.

"Our presentations and workshops are valuable to writers and interesting to readers."

COSTS Costs available online; prices vary depending on how long attendees stay and if they attend the banquet dinner.

ADDITIONAL INFORMATION Multiple literary agents are flown in to the event every year to meet with writers and take pitches.

COMMUNITY OF WRITERS AT SQUAW VALLEY

Community of Writers at Squaw Valley, P.O. Box 1416, Nevada City CA 95959. (530)470-8440 or (530)583-5200 (summer). **E-mail:** info@communityofwriters.org. **Website:** www.communityofwriters.org. **Contact:** Brett Hall Jones, Executive Director. P.O. Box 2352, Olympic Valley CA 96146 (summer) Estab. 1969.

COSTS Tuition is $1,075, which includes 6 dinners. Limited financial aid is available.

ACCOMMODATIONS The Community of Writers rents houses and condominiums in the Squaw Valley for participants to live in during the week of the conference. Single room (1 participant): $700/week. Double room (twin beds, room shared by conference participant of the same gender): $465/week. Multiple room (bunk beds, room shared with 2 or more participants of the same gender): $295/week. All rooms subject to availability; early requests are recommended. Can arrange airport shuttle pickups for a fee.

DESERT DREAMS WRITERS CONFERENCE

Desert Rose Chapter of Romance Writers of America, P.O. Box 14601, Tempe AZ 85285. **E-mail:** desertdreams@desertroserwa.org. **E-mail:** desertdreams@desertroserwa.org. **Website:** desertroserwa.org/desertdreams. **Contact:** Kris Tualla. Estab. 1986. Annual conference held in summer. 2017 dates: June 1-4. Desert Dreams Writers Conference provides authors of all skill levels, from beginner to multipublished, with the tools to take their writing to the next level. Sessions will include general writing, career development, genre-specific, agent/publisher spotlights, and an agent/editor panel. The conference also offers one-on-one appointments with editors or agents (included in registration), an all-author book signing, and a keynote address.

COSTS $299 for regular registration, which includes 3-1/2 days of sessions plus extra opportunities (see website), 2 sit-down dinners, keynote, and an awards gala announcing the winners of the event's 3 contests.

ACCOMMODATIONS Embassy Suites Phoenix-Scottsdale. "Enter the code DRE to receive the $104 per night conference rate."

ADDITIONAL INFORMATION 2017 keynote speaker: Diana Gabaldon.

DETROIT WORKING WRITERS ANNUAL WRITERS CONFERENCE

Detroit Working Writers, P.O. Box 82395, Rochester MI 48308. **E-mail:** conference@detworkingwriters.org. **Website:** dww-writers-conference.org. Estab. 1961. Annual conference held in spring. Site: Michigan State University Management Education Center in Troy, Michigan. Conference is 1 day, with breakfast, luncheon, keynote speaker, 4 breakout sessions, and 3 workshop choices. Details available online. There are 5 writing competitions with cash prizes in different categories: young adult/new adult, creative nonfiction, poetry, children's, and adult fiction. Registration and competition open in January, online.

COSTS Costs vary, depending on early bird registration and membership status within the organization.

ERMA BOMBECK WRITERS' WORKSHOP

University of Dayton, 300 College Park, Dayton OH 45469. (937)229-3255. **E-mail:** erma@udayton.edu. **Website:** humorwriters.org. **Contact:** Teri Rizvi. Estab. 2000. Biennial conference held in even-numbered years. 2018 dates: April 5-7. This is a specialized writing conference for writers of humor (books, articles, essays, blogs, and film/television). "The Bombeck Workshop is the only one in the country devoted to both humor and human interest writing. Through the workshop, the University of Dayton and the Bombeck family honor one of America's most celebrated storytellers and humorists. Over the past decade, the workshop has attracted such household names as Dave Barry, Art Buchwald, Phil Donahue, Roy Blount Jr., Nancy Cartwright, Don Novello, Garrison Keillor, Gail Collins, Connie Schultz, Adriana Trigiani, and Alan Zweibel. The workshop draws approximately 350 writers from around the country and typically sells out very quickly, so don't wait once registration opens."

ADDITIONAL INFORMATION Connect with the event on social media: facebook.com/ermabombeck and @ebww.

FLORIDA CHRISTIAN WRITERS CONFERENCE

Word Weavers International, Inc., 504 Spoonbill Court, Winter Springs FL 32708. (386)295-3902. **E-mail:** floridacwc@aol.com. **Website:** floridacwc.net. Jessica Everson, Taryn Souders **Contact:** Eva Marie Everson and Mark T. Hancock. Estab. 1988. Annual conference held from the last Wednesday of February to the first Sunday in March at Lake Yale Conference Center in Leesburg, Florida. Workshops/classes geared toward all levels, from beginners to published authors. Open to students. Offers 6 keynote addresses, 10 continuing classes (including teen and pastor tracks), and a number of 3-hour workshops, 1-hour workshops, and after-hours workshops. "FCWC brings in the finest the industry has to offer in editors, agents, freelancers, and marketing and media experts." Additionally, the conference offers a book proposal studio, a pitch and networking studio, and advanced critique services.

COSTS Ranges: $275 (daily rate—in advance, includes lunch and dinner; specify days) to $1,495 (attendee and participating spouse/family member staying in same room). Scholarships offered. For more information or to register, go to the conference website.

ACCOMMODATIONS Offers private rooms and double occupancy as well as accommodations for participating and nonparticipating family members. Meals provided, including awards dessert banquet Saturday evening. For those flying into Orlando or Sanford airports, FCWC provides a shuttle to and from the conference center.

FLORIDA ROMANCE WRITERS FUN IN THE SUN CONFERENCE

Florida Romance Writers, P.O. Box 550562, Fort Lauderdale FL 33355. **E-mail:** frwfuninthesun@yahoo.com. **Website:** frwfuninthesunmain.blogspot.com. Estab. 1986. Annual conference held in February. 2017 dates: February 16-20. "Set sail with Florida Romance Writers and our special guests. Inspiring workshops and panels will keep your muse buzzing with plot turns. For those with a well-behaved muse who continues to do her job, schedule an appointment with our guest agents and editors. Also, take advantage of the opportunities to build a website and create a marketing plan while at sea." Space is limited.

GREEN MOUNTAIN WRITERS CONFERENCE

47 Hazel St., Rutland VT 05701. (802)236-6133. **E-mail:** ydaley@sbcglobal.net. **E-mail:** yvonnedaley@me.com. **Website:** vermontwriters.com. **Contact:** Yvonne Daley, director. Estab. 1998. Annual conference held in the summer. Covers fiction, creative nonfiction, poetry, young adult fiction, journalism, nature writing, essay, memoir, personal narrative, and biography. Held at the Mountain Top Inn and Resort, a beautiful lakeside inn located in Chittenden, Vermont. Speakers have included Grace Paley, Ruth Stone, Howard Frank Mosher, Chris Bohjalian, Yvonne Daley, David Huddle, David Budbill, Jeffrey Lent, Verandah Porche, Tom Smith, and Chuck Clarino.

COSTS $525 before April 15; $575 before May 15; $600 before June 1. Partial scholarships are available.

ACCOMMODATIONS Dramatically reduced rates at the Mountain Top Inn and Resort for attendees. Close to other area hotels and bed-and-breakfasts in Rutland County, Vermont.

ADDITIONAL INFORMATION Participants' mss can be read and commented on at a cost. Sponsors contests and publishes a literary magazine featuring work of participants. Brochures available on website or e-mail.

HAMPTON ROADS WRITERS CONFERENCE

P.O. Box 56228, Virginia Beach VA 23456. **E-mail:** hrwriters@cox.net. **Website:** hamptonroadswriters.org. Annual conference held in September. 2017 dates: September 14-16. Workshops cover fiction, nonfiction, memoir, poetry, and the business of getting published. A bookshop, 3 free contests with cash prizes, free evening networking social, and many networking opportunities will be available. Multiple literary agents are in attendance each year to meet with writers and hear 10-minute pitches. Much more information available on the website.

COSTS Costs vary. There are discounts for members, early bird registration, students, and more.

HOUSTON WRITERS GUILD CONFERENCE

P.O. Box 42255, Houston TX 77242. (281)736-7168. **E-mail:** info@houstonwritersguild.org. **Website:** houstonwritersguild.org. This annual conference, organized by the Houston Writers Guild, happens in the spring and has concurrent sessions and tracks on the craft and business of writing. Each year, multiple agents are in attendance taking pitches from writers.

COSTS Costs are different for members and non-members. Costs depend on how many days and events you sign up for.

ADDITIONAL INFORMATION There is a writing contest at the event. There is also a preconference workshop the day before the event, for an additional cost.

IDAHO WRITERS LEAGUE WRITERS' CONFERENCE

601 W. 75 St., Blackfoot ID 83221. (208)684-4200. **Website:** www.idahowritersleague.org. Estab. 1940. Annual floating conference, usually held in September. This conference has at least one agent in attendance every year, along with other writers and presenters.

COSTS Pricing varies. Check website for more information.

🔄 INTERNATIONAL WOMEN'S FICTION FESTIVAL

Via Cappuccini 8E, Matera Italy. (39)0835-312044. **Fax:** (39)333-5857933. **E-mail:** contact@womensfictionfestival.com. **Website:** www.womensfictionfestival.com. **Contact:** Elizabeth Jennings. Estab. 2004. Annual conference usually held in September. 2017 dates: September 28-30. Average attendance: 100. International writers conference with a strong focus on fiction and marketing to international markets. Numerous literary agents and editors are in attendance, both from the United States and from Europe.

COSTS Registration costs vary. Check website for full details.

ACCOMMODATIONS The conference is held at Le Monacelle, a restored 17th century convent. Conference travel agency will find reasonably priced accommodation. A paid shuttle is available from the Bari Airport to the hotel in Matera.

IWWG ANNUAL SUMMER CONFERENCE

(917)720-6959. **E-mail:** iwwgquestions@gmail.com. **Website:** https://iwwg.wildapricot.org/events. Marj Hahne, Interim Director of Operations **Contact:** Dixie King, executive director. Estab. 1976.

ACCOMMODATIONS Check website for updated pricing.

ADDITIONAL INFORMATION Choose from 30 workshops in poetry, fiction, memoir and personal narrative, social action/advocacy, and mind-body-spirit. Critique sessions, book fair, salons, and open readings are also available. No portfolio required.

JACKSON HOLE WRITERS CONFERENCE

P.O. Box 1974, Jackson WY 83001. (307)413-3332. E-mail: connie@blackhen.com. **Website:** jacksonhole-writersconference.com. Estab. 1991. Annual conference held in June. 2017 dates: June 22-24. Conference duration: 3-4 days. Average attendance: 110. Covers fiction, creative nonfiction, and young adult and offers ms critiques from authors, agents, and editors. Agents in attendance will take pitches from writers. Paid ms critique programs are available.

ADDITIONAL INFORMATION Held at the Center for the Arts in Jackson, Wyoming, and online.

JAMES RIVER WRITERS CONFERENCE

2319 E. Broad St., Richmond VA 23223. (804)433-3790. **Fax:** (804)291-1466. **E-mail:** info@jamesriver-writers.org, fallconference@jamesriverwriters.org. **Website:** www.jamesriverwriters.org. Estab. 2003. Annual conference held in October. The event has master classes, agent pitching, editor pitching, critiques, sessions, panels, and more. Previous attending agents have included Kimiko Nakamura, Kaylee Davis, Peter Knapp, and more.

COSTS Check website for updated pricing.

KACHEMAK BAY WRITERS' CONFERENCE

Kachemak Bay Campus-Kenai Peninsula College/University of Alaska Anchorage, Kenai Peninsula College-Kachemak Bay Campus, 533 E. Pioneer Ave., Homer AK 99603. (907)235-7743. **E-mail:** iyconf@uaa.alaska.edu. **Website:** writersconf.kpc.alaska.edu. Annual conference held in June. 2017 dates: June 9-13. 2017 keynote speaker is Jane Smiley. This nationally recognized writing conference features workshops, readings, and panel presentations in fiction, poetry, nonfiction, and the business of writing. There are open mic sessions for conference registrants, evening readings open to the public, agent/editor consultations, and more.

COSTS See the website. Some scholarships available.

ACCOMMODATIONS Homer is 225 miles south of Anchorage, Alaska, on the southern tip of the Kenai Peninsula and the shores of Kachemak Bay. There are multiple hotels in the area.

KENTUCKY WOMEN WRITERS CONFERENCE

University of Kentucky College of Arts & Sciences, 232 E. Maxwell St., Lexington KY 40506. (859)257-2874. **E-mail:** kentuckywomenwriters@gmail.com. **Website:** kentuckywomenwriters.org. **Contact:**

Julie Wrinn, director. Estab. 1979. Conference held second or third weekend of September. 2017 dates: September 15-16. Duration: 2 days. Site: Carnegie Center for Literacy in Lexington, Kentucky. Average attendance: 150-200. Conference covers poetry, fiction, creative nonfiction, and playwriting. Includes writing workshops, panels, and readings featuring contemporary women writers.

COSTS $200 for general admission and a workshop and $125 for admission with no workshop.

ADDITIONAL INFORMATION Sponsors prizes in poetry ($200), fiction ($200), nonfiction ($200), playwriting ($500), and spoken word ($500). Winners are also invited to read during the conference. Preregistration opens May 1.

KENTUCKY WRITERS CONFERENCE

Southern Kentucky Book Fest, Knicely Conference Center, 2355 Nashville Rd., Bowling Green KY 42101. (270)745-4502. **E-mail:** sara.volpi@wku.edu. **Website:** www.sokybookfest.org. **Contact:** Sara Volpi. This event is entirely free to the public. 2017 date: April 21. Duration: 1 day. Part of the 2-day Southern Kentucky Book Fest. Authors who will be participating in the Book Fest on Saturday will give attendees at the conference the benefit of their wisdom on Friday. Free workshops on a variety of writing topics will be presented. Sessions run for 75 minutes, and the day begins at 9 a.m. and ends at 3:30 p.m. The conference is open to anyone who would like to attend, including high school students, college students, teachers, and the general public.

KILLER NASHVILLE

P.O. Box 680759, Franklin TN 37068. (615)599-4032. **E-mail:** contact@killernashville.com. **Website:** www.killernashville.com. Estab. 2006. Annual conference held late summer or fall. Duration: 3 days. Average attendance: more than 400. The event draws in literary agents seeking thrillers, as well as some of the industry's top thriller authors. Designed for writers and fans of mysteries and thrillers, including fiction and nonfiction authors, playwrights, and screenwriters. There are many opportunities for authors to sign books. Distinct session tracks may include general writing, genre-specific writing, publishing, publicity and promotion, forensics, and ms critiques (fiction, nonfiction, short stories, screenplays, and queries). The conference also offers a realistic mock crime scene for guests to solve and an opportunity for networking with best-selling authors, agents, editors, publishers, attorneys, publicists, and representatives from law and emergency services. Other activities include mystery games, an authors' bar, a wine tasting event, 2 cocktail receptions, a guest of honor dinner and awards program, and giveways.

COSTS $375 for general registration, includes network lunches on Friday and Saturday and special sessions with best-selling authors and industry professionals.

ADDITIONAL INFORMATION Additional information about registration is provided online.

LA JOLLA WRITERS CONFERENCE

P.O. Box 178122, San Diego CA 92177. **E-mail:** akuritz@san.rr.com. **Website:** www.lajollawritersconference.com. **Contact:** Jared Kuritz, director. Estab. 2001. Annual conference held in fall. 2017 dates: October 27-29. Conference duration: 3 days. Attendance: 200 maximum. The LaJolla Writers Conference covers all genres and both fiction and nonfiction, as well as the business of writing. "We take particular pride in educating our attendees on the business aspect of the book industry and have agents, editors, publishers, publicists, and distributors teach classes. There is unprecedented access to faculty. Our conference offers lecture sessions that run for 50 minutes and workshops that run for 110 minutes. Each block period is dedicated to either workshop or lecture-style classes, with 6-8 classes on various topics available each block. For most workshop classes, you are encouraged to bring written work for review. Literary agents from prestigious agencies such as the Andrea Brown Literary Agency, the Dijkstra Agency, the McBride Agency, Full Circle Literary Group, the Zimmerman Literary Agency, the Van Haitsma Literary Agency, the Farris Literary Agency, and more have participated in the past, teaching workshops in which they are familiarized with attendee work. Late night and early bird sessions are also available. The conference creates a strong sense of community, and it has seen many of its attendees successfully published."

COSTS $395 for full 2017 conference registration (doesn't include lodging or breakfast).

LAS VEGAS WRITERS CONFERENCE

Henderson Writers' Group, P.O. Box 92032, Henderson NV 89009. (702)953-5675. **E-mail:** info@lasvegaswritersconference.com. **Website:** www.lasvegaswritersconference.com. Annual event held in spring. 2017 dates: April 20-22. Conference duration: 3 days. Attendance: 150 maximum. "Join writing professionals, agents, industry experts, and your colleagues for 3 days in Las Vegas as they share their knowledge on all aspects of the writer's craft. While there are formal pitch sessions, panels, workshops, and seminars, the faculty is also available throughout the conference for informal discussions and advice. Workshops, seminars, and expert panels cover topics in both fiction and nonfiction, screenwriting, marketing, indie publishing, and the craft of writing itself. There will be many question-and-answer panels for you to ask the experts all your questions." Site: Sam's Town Hotel and Gambling Hall in Las Vegas (Henderson, Nevada). 2017 keynote speaker: Donald Maass.

COSTS Costs vary depending on the package. See the website. There are early bird rates and deep discounts for Clark County high school students.

ADDITIONAL INFORMATION Sponsors contest. Agents and editors also participate in conference.

MENDOCINO COAST WRITERS CONFERENCE

1211 Del Mar Drive, P.O. Box 2087, Fort Bragg CA 95437. (707)485-4031. **E-mail:** info@mcwc.org. **Website:** www.mcwc.org. **Contact:** Barbara Lee, registrar; Karen Lewis, executive director. Estab. 1989. 27th annual summer writers conference where established and emerging writers find inspiration and work closely with notable authors. 2016 dates: August 4-7. Average attendance: 90. Offers intensive workshops on fiction, creative nonfiction, poetry, writing for children/young adults, and emerging writers, and afternoon craft sessions. Located at Mendocino College on the scenic northern California coast. Faculty from 2016: Les Standiford, Lori Ostlund, Jessica Piazza, James W. Hall, Reyna Grande, Jordan Rosenfeld, Laura Atkins, Brooke Warner, and Shirin Yim Bridges. Attendees work closely with editors, literary agents, and special guests. New in 2016: all-day Publishing Boot Camp on August 7, open to all. CEUs and scholarships available. Optional consultations and writing contests.

COSTS $575 early bird registration includes morning intensives, afternoon panels and seminars, social events, and most meals. Scholarships available. Opt-in for consultations and Publishing Boot Camp. Early application advised.

ACCOMMODATIONS Many lodging options in the scenic coastal area.

ADDITIONAL INFORMATION "Take your writing to the next level with encouragement, expertise, and inspiration in a literary community where authors are also fantastic teachers." Registration opens March 15.

MIDWEST WRITERS WORKSHOP

Muncie IN 47306. (765)282-1055. **E-mail:** midwestwriters@yahoo.com. **Website:** www.midwestwriters.org. **Contact:** Jama Kehoe Bigger, director. Annual workshop held in July in east-central Indiana. Writer workshops geared toward writers of all levels include craft and business sessions. Topics include most genres. Faculty/speakers have included Joyce Carol Oates, George Plimpton, Clive Cussler, Haven Kimmel, William Kent Krueger, William Zinsser, John Gilstrap, Lee Martin, Jane Friedman, Chuck Sambuchino, and numerous best-selling mystery, literary fiction, young adult, and children's authors. Workshop also includes agent pitch sessions, ms evaluation, query letter critiques, and social media tutoring. Registration tentatively limited to 240.

COSTS $155-400. Most meals included.

ADDITIONAL INFORMATION Offers scholarships. See website for more information. Keep in touch with MWW at facebook.com/midwestwriters and twitter.com/midwestwriters.

MISSOURI WRITERS' GUILD CONFERENCE

St. Louis MO **E-mail:** mwgconferenceinfo@gmail.com. **Website:** www.missouriwritersguild.org. **Contact:** Tricia Sanders, vice president/conference chair. Annual conference held in spring. 2017 dates: May 5-7. Writer and illustrator workshops geared to all levels. Open to students. "Gives writers the opportunity to hear outstanding speakers and to receive information on marketing, research, and writing techniques." Agents, editors, and published authors in attendance.

ADDITIONAL INFORMATION The primary contact individual changes every year, because the conference chair changes every year. See the website for contact info.

MOONLIGHT AND MAGNOLIAS WRITER'S CONFERENCE

Georgia Romance Writers, 3741 Casteel Park Drive, Marietta GA 30064. **Website:** www.georgiaromancewriters.org/mm-conference. Estab. 1982. Georgia Romance Writers Annual Conference. 2017 dates: September 28-October 1. "Conference focuses on writing women's fiction with emphasis on romance. Includes agents and editors from major publishing houses. Previous workshops have included beginning writer sessions, research topics, writing basics, and professional issues for the published author, plus specialty sessions on writing young adult, multicultural, paranormal, and Regency. Speakers have included experts in law enforcement, screenwriting, and research."

MUSE AND THE MARKETPLACE

Grub Street, 162 Boylston St., Fifth Floor, Boston MA 02116. (617)695-0075. **E-mail:** info@grubstreet.org. **Website:** museandthemarketplace.com. Grub Street's national conference for writers. Held in the late spring. 2017 dates: May 5-7. Conference duration: 3 days. Average attendance: 400. Dozens of agents are in attendance to meet writers and take pitches. The conference has workshops on all aspects of writing.

ACCOMMODATIONS Boston Park Plaza Hotel.

NAPA VALLEY WRITERS' CONFERENCE

Napa Valley College, 1088 College Ave., St. Helena CA 94574. (707)967-2900 ext. 4. **E-mail:** info@napawritersconference.og. **Website:** www.napawritersconference.org. **Contact:** Catherine Thorpe, managing director. Estab. 1981. Established 1981. Annual weeklong event. 2017 dates: July 23-July 28. Location: Upper Valley Campus in the historic town of St. Helena, 25 miles north of Napa in the heart of the valley's wine-growing community. Average attendance: 48 in poetry and 48 in fiction. "Serious writers of all backgrounds and experience are welcome to apply." Offers poets and fiction writers workshops, lectures, faculty readings at Napa Valley wineries, and one-on-one faculty counseling. "Poetry session provides the opportunity to work both on generating new poems and on revising previously written ones."

COSTS $975; $25 application fee.

NATIONAL WRITERS ASSOCIATION FOUNDATION CONFERENCE

10940 S. Parker Road, #508, Parker CO 80138. **E-mail:** natlwritersassn@hotmail.com. **Website:** www.nationalwriters.com. **Contact:** Sandy Whelchel, executive director. Estab. 1926. Annual conference held the second week of June in Denver. Conference duration: 1 day. Average attendance: 100. Focuses on general writing and marketing.

ADDITIONAL INFORMATION Awards for previous contests will be presented at the conference. Brochures/guidelines are available online or by SASE.

NETWO WRITERS CONFERENCE

Northeast Texas Writers Organization, P.O. Box 962, Mt. Pleasant TX 75456. (469)867-2624 or (903)573-6084. **E-mail:** jimcallan@winnsboro.com. **Website:** www.netwo.org. Estab. 1987. Annual conference held in April. Duration: 2 days. Presenters include agents, writers, editors, and publishers. Agents in attendance will take pitches from writers. The conference features a writing contest, pitch sessions, critiques from professionals, and dozens of workshops and presentations.

COSTS $90 for members before February 29, and $100 after. $112.50 for non-members before February 29, and $125 after.

ACCOMMODATIONS See website for information on area motels and hotels. The conference is held at the Titus County Civic Center in Mt. Pleasant, Texas.

ADDITIONAL INFORMATION Conference is cosponsored by the Texas Commission on the Arts. See website for current updates.

NEW JERSEY ROMANCE WRITERS PUT YOUR HEART IN A BOOK CONFERENCE

P.O. Box 513, Plainsboro NJ 08536. **Website:** www.njromancewriters.org/conference.html. Estab. 1984. Annual conference held in October. 2017 dates: October 13-14. Average attendance: 500. Workshops are offered on various topics for all writers of romance, from beginner to multipublished. Speakers have included Nora Roberts, Kathleen Woodiwiss, Patricia Gaffney, Jill Barnett, and Kay Hooper. Appointments are offered with editors and agents.

NORTH CAROLINA WRITERS' NETWORK FALL CONFERENCE

P.O. Box 21591, Winston-Salem NC 27120. (336)293-8844. **E-mail:** mail@ncwriters.org. **Website:** www.ncwriters.org. Estab. 1985. Annual conference held in November in different North Carolina venues. Average attendance: 250. This organization hosts 2 conferences: 1 in the spring and 1 in the fall. Each conference is a weekend full of workshops, panels, book signings, and readings (including open mic). There will be a keynote speaker, a variety of sessions on the craft and business of writing, and opportunities to meet with agents and editors.

COSTS Approximately $250 (includes 4 meals).

ACCOMMODATIONS Special rates are usually available at the conference hotel, but attendees must make their own reservations.

NORTHERN COLORADO WRITERS CONFERENCE

407 Cormorant Court, Fort Collins CO 80525. (970)227-5746. **E-mail:** april@northerncoloradowriters.com. **Website:** www.northerncoloradowriters.com. Estab. 2006. Annual conference held in Fort Collins. 2017 dates: May 5-6. Duration: 2-3 days. The conference features a variety of speakers, agents, and editors. There are workshops and presentations on fiction, nonfiction, screenwriting, children's books, marketing, magazine writing, staying inspired, and more. Previous agents who have attended and taken pitches from writers include Jessica Regel, Kristen Nelson, Rachelle Gardner, Andrea Brown, Ken Sherman, Jessica Faust, Gordon Warnock, and Taylor Martindale. Each conference features more than 30 workshops from which to choose. Previous keynotes include Andrew McCarthy and Stephen J. Cannell.

COSTS Prices vary depending on a number of factors. See website for details.

ACCOMMODATIONS Conference hotel may offer rooms at a discounted rate.

NORWESCON

100 Andover Park W., Suite 150-165, Tukwila WA 98188. (425)243-4692. **E-mail:** info@norwescon.org. **Website:** www.norwescon.org. Estab. 1978. Annual conference held on Easter weekend. Average attendance: 2,800-3,000. General convention (with multiple tracks) focusing on science fiction and fantasy literature with wide coverage of other media. Tracks cover science, sociocultural, literary, publishing, editing, writing, art, and other media of a science fiction/fantasy orientation. Literary agents will be speaking and available for meetings with attendees.

ACCOMMODATIONS Conference is held at the Doubletree Hotel Seattle Airport.

ODYSSEY FANTASY WRITING WORKSHOP

P.O. Box 75, Mount Vernon NH 03057. (603)673-6234. **E-mail:** jcavelos@sff.net. **Website:** www.odysseyworkshop.org. **Contact:** Jeanne Cavelos. Saint Anselm College, 100 Saint Anselm Dr., Manchester NH 03102 Estab. 1996. Annual workshop held in June (through July). Conference duration: 6 weeks. Average attendance: 15. A workshop for fantasy, science fiction, and horror writers that combines an intensive learning and writing experience with in-depth feedback on students' mss. Held on the campus of Saint Anselm College in Manchester, New Hampshire. Speakers have included George R.R. Martin, Elizabeth Hand, Jane Yolen, Catherynne M. Valente, Holly Black, and Dan Simmons.

COSTS $2,025 tuition, $870 housing (double room), $1,740 housing (single room), $40 application fee, $600 food (approximate), $750 optional processing fee to receive college credit.

ADDITIONAL INFORMATION Students must apply and include a writing sample. Application deadline: April 8. Students' works are critiqued throughout the 6 weeks. Workshop information available in October. For brochure/guidelines, send SASE, e-mail, visit website, or call.

OKLAHOMA WRITERS' FEDERATION, INC. ANNUAL CONFERENCE

9800 South Hwy. 137, Miami OK 74354. **Website:** www.owfi.org. Annual conference held first weekend in May, just outside Oklahoma City. Writer workshops geared toward all levels. "The goal of the conference is to create good stories with strong bones. We will be exploring cultural writing and cultural sensitivity in writing." Several literary agents are in attendance each year to meet with writers and hear pitches.

COSTS Costs vary depending on when registrants sign up. Cost includes awards banquet and famous author banquet. Three extra sessions are available for an extra fee. Visit the event website for more information and a complete faculty list.

OREGON CHRISTIAN WRITERS SUMMER CONFERENCE

1075 Willow Lake Rd. N., Keizer OR 97303. **E-mail:** summerconference@oregonchristianwriters.org. **Website:** www.oregonchristianwriters.org. **Contact:** Lindy Jacobs, summer conference director. Estab. 1989. Annual conference held in August at the Red Lion Hotel on the River, a full-service hotel in Portland. Duration: 4 days. 2017 dates: August 15-18. Average attendance: 225 (175 writers, 50 faculty).

Top national editors, agents, and authors in the field of Christian publishing offer 12 intensive coaching classes and 30 workshops plus critique sessions. Published authors as well as emerging writers have opportunities to improve their craft, get feedback through ms reviews, meet one-on-one with editors and agents, and have half-hour mentoring appointments with published authors. Classes include fiction, nonfiction, memoir, young adult, poetry, magazine articles, devotional writing, children's books, and marketing. Daily general sessions include worship and an inspirational keynote address. Each year contacts made during the OCW summer conference lead to publishing contracts.

COSTS $525 for OCW members, $560 for nonmembers. Registration fee includes all classes, workshops, and 2 lunches and 3 dinners. Lodging additional. Full-time registered attendees may also presubmit 3 proposals for review by an editor (or agent) through the conference, plus sign up for a half-hour mentoring appointment with an author.

ACCOMMODATIONS Conference is held at the Red Lion on the River. Attendees wishing to stay at the hotel must make a reservation through the hotel. A block of rooms is reserved at a special rate and held until mid-July. The hotel reservation link is posted on the website in late spring. Shuttle bus transportation is provided from Portland Airport (PDX) to the hotel, which is 20 minutes away.

ADDITIONAL INFORMATION Conference details posted online beginning in January. All conferees are welcome to attend the Cascade Awards ceremony, which takes place Wednesday evening during the conference. For more information about the Cascade Writing Contest, please check the website.

OZARK CREATIVE WRITERS, INC. CONFERENCE

P.O. Box 9076, Fayetteville AR 72703. **E-mail:** ozarkcreativewriters1@gmail.com. **Website:** www.ozarkcreativewriters.com. The annual event is held in October at the Inn of the Ozarks, in the resort town of Eureka Springs, Arkansas. Approximately 200 writers attend each year; many also enter the creative writing competitions. Open to professional and amateur writers, workshops are geared toward all levels and all forms of the creative process and literary arts; sessions sometimes also include songwriting. Includes presentations by best-selling authors, editors, and agents. Offering writing competitions in all genres.

PENNWRITERS CONFERENCE

P.O. Box 685, Dalton PA 18414. **E-mail:** conference-co@pennwriters.org, info@pennwriters.org. **Website:** pennwriters.org/conference. Estab. 1987. The Mission of Pennwriters, Inc. is to help writers of all levels, from the novice to the award-winning and multipublished, improve and succeed in their craft. The annual Pennwriters conference is held every year in May in Pennsylvania, switching between locations—Lancaster in even-numbered years and Pittsburgh in odd-numbered years. 2017 dates: May 19-21 at the Pittsburgh Airport Marriott. Literary agents are in attendance to meet with writers.

ACCOMMODATIONS Costs vary. Pennwriters members in good standing get a slightly reduced rate.

ADDITIONAL INFORMATION Sponsors contest. Published authors judge fiction in various categories. Agent/editor appointments are available on a first-come, first-served basis.

PHILADELPHIA WRITERS' CONFERENCE

P.O. Box 7171, Elkins Park PA 19027. (215)619-7422. **E-mail:** info@pwcwriters.org. **Website:** pwcwriters.org. Estab. 1949. Annual conference held in June. Duration: 3 days. Average attendance: 160-200. Conference covers many forms of writing: novel, short story, genre fiction, nonfiction book, magazine writing, blogging, juvenile, poetry.

ACCOMMODATIONS See website for details. Hotel may offer discount for early registration.

ADDITIONAL INFORMATION Accepts inquiries by e-mail. Agents and editors attend the conference. Many questions are answered online.

PIKES PEAK WRITERS CONFERENCE

Pikes Peak Writers, P.O. Box 64273, Colorado Springs CO 80962. (719)244-6220. **E-mail:** registrar@pikespeakwriters.com. **Website:** www.pikespeakwriters.com/ppwc. Estab. 1993. Annual conference held in April. 2017 dates: April 28-30. Conference duration: 3 days. Average attendance: 300. Workshops, presentations, and panels focus on writing and publishing mainstream and genre fiction (romance, science fiction/fantasy, suspense/thrillers, action/adventure, mysteries, children's, young adult). Agents and editors are available for meetings with attendees on Saturday. Speakers have included Jeff Lindsay, Rachel Caine, and Kevin J. Anderson.

COSTS $395-465 (includes all 7 meals).

ACCOMMODATIONS Marriott Colorado Springs holds a block of rooms at a special rate for attendees until late March.

ADDITIONAL INFORMATION Readings with critiques are available on Friday afternoon. Registration forms are online; brochures are available in January. Send inquiries via e-mail.

PNWA SUMMER WRITERS CONFERENCE

Writers' Cottage, 317 NW Gilman Blvd., Suite 8, Issaquah WA 98027. (425)673-2665. **E-mail:** pnwa@pnwa.org. **Website:** www.pnwa.org. Estab. 1955. Annual conference held in July. 2017 dates: July 20-23. Duration: 4 days. Average attendance: 400. Attendees have the chance to meet agents and editors, learn craft from authors, and uncover marketing secrets. Speakers have included J.A. Jance, Sheree Bykofsky, Kimberley Cameron, Jennie Dunham, Donald Maass, Jandy Nelson, Robert Dugoni, and Terry Brooks.

ROCKY MOUNTAIN FICTION WRITERS COLORADO GOLD CONFERENCE (SEPTEMBER)

Rocky Mountain Fiction Writers, P.O. Box 711, Montrose CO 81402 USA. **E-mail:** conference@rmfw.org. **Website:** www.rmfw.org. Estab. 1982. Annual conference held in September. Duration: 3 days. Average attendance: 400+. Themes include general fiction, genre fiction, contemporary romance, mystery, science fiction/fantasy, mainstream, young adult, screenwriting, short stories, and historical fiction, as well as marketing and career management. 2017 keynote speakers are Diana Gabaldon, Sherry Thomas, and Lori Rader-Day. Past speakers have included Ann Hood, Robert J. Sawyer, Jeffery Deaver, William Kent Krueger, Margaret George, Jodi Thomas, Bernard Cornwell, Terry Brooks, Dorothy Cannell, Patricia Gardner Evans, Diane Mott Davidson, Constance O'Day, and Connie Willis. Approximately 8 editors and 8 agents attend annually.

COSTS Available on website.

ACCOMMODATIONS Special rates will be available at conference hotel.

ADDITIONAL INFORMATION Editor-conducted critiques are limited to 8 participants, with auditing available. Craft workshops include beginner through professional levels. Pitch appointments and book blurb critiques available at no charge. Also available for an extra charge are master classes, pitch coaching, query letter coaching, special critiques, and more.

ROMANCE WRITERS OF AMERICA NATIONAL CONFERENCE

14615 Benfer Rd., Houston TX 77069. (832)717-5200. **Fax:** (832)717-5201. **E-mail:** info@rwa.org. **Website:** www.rwa.org/conference. Estab. 1981. Annual conference held in July. 2017 conference: Walt Disney World Swan & Dolphin Resort Orlando, Florida, July 26-29. Average attendance: 2,000. More than 100 workshops on writing, researching, and the business side of being a working writer. Publishing professionals attend and accept appointments. The keynote speaker is a renowned romance writer. "Romance Writers of America (RWA) is a nonprofit trade association with a membership of more than 10,000 romance writers and related industry professionals our mission is to advance the professional interests of career-focused romance writers through networking and advocacy."

COSTS $450-675 depending on your membership status and when you register.

ADDITIONAL INFORMATION Annual RTA awards are presented for romance authors. Annual Golden Heart awards are presented for unpublished writers. Numerous literary agents are in attendance to meet with writers and hear book pitches.

RT BOOKLOVERS CONVENTION

81 Willoughby Street, Suite 701, Brooklyn NY 11201. **E-mail:** tere@rtconvention.com. **Website:** rtconvention.com. **Contact:** Tere Michaels. Annual conference with a varying location. 2017 conference: May 2-7, Atlanta. Features 200 workshops, agent and editor appointments, Giant Book Fair, and more. More than 1,000 authors attend the event.

COSTS $495 for normal registration; $425 for industry professionals (agents and editors). Special discounted rate for readers, $450. Many other pricing options available. See website.

ACCOMMODATIONS Rooms available at the 2017 hotel, the Atlanta Hyatt Regency.

⬤ SALT CAY WRITERS RETREAT

Salt Cay, Bahamas. (732)267-6449. **E-mail:** admin@saltcaywritersretreat.com. **Website:** www.saltcaywritersretreat.com. **Contact:** Karen Dionne and Christopher Graham. Annual retreat held in the Bahamas in May. Duration: 5 days. "The Salt Cay Writers Retreat is particularly suited for novelists (especially those writing literary and upmarket commercial fiction, or genre novelists wanting to write a breakout book), memoirists, and narrative nonfiction writers. However, any author (published or not yet published) who wishes to take their writing to the next level is welcome to apply." Speakers have included editors Chuck Adams (Algonquin Books) and Amy Einhorn (Amy Einhorn Books); agents Jeff Kleinman, Michelle Brower, Erin Niumata, and Erin Harris (all of Folio Literary Management); and authors Robert Goolrick and Jacquelyn Mitchard.

COSTS $2,450 through May 1; $2,950 after.

ACCOMMODATIONS Comfort Suites, Paradise Island, Nassau, Bahamas.

SAN DIEGO STATE UNIVERSITY WRITERS' CONFERENCE

SDSU College of Extended Studies, 5250 Campanile Drive, San Diego State University, San Diego CA 92182. (619)594-2099. **Fax:** (619)594-8566. **E-mail:** sdsuwritersconference@mail.sdsu.edu. **Website:** ces.sdsu.edu/writers. Estab. 1984. Annual conference held in January. 2017 dates: January 20-22. Conference duration: 2.5 days. Average attendance: 350. Covers fiction, nonfiction, scriptwriting, and e-books. Held at the San Diego Marriott Mission Valley Hotel. Each year the conference offers a variety of workshops for beginner and advanced writers. This conference allows writers to choose which workshops best suit their needs. In addition to the workshops, editor reading appointments and agent/editor consultation appointments are provided so attendees may meet with editors and agents one-on-one to discuss specific questions. A reception is offered Saturday immediately following the workshops, offering attendees the opportunity to socialize with the faculty in a relaxed atmosphere. In previous years, approximately 60 faculty members have attended.

COSTS $495-549. Extra costs for consultations.

ACCOMMODATIONS Attendees must make their own travel arrangements. A conference rate for attendees is available at the event hotel (Marriott Mission Valley Hotel).

SAN FRANCISCO WRITERS CONFERENCE

1029 Jones St., San Francisco CA 94109. (415)673-0939. **E-mail:** barbara@sfwriters.org, sfwriterscon@aol.com. **E-mail:** See website for online contest and scholarship submissions and other details.. **Website:** sfwriters.org. **Contact:** Barbara Santos, marketing director. Estab. 2003. 2017 dates: February 16-19. Annual conference held President's Day weekend in February. Average attendance: 700. "More than 100 top authors, respected literary agents, and major publishing houses are at the event so attendees can make face-to-face contact with all the right people. Writers of nonfiction, fiction, poetry, and specialty writing (children's books, cookbooks, travel, etc.) will all benefit from the event. There are important sessions on marketing, self-publishing, technology, and trends in the publishing industry. Plus, there's an optional session called Speed Dating with Agents where attendees can meet with more than 20 agents. Past speakers have included Jane Smiley, Debbie Macomber, Clive Cussler, Guy Kawasaki, Jennifer Crusie, R.L. Stine, Lisa See, Steve Berry, and Jacquelyn Mitchard. More than 20 agents and several editors from traditional publishing houses participate each year, and most will be available for meetings with attendees."

COSTS Full registration is $795 (as of the 2017 event) with early bird registration discounts through February 1.

ACCOMMODATIONS The Intercontinental Mark Hopkins Hotel offers a discounted SFWC rate (based on availability). Call directly: (415)392-3434. The Mark is a historic landmark at the top of Nob Hill in San Francisco. The hotel is located so that everyone arriving at the Oakland or San Francisco airport can take the BART to either the Embarcadero or Powell Street exits, then walk or take a cable car or taxi directly to the hotel.

ADDITIONAL INFORMATION "Present yourself in a professional manner, and the contacts you will make will be invaluable to your writing career. Fliers, details, and registration information are online."

SAN FRANCISCO WRITING FOR CHANGE CONFERENCE

San Francisco Writers Conference, 1029 Jones Street, San Francisco CA 94109. (415)673-0939. **E-mail:** barbara@sfwriters.org. **Website:** SFWritingforChange.org. **Contact:** Barbara Santos, marketing director; Michael Larsen, codirector. Estab. 2004. Annual conference in September held at Unitarian Universalist Center in San Francisco. Average attendance: 100 attendees and 25 presenters. Early discounts available. Includes panels, workshops, keynote address, lunch, and editor consultations.

COSTS $199. Early registration discounts available. Please visit the website for details.

ACCOMMODATIONS Check website for event details, accommodations, directions, and parking.

ADDITIONAL INFORMATION "The limited number of attendees (150 maximum) makes this a truly interactive event and a highly effective and productive conference. The presenters are major names in the publishing business, but they take personal interest in the projects discovered at this event each year." Guidelines available on website.

SCBWI; ANNUAL CONFERENCES ON WRITING AND ILLUSTRATING FOR CHILDREN

8271 Beverly Blvd., Los Angeles CA 90048. **E-mail:** scbwi@scbwi.org. **Website:** www.scbwi.org. **Contact:** Lin Oliver, conference director. Writer and illustrator workshops geared toward all levels. Open to students. Covers all aspects of children's book and magazine publishing—the novel, illustration techniques, marketing, etc. Annual conferences held in April in Los Angeles and in New York in February. Cost of conference includes all 4 days and q banquet meal. Write for more information or visit website.

⊕ SCBWI—AUSTIN CONFERENCE

E-mail: austin@scbwi.org. **Website:** austin.scbwi. org. **Contact:** Samantha Clark, regional advisor. Annual conference features a faculty of published authors and illustrators. Past years have featured National Book Award winner William Alexander, Caldecott Honors Liz Garton Scanlon and Molly Idle, *New York Times* best-selling author Cynthia Leitich Smith, and more. Editors and agents are in attendance to meet with writers. The schedule consists of keynotes and breakout sessions with tracks for writing (picture book and novel), illustrating, and professional development.

COSTS Costs vary for members, students, and nonmembers, and discounted early bird pricing is available. Visit website for full pricing options.

◐ SCBWI—CANADA EAST

Canada. **E-mail:** canadaeast@scbwi.org, almafullerton@almafullerton.com. **Website:** www.canadaeast. scbwi.org. **Contact:** Alma Fullerton, regional advisor. Writer and illustrator events geared toward all levels. Usually offers one event in spring and another in the fall. Check website for updated information.

SCBWI—MID-ATLANTIC; ANNUAL FALL CONFERENCE

P.O. Box 3215, Reston VA 20195. **E-mail:** midatlantic@scbwi.org. **Website:** midatlantic.scbwi.org/. **Contact:** Ellen R. Braaf, regional advisor. For updates and details, visit website. Registration limited to 250. Conference fills quickly. Includes continental breakfast and boxed lunch. Optional craft-focused workshops and individual consultations with conference faculty are available for additional fees.

SCBWI—NORTHERN OHIO; ANNUAL CONFERENCE

225 N. Willow St., Kent OH 44240-2561. **E-mail:** vselvaggio@windstream.net. **Website:** http://ohionorth. scbwi.org. **Contact:** Victoria A. Selvaggio, regional advisor. Northern Ohio's conference is crafted for all levels of writers and illustrators of children's literature. 2015 dates: September 18-19. "Our annual event will be held at the Sheraton Cleveland Airport Hotel. Conference costs will be posted on our website with registration information. SCBWI members receive a discount. Additional fees apply for late registration, critiques, or portfolio reviews. Cost includes an optional Friday evening Opening Banquet from 6-10 p.m. with a keynote speaker; Saturday event from 8:30 a.m. to 5 p.m. which includes breakfast snack, full-day conference with headliner presentations, general sessions, breakout workshops, lunch, panel discussion, and autograph session. The Illustrator Showcase is open to all attendees at no additional cost. Grand door prize drawn at the end of the day Saturday, is free admission to the following year's conference. Further information, including Headliner Speakers will be posted on our website."

SCBWI WINTER CONFERENCE ON WRITING AND ILLUSTRATING FOR CHILDREN

4727 Wilshire Blvd. #301, Los Angeles CA 90010. (323)782-1010. **Fax:** (323)782-1892. **E-mail:** scbwi@scbwi.org. **Website:** www.scbwi.org. **Contact:** Stephen Mooser. Estab. 2000. Annual conference held in February. Average attendance: 1,000. Conference is to promote writing and illustrating for children (picture books, middle-grade, and young adult) and to give participants an opportunity to network with professionals. Covers financial planning for writers, marketing your book, art exhibitions, and more. The winter conference is held in Manhattan.

COSTS See website for current cost and conference information.

ADDITIONAL INFORMATION SCBWI also holds an annual summer conference in August in Los Angeles.

SEWANEE WRITERS' CONFERENCE

735 University Ave., 119 Gailor Hall, Stamler Center, Sewanee TN 37383. (931)598-1654. **E-mail:** swc@sewanee.edu. **Website:** www.sewaneewriters.org. **Contact:** Adam Latham. Estab. 1990. Annual conference. 2017 dates: July 18-30. Average attendance: 150. Accepting applications January 16-April 17. The University of the South will host the 28th session of the Sewanee Writers' Conference. Thanks to the generosity of the Walter E. Dakin Memorial Fund, supported by the estate of the late Tennessee Williams, the Conference will gather a distinguished faculty to provide instruction and criticism through workshops and craft lectures in poetry, fiction, and playwriting. During a 12-day period, participants will read and critique workshop manuscripts under the leadership of some of our country's finest fiction writers, poets, and playwrights. Faculty members and fellows give scheduled readings; senior faculty members offer craft lectures; open mic readings accommodate many others. Additional writers, along with a host of writing professionals, visit to give readings, participate in panel discussions, and answer questions from the audience. Receptions and mealtimes offer ample social opportunities. Recent and forthcoming faculty include fiction writers Richard Bausch, John Casey, Tony Earley, Randall Kenan, Jill McCorkle, Alice McDermott, Erin McGraw, Christine Schutt, Allen Wier, and Steve Yarbrough; poets Daniel Anderson, B.H. Fairchild, Robert Hass, Mark Jarman, Maurice Manning, Marilyn Nelson, A.E. Stallings, and Sidney Wade; and playwrights Naomi Iizuka, Dan O'Brien, and Ken Weitzman.

COSTS $1,100 for tuition, and $700 for room, board, and activity costs.

ACCOMMODATIONS Participants are housed in single rooms in university dormitories. Bathrooms are shared by small groups.

SLEUTHFEST

Mystery Writers of America Florida, **E-mail:** sleuthfestinfo@gmail.com. **Website:** sleuthfest.com. Annual conference held in February/March, at the Deerfield Beach Hilton, Florida. 2017 dates: February 23-26. Conference duration: 4 days. Hands-on workshops, 4 tracks of writing and business panels, and 2 keynote speakers for writers of mystery and crime fiction. 2017 keynote speaker: David Baldacci. Also offers agent and editor appointments and paid ms critiques. A full list of attending speakers, as well as agents and editors, is online. This event is put on by the local chapter of the Mystery Writers of America.

SOUTH CAROLINA WRITERS WORKSHOP

4711 Forest Drive, Suite 3, P.M.B. 189, Columbia SC 29206. **E-mail:** scwwliaison@gmail.com. **Website:** www.myscwa.org. Estab. 1991. Conference held in October at the Metropolitan Conference Center in Columbia. Held almost every year. Conference duration: 3 days. Features critique sessions, open mic readings, and presentations from agents and editors. More than 50 different workshops for writers to choose from dealing with all subjects of writing craft, writing business, getting an agent, and more. Agents will be in attendance.

SOUTHEASTERN WRITERS ASSOCIATION— ANNUAL WRITERS WORKSHOP

E-mail: purple@southeasternwriters.org. **Website:** www.southeasternwriters.org. Estab. 1975. Annual 4-day workshop, held in Epworth by the Sea, St. Simons Island, Georgia. Open to all writers. 2017 dates: June 16-20. Tuition includes 3 evaluation conferences with instructors (minimum 2-day registration). Offers contests with cash prizes. Manuscript deadlines: May 15 for contests and May 25 for evaluations.

COSTS Cost of workshop: $445 for 4 days or lower prices for daily tuition or early bird special. (See website for tuition pricing.)

ACCOMMODATIONS Lodging at Epworth and throughout St. Simons Island. Visit website for more information.

SPACE COAST WRITERS GUILD ANNUAL CONFERENCE

P.O. Box 262, Melbourne FL 32902. **E-mail:** stilley@scwg.org. **Website:** www.scwg.org. Conference held along the east coast of central Florida in the last weekend of January, though not necessarily every year. Check website for up-to-date information. Conference duration: 2 days. Average attendance: 150+. This conference is hosted in Florida and features a variety of presenters on all topics. Critiques are available for a price, and agents in attendance will take pitches from writers. Previous presenters

have included Debra Dixon, Davis Bunn (writer), Ellen Pepus (agent), Jennifer Crusie, Chuck Sambuchino, Madeline Smoot, Mike Resnick, Christina York, Ben Bova, and Elizabeth Sinclair.

COSTS Check website for current pricing.

ACCOMMODATIONS The conference is hosted in a beachside hotel, with special room rates available.

✪ SURREY INTERNATIONAL WRITERS' CONFERENCE

SiWC, 151-10090 152 St., Suite 544, Surrey British Columbia V3R 8X8 Canada. **E-mail:** kathychung@siwc.ca. **Website:** www.siwc.ca. **Contact:** Kathy Chung, proposals contact and conference coordinator. Annual professional development writing conference outside Vancouver, Canada, held every October. Writing workshops geared toward beginner, intermediate, and advanced levels. More than 80 workshops and panels, on all topics and genres, plus preconference master classes. Blue Pencil and agent/editor pitch sessions included. Different conference price packages available. Check the conference website for more information. This event has many literary agents in attendance taking pitches. Annual fiction writing contest open to all with $1000 prize for first place. Conference registration opens in early June every year. Register early to avoid disappointment, as the conference is likely to sell out.

TAOS SUMMER WRITERS' CONFERENCE

Department of English Language and Literature, MSC 03 2170, 1 University of New Mexico, Albuquerque NM 87131. (505)277-5572. **E-mail:** nmwriter@unm.edu. **Website:** taosconf.unm.edu. **Contact:** Sharon Oard Warner, founding director. Estab. 1999. Annual conference held in July. Offers workshops and master classes in the novel, short story, poetry, creative nonfiction, memoir, prose style, screenwriting, humor writing, yoga and writing, literary translation, book proposal, the query letter, and revision. Participants may also schedule a consultation with a visiting agent/editor.

COSTS Weeklong workshop registration: $700. Weekend workshop registration: $400. Master classes: $1,350-1,625. Publishing consultations: $175.

TEXAS WRITING RETREAT

Navasota TX **E-mail:** paultcuclis@gmail.com. **Website:** www.texaswritingretreat.com. **Contact:** Paul Cuclis, coordinator. Estab. 2013. The Texas Writing Retreat is an intimate event with a limited number of attendees. 2017 dates: January 11-16. Held on a private residence ranch an hour outside of Houston, the retreat has an agent and editor in attendance teaching. All attendees get to pitch the attending agent. Meals, excursions, and amenities are included. This is a unique event that combines craft sessions, business sessions, time for writing, relaxation, and more. The retreat is not held every year; it's best to check the website.

COSTS Costs vary per event. There are different pricing options for those staying on-site versus commuters.

THRILLERFEST

P.O. Box 311, Eureka CA 95502. **E-mail:** kimberlyhowe@thrillerwriters.org, infocentral@thrillerwriters.org. **Website:** www.thrillerfest.com. **Contact:** Kimberley Howe, executive director. Grand Hyatt New York, 109 E. 42nd St., New York, NY 10017 Estab. 2006. Annual workshop/conference/festival. 2017 dates: July 11-15 at the Grand Hyatt in New York. Conference duration: 5 days. Average attendance: 1,000. "A great place to learn the craft of writing the thriller. Classes taught by best-selling authors." Speakers have included David Morrell, James Patterson, Sandra Brown, Ken Follett, Eric Van Lustbader, David Baldacci, Brad Meltzer, Steve Martini, R.L. Stine, Steve Berry, Kathleen Antrim, Douglas Preston, Gayle Lynds, Harlan Coben, Lee Child, Lisa Scottolini, Katherine Neville, Robin Cook, Andrew Gross, Kathy Reichs, Brad Thor, Clive Cussler, Donald Maass, M.J. Rose, and Al Zuckerman. Three days of the conference are CraftFest, where the focus is on the craft of writing, and 2 days are ThrillerFest, which showcase the author-fan relationship. Also featured: PitchFest, a unique event where authors can pitch their work face-to-face to 50 top literary agents. Lastly, there is the International Thriller Awards and Banquet.

COSTS $475-1,199, depending on which events are selected. Various package deals are available, and early bird pricing is offered beginning September of each year.

TMCC WRITERS' CONFERENCE

Truckee Meadows Community College, 7000 Dandini Blvd., Reno NV 89512. (775)673-7111. **E-mail:** wdce@tmcc.edu. **Website:** wdce.tmcc.edu. Estab. 1991. Annual conference held in April. 2017 date: April 8. Average attendance: 150. Conference focuses on strengthening mainstream/literary fiction and nonfiction works and how to market them to

agents and publishers. Site: Truckee Meadows Community College in Reno. "There is always an array of speakers and presenters with impressive literary credentials, including agents and editors." Speakers have included Chuck Sambuchino, Sheree Bykofsky, Andrea Brown, Dorothy Allison, Karen Joy Fowler, James D. Houston, James N. Frey, Gary Short, Jane Hirschfield, Dorrianne Laux, and Kim Addonizio. Literary agents are on site to take pitches from writers.

ACCOMMODATIONS Contact the conference manager to learn about accommodation discounts.

ADDITIONAL INFORMATION "The conference is open to all writers, regardless of their level of experience. Brochures are available online and mailed in January. Send inquiries via e-mail."

UNICORN WRITERS CONFERENCE

17 Church Hill Rd., Redding CT 06896. (203)938-7405. **E-mail:** unicornwritersconference@gmail.com. **Website:** www.unicornwritersconference.com. **Contact:** Jan L. Kardys, chair. Estab. 2010. This writers conference draws upon its close proximity to New York and pulls in over 40 literary agents and 15 major New York editors to pitch each year. There are manuscript review sessions (40 pages equals 30 minutes with an agent/editor), query/manuscript review sessions, and 6 different workshops every hour. Cost: $325, includes all workshops and 3 meals.

COSTS $325 includes all workshops (6 every hour to select on the day of the conference), gift bag, and 3 meals. Additional cost for manuscript reviews: $60 each.

ACCOMMODATIONS Held at Reid Castle, Purchase, New York. Directions available on event website.

ADDITIONAL INFORMATION The first self-published authors will be featured on the website, and the bookstore will sell their books at the event.

UNIVERSITY OF NORTH DAKOTA WRITERS CONFERENCE

Department of English, Merrifield Hall, Room 1D, 276 Centennial Drive, Stop 7209, Grand Forks ND 58202. (701)777-2393. **Fax:** (701)777-2373. **E-mail:** crystal.alberts@und.edu. **Website:** und.edu/orgs/writers-conference. **Contact:** Crystal Alberts, director. Estab. 1970. Annual event. 2017 dates: March 22-24. Duration: 3-5 days. Offers panels, readings, and films focused around a specific theme. Almost all events take place in the University of North Dakota Memorial Union, which has a variety of small rooms and a thousand-seat main hall. Past speakers have included Art Spiegelman, Truman Capote, Sir Salman Rushdie, Allen Ginsberg, Alice Walker, and Louise Erdrich.

COSTS All events are free and open to the public. Donations accepted.

ACCOMMODATIONS Accommodations available at area hotels. Information on overnight accommodations available on website.

ADDITIONAL INFORMATION Schedule and other information available on website.

UNIVERSITY OF WISCONSIN AT MADISON WRITERS INSTITUTE

21 N. Park St., Madison WI 53715. (608)265-3972. **E-mail:** laurie.scheer@wisc.edu. **Website:** uwwritersinstitute.wisc.edu. Estab. 1990. Annual conference. 2017 dates: March 24-26. Conference on fiction and nonfiction held at the University of Wisconsin at Madison. Guest speakers are published authors and publishing executives. Agents and editors take pitches.

COSTS $195-345, depending on discounts and if you attend 1 day or multiple days.

WESTERN RESERVE WRITERS & FREELANCE CONFERENCE

Cuyahoga County Public Library South Euclid-Lyndhurst Branch, 4645 Mayfield Road, South Euclid OH 44121. (216)382-4880. **E-mail:** deencr@aol.com. **Website:** www.deannaadams.com. Laurie Kincer, program coordinator, South Euclid-Lyndhurst Library **Contact:** Deanna Adams, director/conference coordinator. Estab. 1983. Annual conference held in the fall. Duration: 1 day. Average attendance: 120. "The Western Reserve Writers Conference is designed for all writers, aspiring and professional, and offers presentations in all genres—nonfiction, fiction, poetry, essays, creative nonfiction, and the business of writing, including successful freelance writing." Site: "Formerly located at Lakeland Community College, the conference is now held at the new Writers' Center at the South Euclid-Lyndhurst Library. Included throughout the day are one-on-one editing consults, a question and answer panel, and book sale/author signings." See Deanna's website for updates: www.deannaadams.com.

COSTS The conference is now free but does not include lunch.

ADDITIONAL INFORMATION Brochures for the conferences are available by January (for spring conference) and July (for fall). Also accepts inquiries by e-mail and phone. Check Ms. Adams' website for all updates. Editors always attend the conferences. Private editing consultations are available as well.

☼ WRITE CANADA

The Word Guild, Suite 226, 245 King George Road, Brantford Ontario N3R 7N7 Canada. **E-mail:** writecanada@thewordguild.com. **Website:** thewordguild.com/events/write-canada. Annual conference in Ontario for Christian writers of all types and at all stages. Conference duration: 3 days. Offers solid instruction, stimulating interaction, exciting challenges, and worshipful community.

WRITE ON THE SOUND

WOTS, City of Edmonds Arts Commission, Frances Anderson Center, 700 Main St., Edmonds WA 98020. (425)771-0228. **E-mail:** wots@edmondswa.gov. **Website:** www.writeonthesound.com. **Contact:** Laurie Rose or Frances Chapin. Estab. 1985. Small, affordable annual conference focused on the craft of writing. Held the first weekend in October. 2017 dates: October 6-8. Conference duration: 2.5 days. Average attendance: 275. Features over 30 presenters, keynote, literary contest, ms critiques, roundtable discussions, book signing reception, on-site bookstore, and opportunity to network with faculty and attendees. Edmonds is located just north of Seattle on the Puget Sound.

COSTS $80-155 (not including optional fees).

ACCOMMODATIONS Best Western Plus/Edmonds Harbor Inn.

ADDITIONAL INFORMATION Schedule posted on website late spring/early summer. Registration opens mid-July. Review the schedule and register early. Attendees are required to select the sessions they wish to attend at the time of registration. Registration fills quickly, and day-of, on-site registration is not available. Waiting lists for conference and manuscript appointments are available.

WRITERS@WORK WRITING RETREAT

P.O. Box 711191, Salt Lake City UT 84171. (801)996-3313. **E-mail:** jennifer@writersatwork.org. **Website:** www.writersatwork.org. Estab. 1985. Annual conference held in June. Duration: 4 days. Average attendance: 45. Morning workshops (3 hours/day) focus on novel, advanced fiction, generative fiction, nonfiction, poetry, and young adult fiction. Afternoon sessions include craft lectures, discussions, and directed interviews with authors and editors. In addition to the traditional, one-on-one ms consultations, there will be many opportunities to mingle informally with visiting writers and editors. Site: Alta Lodge in Alta Lodge, Utah. Speakers have included Steve Almond, Bret Lott, Shannon Hale, Emily Forland (Wendy Weil Agency), Julie Culver (Folio Literary Management), Chuck Adams (Algonquin Press), and Mark A. Taylor (Juniper Press). **COSTS** $650-1,000, based on housing type and consultations.

ACCOMMODATIONS On-site housing available. Additional lodging information is on the website.

WRITERS CONFERENCE AT OCEAN PARK

P.O. Box 172, Assonet ME 02702. (401)598-1424. **E-mail:** jbrosnan@jwu.edu. **Website:** www.oceanpark. org/programs/education/writers/writers.html. Estab. 1941. Annual conference held in mid-August. Conference duration: 4 days. Average attendance: 50. "We try to present a balanced and eclectic conference. In addition to time and attention given to poetry, we also have children's literature, mystery writing, travel, fiction, nonfiction, journalism, and other issues of interest to writers. Our speakers are editors, writers, and other professionals. Our concentration is, by intention, a general view of writing to publish with supportive encouragement. We are located in Ocean Park, a small seashore village 14 miles south of Portland. Ours is a summer assembly center with many buildings from the Victorian age. The conference meets in Porter Hall, one of the assembly buildings which is listed in the National Register of Historic Places." Speakers have included Michael C. White (novelist/short story writer), Betsy Shool (poet), Suzanne Strempek Shea (novelist), John Perrault (poet), Anita Shreve (novelist), Dawn Potter (poet), Bruce Pratt (fiction writer), Amy McDonald (children's author), Sandell Morse (memoirist), Kate Chadbourne (singer/songwriter), and Wesley McNair (poet and Maine faculty member). "We usually have about 8 guest presenters each year." Writers/editors lead workshops and are available for meetings with attendees. Workshops start at 8:30 a.m. on Tuesday and continue through Friday until early afternoon. Opening event is Monday at 4 p.m.

COSTS $200. The fee does not include housing or meals, which must be arranged separately.

ACCOMMODATIONS "An accommodations list is available. We are in a summer resort area where motels, guest houses, and restaurants abound."

ADDITIONAL INFORMATION 2017 marks the conference's 77th anniversary.

WRITER'S DIGEST ANNUAL CONFERENCE

F+W Media, Inc., 10151 Carver Road., Suite 200, Blue Ash OH 45242. (877)436-7764 (option 2). **E-mail:** writersdigestconference@fwmedia.com. **E-mail:** phil.sexton@fwmedia.com. **Website:** www. writersdigestconference.com. **Contact:** Taylor Sferra. Estab. 1995. The Writer's Digest conferences feature an amazing lineup of speakers to help writers with the craft and business of writing. Each calendar year typically features multiple conferences around the country. In 2017, the New York conference will be August 18-20 at the New York Hilton Midtown. The most popular feature of the east coast conference is the agent pitch slam which allows potential authors to pitch their books directly to agents. For the 2017 conference, there will be more than 50 agents in attendance. For more details, see the website.

COSTS Cost varies by location and year. There are typically different pricing options for those who just wish attend the pitch slam and those who want to attend the conference.

ACCOMMODATIONS A block of rooms at the event hotel is reserved for guests. See the travel page on the website for more information.

WRITERS IN PARADISE

Eckerd College, 4200 54th Ave. S., St. Petersburg FL 33711. (727)386-2264. **E-mail:** wip@eckerd.edu. **Website:** writersinparadise.com. Estab. 2005. Annual conference held in January. 2017 dates: January 14-21. Conference duration: 8 days. Average attendance: 84 maximum. Workshop. Offers college credit. "Writers in Paradise offers workshop classes in fiction (novel and short story), poetry, and nonfiction. Working closely with our award-winning faculty, students will have stimulating opportunities to ask questions and learn valuable skills from fellow students and authors at the top of their form. Most important, the intimate size and secluded location of the Writers in Paradise experience allows you the time and opportunity to share manuscripts, critique one another's work, and discuss the craft of writing with experts and peers who can help guide you to the next level." Faculty have included Andre Dubus III (*House of Sand and Fog*), Laura Lippman (*Wilde Lake*), Dennis Lehane (*The Given Day*), Ann Hood (*The Book That Matters Most*), Lisa Gallagher (literary agent), and Daniel Halpern (editor). Editors and agents attend the conference.

ADDITIONAL INFORMATION Application materials are due in November and required of all attendees.

WRITE-TO-PUBLISH CONFERENCE

WordPro Communication Services, 9118 W. Elmwood Drive, Suite 1G, Niles IL 60714. (847)296-3964. **E-mail:** lin@writetopublish.com. **Website:** www.writetopublish.com. **Contact:** Lin Johnson, director. Estab. 1971. Annual conference. 2017 dates: June 14-17. Average attendance: 175. Conference is focused on the Christian market and includes classes for writers at all levels. Open to high school students. Site: Wheaton College, Wheaton, Illinois (Chicago area). This is not a function of Wheaton College.

ACCOMMODATIONS Campus residence hall rooms available. See the website for current information and costs.

ADDITIONAL INFORMATION Conference information available in January. For details, visit website, or e-mail brochure@writetopublish.com. Accepts inquiries by e-mail and, phone.

WRITING AND ILLUSTRATING FOR YOUNG READERS CONFERENCE

1480 E. 9400 S., Sandy UT 84093. **E-mail:** staff@wifyr.com. **Website:** www.wifyr.com. Estab. 2000. Annual workshop held in June. 2017 dates: June 12-16. Duration: 5 days. Average attendance: more than 100. Learn how to write, illustrate, and publish in the children's and young adult markets. Beginning and advanced writers and illustrators are tutored in a small-group workshop setting by published authors and artists and receive instruction from and network with editors, major publishing house representatives, and literary agents. Afternoon attendees get to hear practical writing and publishing tips from published authors, literary agents, and editors. Site: Waterford School in Sandy, UT. Speakers have included John Cusick, Stephen Fraser, Alyson Heller, and Ruth Katcher.

ACCOMMODATIONS A block of rooms is available at the Best Western Cotton Tree Inn in Sandy, UT, at a discounted rate. This rate is good as long as there are available rooms.

ADDITIONAL INFORMATION There is an online form for contacting this event.

WYOMING WRITERS CONFERENCE

Cheyenne WY **E-mail:** president@wyowriters.org. **Website:** wyowriters.org. **Contact:** Chris Williams. This is a statewide writing conference for writers of Wyoming and neighboring states. Each year, multiple published authors, editors, and literary agents are in attendance to meet with writers and take pitches.

LITERARY AGENT SPECIALTIES INDEX

Gallt and Zacker Literary Agency 180
Glass Literary Management 183
Green, Kathryn, Literary Agency, LLC 185
Greenhouse Literary Agency 187
Grinberg, Jill, Literary Management 188
Herman, Ronnie Ann 192
HGS Agency 194
Inklings Literary Agency 195
J De S Associates, Inc. 159
Jabberwocky Literary Agency 197
Jenks, Carolyn, Agency 198
Klinger, Harvey, Inc. 202
Knight Agency 202
Kroll, Edite, Literary Agency, Inc. 204
Lord, Sterling, Literistic, Inc. 213
Maass, Donald, Literary Agency 214
MacCoby, Gina, Literary Agency 215
Mansion Street Literary Management 217
Marsal Lyon Literary Agency, LLC 218
Martin Literary and Media Management 220
McBride, Margret, Literary Agency 220
McCarthy, Sean, Literary Agency 222
Mendel Media Group, LLC 224
Mura, Dee, Literary 226
Park Literary Group, LLC 230
Pfeffer, Rubin, Content 232
Prospect Agency 233
P.S. Literary Agency 234
Purcell Agency 234
Red Sofa Literary 235
Rights Factory 238
Rittenberg, Ann, Literary Agency, Inc. 239
Rodeen Literary Management 240
Ross, Andy, Literary Agency 242
Sanders, Victoria, & Associates 244
Schulman, Susan, Literary Agency LLC 246
Spitzer Philip G., Literary Agency, Inc. 253
Stonesong 254
Tallcott Notch Literary 258
Thompson Literary Agency 259
Triada US 261
Trident Media Group 261
Unter Agency 263
Wells Arms Literary 265
Westwood Creative Artists, Ltd. 266
Writers House 268

LESBIAN

Barone Literary Agency 132
Bookends Literary Agency 137
Bradford Literary Agency 138
Corvisiero Literary Agency 153
Dawson, Liza, Associates 155
De Chiara, Jennifer, Literary Agency 156
DeFiore & Company 157
Donaghy Literary Group 160
Dystel, Goderich & Bourret LLC 163
Fairbank Literary Representation 169
Inklings Literary Agency 195
International Transactions, Inc. 197
Jabberwocky Literary Agency 197
Jenks, Carolyn, Agency 198
Klinger, Harvey, Inc. 202
Knight Agency 202
Maass, Donald, Literary Agency 214
Marshall, Evan, Agency 219
Mendel Media Group, LLC 224
Mizell, Robin, Ltd. 225
Mura, Dee, Literary 226
Perkins, L., Agency 230
Prospect Agency 233
P.S. Literary Agency 234
Red Sofa Literary 235
Rights Factory 238
Sanders, Victoria, & Associates 244
Serendipity Literary Agency LLC 247
Stonesong 254

Tallcott Notch Literary 258
Triada US 261

LGBTQ

Cameron, Kimberley, & Associates 147
Fuse Literary 179

LGBTQ YOUNG ADULT

Morhaim, Howard, Literary Agency 225

LITERARY

Aitken Alexander Associates 129
Amster, Betsy, Literary Enterprises 130
Barone Literary Agency 132
Baror International, Inc. 132
Belli, Lorella, Literary Agency (LBLA) 133
Bent Agency 133
Bijur, Vicky, Literary Agency 134
Black, David, Literary Agency 134
Bond Literary Agency 135
Book Cents Literary Agency, LLC 135
Book Group 136
Books & Such Literary Management 137
Borchardt, Georges, Inc. 138
Bradford Literary Agency 138
Brandt & Hochman Literary Agents, Inc. 139
Brattle Agency 140
Braun, Barbara, Associates, Inc. 140
Bresnick Weil Literary Agency 140
Brower Literary & Management 142
Brown, Curtis, Ltd. 143
Brown, Marie, Associates Ltd. 144
Browne & Miller Literary Associates 144
Bykofsky, Sheree, Associates, Inc. 145
Cameron, Kimberley, & Associates 147
Cannell, Cynthia, Literary Agency 147
Carvainis, Maria, Agency 148
Chalberg & Sussman 148
Chase Literary Agency 149
Cheney Associates, LLC 149
Chudney Agency, The 150
Clark, Wm. Associates 150
Collin, Frances, Literary Agent 150
Compass Talent 151
Congdon, Don, Associates, Inc. 152
Coover, Doe, Agency 152
Cunow, Carlson, & Lerner Agency 163
D4EO Literary Agency 154
Darhansoff & Verrill Literary Agents 155
De Chiara, Jennifer, Literary Agency 156
DeFiore & Company 157
Delbourgo, Joelle, Associates, Inc. 158
Dijkstra, Sandra, Literary Agency 159
Donadio & Olson, Inc. 160
Donaghy Literary Group 160
Dunham Literary, Inc. 162
Dystel, Goderich & Bourret LLC 163
Ehrlich, Judith, Literary Management,
    LLC 165
Einstein Literary Management 165
Ellenberg, Ethan, Literary Agency 167
Eth, Felicia, Literary Representation 168
Evans, Mary, Inc. 168
Fairbank Literary Representation 169
Finch, Diana, Literary Agency 170
Fineprint Literary Management 170
Fletcher & Co. 172
Folio Literary Management, LLC 172
Foundry Literary + Media 173
Freymann, Sarah Jane, Literary Agency 177
Friedman, Rebecca, Literary Agency 178
Friedrich Agency 178
Full Circle Literary, LLC 178
Fuse Literary 179
Gelfman Schneider/ICM Partners 182
Gernert Company 182
Glass Literary Management 183

Goldin, Frances, Literary Agency, Inc. 184
Grad, Doug, Literary Agency 185
Green, Kathryn, Literary Agency, LLC 185
Greenburger, Sanford J., Associates, Inc. 187
Grinberg, Jill, Literary Management 188
Grosjean, Jill, Literary Agency 189
Harris, Joy, Literary Agency, Inc. 189
Hawkins, John, & Associates, Inc. 190
Heller, Helen, Agency, Inc. 190
Henshaw, Richard, Group 192
HGS Agency 194
Holloway Literary 193
Inkwell Management, LLC 196
International Transactions, Inc. 197
J De S Associates, Inc. 159
Jabberwocky Literary Agency 197
Janklow & Nesbit Associates 198
Jenks, Carolyn, Agency 198
Keller Media Inc. 199
Klinger, Harvey, Inc. 202
Knight Agency 202
Krichevsky, Stuart, Literary Agency, Inc. 203
LA Literary Agency 205
Lampack, Peter, Agency, Inc. 205
Lazin, Sarah, Books 207
Lecker, Robert, Agency 208
Levine Greenberg Rostan Literary Agency,
    Inc. 208
Lippincott Massie McQuilkin 210
Literary Services, Inc. 212
Lord, Sterling, Literistic, Inc. 213
Lowenstein Associates Inc. 214
Maass, Donald, Literary Agency 214
MacCoby, Gina, Literary Agency 215
MacGregor Literary Inc. 215
Mann, Carol, Agency 217
Marsal Lyon Literary Agency, LLC 218
Marshall, Evan, Agency 219
Martell Agency 220
McCormick Literary 223
McDermid, Anne, & Associates 223
McIntosh & Otis, Inc. 223
Mendel Media Group, LLC 224
Mizell, Robin, Ltd. 225
Morhaim, Howard, Literary Agency 225
Moveable Type Management 225
Mura, Dee, Literary 226
Naggar, Jean V., Literary Agency, Inc. 227
Nelson Literary Agency 228
New Leaf Literary & Media 228
Newman, Dana, Literary 229
Perkins, L., Agency 230
Priest, Aaron M., Literary Agency 233
Prospect Agency 233
P.S. Literary Agency 234
Queen Literary Agency 234
Red Sofa Literary 235
Rees Literary Agency 237
Regal Hoffman & Associates 237
Rennert, Amy, Agency 238
Rights Factory 238
Rinaldi, Angela, Literary Agency 239
RLR Associates, Ltd. 239
Robbins, B.J., Literary Agency 240
Ross, Andy, Literary Agency 242
Rotrosen, Janet, Agency LLC 243
Rudy Agency 244
Sanders, Victoria, & Associates 244
Schiavone Literary Agency, Inc. 245
Schmalz, Wendy, Agency 245
Schulman, Susan, Literary Agency LLC 246
Seligman, Lynn, Literary Agent 247
Serendipity Literary Agency LLC 247
Shannon, Denise, Literary Agency, Inc. 249
Sherman, Ken, & Associates 249
Slopen, Beverly, Literary Agency 250
Spencerhill Associates 252

YOUNG ADULT

NONFICTION

ADVENTURE

AFRICAN-AMERICAN ISSUES

AGRICULTURE

ALTERNATIVE MEDICINE

AMERICAN STUDIES

AMERICANA

ANGLOPHILIA

ANIMALS

(*see also* Pets)

ANTHROPOLOGY

ARCHEOLOGY

ARCHITECTURE

ART

MEN'S ISSUES

METAPHYSICS

MIDDLE-GRADE

MILITARY

MIND/BODY/SPIRIT

MONEY

MULTICULTURAL

Amster, Betsy, Literary Enterprises 130
Belli, Lorella, Literary Agency (LBLA) 133
Brown, Marie, Associates Ltd. 144
Bykofsky, Sheree, Associates, Inc. 145
Chase Literary Agency 149
Congdon, Don, Associates, Inc. 152
Dail, Laura, Literary Agency, Inc. 154
Dawson, Liza, Associates 155
De Chiara, Jennifer, Literary Agency 156
DeFiore & Company 157
Delbourgo, Joelle, Associates, Inc. 158
Dijkstra, Sandra, Literary Agency 159
Dunham Literary, Inc. 162
Freedson's, Grace, Publishing Network 177
Freymann, Sarah Jane, Literary Agency 177
Full Circle Literary, LLC 178
Herman, Jeff, Agency, LLC 192
HGS Agency 194
International Transactions, Inc. 197
Knight Agency 202
LA Literary Agency 205
Lord, Sterling, Literistic, Inc. 213
Lowenstein Associates Inc. 214
Martell Agency 220
McBride, Margret, Literary Agency 220
Mendel Media Group, LLC 224
Mura, Dee, Literary 226
Newman, Dana, Literary 229
Purcell Agency 234
Red Sofa Literary 235
Robbins, B.J., Literary Agency 240
Sherman, Ken, & Associates 249
Straus, Robin, Agency, Inc. 255
Tallcott Notch Literary 258
Thompson Literary Agency 259

MUSIC

Aitken Alexander Associates 129
Black, David, Literary Agency 134
Brandt & Hochman Literary Agents, Inc. 139
Bresnick Weil Literary Agency 140
Bykofsky, Sheree, Associates, Inc. 145
Chase Literary Agency 149
Clark, Wm. Associates 150
Congdon, Don, Associates, Inc. 152
Cunow, Carlson, & Lerner Agency 163
Curtis, Richard, Associates, Inc. 153
Delbourgo, Joelle, Associates, Inc. 158
Finch, Diana, Literary Agency 170
Fineprint Literary Management 170
Foundry Literary + Media 173
Fuse Literary 179
Gartenberg, Max, Literary Agency 182
Goldin, Frances, Literary Agency, Inc. 184
Grad, Doug, Literary Agency 185
Greenburger, Sanford J., Associates, Inc. 187
HGS Agency 194
International Transactions, Inc. 197
Jabberwocky Literary Agency 197
Klinger, Harvey, Inc. 202
LA Literary Agency 205
Launchbooks Literary Agency 207
Lazin, Sarah, Books 207
Lecker, Robert, Agency 208
Levine, Paul S., Literary Agency 209
Mann, Carol, Agency 217
McBride, Margret, Literary Agency 220
Mendel Media Group, LLC 224
Moveable Type Management 225
Mura, Dee, Literary 226
Naggar, Jean V., Literary Agency, Inc. 227
Newman, Dana, Literary 229
Perkins, L., Agency 230
P.S. Literary Agency 234
Regal Hoffman & Associates 237
Rights Factory 238

Robbins, B.J., Literary Agency 240
Rosenberg Group 241
Rosenkranz, Rita, Literary Agency 242
Rudy Agency 244
Sanders, Victoria, & Associates 244
Seligman, Lynn, Literary Agent 247
Serendipity Literary Agency LLC 247
Sherman, Ken, & Associates 249
Speilburg Literary Agency 252
Stonesong 254
Straus, Robin, Agency, Inc. 255
Triada US 261
Weingel-Fidel Agency 265
Zimmerman, Helen, Literary Agency 269

NARRATIVE NONFICTION

(*see also* Creative Nonfiction)
August Agency 131
Brandt & Hochman Literary Agents, Inc. 139
Braun, Barbara, Associates, Inc. 140
Brown, Andrea, Literary Agency, Inc. 142
Cameron, Kimberley, & Associates 147
Cheney Associates, LLC 149
Darhansoff & Verrill Literary Agents 155
DeFiore & Company 157
Dijkstra, Sandra, Literary Agency 159
Glass Literary Management 183
Holloway Literary 193
Janklow & Nesbit Associates 198
Lippincott Massie McQuilkin 210
Naggar, Jean V., Literary Agency, Inc. 227
Newman, Dana, Literary 229
Rabiner, Susan, Literary Agency, Inc. 235
Rinaldi, Angela, Literary Agency 239
Ross Yoon Agency 243
Rotrosen, Janet, Agency LLC 243
Shannon, Denise, Literary Agency, Inc. 249
Sherman, Wendy, Associates, Inc. 249
Tade, Stephanie, Agency 257
Transatlantic Literary Agency 260
Union Literary 262
United Talent Agency 262
Wales Literary Agency, Inc. 264

NARRATIVE REPORTAGE

Cheney Associates, LLC 149

NARRATIVE SCIENCE

McDermid, Anne, & Associates 223

NATURAL HISTORY

Broadhead, Rick, & Associates Literary Agency 141

NATURE SUBJECTS

Freymann, Sarah Jane, Literary Agency 177
Unter Agency 263
Wales Literary Agency, Inc. 264

NEW AGE

Bykofsky, Sheree, Associates, Inc. 145
Dystel, Goderich & Bourret LLC 163
Ellenberg, Ethan, Literary Agency 167
Herman, Jeff, Agency, LLC 192
Hill, Julie A., and Associates, LLC 193
J De S Associates, Inc. 159
Levine, Paul S., Literary Agency 209
Marcil, Denise, Literary Agency, LLC 218
Mura, Dee, Literary 226
Newman, Dana, Literary 229
O'Shea, Allen, Literary Agency 229
P.S. Literary Agency 234
Rosenkranz, Rita, Literary Agency 242
Sherman, Ken, & Associates 249
Stonesong 254

Whimsy Literary Agency, LLC 266

NEW JOURNALISM

Holloway Literary 193

PARANORMAL

Congdon, Don, Associates, Inc. 152

PARENTING

Amster, Betsy, Literary Enterprises 130
Black, David, Literary Agency 134
Books & Such Literary Management 137
Bradford Literary Agency 138
Bykofsky, Sheree, Associates, Inc. 145
Daniel Literary Group 154
Dawson, Liza, Associates 155
De Chiara, Jennifer, Literary Agency 156
DeFiore & Company 157
Delbourgo, Joelle, Associates, Inc. 158
Dijkstra, Sandra, Literary Agency 159
Donovan, Jim, Literary 162
Doyen Literary Services, Inc. 162
Dunham Literary, Inc. 162
Dystel, Goderich & Bourret LLC 163
Ehrlich, Judith, Literary Management, LLC 165
Eth, Felicia, Literary Representation 168
Finch, Diana, Literary Agency 170
Fineprint Literary Management 170
Folio Literary Management, LLC 172
Foundry Literary + Media 173
Fredericks, Jeanne, Literary Agency, Inc. 175
Freedson's, Grace, Publishing Network 177
Freymann, Sarah Jane, Literary Agency 177
Garamond Agency, Inc. 180
Goodman, Irene, Literary Agency 185
Green, Kathryn, Literary Agency, LLC 185
Grinberg, Jill, Literary Management 188
Hartline Literary Agency 189
Herman, Jeff, Agency, LLC 192
HGS Agency 194
Keller Media Inc. 199
Knight Agency 202
LA Literary Agency 205
Launchbooks Literary Agency 207
Lazin, Sarah, Books 207
Leshne Agency 208
Levine, Paul S., Literary Agency 209
Levine Greenberg Rostan Literary Agency, Inc. 208
Literary Management Group, Inc. 211
Literary Services, Inc. 212
LKG Agency 213
Lord, Sterling, Literistic, Inc. 213
MacGregor Literary Inc. 215
Mann, Carol, Agency 217
Marsal Lyon Literary Agency, LLC 218
Martin Literary and Media Management 220
Mendel Media Group, LLC 224
Morhaim, Howard, Literary Agency 225
Mura, Dee, Literary 226
Newman, Dana, Literary 229
O'Shea, Allen, Literary Agency 229
Purcell Agency 234
Rinaldi, Angela, Literary Agency 239
Rosenkranz, Rita, Literary Agency 242
Ross, Andy, Literary Agency 242
Rudy Agency 244
Seligman, Lynn, Literary Agent 247
Serendipity Literary Agency LLC 247
Sherman, Wendy, Associates, Inc. 249
Snell, Michael, Literary Agency 250
Stonesong 254
Straus, Robin, Agency, Inc. 255
Tallcott Notch Literary 258
Triada US 261
Westwood Creative Artists, Ltd. 266

AGENT NAME INDEX

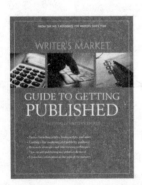